Flesh of My Flesh

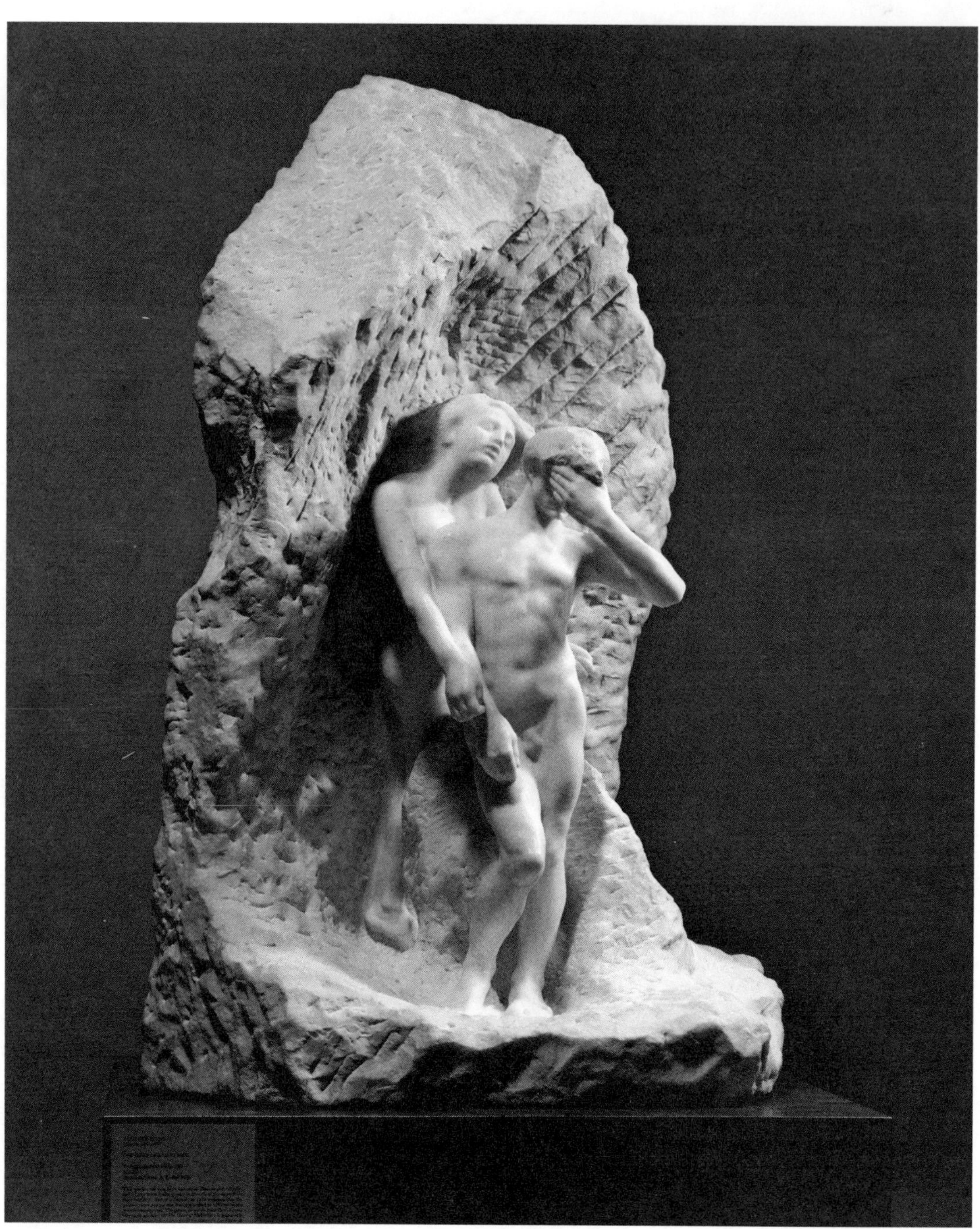

Flesh of My Flesh

Kaja Silverman

Stanford University Press
Stanford, California

Stanford University Press
Stanford, California

This book has been published with the assistance of the Committee on Research at the University of California, Berkeley.

Printed in the United States of America on acid-free, archival-quality paper

Library of Congress Cataloging-in-Publication Data has been requested.

ISBN (cloth) 978-0-8047-6207-6
ISBN (paper) 978-0-8047-6208-3

Designed by Bruce Lundquist
Typeset at Stanford University Press in 10/15 Minion

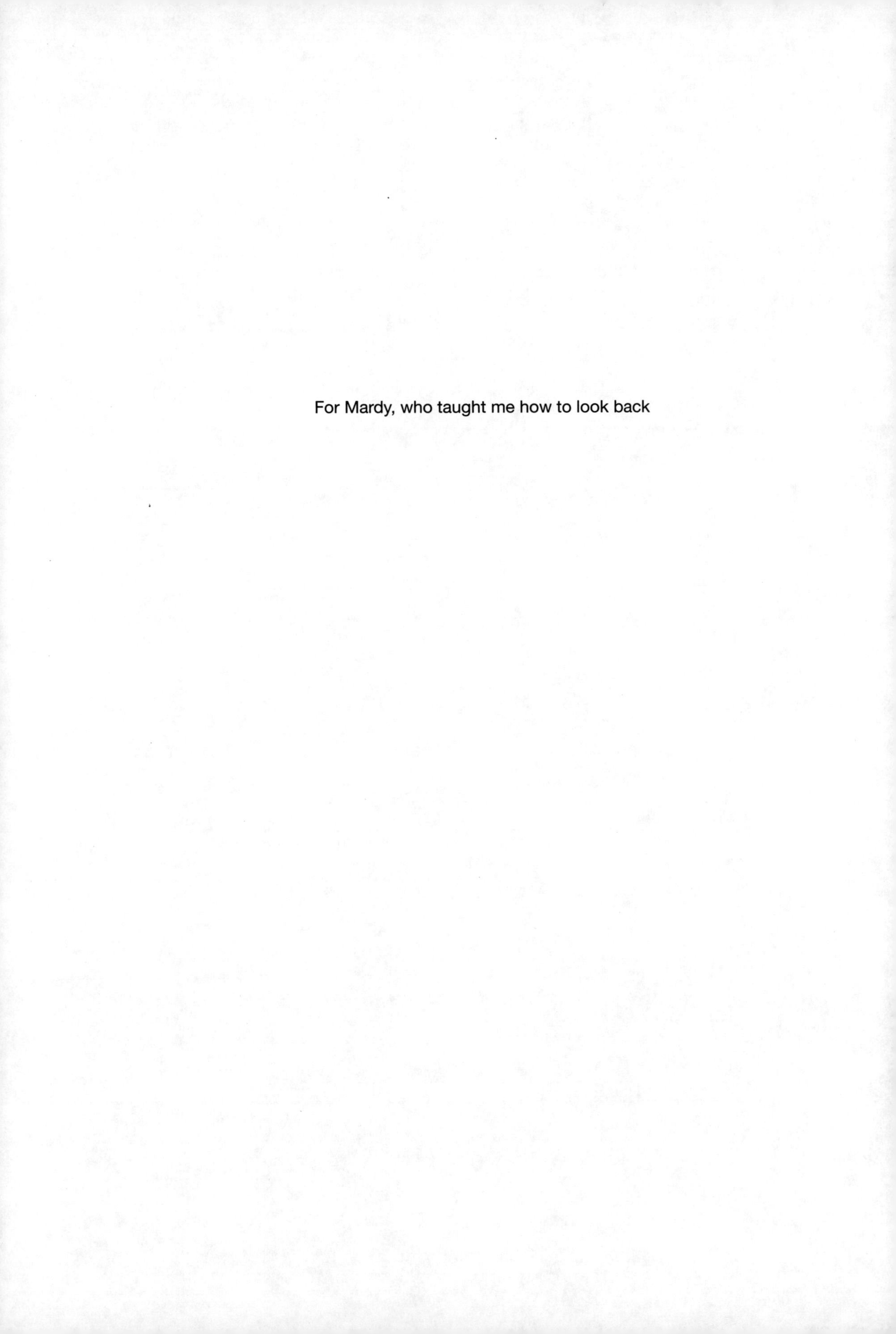

For Mardy, who taught me how to look back

Contents

Acknowledgements ix

Introduction 1

THEN

1 The Oceanic Feeling 17

2 Orpheus Rex 37

3 The Book of Life 59

4 Mutually Embracing 81

NOW

5 All Things Shining 107

6 The Twilight of Posterity 133

7 Photography by Other Means 168

Notes 223

Index 259

Illustration Captions and Credits 267

Acknowledgments

"Even in the darkest times we have the right to expect some illumination," writes Hannah Arendt, "and that illumination may well come less from theories and concepts than from the . . . light that some men and women, in their lives and their works, will kindle under almost all circumstances and shed over the time span that was given them on earth." I want to begin by thanking the friends who provided this illumination for me during some very dark times: Patrick Anderson, Elise Archias, George Baker, Brooke Belisle, Leo Bersani, Wendy Brown, Judith Butler, Renu Capelli, Steve Choe, Tim Clark, Douglas Crimp, Silvia DiPierdemenico, David Eng, Samera Esmeir, Maxine Fredrickson, Ruth Fyer, Saidiya Hartman, Amy Huber, Homay King, Jim Longenbach, Susan Lurie, Eve Meltzer, Richard Meyer, Rob Miotke, Andrew Moisey, Omri Moses, Kyle Parry, Gayle Salomon, Joanna Scott, Jane Taylorson, Domietta Torlasco, Anne Wagner, Linda Williams, Ulla Ziemann, and my mother. I am indebted to each of these people in a way that is utterly unique—and private.

I also want to thank Michael Ann Holly for inviting me to spend a semester at the Clark Art Institute; Mieke Bal for her fierce and unflagging intellectual support, of both this book and my earlier work; Kyle Parry for the enormous help he gave me in the final weeks of writing; and Andrew Moisey for all of the many ways in which he aided and abetted this project, from the very beginning to the very end.

I owe a tremendous debt of gratitude to Gerhard Richter, who allowed me to reproduce dozens of his works free of charge, including the painting on the cover; to his assistant, Konstanze El, who helped me in myriad ways; and to Françoise Viatte and Varena Forcione, who made it possible for me to write Chapter 6. I am also grateful to Emily-Jane Cohen for supporting this project; to Sarah Crane Newman for her organizational prowess; to Jan McInroy for her fastidious copy-editing; to Bruce Lundquist for the beautiful design of this book; and to Emily Smith for being the world's best production editor.

Finally, I want to thank David Eng for reading and discussing parts of this book with me on numerous occasions, and Homay King, Brooke Belisle, Jim Longenbach, George Baker, and Leo Bersani for the exquisite care with which they read the penultimate draft of this book, and for their extraordinarily generous, insightful, and constructive feedback. I hope that they will be able to see some traces of all of their hard work.

Flesh of My Flesh

Introduction

SOMEWHERE BETWEEN the ages of six and eighteen months, we have been told, the typical infant is held up to a mirror by a parent or caretaker and encouraged to identify with its reflection. This identification creates something that did not previously exist: a self. But since the child is sunk in "nursling dependence" and is little more than a disorganized mass of motor responses, this identification is impossible to sustain.[1] As soon as the mirror asserts its exteriority, the infant self begins to disintegrate. Only by overcoming the otherness of its newly emergent rival can the child reassemble the pieces. And because the subject's identity will continue to be propped upon external images, its battle-to-the-death with its own mirror image is only the first installment in a lifelong war between itself and everything else. This rivalry makes similarity even harder to tolerate than alterity, since the more an external object resembles the subject, the more it undercuts the latter's claim to be unique and autonomous. Sometimes all that it takes to get the war machine up and running is a whiff of likeness.[2]

However, the notion that we cannot be ourselves unless we are different from everyone else is relatively new. From Plato until the end of the sixteenth century, resemblance, not difference, was the organizing principle of the universe. As Foucault observes in *The Order of Things*, the "earth echo[ed] the sky, faces [saw] themselves reflected in the stars, and plants [held] within their stems the secrets that were of use to man."[3] Not all of these echoes and reflections were as egalitarian as this passage suggests. Christian analogies subordinate our world to a higher world and institute hierarchical and nonreciprocal relationships within it. They are also divinely authored and bound within the covers of two already-written volumes: the Bible and the Book of Nature. Platonic analogies work in a similar way; the earth is a pale reflection or a degraded copy of the Realm of Ideas. But in Ovid's *Metamorphoses*, every phenomenal form rhymes with many others. These rhymes also teach us that we should "revere" all creatures and "keep [them] safe," because everything emerges from the same "flesh" and has the same ontological weight.[4] We also relate to *ourselves* analogically. We do not have an "identity" because we are constantly changing, but we also do not break into a million pieces because each of our "shapes" resembles the others. Analogy works differently in *The Metamorphoses* than it does in Christianity and Platonism because Ovid makes room for death. "Nature, ever renewing the world, creates new forms from old ones endlessly," he writes in Book XV (258).[5]

Analogy has a similar status in Leonardo's paintings, drawings, and writings, and his analogies differ from Christian and Platonic analogies for the same reason Ovid's do: because he saw death as an indispensable part of life. Leonardo was fascinated by the aging process and dissected and drew many corpses. He also repeats one of Ovid's central claims: that everything derives from the same flesh. These correspondences connect us to both ourselves and others, promoting transformation rather than stasis, equality rather than hierarchy, and an "unfinished universality" rather than a closed order.[6]

Descartes's *Meditations* dramatizes the end of this way of thinking and the emergence of what Heidegger calls "representation."[7] The world ceased to be a book that man must learn to read and became a picture constructed by his look. The human subject also stopped tracing the similarities between himself and other beings; he strove to be unique, freestanding, and identical to himself. Descartes tried to reach these goals by retreating to his "stove-heated room," purging his mind of all thoughts that might have originated elsewhere, and making himself the foundation of his knowledge and being.[8] But far from consolidating his identity, this experiment atomized it. "But what then am I?" the philosopher asks in a famous passage from the *Meditations*. "A thing which thinks. What is a thing which thinks? It is a thing which doubts, understands, [conceives], affirms, denies, wills, refuses, which also imagines and feels."[9] Unnerved by his own heterogeneity, Descartes abandoned his claim to be the origin of his thoughts and restored God to that position.

But there is also another modernity—one that looks back to Ovid and Leonardo, instead of Descartes, and that emphasizes kinship, instead of separation. In 1758 Emanuel Swedenborg published *Heaven and Hell*, a book that offers a modified version of the Great Chain of Being.[10] Swedenborg argues that there are three levels of meaning in the Bible, corresponding to three worlds—one natural, one spiritual, and one celestial—and that many other analogies are contained within these overarching correspondences.[11] *Heaven and Hell* was an enormously influential book, which helped to shape Balzac's account of society in *The Human Comedy*[12] and inspired many other nineteenth-century authors, including Alphonse-Louis Constant, Charles Baudelaire, and Ralph

Waldo Emerson.[13] As Emerson notes, there are also striking similarities between Swedenborg's correspondences and Fourier's Universal Analogies.[14]

Similarity also reappeared in a number of other nineteenth-century venues, including Darwin's evolutionary theory and Walt Whitman's *Leaves of Grass.* Like Ovid's and Leonardo's analogies, Whitman's extend to the farthest reaches of space and time, and connect even the most categorically disparate of things. "A vast similitude interlocks all, / " he exults. "All spheres, grown, ungrown, small, large, suns, moons, planets, / All distances of place however wide, / All distances of time, all inanimate forms, / All souls, all living bodies though they be ever so different, or in different worlds, / All gaseous, watery, vegetable, mineral processes, the fishes, the brutes, / All nations, colors, barbarisms, civilizations, languages, / All identities that have existed or may exist on this globe, or any globe, / All lives and deaths, all of the past, present, future."[15]

Darwin also sees analogies everywhere he looks, and his analogies are even closer to those described by Ovid and Leonardo. Not only do they span vast distances in time and space, they also do so through corporeal links. Every being bears a physical resemblance to many others, and all beings derive from the same flesh. "Throughout whole classes various structures are formed on the same pattern, and at an embryonic age the species closely resemble each other," Darwin writes near the end of *The Origin of Species.* "Therefore I cannot doubt that the theory of descent with modification embraces all the members of the same class. . . . Analogy would lead me one step further, namely, to the belief that . . . all the organic beings which have ever lived on this earth have descended from some one primordial form."[16]

Fourier, Balzac, and Baudelaire were interested in correspondences because they saw them as the basis for an ideal social order.[17] Several of the other nineteenth-century writers who were attracted to analogies also saw them as a blueprint for, or a vehicle of, social transformation. Although most of the anger that has been directed against Darwin has been motivated by the challenges that his theory of evolution poses to the biblical story of creation, his primary target was slavery[18] rather than Christianity, and when we look at the title of the penultimate chapter in *The Origin of Species*—"Mutual Affinities of Organic Beings"—we can see the political work that analogy is asked to do. Whitman did not support the abolitionist movement, and he swung back and forth between "the antislavery rhetoric of the American Revolution" and the "anti-Negro phobia of his age."[19] However, it would be difficult to imagine a more comprehensive repudiation of social hierarchy and privilege than his inclusion in the totality described above of "all identities that have existed or may exist on this globe, or any globe."

In spite of the fact that it has been discredited by Russian formalism, Saussurean semiotics, structuralism, post-structuralism, and most of the Frankfurt School writers, analogy has also been embraced by an impressive group of later writers and artists. Rainer Maria Rilke, Lou Andreas-Salomé, Aby Warburg, Marcel Proust, Paul Valéry, Wilhelm Jensen, Walter Benjamin, Maurice Merleau-Ponty, James Agee, Roland Barthes, W. G. Sebald, Jean-Luc Godard, Gerhard Richter, James Coleman, and Terrence Malick all privilege similarity above all other relationships. A number of these figures also think of it as a kind of "flesh," and see this ontological kinship as the starting point for another kind of human relationality. Analogy has lived on in this way because it is the structure of Being, and it gleams with promise because it does indeed have the power to save us.

But I do not mean to suggest that Jacques Lacan is *wrong*. Although we are linked to each other through reversible and ontologically equalizing similarities, these similarities have no social efficacy unless they are acknowledged, and there is something within us that does not want to provide such acknowledgment. As Lacan helps us to see, this resistant force is the desire awakened in us by the impossible-to-satisfy demand that humanism makes upon us: the demand to be an "individual."[20] Since this aspiration cannot be satisfied as long as there are other beings, it turns them into rivals and enemies. It also gives us a dystopic view of our own multiplicity; when we fail to coincide with the mirrors in which we seek to find ourselves, we feel as if we are falling into "bits" and "pieces."[21]

Finitude is the most capacious and enabling of the attributes we share with others, because unlike the particular way in which each of us looks, thinks, walks, and speaks, that connects us to a few other beings, it connects us to *every* other being. Since finitude marks the point where we end and others begin, spatially and temporally, it is also what makes room for them—and acknowledging these limits allows us to experience the expansiveness for which we yearn, because it gives us a powerful sense of our emplacement within a larger Whole. Unfortunately, though, finitude is the most narcissistically injurious of all of the qualities we share with others, and therefore the one we are most likely to see in them, and deny in ourselves. Our refusal to acknowledge that we are limited beings has devastating and often fatal consequences for others.

Ovid spells all of this out for us in *The Metamorphoses*, through the story of Orpheus and Eurydice. Shortly after her marriage to Orpheus, we read in Book X, Eurydice is bitten by a poisonous snake and dies. Orpheus descends to Hades to plead for her life, but when he arrives, he seems less interested in her than in conquering death. He is so eloquent that the gods of the underworld allow him to take Eurydice back to earth, provided that he not look at her during their return journey. He walks ahead as they travel, so as to avoid violating this prohibition, but as they approach their destination, he is overwhelmed by the desire to see her and turns around. Eurydice is immediately transported back to Hades, and Orpheus is terrified by her sudden disappearance, which makes death real to him. He attempts to rid himself of his mortality by feminizing it, and since this projection renders women repugnant to him, he transfers his desire to young men. Orpheus also retreats to nature and uses his music to overcome it.[22] But Ovid gives this story a redemptive coda. At the beginning of Book XI of *The Metamorphoses*, Orpheus is killed and dismembered by a group of women, who resent his misogyny, and death transforms him. When he arrives in Hades, he sees again what he has seen before, but now he sees it differently. He also looks for Eurydice, and when he finds her, clasps her "tightly in his loving arms" and acknowledges her ontological equality. Sometimes they stroll "side by side" through Hades. At other times she walks ahead and he follows, or he walks ahead and she follows (182–183).

I did not choose this example at random. The first part of the myth has a firm hold on the Western imagination. It was allegorically assimilated by paganism, Christianity, courtly love, Neoplatonism, humanism, romanticism, modernism,[23] and even postmodernism.[24] It provides the storyline for the first three operas,[25] and many nineteenth-century artists painted scenes from it, including Eugène Delacroix, Camille Corot, Gustave Moreau, and Jean Delville.[26] The myth was the launching pad for Jean Cocteau's *Orphic Trilogy*, two of Balanchine's ballets, for one of which Isamu Noguchi designed the sets and costumes, and a number of Max Beckmann's lithographs.[27] Although it may seem to have little or nothing to do with our contemporary world, John Ashbery, Muriel Rukeyser, Margaret Atwood, and Adrienne Rich have all written poems about it,[28] and it still forms a central—albeit unacknowledged—part of our psychic reality.

As the myth journeyed through time, Eurydice's second death stopped mattering; what was important about Orpheus's backward look was the threat it posed to *him*. For Boethius, this threat was spiritual; the musician represented the "higher powers of the soul" and his wife, the "earthbound passions." For the Christian Ovidians, it was moral; Orpheus was "a type of Christ, overcoming death," and Eurydice a signifier for the world, the devil, and/or the flesh. When the myth was interpreted in this last way, Eurydice's death became a "fortunate loss"—something that had to happen in order for Orpheus to succeed in his mission.[29] And although many later writers saw Orpheus as the prototypical artist, rather than as a Christ-figure or a virtuous man, they continued to stress the danger to him of looking at her. Maurice Blanchot presents one of the many variations on this last theme in "The Gaze of Orpheus." Eurydice is "the profoundly dark point towards which art, desire, death, and the night all seem to lead."[30] Orpheus cannot create without approaching her, but he must do so without looking at her, because if he turns around to face her, his work will be ruined.

Eurydice has also been marginalized in other ways. In an important humanist reworking of the myth, Angelo Poliziano's *Orfeo*, she dies offstage, while fleeing Aristaeus, an unwanted suitor, and Orpheus turns around to look at her while boasting of his triumph over death. Act 5 begins with his "woeful dirge" for the "great loss" of Eurydice, but after a few sentences he renounces—and then denounces—heterosexuality, urging "the married man . . . to seek divorce, and all to flee the company of women."[31] And in many of its retellings, the myth is reduced to the scene in which Orpheus retreats to a *locus amoenus*, and plays music for a nonhuman audience. (This scene is much older than the scenes with Eurydice,[32] but its meaning shifted when she was added to the myth, since it was structured thereafter by her absence.) The only part of the coda that is a regular component in later versions of the myth is the one that can be used to sharpen the gender antimony: the scene in which Orpheus is killed and dismembered.[33]

Fascinatingly, though, the entire story is present in Leonardo's work, and he (like Ovid) uses the second half to undo the first. He designed an "Orpheus machine" for a production of Poliziano's *Orfeo* that allows the encounter between the musician and the gods of the underworld to be staged—but rather than carrying Orpheus down to Hades, it lifts Pluto and Prosperina up into the world.[34] Leonardo also levels the opposition between life and death in *The Last Supper*, this time by restaging the scene in which Orpheus is killed and dismembered. The painting portrays Christ's final meal before his Crucifixion, during which he anticipates his death and invites his disciples to tear his body apart by introducing them to the sacrament.[35] *The Last Supper* also references this scene in another way: because the fresco does not adhere tightly to the wall on which it was painted, it has been "decomposing" ever since the artist stopped working on it. And in another important painting, *Virgin and Child with Saint Anne*, Leonardo reprises the most sublime part of Ovid's story; he links three human figures and a lamb to each other through a series of reversible and democratizing analogies.

Ovid's coda resurfaced again in the period between the first version of Nietzsche's *The Gay Science* (1882) and the posthumous publication of Freud's *Moses and Monotheism* (1939). When it did, it opened the door to some vitally important questions: What is a woman? What is a man? How do they—and how *should* they—relate to each other? Is our yearning for wholeness merely a remnant of our infantile narcissism or does it refer to something real? If there is a Whole, what is it, and why do we feel so estranged from it? Some surprising and profoundly enabling answers were given to these questions. The second part of Ovid's story also appears in the work of three contemporary artists, who address many of the same issues and raise the stakes even higher: Terrence Malick, James Coleman, and Gerhard Richter.

Although I will have more to say about Leonardo in the penultimate chapter of this book, and Ovid will be a constant point of reference, the first four chapters are primarily devoted to the years between 1882 and 1939, and the last three to the years between 1965 and 2003.[36] The earlier of these periods could have been the starting point for a very different history than the one in which we find ourselves, and the works discussed in chapters 5–7 reactivate this unrealized potential. I will therefore be talking not only about *what was* but also about *what might have been and could yet be.*

LIKE THE CENTURY in which Leonardo painted, drew, and wrote, the years between *The Gay Science* and *Moses and Monotheism* were a time of waning belief in the Christian narrative, and as its sun set, Western man felt the chill of the approaching night. One of the most famous representatives of this new secularism—Nietzsche—tried to overcome his finitude through will, but the only way he could accomplish this was by affirming what he wanted to transcend. The other—Freud—attempted to reconcile himself to his limits through reason, but he also could not stop wishing for *more.* However, reason was not the psychoanalyst's first, or even last, line of defense. Before mobilizing this mental faculty, he did what Orpheus did: he put a female surrogate in his place. Like Orpheus, he also concealed this crime behind a different account of gender—one based on corporeal variation instead of finitude, and castration instead of murder.

Freud wrote "Some Psychical Consequences of the Anatomical Distinction between the Sexes," "Female Sexuality," and "Femininity" after undergoing several operations for cancer of the jaw, including one that removed his right upper jaw and palate, seriously impaired his speech and hearing, and left him extraordinarily dependent on his daughter, Anna.[37] In these essays he attributes a "small" and "inferior" organ to the mother and the daughter, adduces this "mutilation" as proof of a more general lack, and uses this lack to separate them from each other and provide himself with a limitless supply of love.[38] In his last book, *Moses and Monotheism*, Freud returns to the "just so" story he recounts in *Totem and Taboo*,[39] and uses it to disguise the myth he has been restaging. It is not the mother who dies and is dismembered, he loudly proclaims; it is the father. And it is not Orpheus who commits this crime. It is Oedipus. We are still living in the shadow of this narrative, with its hidden knife and clitoral "wound."

Lou Andreas-Salomé responded differently when she was touched by the angel of death. An early encounter with mortality gave her "*the profound feeling of a deeply shared destiny with all things*," and—because of this—an "indwelling reverence" for everything "that 'is.'"[40] Salomé believed that most people are unable to experience this feeling because they have repudiated one of their "partners" and that the goal of analysis should be to reawaken this affect in those who have lost it. She organized her therapeutic practice accordingly. Instead of focusing on her patients' Oedipal problems, she helped them turn around and claim the one they had left behind—and she did this by occupying the symbolic position of Eurydice.[41] In her memoir, she also turns around to claim the mother *she* had left behind.[42]

Salomé corresponded with Ovid's coda in other ways as well. The title of her memoir is *Looking Back*, and retro-vision has a privileged status in her *Freud Journal*, her exchanges with Rilke, and her homage to Freud. She attributes a redemptive power to this kind of looking—the capacity to make the past happen again, in a new way. She also suggests that transformations in a person's private past can precipitate changes in the historical past. When we turn around and embrace the "partner" we have repudiated, Salomé writes in her *Freud Journal*, "*all* the vanished people of the past arise anew" (193; my emphasis).

Rilke spent many years trying to isolate himself and his poetry from the world because he wanted to be autonomous and because he was terrified of dying. As he notes in a 1912 letter, these were two sides of the same thing: his finitude.[43] Eventually, though, he also came to believe that he was part of a larger Whole. "Though we are unaware of our true status, /" he writes in the *Sonnets to Orpheus*, "our actions stem from pure relationship. / Far away, antennas hear antennas / and the empty distances transmit."[44] Finitude was the door that opened onto this expanded universe, and the second half of Ovid's story was the key that unlocked it.

Rilke devoted three poems and a sonnet sequence to the myth of Orpheus and Eurydice, and he used it to work through his relationships with his dead sister and the mother he had cast away. In the first two poems, "Orpheus. Eurydice. Hermes" and *Requiem for a Friend*, he is unable to get past the first half of Ovid's story, but in the *Sonnets to Orpheus* he finally descends to Hades and takes his sister's hand. "*Death* is the *side of life* averted from us, unshone upon by us," he wrote thereafter. "We must try to achieve the greatest consciousness of our existence which is at home in *both unbounded realms, inexhaustibly nourished from both*. . . . The true figure of life extends through *both* spheres."[45]

Rilke thought of this totality as a vast, unauthored book, written in the language of analogy.[46] His task as a poet was to transcribe what his experiences "dictated" to him[47] so that others could read it and discover that their lives were part of the same volume. In a 1914 letter, Rilke talks about how wonderful it would be to participate in a group reading of Proust's novel, *Swann's Way*, spread out over many evenings, because it would connect the author to the reader, and every reader to every other—not *in spite of* the particularities of their lives but rather *through* them.[48] The same is true of his own writing, Rilke suggests in a 1925 letter; the completion of the *Duino Elegies* after almost a decade of creative paralysis was "more than just a private event," because all of those "who *for one reason or another* believe themselves cleft apart might draw from this *example* of *possible* continuation a *singular* comfort" (my emphasis).[49]

Since so much of the story recounted in *Swann's Way* is Oedipal in nature, it's not hard to imagine a group of readers interacting with it in the way Rilke describes. However, the poet's life is representative not because he desires his mother but because he wants to get rid of her, and because by repudiating her he has lost his capacity to love. Women have a "diploma" in this affect, Rilke argues in a 1912 letter, but all that men have ever done is mouth meaningless phrases. Over the centuries, the male subject has become increasingly a-relational, and now a "man of the 'new grain'" has emerged, whose defining attribute is solitude. Since it is neither psychically nor ontologically possible for any of us to be alone, this man is "going to pieces." When this "salutary" process of decomposition is complete, he will finally start learning how to love, and at some point in the future we will witness something that we have not yet seen: the heterosexual couple.[50]

Like Rilke, Nietzsche, Rodin, Cézanne, and Proust are all striking examples of this "man of the 'new grain,'" and the a-relational male subject also occupies an important place in Paul Valéry's writings. Nietzsche, Rodin, and Proust share Rilke's preoccupation with corporeal disintegration, as well. Zarathustra tells his disciples that mankind is "in ruins and scattered about as if on a battle field or a butcher field."[51] One of the most basic principles of Rodin's work is the "repetition and exploitation of fragments, constantly metamorphosed and renewed in context and meaning,"[52] and in the opening section of *Swann's Way*, a solitary male subject offers a detailed description of the numerous "pieces" into which his ego falls whenever he enters the indeterminate zone between sleeping and waking.[53] Like Rilke, Proust seems to find this decomposition "salutary," because he treats it as the prelude to an almost unimaginably capacious relationality. In an important passage early in *Swann's Way*, Marcel describes the process of coming to consciousness as a vertiginous journey not just through his own memories but also through a much larger past (5).

Rilke was in such an acute crisis when he produced this diagnosis of the masculine condition that he had been thinking of seeing a psychoanalyst. But since so many of his contemporaries were afflicted by the same malady, he opted for a different kind of treatment; he decided to conduct his analysis out in the open, through his poetry, so that others could participate in it.[54] His "self-treatment" was based on the same myth as Salomé's psychoanalysis—and we can see why he imputes a curative value to it. Ovid's version of the story can be mapped with uncanny precision onto the history that Rilke recounts in his 1912 letter about masculinity. Orpheus's repudiation of Eurydice dramatizes man's inability to love women; his retreat to a remote location symbolizes the latter's increasing solitude; the dismemberment of his body signifies the salutary disintegration of the male ego; and his descent to Hades and reunion with Eurydice stands for the arrival of the heterosexual couple.

The first part of Ovid's story also appears in the works of Proust, Valéry, Nietzsche, and Rodin. The narrator of Proust's *In Search of Lost Time* uses it to punish his grandmother for continuing to exist when he is not present; Valéry wrote three poems about the scene in which Orpheus isolates himself from human companionship;[55] and Nietzsche's *Thus Spoke Zarathustra* is an extended dramatization of the same scene. Rodin returned to the myth repeatedly, producing plaster, marble, and/or bronze versions of Orpheus and Eurydice leaving Hades, of Orpheus immediately after losing Eurydice, and of Orpheus being killed by the Ciconian women. A bronze rendition of the second motif echoes a plaster version of the first, in which Eurydice hovers above Orpheus's lyre. It includes the lyre and her severed hand, testifying to the violence of her removal.[56] Dorothy M. Kosinski sees this statue as a self-portrait—as "a symbolic embodiment of Rodin and his creative mission" (162).

And Rilke was not the only "man of the 'new grain'" who drew on Ovid's coda. Rodin often combined the best parts of one model with the best parts of another, regardless of gender. Proust looks at the past in a way that reanimates it, relying for this purpose on the "miracle of an analogy."[57] The coda also appears in the work of two of Rilke's other contemporaries. It figures prominently in Jensen's *Gradiva* and in Freud's interpretation of the novella, and the psychoanalyst continued to correspond with it structurally even after elaborating his theory of sexual difference. His therapeutic practice is based on the act of turning around to look at the past and the belief that this can make the past happen again, in a new way—and although Freud refers to analogy as a "false connection,"[58] he cannot proceed without it.

Martin Heidegger and Walter Benjamin also attribute a redemptive power to the act of turning around, and they echo Ovid's argument in other ways as well. The Heideggerian "turn" is a turn toward finitude, and in one of the philosopher's most moving descriptions of this act, he quotes extensively from the *Sonnets to Orpheus* and Rilke's late letters.[59] The Benjaminian "turn" is also a turn toward analogy.[60] The present is connected to the past through unauthored correspondences, the philosopher argues in *The Arcades Project* and "On The Concept of History."[61] These correspondences are revealed to us at moments of danger through objects that are "blasted" out of the "continuum of historical succession" and journey toward us.[62] They are warnings rather than declarations; they show us not who we are, or who we will be, but rather who we are in the process of becoming.[63] They are issued by our predecessors, who want to prevent us from reenacting their mistakes. If we are able to see the parallels between what they did and what we are on the verge of doing, we will not only prevent a new catastrophe from occurring but also change the "character" of the past.[64]

Heidegger and Benjamin help us to see that the story of Orpheus and Eurydice is not just about hetero-relationality; it is about relationality *tout court.* Heidegger also deepens our understanding of finitude, gives us a more complex account of Being, and teaches us to think ontologically about affect. Benjamin shows us that retroactivity is a historical as well as a psychic possibility and that we are therefore dependent upon and answerable to not just our contemporaries but our predecessors and successors as well. However, because neither philosopher makes room for Eurydice, each falters at a crucial point in his argument. Heidegger's description of the "turn" remains strangely nebulous, and he shifts more and more of the responsibility for performing it onto Being. Benjamin is unable to explain why we are so reluctant to acknowledge the similarities that connect us to our predecessors, how we turn away, or what it would mean to turn back, "awaken the dead, and make whole what has been smashed."[65]

THE FIRST FOUR CHAPTERS of this book are almost as tightly interwoven as the lives of the figures I discuss in them. The second half of the book is more heterogeneous. Chapter 5 is devoted to Malick's 1998 film, *The Thin Red Line,* Chapter 6 to Coleman's "intervention" in the Louvre's 2003 exhibition of Leonardo's drawings and manuscripts, and Chapter 7 to the constellation of paintings and photographs through which Richter responded to an urgent historical summons. However, these works also have many things in common. They are all shadowed by war: *The Thin Red Line* by World War II, Coleman's intervention in the Leonardo exhibition by the Iraq War, and Richter's paintings and photographic practice by Auschwitz and the "war on terrorism." They also show this violence to be the inevitable result of our refusal to think analogically, characterize finitude as the most capacious and enabling of all analogies, use the first part of the Orpheus and Eurydice story to dramatize the fateful moment when the subject repudiates the first of its "partners," and reverse this deadly act by restaging Ovid's coda. All three artists also correspond with *The Metamorphoses* in another way: they show that we are all flesh of the same flesh, and they arrive at this ontological understanding of kinship through a literal instantiation of the same principle. Finally, each is in passionate dialogue with several of his predecessors—Malick with Salomé, Heidegger, and Rolland; Coleman with Leonardo and Valéry; and Richter with Freud and Benjamin.

In *The Thin Red Line*, Malick explores and ultimately dispenses with a number of the fictions through which we attempt to shield ourselves from our mortality. Although this exploration takes place during the Battle of Guadalcanal, and includes several scenes in which a character tries to "outsource" death, it is primarily focused on fantasies of wholeness. Malick disabuses the captain (Staros) who prays for divine guidance of the notion that God is his copilot, and shows the private (Witt) who goes AWOL on a Melanesian island that it is not the earthly paradise he imagines it to be. He also weans the soldier (Bell) who seeks refuge in memories of his wife away from the fantasy that their love will overcome all obstacles and outlast death. Instead of dismissing these fantasies as simple illusions, however, Malick treats them as misrecognitions of another kind of totality, whose basis is finitude.

This totality is what Heidegger calls "beings as a whole,"[66] and there are also many other traces of the philosopher's thought in *The Thin Red Line*. But although the film is close to Heidegger's thought in certain respects, it is distant in others. It privileges wonder rather than anxiety, and women figure prominently both in its narrative and in its phenomenology. Early in the film, Witt talks about his mother's tranquillity at the moment of her death, acknowledges his reluctance to "touch" the mortality he saw "in" her, and expresses the hope that he will be able to meet death in the same way. After trying several times to localize "wholeness" in the Melanesian Islands, he eventually comes to see that it defies localization, because all beings are "features of the same face." As he waits for the Japanese soldiers to shoot him at the end of the film, he experiences the same affects that his mother experienced during the last days of her life—affects that are shown to be enworlding. And although Bell's marriage does not even survive the war, let alone death, Malick nevertheless affirms the soldier's love for his wife in one of the most extraordinary sequences in the film.

James Coleman's "intervention" in the Louvre's 2003 exhibition of Leonardo's work also gave the mother pride of place. In addition to a large number of manuscripts and drawings, the exhibition included the painting that led Freud to conclude that Leonardo, unlike the "normal" male subject, never turned away from his mother: *Virgin and Child with Saint Anne.*[67] Coleman corresponded with this painting by doing what it does: linking things to each other through their similarities. His intervention had six components—four sets of video editing monitors, a large-screen projection of a series of digital images of *The Last Supper*, and a wall text. The editing monitors displayed digital versions of some Leonardo works that were not included in the show, and these images related to the works they reprised and to the rest of the exhibition through a complex series of analogies. One of these works was Leonardo's design for an Orpheus machine, and several of the others referred to the same myth.

Coleman corresponded with another of Leonardo's paintings through his large-screen projection *The Last Supper.* Each image of this famous—and famously deteriorating—fresco remained on the screen for about a minute and then yielded to another. Since some of these images displayed the whole painting and others only a section or a small detail, it was impossible to say what one was seeing. Coleman used these digital metamorphoses to show that change is internal to the fresco's being, and not an external corruption of its original "essence." He also built decay and expiration into his *own* images, by destroying them when the exhibition ended and by using them to absolutize the concepts of absence and presence. And because his intervention was an "ephemeral memorial"[68] to Leonardo's work, instead of a lasting monument, it could not be added to the paternal legacy.

Analogy has been the basis of Richter's work ever since he painted his first photo pictures. He has used it to connect photography to painting, figuration to abstraction, art to the world, the past to the present, and what is knowable to what is unknowable. It is closely linked in his mind to photography, both because he regards photography as an analogical medium, and because he sees it as the primary agency through which the past communicates with the present. In the mid-sixties, a group of concentration camp photographs burst out of the continuum of time and landed on Richter's doorstep. They made a demand on him that he couldn't meet: they asked him to acknowledge his kinship both with the emaciated prisoners and with those responsible for their suffering. Richter was unable either to paint these photographs or to ignore them, so he processed them in various ways and put them in the *Atlas.* He also attempted to silence their call through a false analogy: he paired six of them with some pornographic photographs.

Twenty years later, another group of photographs sought Richter out—those documenting the imprisonment and deaths of three German terrorists: Ulrike Meinhof, Gudrun Ensslin, and Andreas Baader. They made a similar demand on him—and he met that demand by painting *October 18, 1977.* Richter was able to respond to this second solicitation because of some striking formal analogies that permitted him first to extend the category of "kin" from his daughter to Meinhof and Ensslin, then to acknowledge the analogies linking *him* to the terrorists and the police, and—finally—to recognize aspects of himself both in the concentration camp inmates and in their captors. He made these acknowledgments publicly, through a series of photographic self-portraits. Since then, this constellation of photographs and paintings has expanded to include Richter's great abstract triptych, *January, December,* and *November;* several more self-portraits; and a date etched in black in our own memories: September 11, 2001. Although this last analogy cannot be rationally explained, it is no more mysterious than the others. All of our stories really are part of the same great volume: the Book of Life. And unlike the *logos,* the words in this book do not have to become flesh in order to save us. They *are* flesh.

THEN

1 The Oceanic Feeling

You can check out anytime you want, but you can never leave.

—The Eagles

IN THE MOST FAMOUS PASSAGE in Nietzsche's 1882 book *The Gay Science*, a madman runs into a marketplace before dawn, crying, "I'm looking for God!"[1] Since those who hear his words are atheists, they ridicule him. A moment later, the madman also acknowledges the vanity of his search, although for a different reason: the God for whom he is looking is already dead. He and his auditors are responsible for this death, which violates the most sacrosanct of taboos. "God is dead!" the madman cries. "God remains dead! And we have killed him! How can we console ourselves, the murderers of all murderers! The holiest and mightiest thing the world has ever possessed has bled to death under our knives: who will wipe this blood from us?" (120).

But the event described by the madman is both temporally unlocatable and unthinkable within the coordinates of an "action." Although his listeners do not believe in God, Nietzsche writes, and have therefore already killed him, he is not yet dead for them. Their deed is "still more remote to them than the remotest stars" (120). It will "need time . . . in order to be seen and heard," and until this time has passed, it will not really occur. The madman therefore arrives not only too late to find God, but also too early to attend his funeral. The "tremendous event" that he proclaims is "still on its way, wandering" (120).

Midway through this section of *The Gay Science*, Nietzsche also changes another crucial element of the story. The madman and his auditors are guilty not because they have killed God but because their crime outstrips them—because they are not big enough to fill the throne that they have emptied. No ritual feast can rectify this situation; in order to wash the blood off their hands, they must become gods themselves. "With what water could we clean ourselves?" the madman asks those who have gathered in the marketplace. "What festivals of atonement, what holy games will we have to invent for ourselves? Is the magnitude of this deed not too great for us? Do not we ourselves have to become gods merely to appear worthy of it?" (120).

This is an odd account of guilt. Since placing oneself on the same level as God is often seen as the most grievous of sins, the madman's inability to commit it would seem a good thing—commendable, if not virtuous. And the affect we experience when our megalomania outstrips our capacity to act is usually shame rather than remorse. However, Nietzsche is not thinking within moral or psychoanalytic coordinates; he is offering an *ontological* account of guilt. The madman is guilty because of the limits that define him—because he is a finite being. His guilt is consequently irredeemable.

Nietzsche's doppelgänger disappears after acknowledging that God's death has not yet "arrived," but his creator continues to scan the horizon of the future for the "greatness" he needs to complete his task. In *Thus Spoke Zarathustra*,[2] the philosopher tries to become equal to the event proclaimed by his madman by overcoming *himself*—by being both an obedient slave and the exacting master to whom this slave submits. "Ten times a day you must overcome yourself," he says to himself at one point, through another thinly veiled alter ego.[3] "You must want to burn yourself up in your own flame," he declares at another. "How could you become new if you did not first become ashes?" (47).

The first limit Zarathustra attempts to overcome is death. His desire for immortality surfaces repeatedly in part 3, through the declaration "joy wants eternity," and he attributes the capacity to satisfy this desire to his will. "You are still the shatterer of all graves," he says to this faculty, immediately before the chapter devoted to self-overcoming. "And only where there are graves are there resurrections" (88). The second limit that Zarathustra seeks to transcend is time. Since he is not yet the overman he yearns to become, he finds the present intolerable, so he turns to the past, hoping to enlist "what was" as an ally against "what is." However, he only finds more of the same: "fragments and limbs and grisly accidents—but no human beings" (110). In fact, the past is even more intractable than the present, because "the will cannot will backward" (111). Since Zarathustra can neither destroy nor modify what has already occurred, he tries to triumph over it by altering his affective relationship to it—by converting every "'it was'" into an "'I will it thus'" (112). He affirms the past from which he would so gladly escape in the most radical way imaginable: by willing it to happen over and over again, in exactly the same way.

By remaking the future in the image of the past, Zarathustra achieves a strange kind of immortality; yes, he will die, but only to return to the world and begin his life anew. When it ends, he will die again, and be resurrected again—

and this process will continue for all eternity. "Now I die and disappear," Zarathustra's animals say on his behalf, "and in an instant I will be a nothing. . . . But the knot of causes in which I am entangled recurs—it will create me again! . . . I will return to this same and selfsame life, in what is greatest as well as in what is smallest, to once again teach the eternal recurrence of all things'" (178). But the only thing that separates the eternal recurrence from a compulsory repetition is the hairsbreadth of will, and will cannot prevent desire from wanting something else.

Freud was clearly fascinated by this project, because he also spends a lot of time talking about the impossibility of killing God, and often in ways that reference Nietzsche.[4] In his 1913 book *Totem and Taboo*, he recounts another version of the madman's story. There was once a primal father, we read there, who ruled over a horde of brothers. He kept all of the women for himself and drove his sons away when they became adults. The brothers banded together and killed the primal father, but as soon as they secured their freedom, they were overcome with remorse. They prohibited parricide, asserted the rights of the group over those of the individual, and internalized the father as their ego ideal by ritually ingesting him. As a result of their "deferred obedience," the father became far stronger in death than he ever was in life. Since the ceremonial meal through which the brothers atoned for their crime permitted them to repeat it, their obedience also reinforced their guilt.[5]

But Freud is not content to echo Nietzsche; he presents his own story as the explanatory key to the one narrated in *The Gay Science*. God cannot be killed because murder is his life's blood—because he is a derivative of the primal father, the exalted fantasm into which the latter grew at the moment of his death. Freud also levels an implicit critique of Nietzschean will. He devotes chapter 3 of *Totem and Taboo* to "the omnipotence of thoughts," which he defines as "an unshakeable confidence in the possibility of controlling the world" and an "inaccessibility to the experiences, so easily obtainable, which could teach them man's true position in the universe" (89).

However, Freud struggles with the same enemy as Nietzsche—and his battle also ends in defeat. Since mortality is the most powerful of all limits, he argues in *Totem and Taboo*, the primary goal for all such "theorizing" is to solve the "problem of death" (76). The animist tries to do this by transposing "the structural conditions of his own mind into the external world" (91) and grasping the "whole universe as a single unity from a single point of view" (77). The religious believer attempts to accomplish the same thing by ascribing omnipotence to gods whom he is able to influence "in a variety of ways," according to his "wishes" (88). Although they are more conflicted in this respect, neurotics also attribute a magical value to their thoughts, and artistic illusion is yet another way in which human beings deny their mortality. The only people who acknowledge their "smallness and [submit] resignedly to death and the other necessities of nature," and whose thought is therefore untainted by the will to power, are those who subscribe to a "scientific view of the universe" (88).

Freud clearly means us to see him as a member of the last group and Nietzsche as a throwback to the first. However, after telling us that the "scientific view of the universe no longer affords any room for human omnipotence," he concedes that "some of the primitive belief in omnipotence still survives in men's faith in the power of the human mind, which grapples with the laws of reality" (88), and by the time he arrives at his "just-so" story, he has completely forgotten about mortality. What prevents the sons from satisfying their desire for omnipotence is now the primal father. This figure is human yet limitless; he possesses *all* of the woman and other "goods" and shares *none* of his power with his sons. He is also impossible to kill, because each time his corpse is lowered into the ground, he springs back to life in an even more exalted form. This fantasmatic figure attests to Freud's unconscious desire for the omnipotence he has supposedly renounced. The rest of *Totem and Taboo* is cut from the same cloth. When Freud claims that the murder and cannibalization of the primal father by the band of brothers was "the beginning of so many things—of social organization, of moral restrictions and of religion" (142), he does exactly what he accuses the animist of doing: he explains the "whole universe" as a "single unity" from a "single point of view."

There are also a number of striking parallels between chapter 4 of *Totem and Taboo* and section 125 of *The Gay Science*. Freud's account of human guilt is as bizarre as Nietzsche's; it is transmitted from generation to generation, derives from a crime committed long ago, and "has not allowed mankind a moment's rest" (145). Like the death of God, the murder of the father is also unlocalizable, since it is unclear whether it was an actual "deed," committed long ago, or merely a "thought" that every subject entertains. Freud tries to rationalize this equivocation through the Oedipus complex, but the resulting argument reads like a parody of reason. Because "primitive men" were "uninhibited," he argues in the closing pages of *Totem and Taboo*, their thoughts passed directly into actions. We are "weighed down under the burden of an excessive morality," so our thoughts remain thoughts. But although we have not committed patricide, there is still a "*historical* reality" to our guilt, because in our childhood we had "these evil impulses pure and simple" and "turned them into acts so far as the impotence of childhood allowed" (160–161).

Freud must have seen that the story of the primal father and the band of brothers contradicts much of what he writes in the preceding chapter of *Totem and Taboo*, because he offers a different account of the omnipotence of thoughts in his essay on narcissism. Instead of weaving ethnographic fantasies about a primal father who lived long ago and was all-powerful, although human, he focuses on a tyrant who is alive and kicking, and whose power is manifestly illusory. He calls this tyrant "His Majesty, the Baby," thereby identifying him with the infant subject, but he also suggests that this infant may live on long after the subject reaches adulthood. In an extraordinary passage in "On Narcissism," Freud talks about parents who "renew" their "claim" to omnipotence through their offspring. He also characterizes this parental narcissism as yet another of the ways in which human beings attempt to escape their finitude. "The child . . . shall not be subject to the necessities which they have recognized as paramount in life," he writes. "Illness, death, renunciation of enjoyment, restrictions on his own will, shall not touch him; the laws of nature and society shall be abrogated in his favor; he shall once more really be the center and core of creation."[6]

Freud offers a similar account of religion in *The Future of an Illusion* (1927). Human beings create religion to protect themselves from the forces threatening their "self regard," not because they are guilty of a crime someone else committed long ago. Some of these adversaries are human, but others are "natural." The latter—which are much harder to combat than the former—are all variations on a single theme—death: "[Nature] has her own particularly effective method of restricting us. She destroys us—coldly, cruelly, relentlessly. . . . There are the elements, which seem to mock at all human control: the earth, which quakes and is torn apart and buries all human life and its works; water, which deluges and drowns everything in a turmoil; [and] storms, which blow everything before them" (15–16). Although far mightier than even the mightiest of fathers, floods and earthquakes are an external threat, and therefore are something against which we could at least hypothetically protect ourselves. But midway through the passage from which I have just quoted, this destructive force assumes an internal form: "There are diseases, which we have only recently recognized as attacks by other organisms; and finally there is the painful riddle of death, against which no medicine has yet been found, nor probably will be" (15–16).

It was only after a protracted period of time, and many reshufflings of the familial deck, Freud asserts, that mankind devised a religion capable of conjuring away its finitude. Our earliest ancestors tried to get around the problem of death by anthropomorphizing the forces that threatened them; they transformed nature from an impersonal agency, beyond their power to understand or control, into a larger-than-life version of themselves, susceptible to bribes and other gestures of appeasement (16–17). While fashioning their gods, these early believers drew upon an "infantile prototype"—upon the father of their childhood, whom they feared but to whom they also turned for protection (17). However, since these contradictory qualities reflected the ambivalence of the son's relationship to the father, it was a synthesis waiting to come apart.

There were also aspects of nature that could not be assimilated to a human model. Western man attempted to fix both of these problems by detaching his gods from nature and soliciting the protection of the former against the threat posed by the latter. But these benevolent deities failed to do everything their worshipers asked of them, indicating that they were subject to a higher being, so eventually they, too, lost their luster. Mankind then resurrected the feared side of the father and used it as the model for this higher being, which it called "Fate" or "Moira." Instead of a Janus-faced god, who represented opposing qualities, or a purely benevolent god, there were now two kinds of paternal deities: one that destroyed and one that protected (18). Unfortunately, though, the destruction threatened by the first of these father-gods was in excess of the protection offered by the second, so our ancestors soon began looking for a new way of shielding themselves from destruction.

It was at this point, according to Freud, that morality entered the world. By transforming the "precepts of civilization" into a sacred law, our predecessors devised a reassuring explanation for why catastrophes occur (19). When someone suffered or died, it was because he had violated the edicts of the gods. By scrupulously obeying these edicts, one could avoid such a fate. When it was no longer possible to deny that even the most exemplary of human beings suffer and die, there was only one way in which mankind could protect itself from death, and that was by positing an afterlife.

The Christian version of the two-world theory does away not just with mortality but also with every other kind of limit. Our Heavenly Father "orders everything for the best—that is, to make it enjoyable for us" (19). Through the crucifixion, Christianity shows that there is nothing God the Father will not do for us—no sacrifice that he is not prepared to make. And through the figure of Christ, it reduces the category of the "Chosen People" from a group to an individual. These two additions provide the support for a powerful new fantasy: the fantasy of the "only beloved child." "Now that God was a single person, man's relations to him could recover the intimacy and intensity of the child's relation to his father. But if one had done so much for one's father, one wanted to . . . be his only beloved child" (19).

Two years later, Freud added an epilogue to this story. "Long ago [man] formed an ideal conception of omnipotence and omniscience which he embodied in his god," he writes in a riveting passage from *Civilization and Its Discontents.* "To these gods he attributed everything that seemed unattainable to his wishes, or that was forbidden to him. . . . Today he has come very close to the attainment of this ideal, he has almost become a god himself . . . [but he] does not feel happy in his Godlike character."[7] Although Freud embeds these remarks in a discussion of the technological prostheses through which modern man attempts to extend his power, he is clearly thinking primarily about Nietzsche.

The philosopher also haunts the pages of *The Future of an Illusion.* This book has several important subtexts, one of which goes something like this: Nietzsche believed that Christianity promotes a slave mentality, and since he wanted to be a master, he tried to kill its God. He failed to see that what looks like servitude *feels* like mastery. Christianity is the product of man's belated realization that it is much more satisfying to be God's child than to be God himself. Those who purport to have absolute power are quickly discredited; no human being can pretend for very long to control the universe. It is far wiser to admit that we are helpless and dependent beings, and pay homage to the power and glory of our Almighty Protector. Because he is our father, we will be able to bask in the light of his greatness—and because he is God, he will never need to prove that he deserves our praise. Anyone who tries to kill this divinity will be thrown into a profound narcissistic crisis, because he will immediately be confronted with his own limits.

But although Freud is very adept at pointing out the errors of Nietzsche's ways, he is unable to prevent himself from repeating them. In *The Future of an Illusion*, he tries to do exactly what the philosopher sets out to do in *The Gay Science*: eliminate God. And although he refers to his weapon of choice as "reason" instead of the "will to power," it is another variant of the same thing: the omnipotence of thoughts.[8] "The greater the number of men to whom the treasures of knowledge become accessible," Freud writes in one passage from *The Future of an Illusion*, "the more widespread is the falling away from religious belief" (38). "In the long run nothing can withstand reason and experience, and the contradiction which religion offers to both is all too palpable," he argues in a second. "Even purified religious ideas cannot escape this fate, so long as they try to preserve anything of the consolation of religion" (54).

Pages before Freud launches into his celebration of reason, he acknowledges that illusions set no "store" on "verification" (31). If some prove more robust and durable than others, it is because they deliver more pleasure, not because they pitch their tent closer to reality. Eventually, Freud realizes that the opposition between reason and religious illusion cannot be sustained. Even his own atheism may be based on unconscious desire, rather than the unimpeachable logic he imputes to it (53). He now establishes a new line of defense: although his claim that there is no God may be an illusion, it is certainly not a delusion (53).

But midway through *The Future of an Illusion*, Freud breaks into two adversarial parts, much as Nietzsche does in *Zarathustra*. He begins imputing objections to the reader that the latter has not voiced (21–56). The words in question constitute a more and more heated refutation of the claims Freud makes on behalf of reason, and the psychoanalyst responds to them as though he is being persecuted.[9] "What a lot of accusations all at once!" he protests at a key point in this "dialogue." "Nevertheless I am ready with rebuttals for them all. . . . But I hardly know where to begin my reply" (35). This would be a textbook instance of paranoia were it not for the fact that what the father of psychoanalysis exteriorizes in his attempt to disprove religion is *himself as psychoanalyst*.

We come next to the title of the work under discussion. If we were to excerpt from *The Future of an Illusion* only the parts that Freud imputes to himself, we would expect the work to be called *The End of an Illusion* or *The Beginning of Reason*. Instead, Freud projects into the future what he purports to be effecting in the present, just as Nietzsche does in *The Gay Science*. "The voice of the intellect is a soft one, but it does not rest till it has gained a hearing," he says to his "opponent." "Finally . . . it succeeds. This is one of the few points on which one may be optimistic about the future of mankind. And from it one can derive yet other hopes. The primacy of the intellect lies, it is true, in a distant, distant future, but probably not in an *infinitely* distant one" (53).

Near the end of *The Future of an Illusion*, Freud urges us to live within the narrow limits of our individual means by comparing us to humble farmers. "Of what use to [us] is the mirage of wide acres in the moon, whose harvest no one has ever yet seen?" he asks. "As honest smallholders on this earth [we] will know how to cultivate [our] plot in such a way that it supports [us]" (50). Tilling the small scrap of land that is our own will not make our lives enjoyable, Freud acknowledges, but it will make them "tolerable." This passage is a step-by-step rebuttal of another famous passage from *The Gay Science*. In section 124 of the latter work, Nietzsche also thematizes finitude as the ground beneath our feet and anticipates the moment at which humanity will be delivered from religious illusion. However, rather than encouraging us to work this soil and to make do with the meager crops it yields, he appeals to that force within us which seeks to override our limits. Nietzsche metaphorizes this expansion as a boundless sea. "We have forsaken the land and gone to sea!" he exults. "We have destroyed the bridge behind us—more so, we have demolished the land behind us! Now, little ship, look out! Beside you is the ocean: it is true, it does not always roar, and at times it lies there like silk and gold and dreams of goodness. But there will be hours when you realize that it is infinite and that there is nothing more awesome than infinity."[10]

But Nietzsche is the clear winner in this exchange. No one would relinquish the expansionary pleasures of Christian narcissism if the only alternative were a dispiriting sense of diminishment. And although the ocean represents a boundless ego at the beginning of the passage I have just quoted, its meaning shifts dramatically in the third sentence. When Nietzsche compares the postmodern subject to a "little ship" set adrift on a sea that extends infinitely in every direction, he gestures toward another kind of limitlessness: one that is ontological rather than egoic and that is based on finitude instead of transcendence. As I will show later in this chapter, Nietzsche's oceanic metaphor resurfaces in Freud's exchanges with one of his most treasured interlocutors, showing that he too wanted more than the narrow plot of ground beneath his feet. Since this desire is also the driving force behind the recent resurgence of religious belief, we need to start addressing it. That is the project of this book.

NIETZSCHE AND FREUD were not the only figures thinking about these issues at this moment in time. The publication of *The Gay Science* ushered in a period of intense questioning about where religion comes from, whether human beings are capable of living without it, and what such a life would look like. These questions assumed a new urgency with the beginning of World War I and the subsequent rise of fascism. Two other important players in this extraordinary chapter of history—Lou Andreas-Salomé and Rainer Maria Rilke—shared Freud's skepticism about Christianity and his conviction that finitude is the only path leading out of religious illusion. Neither of them, however, believed reason to be the vehicle through which we traverse that path or saw Being-towards-death as a painful but necessary constriction of human existence. On the contrary, both link it to an extraordinary expansion.

Late in life, Salomé wrote an essay called "The God Experience," and in it she also emphasizes the narcissistic bases of religious belief. During the early years of her life, she confides, the only one she really communicated with was God. This figure, whom she thought of as a "grandfather," was an amalgamation of "maternal warmth" and "the perfection of fatherly power." Unlike her actual mother and father, though, his power and love were limitless and benefited only her. He "spoiled [her] mightily," "approved of everything [she] did," and "enjoyed giving [her] gifts so much that it seemed his pockets were overflowing." He could be summoned at any hour of the day or night to listen to her complaints and address her needs, and he made no reciprocal demands on her. Not surprisingly, her relationship to this figure made her feel "almost as omnipotent as he [was]."[11]

Salomé climbed onto the "lap" of her "God-grandfather" in order to avoid surrendering the gratifying fantasy that she was "everything." Like the child about whom Lacan writes in "The Mirror Stage,"[12] she was dependent upon external images for her sense of identity, so every time she passed a mirror, she looked into it. But instead of filling her with an intoxicating sense of plenitude, these glimpses of her reflected form carved away large chunks of what she believed to be her "self." "Whenever I looked into a [mirror]," Salomé writes, "I was disturbed to see so clearly that I was no more than what I beheld: so limited, so restricted; forced to *stop* by everything around me, even what was nearest at hand" (3).

Although it would be difficult to find a more powerful evocation of the limits that constrain us than Salomé's version of the mirror stage, the most frequently reiterated thesis in her letters and public writings is that everything in the world is connected to everything else. The "extra quality" that makes us human is not our reason, she argues, but rather our capacity to participate in this relationality *psychically* as well as *ontologically*.[13] She calls the process by which we do so "identification."[14] Although Salomé clearly took this concept from psychoanalysis, which played a central role in the final decades of her life, she confers upon it a very unpsychoanalytic meaning. To identify with someone or something in the Saloméan sense of the word is not to transform this other into an image of oneself, but rather to *feel* one's togetherness with it in an "unfathomable totality." This totality is unfathomable because it has no limits, either temporally or spatially, and because it defies explanation. It can be affectively registered, but it cannot be *thought*.

All of Salomé's important friendships with men were predicated on this kind of ontological intimacy—something that few of her contemporaries or biographers seem to have understood. Although there was a sexual dimension to her relationship with Rilke that was absent in her relationships with Nietzsche, Freud, Paul Rée, and even her husband, what made her affair with him so intense was not eros but rather the radicality and reciprocity of their identification with each other. In a letter dated January 6, 1913, Rilke told Salomé that it was through her that he was "linked with the human."[15] And years after his death, she wrote him an "open letter," in which she hails him as her "sibling." In this letter, she also provides her most detailed explanation of what this kind of relationality implies. "If for years I was your woman, it was because you were for me the first real truth—indistinguishable body and human spirit, undeniable proof of life itself. Word for word, I could have repeated to you what you said to me as a confession of love: 'You alone are real to me.' With these words we were wed, before we had even become friends. And we became friends hardly by choice but rather through a subliminally consummated marriage. Two halves did not seek completion in each other. But a surprised whole recognized itself in an unfathomable totality. So then we were rather like primal siblings, before incest had become sacrilege."[16]

Although Salomé explains what this primordial kinship means through her "marriage" to Rilke, she insists that it is "not limited [to] human beings alone, but opens simultaneously even to the dust of the cosmos."[17] She also emphasizes its givenness and its irreducibility. Nothing can alter the fact that "a bond of universal destiny" links us to everything else, because it has been forged at the level of our very Being. "Anything that 'is' bears within it the whole weight of existence, as if it were all things," Salomé writes near the end of "The God Experience" (11). Although she uses a conditional construction when formulating the second of these claims, in the immediately preceding paragraph she turns both into simple declaratives. We share the "weight" of everything's "existence," she writes there, because we share its existence and because "it *is* us" (10).

As Salomé explains through another extraordinary anecdote from her early life, it was by becoming aware of her own finitude that she gained psychic access to the limitlessness of Being. One day when she was still very young, and deep in the throes of her "God experience," she learned from a family servant that a couple was standing motionlessly in the garden. This news agitated her, because it was winter and she was afraid that the couple would freeze to death. Over each of the next few days, the servant reported that the man and woman were still standing there but that they were getting smaller and smaller. Eventually they dwindled into nothingness; the only traces of their former presence were the man's "battered hat" and the buttons from the woman's coat.[18]

Later, Salomé discovered that the figures standing in the garden had been snowmen. At the time, though, she took them to be two human beings who had suddenly and inexplicably "dissolved away." Their story brought her up against a new kind of limit, one even more disturbing than those revealed by her mirror reflection. Salomé turned for reassurance to her God-grandfather, but he was strangely mute on this topic. Unable to make any sense of the couple's disappearance, she had no resources with which to construct an egoic defense—no way of denying that she, too, could vanish from the world. At the moment when Salomé understood that her life would eventually come to an end, she stopped believing in God. Although her infantile narcissism lived on for a while in other forms, this initial encounter with her own mortality awakened in her "*the profound feeling of a deeply shared destiny with all things*" (Salomé's emphasis). It also gave her a "*reverence*" for everything that "is."[19] Not only did this reverence never leave Salomé, but it deepened each time she experienced her finitude. It is, finally, what she means when she uses the word "identification."

Rilke offers a similar account of mortality in two letters from 1923. By removing death from life, he argues, Christianity has rendered us "less definite" and "less earthly" and made us forget that we are "akin to tree, flower, and soil."[20] Christianity has also "embezzled" the sense of boundlessness that goes with being inside a family that includes everything, and attributed this feeling to a different kind of limitlessness: the one called "eternity." In so doing, it has transformed ontological "relation" into egoic "possession."[21] Like Salomé, Rilke also distinguishes the primordial connections that link us to other creatures and things from our affirmation of them. There is no getting outside of the unfathomable totality of which we are a part; not only is it spatially unbounded, but it also extends backward and forward in time. Most of us, though, are mentally estranged from this dimension of our Being. We are unable to say "yes" rather than "no" to the existence of other creatures and things because our ego has either incorporated them or excluded them. This will continue to be the case unless we allow the angel of death to graze us with his wing, because only finitude can teach us how to affirm. As Rilke puts it in a contemporaneous poem, our "mortal heart presses out a deathless, inexhaustible wine."[22]

As we have already seen, "reverence" is Salomé's name for this wine; it flows in the quiet of her veins. Since Rilke gives his affirmations a poetic form, thereby making them available to others, he prefers a more outward-turning nomination: "praise." He also maintains that "praising" is "what matters"—that it is the purpose for which we have been "summoned." "Be—and yet know the great void where all things begin, / " Rilke writes in another sonnet from the same sequence. "The infinite source of your own most intense vibration, / So that, this once, you may give it your perfect assent. / To all that is used-up, and to all the muffled and dumb / Creatures in the world's full reserve, the unsayable sums, / Joyfully add your*self*, and cancel the count."[23]

IN THE FALL OF 1912, Salomé went to Vienna to study psychoanalysis with Freud. She attended his Wednesday evening sessions for approximately a year and remained in close contact with him through letters and occasional visits until her death in 1937. She also responded in writing to all of Freud's major studies of religion—*The Future of an Illusion*, *Civilization and Its Discontents*, and *Moses and Monotheism*.[24] Although she often agreed with his criticisms, she repeatedly objected to his rationalism. For Salomé, religion is not so much an illusion as a misrecognition or faulty recollection of the ontological connections that link us to each other and the world. By celebrating reason, she asserts at one point, Freud attempts to dissociate himself from the masses who are deluded by Christianity. In so doing, he repudiates this kinship.[25] Strangely, though, Salomé also defends his rationalism against the objections of her contemporaries, because it led him to the "irrational." "His rational approach to scientific research . . . was such a splendid demonstration of false beliefs," she writes, "that it made a victor of the vanquished, *because* he had remained true to himself. Is this turn of events not a final act of compensation, in which the most mechanized Outwardness involuntarily finds its way back to a home in our most hidden Inwardness, where for the first time the words of Heraclitus about the infinite borders of the soul become true?"[26] It would be startling under any circumstances to hear someone associate Freud with concepts like "soul" and "infinite borders," but to have them conjured forth when *The Future of an Illusion* is still ringing in our ears is utterly mind-boggling. And Salomé does not just link Freud and Heraclitus in a general way; she also suggests that it was only when Freud discovered the unconscious that Heraclitus's words found their referent, because it is through this most seemingly private part of ourselves that we communicate with what resides outside.

Although this account of the unconscious is in part the product of Salomé's own secondary revisions, it is not entirely alien to Freud's own thinking. When he returns to the topic of religion in *Civilization and Its Discontents*, he marches under the banner of disillusionment, rather than reason; nursemaids try to appease us with their "lullaby about heaven," but the father of psychoanalysis knows that all we can expect from the future is more misery, because what drives human existence is a self-serving aggression (122). But an extraordinarily expansive concept emerges in the second paragraph of this book: that of the "oceanic feeling." This concept derives from Romain Rolland, a French playwright, novelist, and professor of musicology; specialist in and proponent of mysticism; and outspoken critic of nationalism and racism. However, although Rolland uses the same metaphor to evoke this sense of limitlessness as Nietzsche does in the passage quoted above, he is not talking about the manic pleasure of an imperial ego; the oceanic feeling is "imposed" upon us as a "fact," and it is a "sensation" instead of a thought—the sensation of the "contact" between ourselves and other beings.[27]

Shortly after Freud wrote *The Future of an Illusion*, he sent the book to Rolland. The latter responded much the way Salomé did: by agreeing with Freud's negative assessment of religion but disagreeing with him about its source.

Churches, Rolland argues, tap into a subterranean source of energy, which manifests itself in the human psyche through a sense of limitlessness. Unfortunately, they also "canalize" and "dry up" this "oceanic feeling"—force it into restricted channels, thereby robbing it of its defining attribute. Because of this, churches are the place where we are *least likely* to experience this boundlessness.[28]

Freud is keenly aware of the challenge the oceanic feeling poses to his thought, and he tries to discredit the concept the same way he tries to discredit Nietzsche: by emphasizing the solidity of the ground beneath his own feet. In 1931 he sent Rolland a copy of *Civilization and Its Discontents* with the humorous inscription "[from] the land-animal (*Landtier*) to his great oceanic friend."[29] In a passage early in *Civilization and Its Discontents*, he also treats the oceanic feeling as a manifestation of infantile narcissism, saying that it is based on a Christian notion of eternity: "If I have understood [Rolland] rightly, he means the same thing by [the oceanic feeling] as the consolation offered by an original and somewhat eccentric dramatist to his hero when facing a self-inflicted death. 'We cannot fall out of this world.' That is to say, a feeling of an indissoluble bond, of being one with the external world as a whole" (65).

Once again, though, something within Freud keeps affirming what he is trying to negate. We learn from a footnote that the text from which he takes this quotation is Christian Dietrich Grabbe's *Hannibal* and that the passage in question reads: "Indeed we shall not fall out of this world. We are in it for once and for all" (63).[30] Far from proving that the oceanic feeling is nothing but infantile narcissism, this passage helps us to see how little the two resemble each other. The narcissist seeks to include everything (good) within himself. Grabbe consoles his hero by reminding him that the opposite is true: the world contains us. The quotation from *Hannibal* also defies the other use to which Freud puts it. If we do not leave the world when we die, then it is all that we can ever experience; the oceanic feeling must consequently be something we access *through our finitude.*

In *The Interpretation of Dreams*, we learn that Hannibal was the psychoanalyst's favorite hero during his "later school days." Since the Carthaginian leader stood in Freud's mind for Jewry, and the opposing Romans for the Catholic Church, his identification with the former allowed him to take revenge upon the latter, which was at that point in time the primary purveyor of Viennese anti-Semitism.[31] Freud's invocation of Hannibal in the passage from *Civilization and Its Discontents* consequently forges a close connection between him and the concept against which he is ostensibly arguing. By replacing the words "shall not" with the word "cannot," Freud also inadvertently strengthens Grabbe's claim.[32] Finally, *two whole years* after reading the letter in which Rolland responded to *The Future of an Illusion*, he wrote the Frenchman that "your remarks about a feeling you describe as 'oceanic' have left me no peace."[33]

There is a fascinating backstory here, which opens onto a whole new dimension of Freud's thought. On February 22, 1923, Rolland wrote Freud to thank him for the complimentary things the psychoanalyst had said about him to a mutual friend.[34] Freud responded with great warmth, and the two men continued to exchange affectively charged letters for well over a decade. In May 1931 Freud described his relationship with Rolland in terms strikingly similar to those used by Salomé to describe her relationship with Rilke. "Approaching life's inevitable end, reminded of it by yet another operation and aware that I am unlikely to see you again," he confided to the other, "I may confess to you that I have rarely experienced that mysterious attraction of one human being for another as vividly as I have with you."[35] Freud wrote this letter after receiving one in which Rolland returned to—and elaborated further upon—his aquatic metaphor. "Since the appearance of my 'Oceanic' works," he writes there, "letters have come forth from all the corners of the earth (including your Austria), like a gushing of waters that had been suppressed."[36]

William B. Parsons maintains that what attracted Freud to Rolland was the latter's opposition to anti-Semitism, and he quotes a passage from one of the Frenchman's essays in support of this claim: "Hitlerism reveals itself to the eyes of the world as a usurpation of power over the great German people by savage illiterates or spiteful malignant creatures like Goebbels, whose weak and violent brain has been turned by Gobinean's ill-digested paradoxes about the 'inequality of Human Races,' and by the fumes of a delirious pride intent on believing in the supremacy of his race" (27). I don't know if Freud was familiar with this particular essay, but if he was, he would obviously have been moved by Rolland's defense of Jewish culture. However, I believe that he would have found another part of the passage even more compelling. Immediately before the lines I have just cited, Rolland "profess[es]" his "aversion and disgust for all racism." He also argues that since civilization is "the product of the efforts and combined achievements of all peoples, of all races which have intermingled with each other," it is "insane and absurd to pretend to sort them out." Freud ends a 1923 letter to Rolland on a similar note: "across all boundaries and bridges, I would like to press your hand."[37]

In 1926, the psychoanalyst also confided that what drew him to the mystic was the latter's "love for mankind" and that he himself had come to believe that unless humanity could find a way of mobilizing this feeling, it was doomed to extinction. "I revered you as an artist and apostle of love for mankind many years before I saw you," he wrote Rolland. "I myself have always advocated the love for mankind not out of sentimentality or idealism but for sober, economic reasons: because in the face of our instinctual drives and the world as it is . . . love [is] as indispensable for the preservation of the human species as . . . technology."[38] It might seem out of character for Freud to champion love for mankind, even for what he calls "sober economic reasons." Although he uses the word "love" from time to time in his early and middle work, it is usually as a derivative of sexuality, one about which he can be very ironic. However, in one of his earliest letters to Rolland, he characterizes it as the "most *precious* of *beautiful* illusions,"[39] a formulation that helps to explain why Freud attributes a futural meaning to the latter noun [my emphasis].

Freud also exchanged many letters with a Swiss pastor, Oskar Pfister, whom he admired for similar reasons. In a 1911 letter to the minister, he characterized his conflict with Alfred Adler as a disagreement about love. "He forgets the saying of the apostle Paul the exact words of which you know better than I: 'And I know that ye have not love in you.'" Freud also complained to Pfister that Adler has created for himself a world system without love and that "I am in the process of carrying out on him the revenge of the offended goddess Libido."[40] If factoring libido out of psychoanalysis led Adler to create a world system without love, then the opposite must also have been true: by making libido the cornerstone of psychoanalysis, Freud was creating—or at least attempting to create—a world system *with* love.

A later letter to Pfister also helps to explain why Freud invested so much hope in Eros. In it he responds to a book in which the pastor criticizes his "sexual theory and [his] ethics" (61). In this book, Pfister takes issue with one of the central theses of *Three Essays on the Theory of Sexuality*—the thesis that adult sexuality is stitched together out of components that are experienced sequentially by the infant, in the form of oral, anal, phallic—and, in the case of the girl—genital pleasure.[41] Since this part of Freud's argument contradicts the still-popular belief that children are "innocent" of sexuality, it is easy to see why a man of the cloth would object to it. But the psychoanalyst does not address this issue at all; what he seeks to defend in his letter to Pfister is rather the integrative capacity of the erotic drive—its ability to reconcile contradictions, overcome differences, and bring warring elements together. "Why on earth do you dispute the splitting up of the sex instinct into its component parts?" he asks the minister. "Do you not see that the multiplicity of these components derives from the multiplicity of the organs, all of which are erotogenic, i.e., fundamentally all aspire to reproduce themselves in the future organism." Together, Freud goes on to say, these organs "combine to form a living unit, all influencing, aiding or checking one another and remaining dependent on one another even in the process of their development" (62). This passage concludes with another surprising claim: the claim that although the concepts of "good" and "evil" may be quite alien to him, he nevertheless subscribes to a "high ideal"—one from which most human beings "depart most lamentably" (61–62).

Freud repeats this definition of the sexual drive in *Beyond the Pleasure Principle* and *Civilization in Its Discontents.* In the first of these works, he characterizes Eros as "constructive and assimilatory,"[42] and in the second he entrusts it with the function of joining "living substance" into "ever-larger units" (118). In *Civilization and Its Discontents,* Freud also expresses something that he only partially communicates in his letters to Pfister: the hope that the erotic drive will be able to do what morality cannot—bind human beings together in a constantly expanding group. Now, however, he no longer seems certain that this force is sexuality. When invoking it, he deploys the language of Necessity, suggesting that he is talking about an ontological imperative rather than a drive. "Civilization is a process in the service of Eros, whose purpose is to combine single human individuals, and after that families, then races, peoples and nations, into one great unity, the unity of mankind," Freud writes. "Why this has to happen, we do not know; the work of Eros is exactly this. These collections of men are to be libidinally bound together" (122).[43]

What makes this passage even more surprising is that it contradicts the central premise of *Civilization and Its Discontents.* Freud found World War I unspeakably depressing, not only because of the massive casualties it inflicted but also because it suggested that human beings may be constitutionally incapable of living together peacefully. "I do not doubt that mankind will survive even this war," he wrote Salomé in 1914, "but I know for certain that for me and my contemporaries the world will never again be a happy place. . . . [S]ince we can only regard the highest present civilization as burdened with an enormous hypocrisy, it follows that we are organically unsuited for it."[44]

The fear that there may be something within our biological constitution that is inimical to civilization remained with Freud and led to his theory of the death drive. In the primary works in which he develops this theory, *Beyond the Pleasure Principle* and *Civilization and Its Discontents,* he describes it as a "destructive" or "dissimilatory" force, which opposes the activity of the erotic drive.[45] In the later of these works, he also spells out the social ramifications of this conflict. Left to its own devices, Eros would create ever larger social units, but no sooner has it formed a group than Thanatos dissolves it, reducing its members to atomized individuals.[46]

Strangely, though, a different kind of Necessity surfaces in the first of these works, as well as the second. In *Beyond the Pleasure Principle*, Freud associates the death drive both with repetition and inertia and with "the production of new forms" (37). He also acknowledges this contradiction and suggests that the only way of resolving it is to assume that there are *two* innate forces calling us back to something more primordial—one that inhibits change and one that promotes it (37). Freud ends his 1914 letter to Salomé on a similar note, with the claim there is something vital within us that we have failed to take note of—an unrealized potentiality for relationality. "We [human beings must] abdicate," he writes her, "and the Great Unknown, He or It, lurking behind this Fate will sometime repeat this experiment with another race" (21).

Rolland's writings clearly struck an answering chord in Freud because he too felt a primordial connectedness to other creatures and things, and knew this feeling to be the only possible basis for social cohesion. Since Freud was a rationalist, and acutely sensitive to the violence lurking in religion, there was only one way to justify his hope, and that was to find a physiological source for this sense of kinship. As his correspondence with Pfister indicates, he turned for this purpose to the sexual drive. Although Freud knew from the very beginning that there are aspects of human existence that cannot be explained through Eros, he struggled for over a decade to ward off this knowledge. He explained anxiety dreams through erotic guilt, sexual difference through the castration crisis, and aggression through narcissism. But with the advent of World War I Freud could no longer deny that there is a counterforce. As the casualties mounted, he came to an even more devastating realization: the realization that the power of this force is far greater than that of the sexual drive.

For several years after writing *Beyond the Pleasure Principle*, Freud still clung to the hope that Eros would eventually prevail; in *The Ego and the Id*, he speculates that it might "fuse" in "serviceable" ways with Thanatos.[47] But by 1932 he no longer believed in the capacity of the sexual drive to domesticate the death drive; in an open letter to Albert Einstein, written on the brink of World War II from within a culture engulfed by anti-Semitism, he points to example after example of the opposite principle: the corruption of Eros by Thanatos.[48] What passes for "right" is never more than the "might" of a particular community. Sexuality also relies upon the death drive to achieve *its* goals, since if a lover wants to possess the object of his desire, he must overcome her. Finally, in order for the members of a group to cohere, they must find an external locus for their violence. Sometimes social unity is forged through war with another country or alliance of countries, but more often it is created by oppressing another entity within the same culture.

As Freud nears the conclusion of his letter to Einstein, he seems once again on the verge of declaring mankind to be "organically unfit" for civilization. But although he has just dispensed with the notion that there is any biological force capable of saving us from the death drive, he does the opposite; he tells Einstein that he still hopes for peace, since that is the direction in which humanity is evolving. Freud also ends his letter to Einstein in the same way he concludes *Beyond the Pleasure Principle*: with the acknowledgment that something here defies rational explanation. All that one can say with any certainty is that it exceeds, and provides the true rationale for, human existence. "How long shall we have to wait before the rest of mankind becomes pacifists too?" he asks, "There is no telling. . . . By what paths or by what side-tracks this will come about we [also] cannot guess. But one thing we *can* say: whatever fosters the growth of civilization works at the same time against war" (214).

As this passage helps us to see, when Freud invokes the concept of love in his correspondence with Rolland and Pfister, he is speaking about neither sexuality nor the emotion that wells up inside us when we allow someone else to incarnate our ideal. It is his word, rather, for what Salomé calls "identification": the psychic affirmation of our primordial kinship with other creatures and things, an affirmation that opens directly onto the oceanic feeling.

IN *CIVILIZATION AND ITS DISCONTENTS*, the death drive is something we direct outward, toward other creatures and things. Only when prevented from exteriorizing it by an external authority or the superego do we turn it back upon ourselves. Culture calls on us to injure ourselves rather than others because it is the only way we can live together peacefully. But since auto-aggression precipitates an intolerable degree of anxiety, it is also the source of our greatest misery and the reason why civilization keeps breaking down. In *Beyond the Pleasure Principle*, on the other hand, the death drive is what orients us toward our *own* mortality. It also reduces psychic tension to the lowest possible level, thereby bringing us to a state of nirvana. Freud tells us that he takes the concept of nirvana from Barbara Low (56), which is an odd claim, since in the passage he cites as his source, Low maintains that *he* is *hers*.[49] Her account of nirvana is also very different from his; she uses the word to refer not to a zero degree of excitation but rather to the manic pleasure we experience when we believe ourselves to be omnipotent. Freud is much likelier to have taken the concept of nirvana from Rolland, who equates it with quiescence.[50] He is reluctant to acknowledge this because nirvana is another name for "oceanic feeling." "'Oceanic' sentiment has nothing to do with my personal yearnings," the Frenchman wrote in a 1927 letter. "Personally, I yearn for eternal rest; survival has no attraction for me at all."[51]

Rolland could also have provided the inspiration for another of the claims Freud advances in *Beyond the Pleasure Principle*: the claim that each of us has to find his own path to the death which nirvana represents. "Let us live our lives knowing who we are," Rolland writes in one of his essays. "Let us place ourselves entirely into our ephemeral role, in the subtlety of its nuances, as well as in the fits of fury that sweep it away. Let us feel, think and act with all of our energy. . . . We must be ourselves, but our whole selves, and (this is the hardest part) without ever becoming the dupes of ourselves."[52] But what motivated Freud to write *Beyond the Pleasure Principle* was finally neither Salomé nor Rolland; it was, rather, his own life. During the last decade of the nineteenth century, he began to record and analyze his own dreams. While doing so he made a surprising discovery: that desire works through analogy. Because repression renders certain objects taboo but immortalizes the feelings that we have for them, the unconscious is constantly searching for socially acceptable substitutes to put in their place. In order for an object to be eligible for this role, it must resemble the taboo object in some respects but differ from it in others.

When dreaming, we are generally "fooled" by this substitution; we treat similarity as identity. For many years Freud believed that the goal of psychoanalysis was to disjoin what the unconscious had brought together. To this end, he distinguished between the manifest and latent content of a dream or a symptom and de-realized the former. The repressed wish was a stable and enduring signified, but the perceptual stimulus or memory through which it expressed itself was only a provisional and disposable signifier. The traumatized veterans whom Freud treated after World War I threw a monkey wrench into this interpretive machine.[53] Like all of the other analysands he had ever treated, they "suffered" from "reminiscences,"[54] and their reminiscences surfaced in their waking and sleeping dreams. However, these dreams could not be traced back to a primordial love object. They were, rather, the perceptual residue and psychic precipitate of a recent historical event.

Working with these shell-shocked soldiers forced Freud to confront something that had been previously unimaginable—and would soon become so again: the possibility that the unconscious might not be the only source of the analogies he had spent his life exploring. He does his utmost to accommodate this thought, even though it means pulling the rug out from under his own feet. By declaring that the aim of life is death, Freud levels the ontological distinction between humans, plants, and animals. He also helps us to see that rather than being a self-contained volume, authored by us, our history is only one chapter in a vast book whose meaning and shape we cannot even begin to grasp, let alone determine.

2

Orpheus Rex

> In [his] house, my imagination could not but listen to the unending monologue of a mind entirely alone, undistracted from itself and from the feeling of its own uniqueness.
>
> —Paul Valéry

> There's a crack in everything; that's how the light gets in.
>
> —Leonard Cohen

"ONLY ONE MAN EVER UNDERSTOOD ME," Hegel is reputed to have said on his deathbed, "and [even] he didn't understand me."[1] Although this story may not be historically verifiable, it conveys an allegorical truth: it reminds us that although the author of *The Phenomenology of Spirit* reifies the categories of master and slave, he never ceases to insist that the former depends upon the recognition of the latter.[2] In Nietzsche's late work, this is no longer the case. Zarathustra's defining attribute is *solitude.* This does not mean that he has opted out of history; on the contrary, he is the *maker* of history. However, he does not need to live among other human beings to effect social change, because he has interiorized the categories of "master" and "slave." Through a series of self-overcomings, in which each master turns into the slave of a new one, he will lift mankind to a higher level of development and bring the past into "*his* sunshine." As Nietzsche remarks in *The Gay Science*, "Every great human being exerts a retroactive force: for his sake all of history is put on the scale again."[3]

Solitude is also the defining attribute of a number of other important figures from this period, including Proust, who spent the last three years of his life in a cork-lined room, and whose great novel begins "For a long time I would go to bed early";[4] Cézanne, who was too busy painting to attend his mother's funeral;[5] and Rodin, whose life was "stunted, like an organ [he] no longer need[ed]."[6] These figures also inhabited the strange liminal temporality described by Nietzsche's madman; they lived after God had died but before his corpse had arrived. Monotheism was in decline, but something closely related had taken its place: something that might be called "monomania." That this self-preoccupation was almost always unhappy only functioned to strengthen its grip on the male psyche—to make it richer, deeper, and more exclusionary.

In 1894 Salomé published a book with the suggestive title *Friedrich Nietzsche: The Man in His Works.* In it she provides a somber account of the philosopher's thought, emphasizing his fear of death (143), his attempt to "unite disciple and master within himself" (52), and the "religious drive" that "always dominated his being and his knowledge" (88). Salomé also acknowledges the destructive sides of a condition she often champions: narcissism.[7] From the very beginning, she observes, Nietzsche "thought and wrote for himself," "describes only himself," and "transposes his own self into his thoughts" (4). By the time he was working on his last books, nothing remained but "the great solitary," who is the "culmination of historical development," and "the peak of everything" (47–48).

Although *Friedrich Nietzsche* appeared two years before Josef Breuer and Sigmund Freud's collaborative book, *Studies on Hysteria,* and six years before Freud's *Interpretation of Dreams,* it is a fully formed psychoanalytic case history. Salomé also treats Nietzsche's writing the way Freud will later treat Leonardo's art:[8] as "an involuntary and unperceived memoir."[9] "The sum of monologues that constitute the many volumes of his aphorisms is a single, great work of memoirs reflective of his intellectuality," she writes. "I wish to attempt a picture of that here: the meaning of the thought-experience in Nietzsche's mental constitution—the confessions in his philosophy" (5). Her account of these "confessions" anticipates Freud's 1908 account of authorship—his claim that "his Majesty the Ego [is] the hero alike of every day-dream and of every story," to whom "nothing can happen."[10] But there is also a historical side to Salomé's study of Nietzsche: she links his subjectivity to "the underlying inner dynamics of [his] time," which she characterizes as "'the anarchy within instincts' of creative and religious forces that so energetically desire satiety that they cannot be content with the crumbs that fall from the table of modern knowledge" (29)—i.e., with the late-nineteenth-century fantasy that man does not need God because he is capable of *being* God.

After Salomé's official turn to psychoanalysis, she seldom speaks directly about Nietzsche; she devotes many entries of her *Freud Journal* to Rilke but none to him, and although she reserves at least one chapter of *Looking Back* for each of the other significant men in her life, she alludes only in passing about the author of *The Gay Science* and *Thus Spoke Zarathustra.* He is, however, a constant reference point. In an important passage from her memoirs, Salomé emphasizes that although her thought diverges sharply from Nietzsche's, it originates in the same source. "I [was] fascinated by something in [his] words and nature that didn't find full expression when he talked with Paul Rée," she confides there. "For me there were memories or half-conscious feelings of the most childlike sort involved, arising from the most personal and indestructible part of my childhood."[11]

Nietzsche is also one of Salomé's primary interlocutors in the final entry of her *Freud Journal*. In this extraordinary passage, which I will quote in its entirety, she represents solitude as a malady, and psychoanalysis as the cure.

> The way in which one beholds a person in psychoanalysis is something that goes beyond all affect toward him, somewhere in the depths both aversion and love become only differences of degree. A relationship is achieved beyond one's own fidelity or infidelity. Approximately this way: if hitherto one had so swiftly and forcefully penetrated the partner that he too soon and to one's own disappointment was left behind, now one would turn quietly, strangely, and see him following and be close to him. And yet not close to him, but close to all. Close anew to all, and in it, to oneself. And all of the vanished persons of the past arise anew, whom one has sinned against by letting them go; they are there as from all eternity, marked by eternity—peaceful, monumental, and one with being itself, as the rock figures of Abu Simbel are one with the Egyptian rock and yet, in the form of men, sit enthroned over the water and the landscape.[12]

The figure of the solitary appears in several different guises in this passage. His most overt—and most Nietzschean—representative is Pharaoh Ramses II, who carved two temples out of solid rock at Abu Simbel, a site on the west bank of the Nile, and adorned one of them with colossal statues of himself and two sun gods. Salomé does not mock Ramses II's attempt to deify himself, nor does she draw attention to his clay feet; she simply points out that the monumental statues are part of the same ontological rock as the river and the cliffs.

The second representative of the solitary man is Adam, who makes his entrance through the very unpsychoanalytic concept of "sin," and the word "partner."[13] After creating the heavens and the earth, we read in Genesis, God fashioned a man in his image and installed him in Eden. He soon concluded, though, that it was not "good" for man to be "alone" and decided to make Adam a "helper" (2:18). Since Eve is generally assumed to be this "helper" and enters the world in an unfallen condition, the word has become the locus for competing definitions of "woman."[14] The Luther Bible feminizes it; the King James Bible qualifies it through the adjective "meet," *Die Heilige Schrift* attaches "*als sein Gegenstück*" ("as his counterpart") to it; and *The New Oxford Annotated Bible* supplements it through the same noun that appears in Salomé's text. Its translation of the contested clause reads: "I will make him a helper as his *partner*" (my emphasis).[15]

Eve is not Yahweh's first attempt at providing this partner. After concluding that it is not good for man to be alone, he creates the "animal[s] of the field" and "bird[s] of the air," and parades them before Adam.[16] But although the latter names these creatures, indicating that he feels addressed by them, and even speaks the same language, he does not find a helper among them. God then puts Adam to sleep, removes one of his ribs, and fashions Eve out of it. When Adam sees her, he exults: "This at last is bone of my bones, and flesh of my flesh; this one shall be called Woman, for out of Man this one was taken" (2:23).[17] The question posed by Genesis 2:18–23 is therefore not "What is woman?" but rather "What is mobilized in the encounter between Adam and Eve that is not there when he meets the animals and birds? What is the basis of human relationality?"

The answer, as the editors of *The New Oxford Annotated Bible* seem to understand, is analogy. "To be fully human," they write in their commentary on these verses, "one needs to be in relation to others who correspond to oneself. Helper not in a relationship of subordination but mutuality and interdependence."[18] Their inclusion of the word "partner" in the body of the text is obviously an attempt to consolidate this reading. Unfortunately, though, the larger passage does not support it. A partner, *The Oxford English Dictionary* tells us, is "one who has a share or part with another or others; one who is associated with another or others in the enjoyment or possession of anything; a partaker, sharer."[19] It is therefore an implicitly plural category. Adam does not relate to Eve in this way; he understands that she is flesh of *his* flesh, but not that he is flesh of *hers*. He thinks of her as a derivative of himself.

The editors of *The New Oxford Annotated Bible* are also working with an inadequate definition of analogy. In the footnote I quoted a moment ago, they characterize it as the correspondence of one thing *to* another, and they limit it to human beings. In actuality, though, analogy is the correspondence of two or more things *with* each other, and it structures every aspect of Being. What distinguishes us from other creatures is our capacity to *affirm* these correspondences. Since we cannot affirm the analogies linking us to other people without acknowledging that we are bound by the same limits, we are reluctant to do so. This refusal takes many forms, one of which is prominently displayed in Genesis 2:18–23: the transformation of a bidirectional analogy into one that is unilateral. This is devastating for Adam as well as Eve, because it renders her incapable of giving him the recognition he needs.

In the conclusion to *Freud Journal*, Salomé subjects the story of Genesis 2:18–23 to some important revisions. The resulting narrative goes something like this: Knowing that it is not good for Adam to be alone, and understanding that they cannot be fully themselves without his affirmation, the birds and animals display themselves to him. Their solicitation strikes an answering chord in him, and he says the word that lets each creature Be. Adam, though, does not find the capacity for a reciprocal acknowledgment in any of the animals or birds. Feeling even lonelier, he turns to psychoanalysis for help. His analyst tells him that the solution to his present problem resides in the past, and she asks him to join her in looking back. When he does so, he finds someone who closely resembles him and who is able to meet his recognition with her own. They spend the rest of their lives ringing variations on the same "fleshly" theme.

But this story is not really about Adam and Eve; it is about us. Like Adam, we have all repudiated at least one of our primal siblings, and most of us have repeated this act over and over again. It is, however, never too late to acquire the art of analogical thinking, and because the analytic relationship is a "partnership," it constitutes an ideal venue for doing so. This might seem a surprising claim, since a classic analysis is as unidirectional as Adam's recognition of Eve, but Salomé insists upon it. She characterizes the analyst as a "partner" and she performs this partnership at the level of her prose. She uses the impersonal pronoun "one" ("*Man*") throughout the conclusion to her *Freud Journal*, making it difficult to determine whether she is speaking about the analyst or the analysand. By the time we arrive at the third sentence, in which the word "partner" appears, we have been weaned of our desire to establish which participant in the analytic drama occupies which position, because each is so clearly situated on both sides of this divide. But there are also many other players in this scene, because the analytic analogy eventually expands to accommodate not just the four people Freud suggests are present in every sexual act[20] but *everyone.*

Salomé offers a fuller version of the same argument in *Mein Dank an Freud.* In this 1931 book, she characterizes the analytic exchange as a "double experience of giving and taking,"[21] and she explains what this means by comparing the feelings of an analyst at the end of a successful analysis to those of the analysand. The analysand experiences "a return home in the feeling of being welcomed and celebrated in the All-Together" she writes (17).[22] The analyst, on the other hand, thinks about how easy it would be to confuse this Whole with the plenitude of the ego, or the false unity promised by religion. She also confronts the very real possibility that if she were to succumb to this confusion, she might never find her way back home. Because of the reciprocal nature of the analogy, each entertains for the other "the most serious respect that one human being can owe another."[23]

The analogy that links the analyst and the analysand is finitude. Because the same analogy links us to every other living being, it is infinitely extendable.

However, although our finitude opens onto an unfathomable totality, it also renders us extraordinarily vulnerable to everything—war, religion, group psychology, nationalism, and the fantasy of a sovereign subjectivity—that promises to render us omnipotent and omnipresent. There is no way of transcending this vulnerability; it is part of what it means to be mortal. In order to illuminate the path leading to the "All-Together," the analyst must consequently not only show the analysand a forgotten aspect of himself, but also recognize in the analysand a disowned part of herself.

Salomé also offers a powerful alternative to Nieztsche's theory of eternal recurrence in the conclusion to *Freud Journal.* In *Project for a Scientific Psychology*, Freud argues that the present has the power not just to change our *recollection* of the past but also to subject its consequences to a corresponding transformation—i.e., to make what has already occurred happen again, in a new way. In the passage in which he theorizes this retroactivity, which he calls "*Nachträglichkeit*," Freud explores the process through which a benign event becomes a trauma.[24] As shown by the case histories in *Studies on Hysteria*, *Nachträglichkeit* can also have the opposite effect: it can render traumatic events benign.[25] This is one of the grounding assumptions of psychoanalysis "proper," and it figures prominently in the conclusion to the *Freud Journal.*

Salomé also imputes a number of other powers to *Nachträglichkeit*: the ability to wash away sin, resurrect the dead, and level the divisions that have sprung up between us. It might seem startling to find concepts like sin and resurrection in a description of analysis, but they play an important role in the transformation to which Salomé subjects the biblical narrative. That story turns upon an original crime, which occurred when Adam and Eve ate fruit from a forbidden tree, but for which we are all somehow responsible. After they violate this prohibition, God expels them from Eden and dooms each to a particular kind of suffering—Eve to the miseries of motherhood and a subordinate position and Adam to the hardship of work. But a far more radical punishment awaits them in the future—a punishment that will fall on both alike, and strip Adam of all claim to ontological superiority. "By the sweat of your face you shall eat bread until you return to the ground," God says to Adam, "for out of it you were taken; you are dust, and to dust you shall return."[26] It is—significantly—only this *last* punishment that Christianity offers to suspend. But the sin to which Salomé refers has nothing to do with serpents or forbidden fruit, nor can it be laid at the feet of Adam and Eve. It inheres, rather, in the act of turning away from the Other. No redeemer can absolve us of this guilt. If we want to liberate ourselves from it, we must turn back to those we have left behind, and tarry with them. Doing so will not make us immortal, but it will permit those who have "vanished" due to our neglect to "arise anew."

There is also another reason why Salomé brings the concepts of "sin" and "redemption" into this discussion. As we have already seen, the notion of an ineradicable guilt figures prominently in both *The Gay Science* and *Totem and Taboo*. Guilt is ineradicable in the first of these texts because it is ontological in nature; man is guilty because he is not capable of replacing God—because he is a finite being (120). Guilt is unredeemable in *Totem and Taboo* because the rituals through which the band of brothers atone for their crime provide the vehicle for its repetition.[27] And although this guilt is Oedipal in nature, it might as well be ontological, because it passes from generation to generation (158). In the last entry of her *Freud Journal*, Salomé doesn't just redefine what it means to sin; she also uses *Nachträglichkeit* to liberate us from this "always-already" guilt. Suddenly nothing is irrevocable.

Salomé also responds to another dimension of Nietzsche's thought in the passage under discussion. In *The Gay Science*, the philosopher urges us to say "no" to metaphysics and "yes" to earthly things by creating new values. We "continually *make* something that is not yet there," he writes, "the whole perpetually growing world of valuations, colors, weights, perspectives, scales, affirmations, and negations. . . . Whatever has *value* in the present world has it not in itself . . . but has rather been given, granted value, and *we* were the givers and granters" (171). However, as Heidegger points out in his monumental study of Nietzsche, the creation of values looks suspiciously like a new form of metaphysics:[28] one that has its locus in the human psyche rather than the Christian God or the Platonic Demiurge. Once again, the physical world pales by comparison with the Idea. The human subject is also a giver and a producer, instead of someone who receives and praises.

It is by "identifying" with other creatures and things, Salomé explains in her *Freud Journal*, that we receive and praise the world. When we notice something with the "senses and intellect," we do not say "I" or "you" to it; rather, we "set it apart for itself"—take our distance from it. When we love something, by contrast, we "rediscover ourselves" (95). Since it would be easy to read this last claim as an endorsement of narcissism, I want to underscore the prefix in its final verb. Salomé does not say "discover ourselves" but rather "*re*discover ourselves." To rediscover oneself in another is to recognize him or her as another embodiment of the same flesh.

ALTHOUGH SALOMÉ takes the concept of *Nachträglichkeit* from Freud, her psychoanalysis is very different from his. Freud seeks to exhume the past so that he can uncover and treat what is pathological or disabling in the analysand's psychic organization. This process depends from start to finish upon analogy. Unconscious desire gets around repression both in dreams and in neurotic symptoms by displacing its affective charge onto "innocent" memories and perceptions.[29] Since displacement is possible only where there is commonality, it is constantly searching for resemblances. The transference is a variation on the same principle; the analysand finds some echo of his mother or father in the analyst and uses it as the "justification" for shifting the feelings he has for the former onto the latter. The analyst gains access to the analysand's unconscious through a reverse process—by moving from the substitutory term to what it replaces. In order to succeed in this task, he, too, must look for resemblances.

These analogies are, however, profoundly undemocratic; the latent term is real, but the manifest term only a temporary stand-in. They are also utterly arbitrary. In *The Interpretation of Dreams*, Freud asks what his dream of the botanical monograph would have looked like if he had not had a conversation with Professor Gärtner on the preceding day about a patient named "Flora," and he answers his own question by saying that "if these chains of thought had been absent others would no doubt have been selected," because "it is easy enough to construct such chains, as is shown by the puns and riddles that people make everyday for their entertainment. The realm of jokes knows no boundaries."[30]

Freud also characterizes the analysand's hunt for similarities as a "compulsion and an illusion which melt[s] away with the conclusion of the analysis."[31] It is a "compulsion" because it provides the vehicle through which involuntary memories return, and an "illusion" because it depends upon the fabrication of a "false connection."[32] In a later text he writes that displacement leads to the "transvaluation of all values," because "*psychical intensity passes over from the thoughts and ideas to which it properly belongs on to others which in our judgment have no claim to any such emphasis*" (his emphasis).[33] Since Freud takes this phrase from Nietzsche, who uses it when talking about our capacity to create values, it permits him once again to emphasize the fabricated nature of similarity. Not surprisingly, then, although a Freudian analysis cannot really begin until the analysand has found some way of linking the analyst to his mother or father, it cannot end until this same analogy has been dismantled.

Finally, although the father of psychoanalysis approaches every psyche with the expectation that he will find some version of the Oedipus complex, he regards each analysand as an "individual," and he looks for personal solutions to private problems. The same is true of the pre-psychoanalytic Freud; the "reminiscences" from which the hysteric "suffers" are unique to her, as are the symptoms through which they return.[34] The circle of those who benefit from the transformation of the past is consequently very small: it consists only of the patient herself, and those in her immediate environment.

Since Salomé was so attuned to the phenomenological dimensions of psychoanalysis, she understood from the very beginning that when the unconscious displaces affect from a repressed wish to a perceptual stimulus or memory, it does not create a new analogy; rather, it acknowledges one that already exists. Infantile memories are precious because they "[unite] us with the world-outside-us," she writes, "bridging the gap which otherwise seems to separate us as individuals from everything around us"—and even "what we term 'objectivity' rather than 'love' is nothing but our conscious mind utilizing *its* methods in opening itself willingly to the unconscious, where we have never ceased denying individual isolation, insisting upon our shared roots with the cosmos."[35] Consequently, if there is something pathological, it is the *refusal* to associate. The goal of analysis is to undo this refusal—to turn its "no" into a "yes."

Since the unconscious is only in a position to affirm the analogies that are perceptually and mnemonically available to it, and always privileges some of them and repudiates others, it might seem difficult to see how it could open onto the All. But since everything is connected to so many other things, and each thing bears within it the weight of all things, if we are able to recognize even *one* of our primal siblings, we will immediately find ourselves surrounded by kin. As Salomé explains in *Looking Back*, "Whoever reaches into a rosebush may seize a handful of flowers; but no matter how many one holds, it's only a small portion of the whole. Nevertheless, a handful is enough to experience the nature of the flowers. Only if we refuse to reach into the bush, because we can't possibly seize all the flowers at once, or if we spread out our handful as if it were the *whole* of the bush itself—only then does it bloom apart from us, unknown to us, and we are left alone" (20).

The unconscious opens onto the world in another way as well; it accommodates not just personal memories but also the "reminiscences of mankind."[36] In the passage in which Salomé advances this claim, she limits it to psychotics and imputes an archetypal status to our recollections, much as Jung does. In a later chapter of the same text, though, she writes that we *all* "live through more than we are." She also imparts some particularity to these inherited reminiscences by describing a woman who retained the intensity of affects that her mother had already "abreacted . . . quite as though [they] were her own," even though they went "far beyond her own experience" (170). And in the final entry of her *Freud Journal*, Salomé jettisons her implicitly synchronic account of history for one that is much more open and dynamic. If we live through more than we are, she argues, it is both because the past lives on in the present and because the present exerts a transformative influence over the past. A psychic *Nachträglichkeit* can also open the door to one that is historical in nature. By turning around to face the partner he has left behind, and tarrying with her, the subject described in this passage also reaches out to all of the others who have been left behind—either by himself or by his predecessors.

As my reader may already have observed, another interlocutor has silently joined the conversation I am having with Freud and Salomé: Walter Benjamin. He also characterizes the past as a book, and he urges us to read this book by recognizing the similarities that connect our moment to earlier moments in time.[37] If we do this, he writes, we will change the "character" of the past—transform its defeats into victories, and awaken the dead.[38] Since there is a specificity to Benjamin's account of history that is missing in the conclusion to the *Freud Journal*, it might seem time to jump theoretical "ships." However, we have not yet learned everything that this passage has to teach us.

AS WE HAVE ALREADY SEEN, Salomé focuses more on recognition than repression; she seeks to facilitate the acknowledgment of previously unacknowledged analogies. Freud left a rich legacy of categories for explaining the refusal to recognize something (projection, disavowal, fetishism, and negation), but she dispenses with those as well. Instead of speaking about exteriorization, splitting, covering over, or denial, she uses a number of terms for which there is no clear psychoanalytic referent: letting go, turning around, and tarrying with. In the sentence beginning "the way in which one beholds a person in psychoanalysis is something that goes beyond all affect toward him," she also chooses a verb connoting a reciprocal perceptual exchange: "*vorsehen*." Literally translated, "*vorsehen*" means "to look ahead," or "in front of oneself," but it derives most of its force here from its opposition to the negatively coded action of "leaving behind." It is also reparative; in order to perform this activity, we must turn around—face what we have left behind. As the English translator helps us to see, *vorsehen* has a similar relationship to another negatively-coded concept: that of "letting go." When we turn away from someone, we cast her away. If we want to undo this destructive act, we must consequently not just turn around to face her but also *behold* her—embrace her with our look.

By imputing a broadly metaphoric meaning to the verbs I have just parsed, I was able to piece together a revisionary account of Genesis 2:18–23, but each of these verbs makes a *direct* reference to the myth of Orpheus and Eurydice. This myth has come down to us primarily through two classical works: Virgil's *Georgics*,[39] and Ovid's *Metamorphoses*.[40] In both works, Orpheus is a musician with magical powers and Eurydice is his wife. She dies after being bitten by a poisonous snake, and he descends to Hades to request that she be restored to him. He appeals to the gods of the underworld through a song, and they grant his wish, on the condition that he not look at Eurydice during their journey back to earth. Orpheus violates this prohibition and loses Eurydice a second time. When he attempts to return to Hades, Charon blocks his way. He then retreats from human society and sings to nature until he is killed and dismembered by a band of women. But Virgil and Ovid impute a very different meaning to each of these shared elements, and their narratives also diverge at a number of important points.[41] Since these distinctions have important ramifications for both gender and heterosexuality, I want to look closely at each of them.

Virgil's version of the myth appears in Book IV of *The Georgics*.[42] It begins with the death of Eurydice, which is precipitated by an extramarital force: she is bitten by the poisonous snake while fleeing another man (Aristaeus), who is attempting to rape her. Devastated by his loss, Orpheus sings about her day and night on a "lonely shore" and then descends to the underworld to rescue her. Virgil focuses on the effects rather than the content of Orpheus's song; we learn that the "insubstantial shades" of "those who lie in darkness" are "stirred," that Cerberus stands "agape," that Ixion's wheel grinds to a halt, and that the Furies are "spellbound," but we are not told what the musician does to provoke these reactions. Virgil also minimizes Orpheus's triumph by not mentioning how Pluto and Proserpine react to his song, eliding the moment in which they grant his wish and moving immediately to the fatal moment in the return journey. The musician tries to avoid "mischance" by walking ahead of Eurydice, but as they approach their destination, he is "seized" by a "sudden frenzy" of love and turns to look at her (251–253). She vanishes, "like smoke mingling with thin air." Thereafter, "no thought of love or wedding song" can "bend" Orpheus's "soul." When he is frustrated in his attempt to return to the underworld, he weeps for seven months "beneath a lofty crag" and "unfold[s]" his piteous tale in "cool dales." He then "roam[s] the frozen north" until he is torn apart by the Ciconian women, who resent his devotion to his wife (255). Even after his death, he continues to mourn her—his severed head calls out, "Eurydice" (257).

This version of the myth is insistently backward-turning; Orpheus journeys to Hades because he cannot forget Eurydice, and he violates the ban on looking at her because his thoughts are directed toward her. There is also nothing inherently different about the second of these looks; it is deadly only because it is prohibited. Virgil emphasizes the arbitrary nature of the prohibition by not mentioning it until it is violated, placing it in parentheses, referring to it as a "ruthless tyrant's pact," and declaring that Orpheus's transgression is "meet for pardon, did Hell know how to pardon." He returns to the topic of the gods' cruelty a few lines later. After describing the bard's failed attempt to return to Hades, he asks: "What could he do? Whither turn, twice robbed of his wife? With what tears move Hell? To what deities address his prayers?" (255).[43] Finally, even after Eurydice's second death, Orpheus has eyes only for her. From the beginning until the end of this version of the myth, these two figures are thus a *couple.*

Virgil also makes room in the myth for Eurydice. He narrates it through Proteus, who recounts it to Aristaeus, and embeds it within a larger narrative of guilt and retribution (251–259). Aristaeus has lost his bees because he is responsible for Eurydice's death, Proteus explains—and although this punishment may seem severe, it is actually "far less" than he "deserve[s]." While describing Orpheus's grief, Proteus also addresses Eurydice, instead of Aristaeus: "But [Orpheus], solacing an aching heart with music from his hollow shell, sang of you, dear wife, sang of you to himself on the lonely shore, as day drew night, of you as day departed" (251–253). As Charles Segal points out, Virgil even gives Eurydice a voice (175), and she uses it to establish her death as a catastrophe for *her*, as well as for *him.* "What madness, Orpheus, what dreadful madness has brought disaster alike upon you and me, poor soul?" she cries out when he turns around to look at her, "See, again the cruel Fates call me back, and sleep seals my swimming eyes. And now farewell! I am borne away, covered in night's vast pall" (255).

Finally, Orpheus's love for Eurydice is both what motivates him to sing and the theme of his songs, and he corresponds with the natural world through his music.[44] His songs attract oaks and charm tigers because his grief is akin to theirs; just as the nightingale "bewails her young ones' loss, when a heartless ploughman . . . pluck[s] them unfledged from the nest," so he "fills all around with plaintive lamentations" (255). His voice also awakens a comparable emotion in them; when his severed head calls out his wife's name, the banks re-echo "Eurydice . . . all along the stream." Consequently, although gender is marked in Virgil's account of the myth, it does not harden into an antithesis. Art and heterosexuality are also complementary. Last, but not least, Orpheus's grief over the loss of Eurydice opens his psyche to the world.

Ovid recounts most of his version of the myth in Book X of *The Metamorphoses* and the rest in Book XI. His narrative begins with Orpheus and Eurydice's wedding—i.e., with the event that should officially establish them as a couple. It is, however, a melancholy affair; Hymnaeus (the god of marriage) attends the ceremony, but his torch "keeps hissing and smoking and making eyes water" and refuses to ignite. Eurydice also dies shortly thereafter, without the intervention of another man; she is bitten by a snake while walking with her "fellow naiads." Orpheus doesn't waste much time grieving before he descends to the underworld, and when he arrives he seems more interested in conquering death than in rescuing his wife; after mourning her death "*long enough* in the world of the living," Ovid writes, he "dare[s]" to go the "realm of the Styx" to "*work* on the shades" (165; my emphasis).[45]

As we can see from the text of Orpheus's song, which Ovid includes in *The Metamorphoses*, this "work" is oratorical in nature.[46] The musician begins by promising not to pull the rhetorical wool over Pluto's and Proserpina's ears, and then proceeds to do just that. He offers a jaunty account of Eurydice's death, admits that he hasn't made much of a fuss about it, yet claims to be "defeated" by love. Orpheus also presents the rape through which Pluto secured Proserpina as another example of love.[47] He spends the remainder of his song trying to outwit the gods of the underworld by pretending to submit to their power:

> O gods of the world beneath the earth . . . if I may lay aside the poet's stock of flowery, false phrases and speak the simple truth . . . I did not come down to the twilight of Tartarus to see what I could see, or chain Medusa's three-headed monster, covered with snakes. The reason I am here is—my wife; she stepped on a viper, and he shot his poison into her and snatched away her life when she was young and blossoming still. I wanted to be able to bear it; I won't deny that I've tried to. Love defeated me. . . . [I]f the story of that long-ago abduction is not false, Love joined the two of you as well. . . . You own us, entirely, and though we may delay a little, sooner or later as we hurry on we come to this one place. . . . When the years that are [Eurydice's] have come and gone and she is old enough to die, she, too, will belong to you by law. . . . I'm only asking you to lend her to me for a little while. (165–166)

Orpheus accomplishes what he sets out to do. The souls of the dead weep, Tantalus stops trying to get a drink of water, Ixion's wheel stops, and the Furies are "overcome." Pluto and Proserpina are also unable to "deny his prayer," and they summon Eurydice, so that Orpheus can be reunited with her. But neither of them seems particularly happy to see the other; Eurydice arrives in the company of the "recent dead" and "walk[s] slowly" toward Orpheus, "limping from her wound." The newlyweds are even more disconnected during their journey back to earth; they "[pick] their way through deathly silent places along a steep upward path, enveloped in thick fog and hard to see," and Eurydice vanishes as soon as her husband looks at her (166).[48] Ovid reduces the substantial speech Virgil gives Eurydice to a barely audible "farewell," and writes that the musician turns to look at his wife because he is "eager to see her" and that she "blame[s]" him "not at all (for what could she blame him for, except for loving her?)" (166).

However, the next few paragraphs undercut the first of these claims and complicate the second, suggesting that Ovid is relaying his characters' thoughts rather than his own. We learn that Orpheus is as rigid with fear when he sees his wife vanish as an unnamed man was when he saw a chained Cerberus being led out of Hades, because this spectacle brings him face-to-face with death: "Orpheus was stunned by the second [disappearance] of his wife just like the man who saw the three-headed dog (with a chain around its middle neck), and was terrified and whose terror did not leave him until his life did, when his body froze into stone" (166).

As this simile also tells us, Orpheus tries to ward off death by transforming Eurydice into the freakish member of another species; when he turns toward her, he therefore "sees" not a fellow human being but rather something more closely resembling what the unnamed man saw: a three-headed dog. This perceptual deformation freights his backward look with a new kind of fatality; the gaze he directs at Eurydice on the slope leading to earth kills her not only because it transgresses a divine prohibition but also because it is *inherently* murderous. Not surprisingly, then, Orpheus is easily dissuaded from returning to Hades to recover his wife, and he mourns for only seven days before withdrawing to "towering Rhodope and to Haemus" to rage against the "cruel gods of the underworld."

At no point in this narrative could Orpheus and Eurydice really be said to be a couple—and what happens during the journey back to earth also makes it impossible for Orpheus to love *other* women. After Eurydice's death, he shifts his desire to "tender males" and encourages other men to do the same (167). At first Ovid claims not to know why Orpheus spurns his female suitors; perhaps it is because the year ended "sadly" for him, or perhaps it is his way of remaining faithful to Eurydice. In the next sentence, though, he remarks that "many women longed for unions with the bard" and "grieved when he rejected them," suggesting that the musician turns to boys because he dislikes women, and he provides further evidence for this reading later in *The Metamorphoses.* Orpheus uses his music not just to celebrate pederasty but also to demonize women; he sings songs about "boys loved by gods and girls gone mad with forbidden desire and rightly punished for their lust" (168). And just before the Ciconian women kill him, one of them cries out: "Look! Look! There he is, the man who hates us!" (182).

Since no one can die in our stead, Orpheus's finitude does not vanish along with Eurydice, and "complaining bitterly" against the "cruel gods of the underworld" proves equally ineffective, so he tries to overcome his limits in another way: by dominating nature. His music is also the vehicle for *this* coercion. Orpheus sits down in an "open field," where there are no trees or auditors, and remedies both of these "lack[s]" by making the "shade" come to him (167). As he "pluck[s] the sweet strings of his lyre," oak, poplar, ash, pine, cypress, palm, and fruit trees assemble around him, and then a "gathering of beasts" and a "flock of birds" (167–168).

However, after comparing Orpheus to the unnamed man who saw the three-headed dog, Ovid factors two more figures into the equation. "Like Olenos, too," he writes, "who took his wife, Lethaea's, crime upon himself and wished to be considered guilty of it; and like you, unhappy Lethaea, too sure of your own beauty: two hearts once joined completely, and now two stones on Ida's rainy summit." Ovid uses this part of the simile both to override the gender binary (he aligns Orpheus with a woman and Eurydice with a man) and to reaffirm the ontological connection between the two characters. Like Lethaea, who was transformed into a stone because she was too proud, he tells us, Orpheus was petrified when confronted with the undefeatable foe he had hubristically imagined he could conquer. Like Olenos, who tried to protect his wife from this fate by assuming her guilt, Eurydice also tried to shield Orpheus from death by maintaining his innocence, and returning uncomplainingly to Hades. But although they are now stranded from each other, Orpheus and Eurydice were "once joined in close embrace," just as Lethaea and Olenos were—and death will bring them together again, just as it did the latter couple.[49]

Ovid also attaches a redemptive coda to this story—a coda that fulfils the prophecy contained in the simile. He begins Book XI by adding some boulders to the group assembled around Orpheus: "With this song, the Thracian bard had gathered trees and animals around him and even boulders bumped along to join them" (182). This is startling as well as comical, because Orpheus recounts so many consecutive stories that by the time we reach the end of Book X, we have forgotten all about him. This sentence also marks the turning of the Wheel of Fortune; when the boulders arrive, so do the Ciconian women, and they strip him of his power to compel. At first the "harmony" of his voice "overcome[s]" the missiles they hurl at him, but before long the stones stop hearing him. The musician then appeals directly to the women, but "for the first time ever" he speaks "in vain" and "move[s] nothing with the sound of his voice." After they dismember him, all that issues from his severed head is "some kind of tearful sound" (182–183).

After Orpheus dies, he descends to Hades and searches through "the field of the blessed" for Eurydice. When he finds her, he "clasp[s] her tightly in his loving arms,"[50] and they celebrate their ontological kinship through a shifting but consistently transformative reenactment of what happened during their journey back to earth. "Here now they stroll together side by side," Ovid writes, "and sometimes she leads the way, and Orpheus follows her, or sometimes he goes in front" (183). Death also clarifies Orpheus's vision, giving him a new kind of "hindsight." When he arrives in Hades, he "[sees] again all of the places he had seen before," and when it is his turn to walk ahead, "he can safely look back at his dear Eurydice."

THE MYTH OF ORPHEUS AND EURYDICE has been retold countless times since it was narrated by Virgil and Ovid, and put to many different uses. "In the Middle Ages," Emmet Robbins writes, "[Orpheus] became a type of Christ, overcoming death, a psalmist or a troubadour, courtly lover and singer of pretty lyrics. From the Renaissance on, [he] is the very incarnation of the power of music . . . [and] presides over the transformations and interaction of poetry and science in the period 1600–1800. . . . To the Romantics and to [the twentieth] century he has been the eternal seeker beyond the threshold" (4). As this passage indicates, most of these "re-editions" allegorize the story and focus on Orpheus—often to the complete exclusion of Eurydice. They also reduce it to one or more of the following components: Orpheus's descent to Hades to rescue Eurydice, Orpheus and Eurydice's ill-fated return, the scene in which Orpheus plays music for a nonhuman audience, and Orpheus's death and dismemberment.

The last of these scenes, which is often treated as a self-contained unit, has a privileged place within the Orphic Mysteries, a mystical religion that dates back at least as far as the fifth century BC and promotes purification of the soul.[51] According to one scholar, Orpheus was a historical figure, who was killed and dismembered by the Ciconian women because he was the founder of this religion and they were devotees of a competing religion.[52] The death and dismemberment of Orpheus have also been used to represent other kinds of loss, violence, and persecution. Bertoldo di Giovanni treats the dying Orpheus as "the sad champion of unhappy love" in a Renaissance plaquette.[53] The death of Orpheus is also the subject of a lost engraving by Andrea Mantegna, that inspired three other representations of the same scene: a drawing by Marco Zoppo, an anonymous engraving, and an Albrecht Dürer pen drawing. Giuseppe Scavizzi suggests that Mantegna may have used it to symbolize "the tragic and unsuccessful side of poetic activity in general, or the lack of success which leads in time to recognition," and that in either case he would have been representing himself.[54] John Milton attributes a similar meaning to this part of the myth in *Lycidas*.[55]

The scene in which Orpheus plays music for a nonhuman audience is as ancient as the one in which he is torn apart, and like the latter, it is often separated from the rest of the story. This scene is also the most invariable part of the myth. Whether or not it is mentioned, Patricia Vicari writes, it never disappears, and it "condition[s] whatever form the fable [takes]" (66). This pastoral Orpheus has been deployed as a type of Adam, as well as Christ, and also construed as a sage and as a courtly lover.[56] Most often, though, he stands for "the artist." Sometimes this artist relates to nature the way Virgil's Orpheus does—by corresponding with it. At other times he behaves more like Ovid's Orpheus, using his art to dominate and control the natural world.[57]

Medieval commentators treated the scene in which Orpheus descends to Hades to rescue Eurydice as an allegory of the harrowing of Hell. Orpheus stood for Christ, but Eurydice was a more labile signifier; sometimes she represented the truth and at other times, concupiscence.[58] The scene on the path leading from Hades to earth was subjected to a similar moralization. In *The Consolation of Philosophy*, the pagan writer Boethius equated Eurydice with the "material world and its enticements" and construed the act of turning toward her as the "backsliding of the unenlightened soul to baser earthly needs and desire." Boethius's Christian followers pushed this argument further; for them, Orpheus was a "would-be-philosopher" who lacked the "will-power to give up the world, the flesh, and the devil" and therefore surrendered to the base pleasure of gazing at Eurydice.

When Ovid's account of the myth was revived in the twelfth century, Orpheus was transformed into an ascetic, and his backward look became a momentary lapse in an otherwise exemplary life; when he gazed at Eurydice, he returned like "'a dog to his vomit,'" but then—fortunately—he abjured her, and "ascend[ed] the mountains of virtue."[59] Although Eurydice continued to pay the price for Orpheus's volte-face, the backward look was no longer treated as a danger to *her*; it was depicted, rather, as a danger to *him*. This placed a new moratorium on the act of looking at her. It also made the act of *turning away* from Eurydice both necessary and commendable.[60]

These allegorical trappings fall away in Angelo Poliziano's humanist version of the myth, which he elaborates in his 1471 play, *Orfeo*.[61] Orpheus and Eurydice are a couple again, and Eurydice dies while trying to escape Aristaeus's unwanted advances, just as she does in *The Georgics*. But woman's fate does not improve when man becomes the measure of all things; Eurydice dies offstage, and the only time she speaks is to bid Orpheus farewell before returning to the underworld. Poliziano is much more interested in her pursuer than he is in her; he devotes most of the first act to Aristaeus's attempts to woo her with song, which he treats with great sympathy. And Orpheus's relationship to Eurydice is even more tenuous than it is in *The Metamorphoses*; he doesn't learn that she is dead until act 3, and when he is informed about it, he laments the bitterness of *his* fate rather than *hers*.

Before descending to Hades, Poliziano's Orpheus announces that he is going there to subjugate death, just as he earlier subjugated nature, and although his song is almost identical to the one in Ovid's text, his interactions with Pluto are much more agonistic. He starts bragging about his victory as soon as he leaves the underworld ("Victorious Laurel, wreathe thou my brow. Eurydice is won—my life restored. This victory deserves a special triumph. Come hither, Triumph, by my skill achieved"),[62] and it is in this state of onanistic exultation that he turns to Eurydice. Orpheus reacts to his wife's disappearance the same way he reacted to her death: by lamenting his bad fortune. He also vows never to love another woman, because women are faithless, or (as he puts it) "lighter than a leaf before the wind" (100). The metaphor is startling, because it evokes the circumstances leading to Eurydice's death—and within that context, flight signified "fidelity," not "faithlessness."

A similar reversal occurs at the level of the enunciation. In the disclaimer Poliziano attached to his opera before putting it into circulation, he compares it to a child who was born "with some maimed members or with strength impaired," and who should be exposed to the elements, or torn limb from limb (71). Although he has just likened this child to both Oedipus and Orpheus, Poliziano describes it as a "little daughter" and begs his readers not to "ascribe" her "imperfections" to her father. The baldness of this antifeminism exposes the "logic" through which Orpheus's many public defenders exonerate him of guilt. "I did not kill Eurydice," they argue on his behalf. "She died, rather, because she was mortal. She also tried to make me mortal, by tempting me to look at her. Because she tried to kill me, I do not love her; instead, I hate her."

THE MYTH OF ORPHEUS AND EURYDICE occupied a prominent place in the European Imaginary in the period between *The Gay Science* and *Moses and Monotheism.* It surfaces not just in Salomé's writings but also in the writings of Nietzsche, Warburg, Freud, Proust, Jensen, Rilke, and Valéry. There are hardly any references in the work of these authors to the scene in which Orpheus descends to Hades to rescue Eurydice, but there are many allusions to his death. Warburg discusses two depictions of it in "Dürer and Italian Antiquity": Dürer's drawing and the anonymous engraving inspired by the lost Mantegna. He also attributes enormous importance to this scene. "The true voice of antiquity, which the Renaissance knew well, chimes with this image," Warburg says of the anonymous engraving, "for the death of Orpheus was more than a studio motif of purely formal interest: it stood for the dark mystery play of Dionysian legend, passionately and knowingly experienced in the spirit and through the words of the ancients."[63] He adduces Poliziano's *Orfeo* as additional proof for these claims.[64]

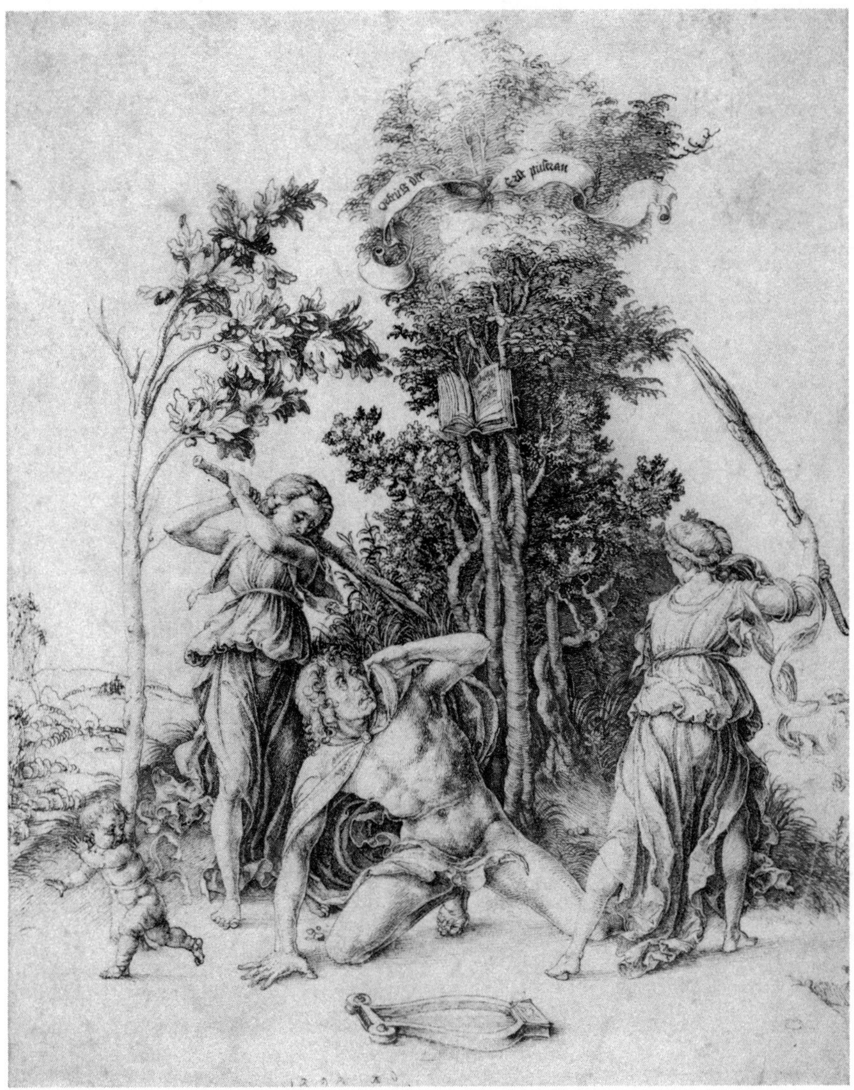

The death of Orpheus is also the central event in Rilke's *Sonnets to Orpheus*, and it haunts every page of *Totem and Taboo. Totem and Taboo* is the text in which Freud makes his boldest claims for the Oedipus complex, and he lifts most of them from Salomon Reinach's account of the Orpheus myth. The story Freud uses to buttress his argument also draws on the narrative recounted by Virgil and Ovid. The band of brothers do to the primal father what the Ciconian women do to Orpheus: they dismember his body. These appropriations are surprisingly easy to discover, because Freud repeatedly invokes Reinach. He also provides an enthusiastic summary of Reinach's account of the death of Orpheus, even though it runs counter to his own account of the Oedipus complex.[65] "The doctrine of original sin was of Orphic origin," Freud writes in the last chapter of *Totem and Taboo.* "It formed part of the mysteries and spread from them to the schools of philosophy of ancient Greece. . . . Mankind, it was said, were descended from the Titans, who had killed the young Dionysus-Zagreus and had torn him to pieces. The burden of this crime weighed on them. A fragment of Anaximander relates how the unity of the world was broken by a primaeval sin, and that whatever issued from it must bear the punishment. The tumultuous mobbing, the killing and the tearing in pieces by the Titans reminds us clearly enough of the totemic sacrifice described by St. Nilus—as . . . do so many other ancient myths, including, for instance, that of the death of Orpheus himself[66] (153–154).

The scene on the slope leading from Hades to earth also appears in many different places in the period between *The Gay Science* and *Moses and Monotheism.* Rilke devotes an entire poem to it: "Orpheus. Eurydice. Hermes." In a later poem, *Requiem for a Friend,* Eurydice refuses to remain where Orpheus's look sends her. She comes back to haunt him, and he does everything in his power to persuade her to return to Hades. This scene is also the concealed subtext of Freud's theory of sexual difference, and it makes a dramatic appearance in Warburg's notes on his journey to the American Southwest. When he was a child, he recalls there, his mother fell gravely ill and seemed to be dying. He "sniffed at her illness like a *frightened* animal," and then looked away both from her, and from his "Jewishness." What Warburg turned toward were images from another religion—a religion based on one man's triumph over death. "[My mother] seemed very strange to me as she was carried in a litter up to Calvarienberg near Ischl," he writes. ". . . It was on this occasion that I saw for the first time with my own eyes . . . scenes from the Passion of Christ's life, whose tragic and naked power I mutely sensed."[67]

The scene in which Orpheus plays music for a nonhuman audience also found its way into many texts in the years between 1882 and 1939. Paul Valéry dedicated an important poem to the solitary musician, and Rilke was so obsessed with him that Baladine Klossowska (Merline) attached a reproduction of Giovanni Battista Cima da Conegliano's drawing of the musician playing his viol for rabbits, deer, and a bird to the wall above his desk before surrendering him to Muzot, his final retreat.[68] *Thus Spoke Zarathustra* is another staging of the same scene. The central figure in this book withdraws from human company, retreats to a secluded spot, surrounds himself with animals, and sings and plays the lyre. Although Zarathustra's refuge is a hut instead of a "broad and open field," it is also situated at the top of an elevation, and the area around it is transformed into a *locus amoenus* through the "arrival" of nature. "Step out of your cave," his animals urge him at the end of a convalescence. "The world awaits you like a garden. The wind is playing with heady fragrances that make their way to you; and all brooks want to run after you" (174).

Nietzsche was clearly drawn to this version of the myth both because Orpheus compels the trees to move and because Eurydice has already been eliminated and the bloodstains washed away. With her removed from the story, his alter ego could be what he wanted it to be: autonomous and self-constituting. But things didn't turn out that way. Zarathustra experiences Eurydice's absence as a deficiency within his *own* subjectivity, and the words through which he

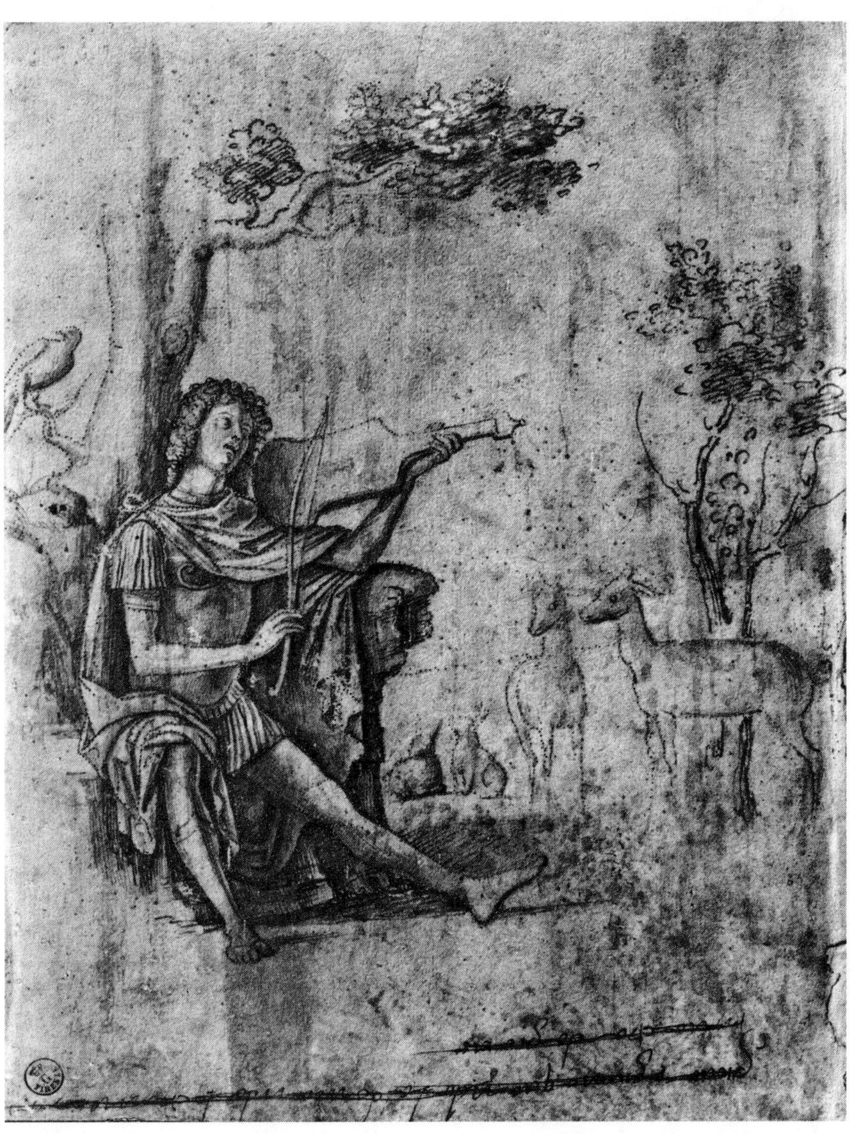

registers this experience echo what Yahweh says in Genesis 2:18. "You are my proper animals," he tells the creatures that have gathered around him. "I love you. But I still lack the proper human beings!" (265). The importation of the biblical story into this scene from the Greek and Roman myth has important temporal consequences; Orpheus is alone because Eurydice is already dead, but Adam lacks company because Eve has not yet been created. In the final pages of *Thus Spoke Zarathustra*, the "already" of the first narrative turns into the "not yet" of the second, and nestled in this futurity is the potential for something new.

Salomé actualizes this potential in the conclusion to her *Freud Journal* by using the second part of the Ovidian narrative to redeem the first. Like Orpheus, she tells us, the analysand has turned his back on someone, with catastrophic consequences for both her and himself. He no longer remembers who she was, though, or even that he let her go. The analyst jogs his memory by positioning herself behind him and returning with him to the scene of the crime. When ascending the slope leading from Hades to earth, he is convulsed with grief and remorse, but then he realizes that he is not alone, and the past ceases to be irrevocable. Turning to Eurydice, he clasps her "tightly" in his "loving" arms.

As I will show in the next two chapters, Salomé was not the only figure in this circle of friends and fellow travelers who was drawn to the final scene in Ovid's version of the myth. Jensen restages it in *Gradiva*, Freud wanders into it while he is working on Jensen's novella, and Rilke dwells there in the *Sonnets to Orpheus*. They were attracted to Ovid's coda for the same reason he wrote it: because *everything* depends on it. The myth of Orpheus and Eurydice is one of the ur-narratives of Western subjectivity—equal in importance to, and perhaps even more important than, the one recounted by Sophocles in *Oedipus Rex*. The latter myth is cloyingly familiar, but few of us could recount what happens in the former. This does not mean, though, that we have ceased to live it. There is an Orpheus inside every Oedipus, and it is *he* who will determine our future.

3

The Book of Life

> The expression "the book of nature" indicates that one can read the real like a text. And that is how the reality of the nineteenth century will be treated here. We open the book of what happened.
>
> —Walter Benjamin

> All the histories that were, or might have been.
>
> —Jean-Luc Godard

SHORTLY AFTER THE PUBLICATION of *Fragment of an Analysis of a Case of Hysteria* and *Three Essays on the Theory of Sexuality*,[1] Freud produced three texts about literary works: "Psychopathic Characters on the Stage," "Creative Writers and Day-Dreaming," and *Delusions and Dreams in Jensen's 'Gradiva'*. In them, he responds to a question with which Salomé and Rilke would also soon be grappling: what is the difference between art and psychoanalysis? The answer he gives to this question keeps changing—not just from one text to another, but also within each of them. The primary thesis of "Psychopathic Characters on the Stage" is that modern tragic drama is a disease for which psychoanalysis has the cure. In premodern tragic drama, the hero revolts against an external authority, which is initially divine and later social.[2] The spectator identifies with this revolt, since he also "longs to feel and to act and to arrange things according to his desires," but because he is "'a poor wretch to whom nothing of importance can happen,'" he never loses sight of the distance between himself and the hero (305). Therefore, instead of being wracked by guilt when the hero falls, he derives masochistic pleasure from the triumph of an authority to which he has already submitted.

In modern tragic drama, by contrast, the hero represents the opposing authority as well as the rebel, and the spectator's identification with him is absolute. Like those sitting in the theater, the hero's psyche houses two competing agencies, one pushing for the satisfaction of unconscious desires and the other prohibiting it. At first these antagonists are kept apart through repression, but later there is a breach in this protective wall, and civil war erupts. The prototype for modern tragic drama is *Hamlet*, and the "repressed impulse" that breaks free in it is "one of those which are similarly repressed in all of us, and the repression of which is part and parcel of the foundation of our personal evolution" (309). The surfacing of this forbidden wish transforms its protagonist from a "normal" person into a neurotic, and "it is the dramatist's business to induce the same illness in us" (310). The psychoanalyst does the reverse: he helps the neurotic patient recover from this illness.

Since psychoanalysis seeks to liberate the same "impulse" as modern tragic drama, this is not a sustainable opposition. Freud tries to reinforce it through the same line of argumentation Lacan will later use to distinguish himself from women:[3] modern tragic drama is blind to its own operations and induces the same oblivion in the spectator, but psychoanalysis knows both what it is doing and what art is doing. "It appears as a necessary precondition of this form of art that the impulse that is struggling into consciousness, however clearly it is recognizable, is never given a definite name," he writes, "so that in the spectator too the process is carried through with his attention averted, and he is in the grip of his emotions instead of taking stock of what is happening. . . . The conflict in *Hamlet* is so effectively concealed that it was left to me to unearth it" (309–310). Curiously, though, the author of "Psychopathic Characters on the Stage" also fails to identify the Oedipus complex.

In the second of his early essays about art, "Creative Writers and Day-Dreaming," Freud argues that we never transcend our infantile narcissism and are constantly looking for imaginary ways of gratifying it.[4] Children satisfy their desire for omnipotence out in the open, through play; ordinary adults in private, through fantasies and dreams; and fiction writers in a public but disguised way, through the heroic stories they recount. Although Freud initially claims to be speaking only about popular fiction, he later maintains that all literature works in this way. He also suggests that what authors most seek to attain is immortality. When we pick up a book, it is for the same reason: "If, at the end of one chapter of my story, I leave the hero unconscious and bleeding from severe wounds," he writes, "I am sure to find him at the beginning of the next being carefully nursed. . . . The feeling of security with which I follow the hero through his perilous journey is . . . the true heroic feeling, which one of our best writers has expressed in the inimitable phrase: "Nothing can happen to *me*!" (149–50). Freud thus imputes to literature the same function he will later impute to religion.[5] He also traces the invulnerability of the hero back to the same delusional source: the belief that the latter is "under the protection of a special Providence" (149).

We keep our daydreams to ourselves because we are ashamed of our egoism. Authors "bribe" us into overlooking theirs through aesthetic pleasure—and this pleasure is so exciting that it also overrides the prohibition against our own. However, in the passage in which Freud develops this part of his argument, he maintains that aesthetic form lowers the walls separating the author from other subjects, thereby suggesting that it militates *against* narcissism, rather than *for* it: "The essential *ars poetica* lies in the technique of overcoming the feeling of repulsion in us which is undoubtedly connected with the barriers that rise between each single ego and the others" (153). In the opening paragraph of "Creative Writers and Day-Dreaming," he also acknowledges that literature stirs up a curiosity in him that psychoanalysis is unable to satisfy, and that far from catering to our self-love, it "arouse[s] in us emotions of which . . . we had not even thought ourselves capable" (143).

In *Delusions and Dreams in Jensen's 'Gradiva'*, Freud focuses on a story that encourages us to turn toward finitude instead of away from it.[6] He also concedes that literature knows "a whole host of things between heaven and earth of which our philosophy has not yet let us dream" (8), and he offers a new account of what distinguishes the former from the latter. The psychoanalyst listens to the eruptions of the unconscious within the analysand's recollections, but the artist listens to his *own* unconscious. He also strains to hear what *could have happened* as well as what *did happen*—the possibilities that his history made available to him but that he failed to actualize. "Our procedure consists in the conscious observation of abnormal mental processes in *other people* so as to be able to elicit and announce their laws," Freud writes in the penultimate paragraph of *Delusions and Dreams in Jensen's 'Gradiva.'* "The author . . . proceeds differently. He directs his attention to the unconscious in his own mind, he listens to its *possible developments* and lends them artistic expression instead of suppressing them by conscious criticism" (92; my emphasis).

The author listens to the possible developments of his own unconscious by attending to the formal affinities it reveals to him. Jensen's *Gradiva* recounts the story of a man who becomes obsessed with a bas-relief of a woman with an unusual gait; as she steps forward with her left foot, "the right, about to follow, touch[es] the ground only lightly with the tips of the toes, while the sole and heel [are] raised almost vertically" (4). It would therefore seem prime grist for the fetishism "mill." But although Freud mentions this psychic phenomenon (45), he does not treat Gradiva's elevated foot as a surrogate for the absent maternal phallus. Instead, he links it to the gait of Jensen's heroine, Zoë. He also suggests that this relationship may point to another: one that connects the living woman to a female inhabitant of Pompeii.

Even more astonishingly, Freud entertains the possibility that we are all enmeshed in the same analogical network: "The different variations of the human form are not independent of one another, and since in fact even among ourselves the ancient types reappear again and again (as we can see in art collections), it would not be totally impossible that a modern [woman's gait] might reproduce the shape of her ancient ancestor in all the other features of her bodily structure as well" (42).[7] If we were to pursue this train of thought a bit further, we would arrive at the following conclusion: it is through its formal affinities, rather than its appeal to our narcissism, that art binds us together.[8] These affinities are not an authorial fabrication; everything really does echo everything else. They also link us in an irrevocable way to each other and the world. The novel that discloses this analogical network to Freud is another edition of the myth discussed in the previous chapter—and this time the heterosexual couple has pride of place.

AS WE HAVE ALREADY SEEN, the "man" in Salomé's study of Nietzsche's "thought" closely resembles the author described in "Creative Writers and Day-Dreaming."[9] She herself, though, subscribes to a different kind of authorship—one similar to that presented in *Delusions and Dreams in Jensen's 'Gradiva'*. Since the unconscious is the wellspring of creativity, art is ineluctably autobiographical, she argues in a 1915 letter to Freud.[10] During the creative process, though, the artist's life ceases to belong to him and becomes something "outside" him (25), and although he may seem extraordinarily self-preoccupied, he is also "quite unaware of the extremely personal and decisive relationship of his work to his own most intimate and infantile nature" (23). This is not a delusional state; he is experiencing his life as what it *is*—a text. The artist also understands what he may later deny: he is not the author of this text. "Human life—indeed all life—*is* poetry," Salomé asserts in another exchange with the same interlocutor. "It's *we* who live it, unconsciously, day by day, like scenes in a play, yet in its inviolable wholeness it lives *us*, it composes *us*. This is something far different from the old cliché 'Turn your life into a work of art'; we are works of art—but we are not the artist."[11] Salomé provides a similar account of her literary production; she attributes *Looking Back* to the "uncontrollable *memories* of life, which in an increasingly forceful way, simply told themselves to [her]" (115).[12] The author is a *listener* (25), rather than a maker.

But when Salomé told Freud that the artist's life ceases to belong to him during the creative process, she was thinking more about Rilke than herself. On

December 28, 1911, the poet wrote her that he had discussed the possibility of treating his long-term depression through psychoanalysis with his wife's analyst, Emil Baron von Gebsattel, but that he was worried that it might damage his writing.[13] Rilke voiced the same concern three weeks later, this time through an odd formulation; he told Salomé that he didn't want to get his soul back, corrected "in red ink like the page of a school-boy's notebook," because that would render art-making impossible.[14] He also wondered whether he really needed psychoanalysis, since his writing was itself a "kind of self-treatment" (184). A moment later, though, he acknowledged that this treatment was unlikely to cure his depression, since as it had "evolved," it had lost "more and more of its therapeutic and solicitous qualities" and was now making "demands" on him that were injurious to his health. It had also assumed an independent existence (184).

Surprisingly, given that she was intimately acquainted with Rilke's sufferings and was about to start attending Freud's evening seminars, Salomé agreed that he should not undergo psychoanalytic treatment. This was no doubt in part because she saw mental disequilibrium as a source of creativity; as Biddy Martin explains, she believed Rilke's genius to be rooted in "pre-Oedipal psychic material that might be damaged by analysis" and thought that "there was something positive and creative in unmastered unconscious life."[15] But Salomé also opted for art over analysis because she thought that if Rilke listened to the possible developments of his past in a form available to others, they might be able to actualize what he could not.

Although he was in pain while writing the *Duino Elegies*, Salomé told him in 1914, they put her into a state of "bliss," because a "new reality" emerges from a work of art,[16] and he received similar testimonials from many other readers.[17] The knowledge that his work gave others "hope" filled Rilke with "overwhelming comfort and reassurance."[18] He also felt enriched by what others made of his life. "Abandoning himself in everything, and thereby making himself superfluous, the benefactor becomes at once the petitioner, the recipients become donors, and [Rilke] hides in their secure existence," Salomé wrote after his death. "And were this loner, who was isolated in death, still with us, I believe he would feel most immediately at home in the deepest anonymity of his work's effects . . . standing there, in deep peace, he too a nameless one among the nameless."[19]

Rilke again referred to his life as a text in a January 14, 1912, letter to Gebsattel, and he described psychoanalysis and art as two very different ways of approaching this text. For the analyst, the "whole written page" of the analysand's life is a provisional series of notations, like the jottings in a schoolboy's notebook. Since he knows that many of these notations are the source of the analysand's sufferings, he helps the latter revise them. For the poet, though, this same "page" is a sacred text, whose "much higher order" he has no right to disturb. His task is to transcribe it and make it available to others. "I am still struck by nothing so much as by the incomprehensible, incredible wonderfulness of my existence," he told Gebsattel, "which from the beginning was so impossibly disposed, and advanced nevertheless from salvation to salvation . . . so that when I think of no longer writing, practically the only thing that upsets me is not to have recorded the utterly wonderful line of this life so strangely carried through."[20]

In one entry in the journal Rilke kept for Salomé, he wrote that "everything that is truly seen *must* become a poem."[21] In another, he chastised himself for having "failed to receive countless poems,"[22] and in the last years of his life he repeatedly characterized his literary production as a compliance with something outside himself. The second half of the *Duino Elegies* and the *Sonnets to Orpheus* "were actually given me as if they were not mine," he told a friend in 1922.[23] The following year Rilke characterized the latter work as "the most enigmatical dictation I have ever sustained and achieved" and added that "the whole first part was written down in a single breathless act of obedience between the second and fifth of February 1922, without one word being in doubt, or having to be changed."[24]

What Rilke believed himself to be obeying changed dramatically over the years. As he explains in an early letter, he initially mistook this authority for God the Father: "In my childish mind I believed myself through my patience near to the virtues of Jesus Christ, and once when I received a hard blow in the face . . . I said to my assailant . . . 'I suffer it because Christ suffered it, silently and without complaint.'"[25] Later, Rilke placed art on the pedestal he had earlier reserved for God; it was otherworldly—a higher and truer reality, to which the artist must sacrifice his life. "One must choose either this or that," he wrote in 1902. "Either happiness or art. . . . The great men have all let their lives become overgrown like an old road and have carried everything into their art. Their lives are stunted like an organ they no longer need."[26] Rilke was horrified when his friend Ellen Key produced a biographical reading of *Stories of God*.[27]

In 1908, however, he wrote a determinedly autobiographical poem, *Requiem for a Friend*; in 1912 he was no longer able to distinguish in an absolute way between art and life; and in 1922 he knew that the "much higher order" to which his life attested was not God or art but rather the unfathomable totality to which we all belong. "A thinking destiny, one cognizant of us . . . yes, often one has wished to be strengthened and confirmed by such a one," he wrote in May of that year. "But would it not at once be one that contemplated us from without, observing us, with which we would no longer be alone? That we are set into a 'blind destiny,' dwell within it, is after all . . . the condition of our own sight. . . . Only through the 'blindness' of our fate are we really deeply related to the wonderful muffledness of the world, that is, with what is whole, vast, and surpassing us."[28]

Rilke's sense that his life was part of a vast "whole" was no more delusional than his belief that his past was an "already written page." Analogies that are not of our making really do connect our lives to many others—to lives that are over, and to lives that have not yet begun, as well as to those proximate to us in time and space. Rather than a self-contained volume, authored by us, our history is only one chapter in an enormous and ever-expanding book, whose overall meaning and shape we cannot even begin to grasp, let alone determine. But this does not mean that there is another kind of author; no one stands outside the Book of Life, to whom it could be imputed. This volume is written from inside, through the analogies we acknowledge and those we refuse. Its production is also a collective process, in which everyone participates and everyone is implicated. As Rilke suggests in a 1924 letter, where there is resemblance, there is also communication, co-endowment, and co-peril.[29] The Book of Life is forever in the making, and later chapters have the capacity to rewrite earlier ones.

Because art privileges similarity above all other relationships, it is able to reveal these connections to us. Not every work of art exercises this capacity; some offer us only fleeting and partial glimpses of the resemblances that connect us to our fellow beings, and others elide them altogether. However, there are songs, poems, paintings, and buildings that help us to see that we have "appointments to keep in the past, in what has gone before and is for the most part extinguished" and that we "must go there in search of places and people who have some connection with us on the far side of time."[30] As Rilke noted, *Swann's Way* is one such work. The entire novel—as well as its companion volumes—hinges upon the completion of an analogy linking a contemporary experience to an earlier one. The narrator neither creates nor controls this analogy; although he senses that something in the present is corresponding with something from the past as soon as he tastes the tea-soaked madeleine, he must patiently wait for the latter to reveal itself. And when the childhood memory *does* surface, it brings with it not only Aunt Léonie's cake and tisane, but "all the flowers in [Marcel's] garden and in M. Swann's park, and the water-lilies on the Vivonne and the good folk of the village and their little dwellings and the parish church and the whole of Combray and its surroundings,"[31] because it is linked to them as well.

In a 1914 letter to Hedwig von Boddien, Rilke talks about how wonderful it would be to participate in a group reading of *Swann's Way*, spread out over many evenings, because the novel also connects the narrator's life to the reader's, and each reader's life to every other's. It does so in the same way it connects Marcel's present to his past: through analogy. "One person or another would read aloud what especially struck home to him out of the inexhaustible pages and would hold it out in a specific way to the general opinion," Rilke writes, "... [and] to many a one his own childhood would appear out of half-oblivion, and one would pass from tale to tale far into the summer night, but also far into the mutually true, rich and alive."[32]

Like Rilke, Proust saw his memories as a "magical scrawl, complex and elaborate," that was "dictated" to him by "reality," and whose "essential character" was that he was "not free to choose" it.[33] Proust also did with his life what Rilke knew he needed to do with *his*: he made it the object of a public analysis. Proust embarked on this project because he believed that his biography was governed by the same laws as everyone else's. "Every reader is, while he is reading, the reader of his own self," he declares in *Time Regained*. "The writer's work is merely a kind of optical instrument which he offers to the reader to enable him to discern what, without this book, he would perhaps never have perceived in himself."[34] Rilke's "self-treatment" had a somewhat different rationale. He decided not to jeopardize the "order" of his life by undergoing psychoanalytic treatment because he knew that many other men were suffering from the same malady. By exploring this malady in his poetry, he also hoped to cure it—in others if not in himself.

LIKE PROUST, Rilke was a card-carrying member of the strange fellowship that sprang up in the last decades of the nineteenth century: the fellowship of solitary men. He stopped living under the same roof with his wife, the German sculptor Clara Westhoff, after a year of marriage, in spite of the fact that she had recently given birth to their daughter, and although their marriage continued for some time thereafter, it was often only through letters. Rilke's later affairs were variations on the same theme. He spoke constantly of his need for solitude, and in 1921 he moved to a castle in a remote part of Switzerland, where he spent the last six years of his life. In a letter written from there, he acknowledged that even a dog would be too much company for him. He had only "one thing" to give: his work.[35]

Rilke was also single-minded in his work. "One seeks in everything new (country or person or thing) only an expression to help some personal confession to greater power or maturity," he wrote in 1899. "All things are there in order that they might become pictures for us."[36] During the brief period when he was Rodin's personal secretary, Rilke became highly critical of this subjectivism and attempted to renegotiate his relationship with the perceptual world.

When looking at external forms, he struggled to see them, and nothing else. But in 1914 he acknowledged that this objectivity was really only another way of turning the world into pictures,[37] and in an extraordinary series of letters extending from December 28, 1911, to January 24, 1912, he not only debated whether to undergo analysis but also diagnosed his condition as the malady of solitude, characterized it as classically "masculine," and addressed its consequences for women.

As we have already seen, Rilke informed Salomé about his conversations with Gebsattel on December 28, 1911. He wrote to her again thirteen days later, and although he does not mention psychoanalysis in this letter, he offers a fascinating account of his psychic difficulties. As the two of them have long known, he tells Salomé, he requires absolute solitude, and is therefore incapable of sustaining a relationship with a woman. Now that he has succeeded in isolating himself from other people, though, he is miserable. In order to be happily alone, he would need to have a woman standing by, "irradiating mere presence" and expecting nothing in return.[38] Rilke also talks about his need for solitude in his January 14 letter to Gebsattel, but acknowledges that it is "not really entirely beneficial" and "not exactly ideal for the inner steadiness I wish for myself."[39] He spends most of the next paragraph complaining about how difficult it is to live in the remote castle to which he has retreated, and then arrives at the already discussed passage in which he characterizes his life as a sacred text and his writing as a "self-treatment." He communicated with Salomé again on January 20, reiterating much of what he said to Gebsattel and elaborating further on the differences between psychoanalysis and art.[40]

Three days after Rilke wrote this last letter to Salomé, he addressed one to Annette Kolb, another of his close female friends. In it he offers a mordant commentary on the a-relationality of the male subject. Woman has earned "the diploma of ability" in love, he muses, but ever since antiquity man has never really "troubled himself" about affairs of the heart; he carries only "an elementary grammar of this discipline in his pocket[,] from which a few words have of necessity gone into him[,] with which he occasionally forms sentences, beautiful and rapturous as the sentences on the first pages of language primers."[41] Rilke also suggests that he and his contemporaries represent a new and even more extreme version of this a-relational male subject. Fortunately, though, this "man of the 'new grain'" is "going to pieces," and when his "salutary" disintegration is complete, he will finally begin the "long" and "difficult" process of becoming a lover (49). Since it will take him a "few thousand years" to reach this goal, woman may "[get] bored," but hopefully she will "find the composure . . . to wait for and to receive this tardy lover" (49). This "man of the 'new grain'" is the one who sprang onto the stage of history with Zarathustra. He is even less relational than his predecessors because he has no desire to overcome the Other; his goal is, rather, to overcome *himself*. This subject is "going to pieces" because he is incapable of mastering his own limits, of transcending his mortality and the fact that he is not an autonomous "whole."

Near the beginning of his January 23, 1912, letter to Kolb, Rilke confesses that he can communicate with other people only through "two finite types": "the woman who loves" and those who die young (46). His privileged example of the first of these finite types is the Portuguese Nun, whose feelings for her lover did not "depend" on how he treated her, but she also surfaces in Rilke's January 20 letter to Salomé as the woman content to stand by, radiating presence and making no demands of her own. As we will see in the next chapter, she was the vehicle through which the poet attempted to overcome the fact that he was not "everything." His second finite type was the instrument through which he tried to overcome the other challenge to his omnipotence: his mortality.

Rilke's work is full of figures who have been struck down prematurely, and almost all of them are also female. So was their biographical prototype. The poet had a baby sister who died before he was born, and his grief-stricken mother tried to resurrect her through him by naming him René Maria and dressing him like a girl. This rendered Rilke exquisitely sensitive to all things feminine, but since his sister could live again only if he took her place in the coffin, it also instilled in him a paralyzing fear of death. When he was a child, he suffered from a recurrent nightmare whose central image continued to haunt him: he dreamt that "he lay near an open grave, before a tall gravestone that threatened to topple into the grave at the slightest movement. . . . [He saw his name] engraved on the precipitous stone, so that it could be mistaken for him, if it disappeared forever into the grave beneath him."[42] There was only one way to remove his name from the gravestone, and that was to replace it with his sister's.

Consequently, although most of Rilke's close friendships were with women, he was emphatically masculine when it came to mortality; death was something that happened on the *other* side of the gender divide. He found support for this claim in a time-honored place: the myth of Orpheus and Eurydice. Rilke organized two early poems around this myth: "Orpheus. Eurydice. Hermes" (1904) and *Requiem for a Friend* (1908). He also came back to it later, through the *Sonnets to Orpheus* (1922) and a poem initially intended for the *Duino Elegies*. Rilke gravitated to this story because Eurydice dies and returns to life but then leaves again, just as he wanted his sister to do. But Eurydice stands for a number of other women as well, and each time the poet restaged the story, he altered it in important ways.

IN "ORPHEUS. EURYDICE. HERMES," Rilke adds the "god of speed and distant messages" to the cast of characters, but reduces the story to the movement of these three figures through a mysterious cavern.[43] He also isolates each of them from the others. Eurydice walks beside Hermes, and behind Orpheus, but she doesn't notice either of them; Orpheus is uncertain whether he is hearing her footsteps or his own; and Hermes is unable to bridge the distance between the two of them. Orpheus has also forgotten that he is a musician: "his hands [hang] at his sides, / tight and heavy, out of the falling folds, / no longer conscious of the delicate lyre / which ha[s] grown into his left arm."

The fifth stanza ends with the word "*she*," and this pronoun ushers in an extended celebration of Eurydice, first as "a woman so loved that from one lyre there came / more lament than from all lamenting women," and then as someone who is no longer "that man's property." Since most of the rest of the poem is also focalized through her,[44] Orpheus drops out of the picture until the very end, when Hermes draws him to her attention, and even then he remains a small figure on the horizon. "And when, abruptly, / the god put out his hand to stop her," Rilke writes, "saying / with sorrow in his voice: He has turned around—, / she could not understand, and softly answered / '*Who*?' / Far away, / dark before the shining exit-gates, / someone or other stood, whose features were unrecognizable."

Since "Orpheus. Eurydice. Hermes" reorganizes the myth of Orpheus and Eurydice around Eurydice, liberates her from the category of a possession, and transforms the forlorn but acquiescent "farewell" she utters in *The Metamorphoses* into an annihilating "who?" it *feels* like a feminist poem. Rilke clearly meant it to be read that way, because in a letter from the same year he presents his ideas about heterosexuality as a kind of feminist manifesto. "We are only just now beginning to consider the relation of one individual to a second individual objectively and without prejudice, and our attempts to live such relationships have no model before them," he wrote to Franz Xaver Kappus. "This humanity of woman . . . will come to light when she has stripped off the conventions of mere femaleness in the transformations of her outward status." When this transformation is complete, man and woman will be "two solitudes," who "protect and border and greet each other."[45]

But Rilke's 1904 version of the Orpheus and Eurydice myth builds to the usual climax: Orpheus turns around to look at Eurydice, and she sinks back to Hades. He also makes no attempt to restore her to the world, or even establish contact with her, and it is not hard to see why: her presence disables his music. Finally, Eurydice escapes "patriarchy" not through work or a more satisfying kind of relationship, but rather by dying—and since "being dead / fill[s] her beyond fulfillment," Orpheus can no longer be blamed for what happens to her. Although Rilke makes no overt references to his life in "Orpheus. Eurydice. Hermes," the poem seems an attempt to pastoralize his sister's death. By returning her to the underworld, he has given her exactly what she wants, and since she is now "filled with her vast death," like a fruit "suffused with its own mystery and sweetness," she will not reach up from the open grave to seize him.

The poet was also working through issues that emerged in his relationship with his wife, Clara. At the beginning of their marriage, he insisted that they live a secluded life, far from their social circle. When Clara's friends protested this arrangement, Rilke responded "for" her, by imputing his wish for solitude to her. He used the same argument with Clara herself later, in order to justify living apart from her,[46] and shortly after completing "Orpheus. Eurydice. Hermes," he wrote her brother that the two of them had "come to an understanding in the very fact that all companionship can consist only in the strengthening of two neighboring solitudes, whereas everything that one is wont to call giving oneself is by nature harmful to companionship."[47]

Since wanting to live apart from one's wife is a far cry from engineering her death, it might not be immediately apparent what "Orpheus. Eurydice. Hermes" has to do with Rilke's marriage to Clara. However, the poet doesn't just claim that Eurydice was fulfilled by death; he also ventriloquizes his horror of relationality through her, just as he did through Clara. She has "come into a new virginity / and [is now] untouchable; her sex ha[s] closed / like a young flower at nightfall, and her hands / [have] grown so unused to marriage that the god's / infinitely gentle touch of guidance / hurt[s] her, like an undesired kiss." It was also because of Rilke's need to establish death as something that happens on the other side of the gender divide that he was unable to remain physically proximate to the women he loved.

The poet returned to his favorite myth in 1908, this time casting the German painter Paula Becker as Eurydice, and himself as Orpheus. He also produced a work—*Requiem for a Friend*—that is relentlessly autobiographical. Rilke met Paula at the same time as Clara—in 1900, in an artists' colony in Worpswede.[48] He was fascinated by both women, but especially by Paula, who unbeknownst to him was already engaged to another painter, Otto Modersohn. After the Modersohn/Becker engagement became public, Rilke proposed to Clara, and the two couples wed in the spring of 1901. Both marriages quickly soured—Rilke and Westhoff's for the reasons I have already discussed, and Modersohn and Becker's because of their aesthetic differences. Modersohn was happy living in Worpswede, producing conventional paintings, but Becker wanted to be in Paris, painting in the space opened up by Cézanne and Gauguin.[49] She moved there in 1906 to pursue the life of a solitary artist, but she depended on Modersohn financially, and he and her family agitated ceaselessly for her return.[50] Becker's situation became more and more desperate, and after about a year[51] she returned to Worpswede. She gave birth to a daughter in 1907 and died eighteen days later, as a result of postnatal complications.

In 1902 Rilke sent Becker a letter explaining why her friendship with his wife had lost its intimacy. Clara, he told her, had taken refuge within a "new solitude." A true friend would accept that, since the "highest task of the union of two people" is for each to "keep watch over the solitude of the other."[52] "Can your love not grasp hold of a similar faith?" Rilke queried Becker near the end of the letter. The person described in this passage bore little relation to Clara. Not only did she want to live with her husband and spend time with her friends; she also found it hard to work in the isolation he imposed on her. Although initially appreciative of her art, Rilke later derided it,[53] and her desire for a more conventional living arrangement made it easy for him to dismiss her as incapable of rising to the heights of the brave new relationality he was offering her.

Becker, though, was a gifted painter, and as committed to her work as Rilke was to his; although she was only thirty-one when she died, she left behind four hundred paintings and more than a thousand graphic works and drawings.[54] The two artists also shared a number of aesthetic assumptions. It was Becker who introduced Rilke to Cézanne's work, which became as important to him as it was to her,[55] and they had similar views about color. "I dream of movement in color, of gentle shimmering, vibration, of one object setting another in motion through color," Becker wrote in 1902.[56] Cézanne shows us that painting "takes place among the colors themselves" and that "one must leave them completely alone so that they may come to terms with each other," Rilke declared five years later. "Their intercourse with one another: that is the whole of painting."[57]

Becker also came closer than any of the other women in Rilke's life to being a "neighboring solitude." Shortly after her marriage, she complained that "marriage does not make one happier," because "it takes away the illusion that has sustained a deep belief in the possibility of a kindred soul."[58] A few years later she concluded that "in art one is usually totally alone with oneself,"[59] and she tried to reconcile Modersohn to her need to spend time apart from him by telling him that being "quiet" and "undisturbed" permitted her to think "good thoughts" about him.[60] When Becker left for Paris, she wrote Rilke the words he had supposedly been longing to hear: "And now, I don't even know how I should sign my name. I'm not Modersohn and I'm not Paula Becker anymore either. I am me and I hope to become me more and more. That is surely the goal of all our struggles."[61] Finally, and most astonishingly, when Modersohn began agitating for Becker's return, she drew an implicit comparison between herself and Rilke's 1904 Eurydice. On March 26, 1906, she made the following entry in her journal: "When I read Otto's letters they are like a voice from the earth. And I seem to myself like someone who has died and now dwells in the Elysian Fields and hears the cry from the earth."[62]

Here, then, was the chance for Rilke to deliver on the feminist claims he made to Kappus—and he made some effort to do so. Although he left on a speaking tour shortly before Becker's arrival, he remained in Paris long enough to welcome her, visited her the day after his return, and sat for her famous portrait of him from May 13 to June 2. When Modersohn suddenly showed up, however, Rilke stopped going to Becker's apartment, and he also went out of his way to avoid encountering her elsewhere, even though she was then in even greater need of his friendship and support. When Paula expressed her desire to accompany the Rilke-Westhoff family on a trip to the Belgian coast, he coldly rebuffed her, and he did not return to Paris until after she had left the city. It was only through letters that Rilke learned about Becker's return to Germany, her subsequent pregnancy, and—finally—her death.[63] On March 17, 1907, he sent her an apologetic letter, acknowledging that he had been "inattentive in a moment in our friendship in which I ought not to have been so."[64]

Rilke also failed Becker in another way. Although he took an immediate interest in Clara's work,[65] it was not until much later that he even looked at Paula's.[66] After Becker's death, he was tormented by the thought that by leaving Paris in the summer of 1906, he had prevented a serious artist from realizing her full potential. In 1908 he wrote her an open letter in the form of a poem. In this poem, *Requiem for a Friend*, he tries to assuage his guilt by attributing Paula's death to her failure to remain "far away from all the world," in the "serene heaven of paintings." In her still-life paintings, he argues early in the poem, she "set" ripe fruit "before the canvas, in white bowls, / and weighed out each one's heaviness with [her] colors." Later, she learned to see women and children as fruit, and eventually she was also able to look at herself this way—to say "this is" rather than "I am that." In so doing, she liberated herself from "curiosity" and "desire," and became "holy." Unfortunately, though, Becker allowed herself to be pulled back into the "world where bodies have their will," and her belly expanded until there was no room left for the artist.

When Rilke exhausts this line of reasoning, he adopts a new one. Becker died because Modersohn would not let her go. Because he, Rilke, was a true friend, he did the opposite: he left Paris in the summer of 1906 so that she would have the freedom she needed. And not only was "letting go" the right thing to do in this particular situation, it is *always* the right thing to do. "For this is wrong, if anything," Rilke proclaims at a climactic moment in *Requiem for a Friend*. "Not to enlarge the freedom of a love / with all the inner freedom one can summon. / We need, in love, to practice only this: / letting each other go. For holding on / comes easily; we do not need to learn it."[67] But this argument collapses before Rilke can even finish making it, because the problem is not that Becker is dead, but rather that she has come back to haunt him and that her presence is unwelcome. "I have my dead, and I have let them go, / and was amazed to see them so soon contented, / so soon at home in being dead, so cheerful, / so unlike their reputation. / Only you return, brush past me, loiter, try to knock against something so that the sound reveals your presence," he says to her irritably at the beginning of the poem, and he spends most of *Requiem for a Friend* trying to persuade her to leave. This makes him—as Robert Hass has already noted—a perverse Orpheus; rather than descending to Hades to retrieve Eurydice, he attempts to talk her "*back down* into the underworld" by "telling her how wonderful it is to be dead."[68]

Although this is the same argument Rilke makes in "Orpheus. Eurydice. Hermes," it sounds very different here, because he is not able to route it through Becker's consciousness. He tries to solve this problem by arguing that she has an aesthetic drive, about which she cannot know because it operates at an unconscious level. This drive impelled her to paint, and later, when her marriage got in the way, to craft her own demise. Since her death was aesthetically fulfilling, she should embrace it. "You turned your tears' / strength and pressure into your ripe gaze, / and were transforming every fluid inside you / into a strong reality," Rilke tells her in stanza 5, when "chance came in and tore you / back from the last step forward on your path." But then "from the night-warm soilbed of your heart, / you dug the seeds still green, from which your death / would sprout: your own, your perfect death, the one / that was your whole life's perfect consummation."

Becker is apparently unpersuaded by these arguments, because later in the poem Rilke asks if she is still there, and then indicates that she is by continuing to talk to her. The painter also went on haunting him long after the publication of *Requiem for a Friend*. In 1913 Rilke told Becker's brother that her departure was "perhaps the first reason why for many years death outweighed life for me, was greater, more just and of more pressing concern to me than all the fullness of this-worldly forces which otherwise so happily occupy us."[69] And in 1923, after reading a German edition of Becker's letters and journals, he had the "feeling" that he should "lay" the *Duino Elegies* and the *Sonnets to Orpheus* "somewhere in a niche to her memory."[70] She loomed so large in the poet's psyche not just because he had failed her but also because she corresponded with the sister *inside* him.

UNTIL NOW, I have talked about analogy as what links us to other beings—what makes all of our stories part of the same great book. But analogy is also internal to our own being—what connects the person we were yesterday with the slightly different person we are today. This is the topic with which Proust begins *Swann's Way*; Marcel is unable to know *who* he is until he knows *where* he is, because sleep slows down the "bioscope" of the self (7), so that he sees his ego for what it is—a discontinuous series of slightly different images that relate to each other in the mode of an "and." This renders him incapable of distinguishing in any absolute way between himself and others. Consequently, until Marcel succeeds in stabilizing the room around him, he shuttles vertiginously not just through his own past but also through the history of mankind. "I had only the most rudimentary sense of existence, such as may lurk and flicker in the depths of an animal's consciousness," he explains. "I was more destitute than the cave dweller; but then the memory—not yet of the place in which I was, but of various other places where I had lived and might now very possibly be—would come like a rope let down from heaven to draw me up out of the abyss of not-being, from which I could never have escaped by myself: in a flash I would traverse centuries of civilization, and out of a blurred glimpse of oil-lamps, then of shirts with turned-down collars, would gradually piece together the original components of my ego" (4–5).

Because of Rilke's unusual formation, he also knew that he had more than one "self." However, because the girl his mother wanted him to be was dead and could live again only if he took her place in the coffin, he saw himself not as a boy *and* a girl but rather as a boy *or* a girl. He offers a thinly veiled account of this egoic battle-to-the-death in *The Notebooks of Malte Laurids Brigge*: "There had been a time when Maman wished I had been a little girl and not the boy that I undeniably was," says the eponymous narrator. "The idea . . . occurred to me of sometimes knocking in the afternoon at Maman's door. Then, when she asked who was there, I would delightedly answer 'Sophie,' making my voice so dainty that it tickled my throat. And when I entered . . . I really was Sophie, Maman's little Sophie, busy with her household chores, whose hair Maman had to braid, so that she wouldn't be mistaken for that naughty Malte, if he should ever come back."[71] Surprisingly, Orpheus dies and Eurydice returns to earth in this telling of the myth. This is, however, only a prophylactic inversion; the poet creates Malte Laurids Brigge so that he can "cast him off and survive him."[72] Later, the poet mapped this fantasmatic battle-to-the-death onto the one he was waging with his own finitude; if he could overcome "Sophie," he imagined, he would also overcome death.

Rilke was fascinated by Becker and Westhoff when he first met them because they were both artists, like him, and "girls," like his sister, but the only way he could imagine this analogy operating was sequentially; at one moment they were artists and at the next, girls. He also turned it into a binary opposition by equating the first of these categories with life and the second with death. In an astonishing journal entry, he describes the two women moving back and forth between this world and a kind of underworld, as their identities first as artists and then as girls come to the fore: "I find them all so moving here in their way of seeing. Half-knowing, that is, painters; half unconscious, that is, Girls. First . . . this mood of muted, beaten silver makes them defenseless and forces them into their Girl-existence, dark and full of longing. . . . Then the artist in them gains the upper hand . . . and they glide gently over into their Girl-lives again."[73] Later, in a poem addressed to Clara and Paula, but sent only to Paula, Rilke acknowledged that he corresponded with them not just as artists but also as girls. He also narrowed the distance between these two "selves" by describing their relationship in spatial rather than temporal terms and imagining a future moment when even this division would be undone: "I am with you. Am thankful to you both / you who are like the sisters of my soul; / for my soul, also, wears a maiden's dress, /and her hair too is silken to the touch. / I am seldom given to see her cool hands, / for she lives far away, behind great walls; / lives as if in a tower and hardly knows / that one day I will come to set her free."[74]

After Rilke finished the January 20, 1912, letter to Salomé in which he distinguished between psychoanalysis and his aesthetic "self-treatment," he took a walk on the cliffs of the Duino and "received the task of the [*Duino Elegies*]."[75] By the time Salomé's January 22 response arrived, the First Elegy was complete. In this poem, as in his January 23 letter to Kolb, Rilke celebrates women who love and those who die young and draws an unflattering contrast between the solitary male subject and the first of these "finite types." Once again, he also maintains that those who die young are fulfilled by death and that he is not responsible for their fate, but this time he admits that they have lost a lot ("Of course, it is strange to inhabit the earth no longer / to give up customs one had barely had time to learn, / not to see roses and other promising Things / in terms of a human future . . . to no longer desire one's desires").[76] He also acknowledges that the living have created this finite type in order to protect themselves from their mortality, to generate the grief that permits their spirits to grow, and to create the void out of which art springs. "In the end," he writes, "those who were carried off early no longer need us. . . . But we, who do need / such great mysteries . . . could we exist without *them*?"

Rilke completed the Second Elegy shortly after the First, two more a year later, and a fifth in 1915, but he had to wait until 1922 for the rest to arrive. He also wrote very few other poems in the period between 1912 and 1922. He talks about the reasons for this in "Wendung" (1914). The title of this poem—which Stephen Mitchell translates as "Turning-Point"—means "turning" and "change." Rilke doesn't just activate both meanings; he also uses the first to clarify the second. What he must change if he wants to write again, he argues, is his way of turning toward the Eurydices in his life. He develops this argument by focusing on a new part of the Ovidian narrative.

As we have already seen, Ovid's Orpheus is much closer to Zarathustra than to his Virgilian counterpart. Although he proclaims the sovereignty of death in the song he sings to the gods of the underworld, he uses his eloquence to "overcome" them and make "tears [run] down the cheeks of the Furies."[77] He is terrified when he sees Eurydice dragged back to Hades, and he mourns her for only seven days before withdrawing to "towering Rhodope and to Haemus, battered by the north wind" (167), in order to rage against the gods. Three years later, he repudiates the "love of women" and begins using his music to dominate nature. Rather than positioning himself under a tree, where there is shade, Ovid writes, Orpheus sits down in an "open field, green and grassy," and forces the "shade" to "come" to him; he "pluck[s] the sweet strings of his lyre," and oaks, poplars, ash, pine, cypress, palm, and fruit trees gather around him (167–168).

Orpheus is in midsong when the Ciconian women attack him. He begs for mercy, but "for the first time ever" he speaks "in vain" and "move[s] nothing with his voice." His loss is nature's gain; when the "breath of life" flies out of "the mouth that stones [have] listened to and wild beasts understood" and into the "wind," his eloquence goes with it. Because of this, birds, wild beasts, and stones are able to weep, rivers are "swollen with their own tears," and "trees shed their leaves in mourning." When Orpheus finds himself once again in Hades, he can no longer deny his mortality, and this has a transformative effect on his vision; he sees "all the places" he has seen before with new eyes and is able to "safely look back at his dear Eurydice" (183).

Rilke begins "Turning-Point" with the scene in which the musician forces the shade to come to him, and he foregrounds the contrast between it and the one with which Ovid concludes his narrative by translating it too into visual terms: "For a long time he attained it in looking, / Stars would fall to their knees / beneath his compelling vision . . . / Towers he would gaze at so they were terrified: / building them up again, suddenly, in an instant!"[78] Birds, animals, and flowers gather around this figure, and eventually women arrive as well. They gaze at him "beseeching[ly]," but instead of responding to their appeal, he "overpower[s]" them and "imprison[s]" their "images" within himself. In the next stanza, we hear the murmuring voices of his victims; they judge him, find him wanting, and decide to deny him "further communions." Without them, he can no longer look, because looking begins with a solicitation from the world. Human vision also has an affective mandate; the world wants to "flourish in love," and unless we provide this affirmation we are not really seeing it.

For most of "Turning-Point," Rilke refers to this loveless spectator in the third person, but in the last stanza he addresses him directly, as his "inner man," and he attributes the latter's inability to respond to the world's solicitation to his repudiation of his female counterpart. He also expands Ovid's coda to include these two parts of himself. If Rilke wants to write again, his internal Orpheus must descend to the place where he has encrypted his internal Eurydice and "clasp" her "tightly in his loving arms." "Work of the eyes is done, now / go and do heart-work," he writes in the last stanza of the poem. ". . . Learn, inner man, to look on your inner woman, / the one attained from a thousand / natures, the merely attained but / not yet beloved form."

"Wendung" is also a turning point in another sense: it completely renegotiates the relationship between art and the world. Instead of two opposed terms, one of which is infinitely "truer" than the other, they are now ontologically equal and mutually enabling. And rather than an atrophied organ, which he no longer uses, the artist's life is both the earphone through which he hears the world's call and what makes him capable of responding to it. Rilke later described this call and response in energic terms—as the "continual conversion of the beloved visible and tangible into the invisible vibrations and excitation of our own nature," which then "introduces new vibration-frequencies into the vibration-spheres of the universe."[79]

ALTHOUGH RILKE KNEW that he was suffering from the malady of solitude and saw it as the source of his creative crisis, he spent the last seven years of his life walled up in a series of increasingly isolated refuges. Baladine Klossowska (Merline) helped him find Muzot, the last of these dwellings, and did her best to make it more habitable. While there, she pinned a postcard reproduction of Cima da Conegliano's pen-and-ink drawing of Orpheus to the wall above her lover's desk.[80] This drawing depicts the scene that Rilke restages in "Turning-Point": Orpheus sitting under a tree playing a musical instrument, surrounded by animals and a bird. It must have reminded him that he had not yet learned to look at his "inner woman," because he opens the *Sonnets to Orpheus* with a reference to this scene.

Rilke begins the first poem the same way he begins "Turning-Point"—by emphasizing Orpheus's will-to-power and his control over nature. This time the musician not only forces the trees to come to him; he also lifts them high into the air. "A tree ascended there. Oh pure transcendence! / Oh Orpheus sings! Oh tall tree in the ear! / And all things hushed."[81] In the fourth line of this poem, though, the "change" for which he earlier called finally "appear[s]"; Orpheus stops using his music to dominate nature and begins responding to the world around him. Transcendence also gives way to immanence; the "tall tree in the ear" turns into a "temple deep inside [the animals'] hearing." Sonnet 1, II unfolds in a similar way. In the opening lines of this poem, Orpheus seems to create Eurydice, as well as his songs; she "[comes] to be / out of [his] single song of joy and lyre." Almost immediately, though, he is shown to be *her* debtor; she builds a bed inside his ear and sleeps there, and her sleep is "everything"— all external phenomena and "all wonders that [have] ever seized [Orpheus's] heart."

In Sonnet 1, XXVI, Rilke moves past the scene where the "creatures of stillness" gather around the musician to the scene where he is killed and dismembered. He uses the latter to dramatize and complete the "salutary" development he described in his 1912 letter to Annette Kolb—i.e., to atomize the "man of the 'new grain'" and to disperse the "pieces." The disintegration and dissemination of Orpheus's bodily ego permits him to be psychically integrated into a much greater Whole—the one Ovid calls "flesh." It also produces a new kind of music—the kind that builds a "temple" inside the world's "hearing." "But you, divine poet, you who sang on to the end / ," Rilke writes, "as the swarm of rejected maenads attacked you, shrieking, / you overpowered their noise with harmony, and / from pure destruction arose your transfigured song / . . . At last they killed you and broke you in pieces . . . / Only because you were torn and scattered through Nature / have *we* become hearers now and [the voice of Nature]."[82]

Sonnet 1, V offers another account of the same events. In this poem, Orpheus ceases to be Rilke's representative and becomes a signifier for the transformations through which the natural world regenerates itself and poetry is renewed: "Erect no gravestone for him. Only this: / let the rose blossom each year for his sake. / For it *is* the god. His metamorphosis / in this and that. We do not need to look / for other names. It is Orpheus once for all / wherever there is song." As the word "metamorphosis" suggests, this is another reference to Ovid. "Everything changes," the Roman poet observes in the final chapter of his book; the soul "wanders here" and "there," passing "from beasts to human beings and back to beasts again" (256).

In Sonnet 2, XII, Rilke focuses on the transformations through which beings perdure, rather than those through which new ones emerge. He urges us to "be inspired for the flame / in which a Thing disappears and bursts into something else," because "the spirit of re-creation which masters this earthly form / loves most the pivoting point where you are no longer yourself." This argument also derives from *The Metamorphoses.* "Our bodies are always changing, too, without any respite, nor shall we be tomorrow what we were, or even what we are today," Ovid remarks in another passage from the same chapter. "At one time we lay hidden in our first mother's womb, merely seed, only a hope for humankind. Then nature touched us with her artful hands" (257).

Since the Roman poet accounts for the renewal of the world through the transmigration of the soul, the latter lives on when "time's decay consumes our bodies." Although it "migrates to different forms," it also remains "the same" (256). In the *Sonnets to Orpheus*, though, it is *forms* that do this work; they are pregnant with the kindred forms that will replace them. Death is also the midwife, as well as the undertaker; it lays the parents in the ground so that it can deliver their progeny. "We, one generation through thousand of lifetimes . . . / ," Rilke writes in Sonnet 2, XXIV, "are more and more filled with the child we will bear / so that through it we may be shattered and overtaken."

But the poet would never have gotten from the postcard Klossowska pinned above his desk to the *Sonnets to Orpheus* if he had not been given another worldly "prompt." In January 1922 he received a letter from Frau Gertrude Ouckama Knoop, describing the death of her eighteen-year-old daughter, Vera, who was a dancer before she was struck down by illness. He wrote back immediately, celebrating the "bigness" of Vera's heart. "Oh how, how she loved, how she reached out with the antennae of her heart beyond all that is graspable and compassable here."[83] A month later, he sent Frau Knoop another letter, announcing the existence of the first half of the *Sonnets to Orpheus* and attributing the "spontaneous emotion" out of which it emerged to his relationship to Vera.[84] He later credited the rest of the *Duino Elegies* and the second half of the *Sonnets to Orpheus*—both of which he had completed by February 22—to the same source.[85]

Rilke hardly knew Vera, but the parallels between her life and Becker's were so striking that he only needed to read the headlines to be moved by it. Like her predecessor, Vera was both an artist and a "girl." Her illness also made her "heavy and massive," like Becker during her pregnancy, and got in the way of her art-making.[86] Last, but not least, she was another instantiation of Rilke's second finite type: "those who die young." But her life also differed in significant ways from Paula's, and these differences unlocked the dungeon in which he had imprisoned his "inner woman." Since at the moment of her death, Vera was "almost still a child" (376), Rilke could not argue that death fulfilled her. Her "incompleteness" also made a demand on him—the demand that he "imprint" her "so deeply, so patiently and passionately" in himself that her "reality" would "arise" in him again, "invisibly" (374). Since the path leading from Hades to earth is a two-way street, this opened "the gate of the grave" to him. As a result, Rilke came to see that there is "*neither a here nor a beyond*," but only one "realm whose depth and influence we share, everywhere unboundaried, with the dead and those to come."[87] The only song that is commensurate with the world's "longing" is one that affirms this unity—that says "*life-AND-death*."[88]

As Rilke points out, Vera also worked in a medium that relies on the living body and leaves no lasting trace: "Dancing girl," he writes in Sonnet 2, XVIII, "transformation / of all transience into steps . . . / And the arm-raised Whirl at the end, that tree made of motion / didn't it fully possess the pivoted year?" When she became too massive to dance, she shifted to a different medium—initially music, and later drawing.[89] The corporeal and ephemeral nature of Vera's aesthetic practice helped Rilke see that "what tightens into survival is already inert" (2, XII), and the metamorphosis of dance into music, and music into drawing, showed him that forms are in constant communication with other forms. Finally, the complementary morphing of Vera's body and her practice conveyed this principle from the domain of art to that of life.

Rilke returned to this last idea in 1926, through a different metaphor. "We of the here and now . . . are incessantly flowing over . . . to those who preceded us . . . and to those who . . . come after us," he told Witold von Hulewicz. What "plunges" us all into the same ontological sea is "the falling away of time."[90] This mysterious pronouncement is yet another reference to *The Metamorphoses*—and one that accounts for both the unpredictability of the future and the alterability of the past. It is not only things that flow, Ovid writes in the last chapter of his book, but time itself. It "glides in endless motion, like a river," and just as "wave drives on wave," so "time runs on, and time pursues." What "was here" has vanished, "what never was now comes to pass," and "every moment is made anew" (257).

4

Mutually Embracing

I knew . . . that everything that was mine, my cares, my wishes, would be buttressed, in my grandmother, by a desire to preserve and enhance my life, and my thoughts were continued and extended in her without undergoing the slightest deflection, since they passed from my mind to hers without any change of atmosphere or of personality.

—Marcel Proust

What is it men in women do require
The lineaments of Gratified Desire
What is it women do in men require
The lineaments of Gratified Desire

—William Blake

SINCE RILKE FINALLY DESCENDS TO HADES in *Sonnets to Orpheus*, we would expect the work's climactic event to be the resurrection of Eurydice. However, not only does she never leave the underworld, but she also sleeps through most of the sequence. Rilke continued to balk at the idea of readmitting Eurydice to the world because she represented his *mother* as well as his *sister*. If he could have separated all of the dead girls who made up the sister side of this figure from the women who constituted the maternal side, he might have been able to accommodate them, but Becker's pregnancy glued them together—and there was no place on earth for the mother.

The poet talks about two of Becker's paintings in *Requiem for a Friend*, both of which date from 1906: *Self-Portrait with Amber Necklace* and *Self-Portrait on Her Sixth Wedding Anniversary*.[1] The first of these paintings offers a tightly framed view of a woman's head and torso, posed against a flowering bush. The woman is nude except for some floral decorations and the eponymous necklace, but so stylized as to be both "impersonal" and "chaste"; her body has the massiveness and pared-down simplicity of some of Picasso's contemporaneous figures, like those in *Self-Portrait with Palette* (1906) and *Portrait of Gertrude Stein* (1906), and her features have the primitivist angularity favored by Gauguin, Picasso, and Matisse.[2] Three small flowers sit atop her head, she holds another in each hand, and several others adorn the bush behind her, all of which have been subjected to a similar stylization; they signify "nature," rather than representing it. There is some modeling of the woman's arms, breast, neck, and face, but the canvas is otherwise two-dimensional. Finally, although she faces the viewer, her glance is oblique and impossible to meet. Rilke is particularly enthusiastic about this last feature of *Self-Portrait with Amber Necklace*, because

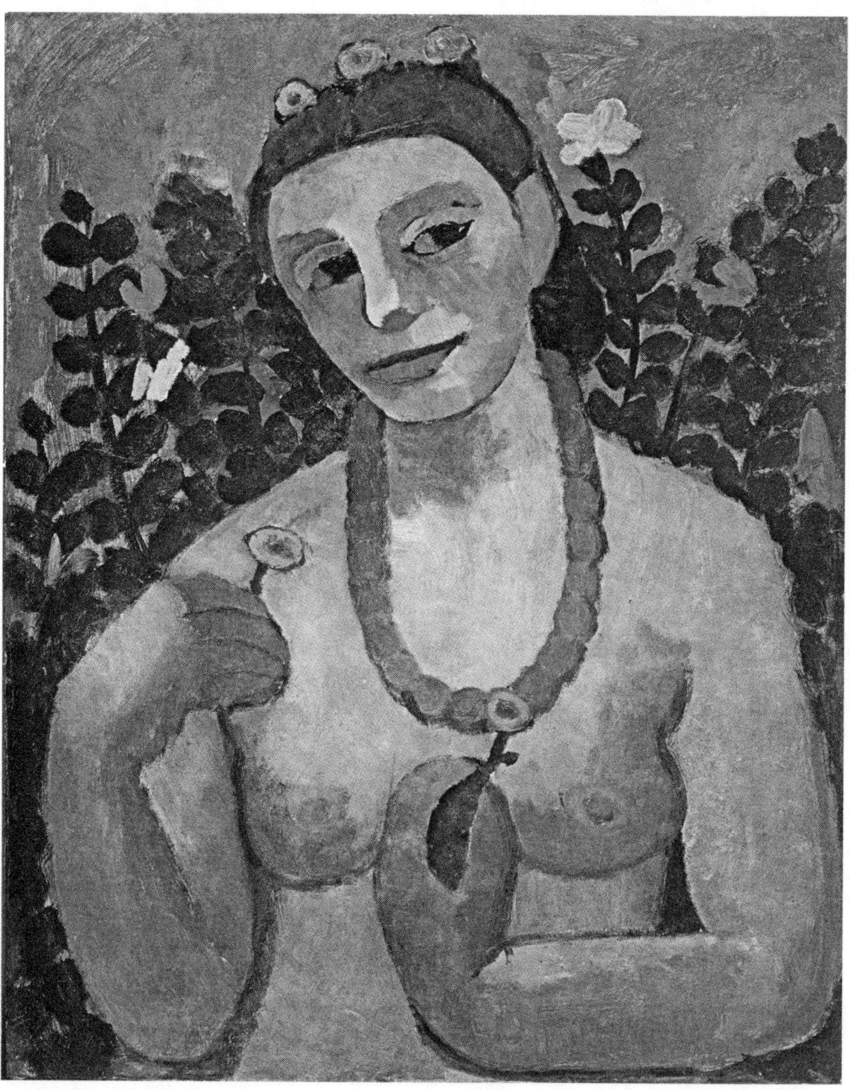

See also Plate 1 in color insert.

it seems to locate the woman in another domain—one as distant from our world as Hades is from earth. "At last," he says to Paula, ". . . you stepped / out of your clothes and brought your naked body / before the mirror, you let yourself inside / down to your gaze."[3]

The woman in *Self-Portrait on her Sixth Wedding Anniversary* is, on the other hand, part of a larger Whole. Although her body is generously framed on both sides by a splotchy backdrop, her head bumps against the upper frame, indicating that she is too tall to fit inside the canvas. She is also much more naturalistically rendered, and recognizably "Becker." The painting's title links it to a specific moment in the artist's life, and the initially abstract backdrop quickly resolves into wallpaper. There is an amber necklace around the woman's neck, and a blue cloth draped around her thighs, but she is otherwise naked, and appears to be in the early stages of pregnancy. This reading is reinforced by both the title and her hands, which frame her rounded belly. Last, but not least, she looks directly at us and blushes in response to our gaze.

Everything about *Self-Portrait on Her Sixth Wedding Anniversary* conflicts with Rilke's 1908 aesthetic—its biographical specificity, its invocation of marriage, its more naturalistic treatment of the body, and its refusal to be an autonomous work of art. Fascinatingly, though, what most offends the poet is the amber necklace. This motif connects *Self-Portrait with Amber Necklace* to *Self-Portrait on Her Sixth Wedding Anniversary*, thereby opening it, too, to the world. It also forces Rilke to see Becker's life as a text, and this revelation undercuts his belief in his *own* autonomy, since it suggests that his life may be part of the same volume. "Why do you want / to make me think that in the amber beads / you wore in your self-portrait, there was still / a kind of heaviness that can't exist / in the serene heaven of painting?" he angrily asks her. "Why do you show me / an evil omen in the way you stand? / What makes you read the contours of your body / like the lines engraved inside a palm, so that / I cannot see them now except as fate?" (83).

Although Rilke does not explicitly address the swollen belly of the figure in this painting, the phrase "contours of your body" is obviously a covert reference to it, and in the middle of *Requiem for a Friend*, he launches into a long and emotionally overwrought description of the violence done to her body by pregnancy and childbirth. By the end of the description, motherhood has mutated into a death drive, which is initially directed outward, against the infant, and then inward, against the mother herself. It slays them because it prevents them from being solitary creatures, because it opens each to the being of the other. "And so you died as women used to die," Rilke says to Becker, ". . . the old-fashioned / death of women in labor, who try to close / themselves again

See also Plate 2
in color insert.

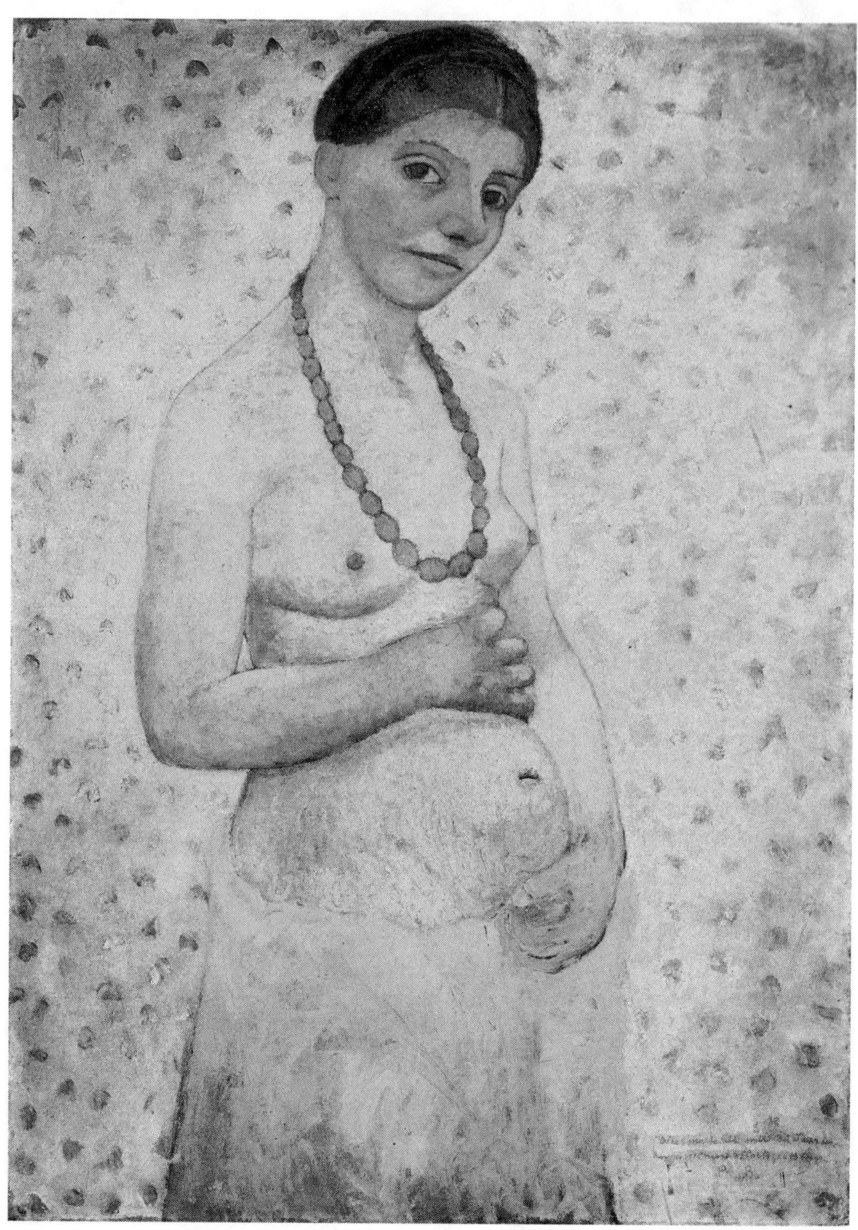

but can't, because that ancient / darkness which they have also given birth to / returns for them, thrusts its way in, and enters" (87).

Two stanzas after the poet inveighs against the "openness" of the maternal body, unwelcome memories from his own childhood burst into his consciousness and must be summarily dismissed: "When somewhere, from deep within me, there arises / the vivid sense of having been a child, / the purity and essence of that childhood / where I once lived: then I don't want to know it" (89).

A few lines later, Rilke introduces a complex simile, ostensibly for the purpose of demonstrating that Becker cannot be held by anyone, since she does not remain still, and that no man can control her arrivals and departures, because she orchestrates them herself. However, rather than selecting a reflexive action for his comparative term, he uses two transitive verbs, "throwing" and "catching": "Who can possess what cannot hold its own self, / but only, now and then, will blissfully / catch itself, then quickly throw itself / away, like a child playing with a ball" (89).

Since the ball is the only thing in this little scenario that comes and goes, it is also the only thing that can be aligned with Becker. The child who plays with the ball must therefore be Rilke himself. I say "be" rather than "represent" because the poet occupies both sides of this comparison; the child he resembles is the child he used to be. What he is doing now is also what he was doing then: trying to get rid of the mother. The poet clearly sees all of this, because he struggles to exonerate himself in the next sentence. I did not do away with "the woman," he argues there; rather, she left. I did not call her back after she left because I did not want to encroach upon her freedom. Therefore I am not just blameless but *good*. However, the last word in this sentence is "*Schuld*," which means both "wrong" and "guilt." "As little as a captain can hold the carved / Niké facing outward from his ship's prow / when the lightness of her godhead suddenly / lifts her up, into the bright sea-wind, / " this sentence reads, "so little can one of us call back the woman / who, now no longer seeing us, walks on / along the narrow strip of her existence, / as though by miracle, in perfect safety— / unless, that is, he wishes to do wrong" (89–91).

Both in her *Freud Journal* and in *Looking Back*, Salomé describes the horror that Rilke's mother aroused in him and his desperate attempts to separate himself from her. These attempts all ended in failure, because he was linked to her through the unbreakable chain of analogy. His "aversion was mixed with despair," she writes in *Looking Back*, "because he was forced to see *himself* grotesquely mirrored in his mother: his devotion as her superstition and hypocrisy, his spiritual creativity as her idle sentimentality."[4] Rilke confides the same thing in a 1904 letter. "When I have to see this lost, unreal woman," he tells Salomé, "I feel how even as a child I struggled to get away from her, and fear deep within me lest after years of running and walking I am still not far enough from her, that somewhere inwardly I still make movements that are the other half of her embittered gestures, bits of memories that she carried about broken within her. . . . And that I am still her child."[5] An even greater panic welled up in Rilke when Becker became pregnant, since he had earlier hailed *this* mother as the "sister" to his "soul." If she does not return to the underworld, he tells her in *Requiem for a Friend,* he will lose everything he has been struggling to "attain" and will "fall back, worthless" into the place from which he came (93).

Rilke later treated this analogy as a general problem for men. He also warns that if the male subject does not separate himself from his mother, he will be "annihilated." The only knife strong enough to cut through this umbilical cord is murder, and Cézanne was exemplary for his willingness to wield it: "I call fate all external events . . . which can inevitably step in to interrupt and annihilate a disposition of mind and training that is by nature solitary. Cézanne must have understood this . . . [when he] gave up going to his mother's funeral so as not to lose a working day. That went through me like an arrow when I learned it, but a flaming arrow that, while it pierced my heart, left in a conflagration of clear sight."[6] Rilke wrote this matricidal letter after completing the *Sonnets to Orpheus,* the work in which he makes his peace with his dead sister. He also addresses it to a "young girl," suggesting that in the battle-to-the-death with the mother, even his sister is a welcome ally.

Although Rilke does not mention it, another of Becker's 1906 paintings also haunts the pages of *Requiem for a Friend: Portrait of Rainer Maria Rilke.* Because the poet stopped sitting for this painting while the artist was still working on it, and because it does not transform the brown swatch beneath his chin into a believable representation of a beard, it is often assumed to be "unfinished." However, what is incomplete is not the painting but rather the person it depicts. As Eric Torgersen notes, Rilke's gaping mouth conveys "the helpless, elemental appetitiveness" that Becker emphasizes in her paintings of children.[7] This hunger attests not just to his physical dependence upon the external world but also to his need for a woman who will love him unreservedly, while making no demands upon him.

As we have already seen, Rilke attempted to overcome his limits through "two finite types"—those who have died young and "the woman who loves."[8] Through the first of these finite types, which he modeled on his dead sister, he attempted to divest himself of his mortality. Through the second, he attempted to recover his infantile narcissism. Like Salomé's God-grandfather, the woman who loves is an almighty servant; she has boundless power and strength, but lives only to serve her mortal creator.[9] However, unlike Salomé's deity, who disappeared along with the melting snowmen, Rilke's second finite type had a long and varied life. Salomé was the most important of the figures he tried to install in this position. He was drawn to her because of their deep ontological kinship, and he also had more of a relationship with her than with any of his subsequent lovers, but their affair was doomed from the start, because instead of acknowledging her as his "primal sibling," he treated her as his own private

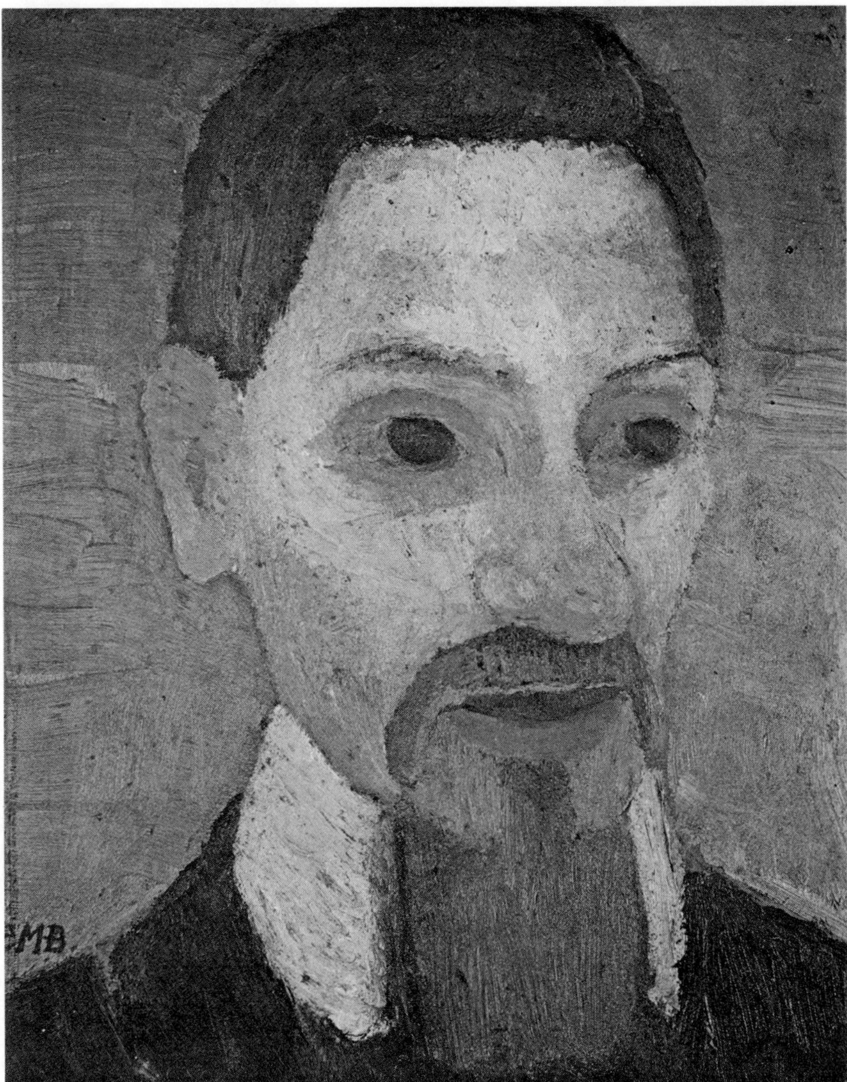

See also Plate 3 in color insert.

deity. "I've never seen you without wanting to pray to you," Rilke told Salomé on June 8, 1897. "I've never heard you without wanting to place my faith in you."[10] "I want to rise in you like a child's prayer in a loud, jubilant morning, like a rocket among the solitary stars," he wrote the next day.[11]

When the unearthly glow of early love receded, Rilke realized that he was no closer to "flying" than he had been before, and as their affair continued, it became harder and harder to believe that he would ever be a "rocket" blasting through the firmament. But rather than moderating the demands he made on Salomé, he increased them. In May 1898, he compared himself to a "child . . . hanging from a precipice" and her to the mother who "grasps it in dear, quiet strength, even if the chasm is below and thorns splay between its cheek and her breast."[12] Salomé found this dependency suffocating, and by the end of 1900 she was yearning to be alone. "Almost the only thing I want from the coming year . . . is quiet," she wrote in her journal on New Year's Eve, "—more being by myself, the way it was four years ago. That will, that *must*, come back" (38).[13] "To make Rainer go away, *go completely away*," she added three weeks later, "I would be capable of brutality. (*He must go*!)"[14]

In February 1901 Salomé compelled Rilke to leave,[15] and although their correspondence resumed in 1903, they did not see each other again until 1914. Only after the completion of the first of the *Duino Elegies* was she able to reaffirm their kinship, and she directed this acknowledgment more to the poet than to the man. "From that Whitsuntide on I read your work on my own, and not just when I was with you. I opened myself to it, welcomed it as an expression of your destiny, which was not to be denied," she says to him in *Looking Back*. "And in so doing I became yours once again, in a second way—in a second maidenhood" (91).

As we can see from Rilke's constant references to Salomé as a "mother" and himself as a "child," his second finite type had a maternal template. Although his written references to his mother, Sophie (Phia) Entz, are extremely unflattering, that is clearly because she failed to satisfy the exorbitant demands he made on her. He devotes several pages of his quasi-autobiographical novel, *The Notebooks of Malte Laurids Brigge*, to the kind of mother he wanted to have, and he gives this figure Entz's birth name.

> O mother: you who are without an equal, who stood before all this silence, long ago in childhood. Who took it upon yourself to say: Don't be afraid; I'm here. Who in the night had the courage to *be* this silence for the child who was frightened, who was dying of fear. You strike a match, and already the noise is you. And you hold the lamp in front of you and say: I'm here; don't be afraid. . . . Does any power equal your power among the lords of the earth?[16]

We can also see from the poet's later affairs what transformed Entz from the deity to whom he addressed his prayers into someone he couldn't be "far enough away from." Unlike his relationship with Salomé, which came to a close when she banished him, Rilke's subsequent relationships ended because of his withdrawal. This also happened very quickly. With the exception of Clara and Paula, whom he initially saw as sisters, the women to whom the poet was attracted all had one thing in common: something about them—most typically their physical remoteness—provided the hook on which he could hang his fantasy of an all-powerful and infinitely loving mother.[17] And as soon as they made reciprocal demands, and/or failed to be the vehicle of his self-realization, he turned away from them.

Several years after Salomé sent Rilke into exile, he expressed the hope that his mouth would one day be allowed to "flow" again like a river into her "hearing" and the "stillness" of her "opened depths."[18] In her portrait of the poet, Becker communicates his desire for self-prolongation and couches it in similar terms; she shows his mouth "flowing" into his beard. But the painter also frustrates the wish of this "*l'hommelette*"[19] to spread in every direction by squeezing a more-or-less life-sized representation of Rilke's head and shoulders into a canvas that is only ten by thirteen inches. By confining the poet to such a small space, she showed him what the mirrors in Salomé's childhood home showed her—that he was "limited," "restricted," and "forced" to "stop" by everything around him.[20] Becker also helped Rilke see that his mother was neither an extension of himself, nor a prototype to which he was forced to conform, but rather the first of a potentially infinite number of partners-in-rhyme, by linking him to her own pregnant body. Like the figure in *Self-Portrait on Her Sixth Wedding Anniversary*, the one in *Portrait of Rainer Maria Rilke* bumps his head against the top of the canvas. Although the poet's eyes were famously blue, Becker gives him large brown irises, like those she gives herself in *Self-Portrait on her Sixth Wedding Anniversary*. Finally—and humorously—she reddens the tip of his nose just as she does her own. Becker also devoted another 1906 painting to this analogy: *Reclining Mother and Child*. In this painting, an infant lies

See also Plate 4 in color insert.

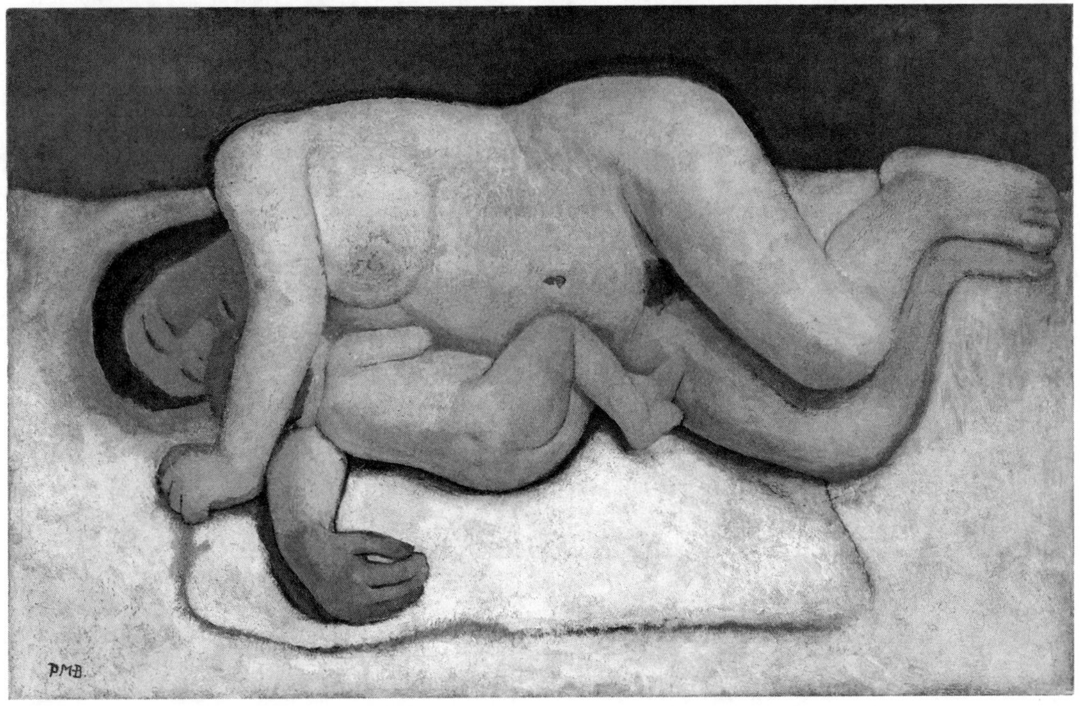

within the enclosure of its mother's arms, its body pressed against hers. Both are naked, and although they face opposite directions, and the child is much smaller than its mother, it crooks its knees the way she crooks hers, and the white cloth on which it lies is a miniature version of the one on which she lies. Becker foregrounds these correspondences by giving them similar flesh tones.

Rilke seems to have registered all of these challenges to his "solitariness," because he did his best to conjure away the painting, both by studiously ignoring it and by generating a counterrepresentation. In a poem stamped with the same date—"Self-Portrait, 1906"—he emphasizes the blueness of his eyes, the downward cast of his gaze, and the maturity and precision of his mouth. He also equips himself with an alternative lineage by locating within his "eyebrows' heavy arches" the "stamina of an old, long-noble race."[21] But Rilke acknowledges that Becker is still standing there at the end of *Requiem for a Friend* (91). Earlier in the poem, he also allows her to talk back. "You're pleading," he says to this maternal revenant. "This penetrates me, to / my very bones, and cuts at me like a saw. / The bitterest rebuke your ghost could bring me, / could scream, at night, when I withdraw / into my lungs, into my intestines, / into the last bare chamber of my heart, - / such bitterness would not chill me half so much / as this mute pleading, / What is it that you want?" (81).

Rilke also produced one other version of the Orpheus and Eurydice story: "Antistrophes."[22] As usual, Orpheus's defining attribute is solitude. The poem also unfolds through a series of gender antinomies: grief is barren for men, but women are able to transform theirs into blessings; men are only familiar with physical distances, but women's hearts contain a "magnificent space"; men are already "disfigured" as children, but women are "unharmed" by rough shoves when they are young; men are like "pieces of rock / that have fallen on flowers" when they grow up, but women are "complete" (221). Now, though, Orpheus represents the poet's contemporaries, as well as the poet himself. Rilke also offers a devastating critique of this "man of the 'new grain,'"[23] whose sadomasochistic preoccupation with self-overcoming leaves no room for anyone else. "We, afflicted by ourselves, / gladly afflicting, gladly / needing to be afflicted," he writes in the penultimate stanza. "We . . . sleep with our anger / laid beside us like a knife." And although the notion of protection figures centrally in "Antistrophes," it is now unavailable, rather than obligatory. "You, who are almost protection / where no one protects," Rilke says to this Eurydice. "The thought of you / is a shade-giving tree of sleep for the restless / creatures of a solitary man" (223).

THE LIMITLESSLY LOVING MOTHER also occupies a prominent position in Proust's great novel, this time in the guise of the narrator's grandmother. Unlike Marcel's mother, who is only intermittently available to him during his childhood and who largely disappears after the "Combray" section of *Swann's Way*, this figure remains at his beck and call until the moment of her death, and he regards her psyche as a simple prolongation of his own. Since Marcel is also "as gluttonous" as "a babe at the breast"[24] when it comes to his grandmother's love, he suffers acutely when he is separated from her for the first time. Although this separation occurs when he is far away from her, visiting Saint-Loup at Doncières, he does not experience it immediately. The catalyst is a faulty telephone connection, which allows the narrator to hear his grandmother's voice but prevents her from hearing his response.[25]

By itself, even the non-reciprocal nature of this telephonic exchange would not have been a problem. However, what Marcel's grandmother says to him freights their one-way communication with significance: she urges him to stay in Doncières longer, showing that she has continued to exist in spite of his absence, and even has "a definite age"—something that has never before occurred to him (183). The revelation that she has an independent existence fills him with "an anxious, insensate longing to return"—the same anguish he had felt "once before in the distant past, when, as a little child, [he] had lost her in a crowd" (177). Marcel attempts to recover his egoic footing the same way Rilke does—by dispatching this enraging mother, who challenges the omnipotence of his thoughts. Like the poet, he also tries to conceal this crime, from both us and himself; instead of acknowledging the cause-and-effect relation between his anguish and his grandmother's death, he represents his feelings as a foretaste of the desolation he will experience later, when the Grim Reaper mows her down.

Marcel also turns for this purpose to the myth of Orpheus and Eurydice, and the passage in which he mobilizes it is as self-incriminating as any passage in *Requiem for a Friend*. "It seemed to me as though it was already a beloved ghost that I had allowed to lose herself in the ghostly world," he confides, "and standing alone before the instrument, I went on vainly repeating: 'Granny! Granny!' as Orpheus, left alone, repeats the name of his dead wife." He tries to place another call to his grandmother, but the "capricious Guardians" refuse to "open the miraculous portals" a second time (178). Marcel rushes back to Balbec, so as to close the distance between himself and his grandmother, but when he arrives he discovers—to his utter horror—that this distance is psychic, as well as physical. He finds her sitting alone in the drawing room, absorbed in thoughts that she has "never allowed" him to "see" (183).[26]

This discovery precipitates the bizarre fantasy that a stranger has just entered the room and is photographing his grandmother as she would appear if Marcel's look were subtracted from her. What this imaginary camera sees is a "red-faced" woman sitting on a sofa beneath a lamp, who is "heavy and vulgar, sick, day-dreaming, [and] letting her slightly crazed eyes wander over a book" (185). Through the resulting "photograph," Marcel kills his Eurydice a second time and installs a madwoman in her place. Although he spends most of the rest of the paragraph deploring the camera's cruelty and describing the visual protection he would have offered his grandmother if he had been in the room, he insists that the unflattering photograph is *objectively* true. He also admits that he would have shielded her from its ravages only if she had still seemed to be part of himself (184–185).

The famous game Freud watched his grandson play also bears a striking resemblance to the one in *Requiem for a Friend* (89), and is based on a similar relationship to the mother. Like the child Rilke once was, and still resembles, this little boy "threw" and "caught" a round object, which was a maternal surrogate. "He had a wooden reel with a piece of string attached to it . . . [and would] hold the reel by the string and very skillfully throw it over the edge of his curtained cot, so that it disappeared into it, at the same time uttering [an] expressive 'o-o-o-o,'" Freud writes in *Beyond the Pleasure Principle.* "He then pulled the reel out of the cot again by the string and hailed its reappearance with a joyful 'da' ['there']. This then was the complete game—disappearance and return. As a rule one only witnessed its first act, which was repeated untiringly in itself."[27]

Freud begins his analysis in the usual way: by looking for the implicitly erotic wish fulfilled by the *fort/da* game. Although the child was "greatly attached" to his mother and found her absences painful, Freud argues, he did not protest when she went away, which shows that the game was compensatory; by drawing the reel into his crib, he brought her back again. But this interpretation does not explain why the child repeated the "distressing experience" of his mother's departure, often without its pleasurable sequel, so Freud replaces it with another. Originally the little boy had a passive relationship to his mother's departure, but by repeating this trauma, he mastered it (16). However, since such a young child would be unlikely to repeat a distressing experience merely for the purpose of mastering it, Freud also abandons this explanation. The original function of the game must have been to punish the mother for leaving, he decides, and it was the deadly form this punishment took that made the game so enjoyable. "Throwing away the object so that it was 'gone' might satisfy an impulse of the child's, which was suppressed in his actual life, to revenge himself on his mother for going away from him. In that case it would have a defiant meaning: 'All right, then, go away! I don't need you. I'm sending you away myself'" (16).

Although this is the only interpretation to which Freud does not subsequently raise an objection, he tries to neutralize it by subjecting the *fort/da* story to an Oedipal "rectification." The little boy did not really hate his mother, or seek to kill her, he announces a few sentences later; on the contrary, he *loved* her. The person he wanted to *kill* was his *father*: "A year later, the same boy . . . used to take a toy, if he was angry at it, and throw it on the floor, exclaiming: 'Go to the fwont!' He had heard at the time that his absent father was 'at the front,' and was far from regretting his absence; on the contrary he made it quite clear that he had no desire to be disturbed in his sole possession of his mother" (16). But immediately after telling us that Ernst was "greatly attached" to his mother, Freud describes an earlier version of the game, in which there was a "*fort*," but no "*da*," and in which the lethal nature of the "gone" was strongly marked: "This good little boy . . . had an occasional disturbing habit of taking any small objects he could get hold of and throwing them away from him, into a corner, under the bed, and so on, so that hunting for his toys . . . was often quite a business" (14).

A footnote at the end of the sentence in which Freud effects his Oedipal rectification also shows that matricide was the goal of the *fort/da* game. From it, we learn that Ernst was unmoved when his mother died, a few years after the events described in *Beyond the Pleasure Principle.* And although the mother who was symbolically dispatched was his own daughter, Sophie,[28] Freud cannot resist the temptation to make a black joke out of her literal disappearance. "When this child was five and three-quarters," he writes, "his mother died. Now that she was really gone ('o-o-o'), the little boy showed no signs of grief" (16n).[29] Lacan completes the process begun by Freud and his grandson. In his influential reading of the *fort/da* game, there is no longer any trace of the mother. What the child throws away and pulls back again is "a small part of [him] that detaches itself from him while still remaining his"—a "self-mutilation on the basis of which the order of significance will be put in perspective."[30]

IT IS GENERALLY AROUND THE FIGURE of the mother that the dream of an infinitely loving and powerful parent first coalesces because she is still the primary caretaker, if not in actuality, then at least within the cultural Imaginary. At the beginning of life, the human subject does not recognize any limits; it is "everything," or—to be more precise—"everything good." When the sand of dissatisfaction starts to jam the gears of this illusion, the child does not moderate its expectations; instead it attempts to take up even more space, so as to incorporate what it needs to be complete. The first serious challenge to the infant subject's omnipotence and omnipresence comes when it registers its mother's absence *as an absence.* When she ceases to be an assemblage of components that are usually part of the child, but sometimes break away, and becomes a separate person, the child realizes that it cannot *be* everything. It can, however, *have* everything, and it is the mother's duty to provide it. This new imperative can be very flattering to the mother's narcissism, since it attributes to her the capacity to satisfy her infant's lack, and so—by extension—her own. Since most women in our culture are egoically wounded, the temptation to bathe in the sun of this idealization often proves irresistible. But there is no room here for the mother, as either a person in her own right or someone with limits, and as long as the child's demands remain unchallenged, there will also be no room for anything else. The only way she can open up a space in the infant's psyche for herself and others is to persist in showing the child that her breast is not the extension of its mouth and that the milk that comes out of it cannot fill every void.

The extraordinarily difficult task imposed upon the child's primary caretaker not only by culture but also by Being itself is to induct it into relationality by saying over and over again, in a multitude of ways, what death will otherwise have to teach it: "This is where you end and others begin." Unfortunately, this lesson seldom "takes," and the mother usually delivers it at enormous cost to herself. Most children respond to the partial satisfaction of their demands with extreme rage, rage that is predicated on the belief that the mother is withholding something that is within her power to provide. Our culture should support her by providing enabling representations of maternal finitude, but instead it keeps alive in all of us the tacit belief that she *could* satisfy our desires if she really *wanted to*. As a result of even more strenuous ideological prompting, a diametrically opposed perception of the mother begins to form in the infant psyche. The mother is not good-for-everything; she is, rather, good-for-nothing. The almighty servant disappears and is replaced by the "red-faced" stranger.

This disillusionment provides the support for a new set of illusions: those constitutive first of the paternal function, and later of God. When the child fails to secure what it wants from the mother, it searches for another source of satisfaction, and because the father is so ready at hand, sometimes physically and ideologically and at other times only ideologically, it is usually to him that it turns.[31] Since he is no more capable of meeting its demands than is the mother, this idealization would also lead to a radical de-idealization if it were not for one crucial aspect of the paternal function: its insistence on deferral. The Oedipus complex permits the father to project far into the future the moment when he must make good on his "promises." The boy classically resolves his rivalry with his father by postponing the moment of satisfaction; although deprived in the present, he will later possess everything he wants, through the paternal legacy. Because the girl classically enters the positive Oedipus complex only by signing away all claim to this legacy, she must accommodate herself to a longer delay; the father will respond to her demands even later, and perhaps never. Through her enforced identification with lack, she also absolves him of guilt for her continuing dissatisfaction.

Christianity adds a formidable new component to the paternal function: God. It posits a father whose love and power know no limits—the Divine Father. It also gives him a son, who for the span of a brief lifetime assumed a finite form, and even became the repository of "sin." Through this figure, Christianity bridges the distance between heaven and earth, and links the actual father to the Divine Father. This dramatically augments his power and authority, and extends until the end of time the date at which his promissory note will come due. Christianity thus provides the actual father with a permanent safeguard against our disappointment and rage.[32]

Freud knows all of this. The "early efflorescence of infantile sexual life is doomed to extinction because its wishes are incompatible with reality," he writes in *Beyond the Pleasure Principle*. No matter how long a child sucks at the maternal breast, it will therefore be "forever unsated," Freud adds in "Female Sexuality." Although the mother is the child's first protector, she is soon replaced by the "stronger father," he observes in *The Future of an Illusion*—and when the "growing individual" requires a more powerful protector, he will "create" a Father God.[33] But the *fort/da* game is not the only matricidal passage in Freud's writings. The phrase "turning away from the mother" ("*Abwendung von der Mutter*") appears so often in "Some Psychical Consequences of the Anatomical Distinction between the Sexes," "Female Sexuality," and "Femininity" that it makes its way into the index of the *Studienausgabe*.[34]

But although the action that is at the heart of the *fort/da* game is also obsessively repeated in these later essays, its agent has changed; instead of a particular boy, it is now a generalized "girl" who turns away from the mother. This action also has a new motive. The girl rejects the mother not because the latter is a separate person, but rather because both of them are corporeally "deficient," and because she blames her mother for her own "castration." As these differences permit us to see, Freud mobilizes an even more disturbing version of the myth of Orpheus and Eurydice in "Some Psychical Consequences," "Female Sexuality," and "Femininity" than he does in *Beyond the Pleasure Principle*; he returns to the one elaborated by the fifteenth-century writer Angelo Poliziano.

When Poliziano released the text of his play, *Orfeo*, he claimed to be doing so under pressure from his patron, Carlo Canale. In a letter to Canale, which he published with the play, he describes the unfavorable circumstances under which he wrote it and recommends that it be exposed to the elements, like an unwanted infant. Although Poliziano does not mention Oedipus by name, he clearly has the latter in mind, because the child to whom he compares his opera has a "maimed membe[r]."[35] However, he makes this wound the justification for, rather than the effect of, the punishment to which he wishes to subject his play.

Poliziano also invokes another mythological figure, this time by name; he tells Canale that his text should be dismembered, just as Orpheus was by the Ciconian women. In the same sentence, though, he maintains that *his* child is a "little daughter," rather than a little son. This permits him to transfer Oedipus's "maimed member" to Eurydice, make her "defect" the justification for abandoning her on the slope leading from Hades to earth, and punish *her* for Orpheus's crime. It also allows him to distance himself from the inadequacies of his play. "It was a custom among the Lacedaemonians . . . when some child of theirs was born either with maimed members or with strength impaired, to expose him immediately . . . for they judged such progeny to be unworthy of Lacedaemonia," Poliziano writes. "Thus I also desired that the fable of Orpheus, which I had composed . . . in two days in the midst of continuous disturbance and in vulgar style . . . should immediately, not unlike Orpheus, be torn piecemeal, knowing that this little daughter of mine was of the kind to bring her father dishonor. . . . But . . . you and some others . . . maintain her in life against my will. . . . Let her, therefore, live, since this is your pleasure . . . [but] I pray you to resist with your authority any one who may attempt to ascribe the imperfection of such a child to the father."[36]

It might seem surprising to find *any* version of the myth of Orpheus and Eurydice in Freud's writings. Unlike a number of the other figures I have discussed in this book, he was not a solitary male subject, but rather an unusually gregarious person. He was also surrounded for most of his adult life by women; had intellectual friendships with Lou-Andreas Salomé, Marie Bonaparte, Sabrina Spielrein, Loe Kahn, and H.D.; and transmitted his psychoanalytic legacy to his daughter, Anna, rather than to one of his sons. As Lisa Appignanesi and John Forrester point out in their excellent book, *Freud's Women*, the "fundamental tenets" of his theory of sexuality also make scant space for and assign "little importance to the differences between the sexes."[37] Indeed, in a number of early texts, Freud often seems on the verge of accounting for human subjectivity analogically—as an infinitely variable "mixture" of "masculinity" and "femininity," which connects every human being to every other, through relationships of greater or lesser similarity.[38]

In "Thoughts for the Times on War and Death," Freud also argues that war is not the opposite of peace, but rather the literalization and collectivization of an everyday practice: the practice of "Othering" our mortality.[39] In a contemporaneous essay, "On Transience," he describes a country walk he took with "a young but already famous poet" in the summer of 1913. This poet—who may have been Rilke[40]—was "disturbed" by the thought that the beauty around him was "fated to extinction, that it would vanish when winter came, like all human beauty and all the beauty and splendor that men have created or may create." Everything seemed "shorn of its worth" by the brevity of its existence.[41] Freud agrees with the first claim, but denies the second. And five years later, he wrote the words that were the inspiration for my own book: "*the aim of all life is death.*"[42]

However, Ernest Jones reports that Freud was more preoccupied with his mortality than any great man he could think of, with the possible exceptions of Montaigne and Sir Thomas Browne. In the early years of their acquaintance, the psychoanalyst "had the disconcerting habit" of saying, at parting, "'Good-bye; you may never see me again.'" Freud was not at all reconciled to the aging process, and he suffered from "repeated attacks of what he called *Todesangst*."[43] When he reached sixty—which was also the year he published "On Transience" (1916)—he was convinced that he would die in February 1918.[44]

Freud's conversation with the young poet was an internal as well as an external argument, and he clearly didn't win it, because it continues unabated in *The Future of an Illusion.* His interlocutor also gets the better of him in the latter text—not because he has God on his side but rather because mortality is not something one can simply "accept." As Freud himself observes in "Thoughts for the Times on War and Death," "our unconscious is just as inaccessible to the idea of our own death, . . . just as murderously inclined toward strangers, just as divided (that is, ambivalent) towards those we love, as was primeval man" (299). There is consequently "a small portion of hostility" even in the "tenderest and most intimate of our love-relations" that can "excite" an unconscious wish for the Other's death (298).

From the very beginning, it was also primarily toward women that Freud directed his unconscious aggression. In the middle of interpreting the dream of Irma's injection, he suddenly realizes that there are two "Mathildes" hidden behind the figure of Irma. One was his oldest daughter, who was born in 1887, and the other was a former patient, whose death he had inadvertently caused. In his dream, he paid for his patient's death by sacrificing his daughter. In his analysis, he divests himself of responsibility for this crime by attributing his daughter's death to the gods. "I had on one occasion produced a severe toxic state in a woman patient by repeatedly prescribing what was at that time regarded as a harmless remedy," Freud writes in the second chapter of his dream book. "My patient—who succumbed to the poison—had the same name as my eldest daughter. . . . It struck me now almost like an act of retribution on the part of destiny. It was as though the replacement of one person for another was to be continued in another sense: this Mathilde for that Mathilde, an eye for an eye and a tooth for a tooth."[45]

As Appignanesi and Forrester note, *The Interpretation of Dreams* contains only one of Freud's childhood dreams, and it is organized around the spectacle of his mother's corpse (12–13). "I saw *my beloved mother, with a peculiarly peaceful, sleeping expression on her features, being carried into the room by two (or three) people with birds' beaks and laid upon the bed*," he writes in chapter 7. "I awoke in tears and screaming, and interrupted my parents' sleep" (Freud's emphasis).[46] Once again, he not only shrugs off his mortality by feminizing it but also imputes this crime to another agency. In this dream and the dream of Irma's injection, the Angel of Death is ungendered, but in "The Theme of the Three Caskets," as in "Some Psychical Consequences of the Anatomical Distinction between the Sexes," "Female Sexuality," and "Femininity," it—too—is female. "Caskets are also women," Freud observes near the beginning of the first of these essays.[47]

And in April 1923 he suffered another narcissistic injury—one that tore away pieces of his face and cost him a number of his *own* teeth. He had the first of thirty-three operations for jaw cancer, the disease that would ultimately kill him. Six months later, a surgeon cut open Freud's right lip and cheek and removed his right upper jaw and palate. This eliminated the partition between his mouth and nasal cavity and seriously impaired his hearing. The resulting cavity was filled with a large prosthesis, which was hard to insert and remove, and extraordinarily uncomfortable to wear; Freud called it "the monster." From this point forward, it was difficult for him to eat, and his speech was "very defective."[48] He also became completely dependent upon his daughter Anna, who served from then until his death in 1939 as his "nurse, a truly 'personal' physician, companion, assistant secretary, co-worker and altogether a shield against the intrusions of the outer world."[49] Eventually, she was the only one (apart from Freud's physician) who was able to handle his prosthesis, and she functioned as her father's mouthpiece[50] when he wanted one of his essays to be read at a professional gathering.

There are striking similarities between the "scabs" and discolored "spots" that Freud saw as he peered into Irma's mouth, and what Anna must have seen as she looked into his mouth.[51] Since he refused to stop smoking, even though he knew that it was the cause of his illness, his physicians must also have said to him what he said to Irma: "If you still get pains, it's really only your fault."[52] But Freud was clearly determined to ignore these analogies, because instead of using them to expand his theory of bisexuality, he started dismantling the theory. In 1925, two years after his first operation, he wrote "Some Psychical Consequences of the Anatomical Distinction between the Sexes." In the years that followed he wrote "Fetishism" (1927), "Female Sexuality" (1931), and "Femininity" (1932).

Not only were all of these essays written after the operation that removed a large part of Freud's right face and left him partly deaf, almost unable to speak, and completely dependent upon his daughter, but they also testify in manifold ways to these humiliations. The "mutilated" creature, who elicited his horror and contempt, was obviously Freud himself. He got rid of this bodily injury by relocating it at the site of the female genitals and by using his daughter's voice to cover over his vocal "lack."[53] Astonishingly, although Freud performed these actions simultaneously, and in a public venue, no one seems to have noticed. According to Jones, the first paper he "entrusted" to Anna was "Some Psychical Consequences of the Anatomical Distinction between the Sexes." She presented it in 1925, to the Hamburg Congress, and "this mark of attention on [her father's] part, the content of the paper, and the way in which it was read, all equally gave general pleasure."[54]

Freud also uses "Femininity" and "Female Sexuality" to provide himself with an inexhaustible supply of maternal love, and—through it—to heal the injuries inflicted on his self-regard by his illness and mortality. But since his mother was eighty-eight when he was diagnosed with jaw cancer, she was not a reliable source of narcissistic sustenance. He consequently needed someone else to love him in the same way—exclusively, permanently, and unreservedly—and he turned for this purpose to his daughter. Freud assured himself of the limitlessness of her love the same way he assured himself of the limitlessness of his mother's love: through the notion of "lack." My mother, my wife, and my daughter are castrated, he announced in the first paper he asked Anna to read for him. Because they have small and inconspicuous organs, their mothers cannot love them as my mother loves me. Anna has also turned away from her mother to me. Since this journey was arduous, and has exhausted her capacity for change, I am all that she will ever desire.

Freud had read *King Lear* many times, and in "The Theme of the Three Caskets" he observes that "it is in vain that an old man yearns for the love of woman as he had it first from his mother; the third of the Fates alone, the silent Goddess of Death, will take him into her arms."[55] But there are already signs of what was to come in this 1913 text. "Goneril and Regan, exhaust themselves in asseverations and laudations of their love for [King Lear]," Freud writes there. "The third, Cordelia, refuses to do so. [Lear] should have recognized the unassuming, speechless love of his third daughter" (292–293). Although Anna was not speechless, she *was* unassuming—at least when it came to her father. She was also his third daughter.[56]

Freud fiercely defended his theory of sexual difference against the criticisms of the "feminists," but he clearly saw that something was constraining his thought, because he was extremely dissatisfied with the books he wrote during the last seventeen years of his life. He didn't think that there was anything new in *Group Psychology and the Analysis of the Ego, The Ego and the Id, or Civilization and Its Discontents.* He also told Ferenzi that *The Future of an Illusion* was "inadequate as a self-confession" and that "fundamentally [he] thought otherwise."[57] Few of us would concur with Freud's blanket dismissal of these four extraordinary works. However, when we place them side by side with the letters he exchanged with Romain Rolland and Oskar Pfister, which I discuss in the first chapter of this book, we can see that they are indeed full of strange blockages and paralyses. These blockages and paralyses derive from the same source as "Femininity," "Female Sexuality," and "Some Psychical Consequences of the Anatomical Distinction between the Sexes": Freud's refusal to think analogically about the women in his life.

BUT TIME IS NOT LINEAR in the Book of Life, and there is no act that cannot be undone, so let us end this chapter by turning back the pages of the calendar. In 1906 Freud wrote an appreciative book about Wilhelm Jensen's 1903 novella, *Gradiva.* As he notes in a 1912 "Postscript" to this book, *Gradiva* "describes the history of a man who 'sees a sister in the woman he loves,'" and Jensen returns to this story in a later novel.[58] Jensen was drawn to stories about brothers and sisters for the same reason Salomé and Rilke were; he saw in the concept of "siblings"[59] the potential for a new kind of heterosexuality. He also sought to actualize this potential through the story of Orpheus and Eurydice. Something extraordinary happens in his telling of the myth: Eurydice finally makes her way back to earth.

The central character in *Gradiva* is Norbert Hanold, a wealthy German man who lives alone in the house he has inherited from his parents.[60] Hanold seeks to "preserve" and "exalt" his "father's name" by following in the latter's antiquarian footsteps, and he is so absorbed by his scientific investigations into the remote past that he scarcely notices the world around him (18). During a trip to Rome, he becomes obsessed with a bas-relief of a woman with an unusual stride. Although he sees nothing of scientific interest in the artifact, he buys a plaster cast of it and hangs it in his workroom. Hanold names the marble woman "Gradiva," which means "the girl splendid in walking," and fantasizes that she was an inhabitant of Pompeii (5). One night, he dreams that he is in this Roman city at the moment of its destruction, and he sees Gradiva moving calmly through the chaos. He calls out to her to save herself, but her uncomprehending face is already turning to stone; she lies down on a step in the Temple of Apollo and is soon covered with a blanket of ashes. When Hanold awakens, he is certain that Gradiva lived in Pompeii and that he was present at her death (11–13).

He departs for Rome, ostensibly to do research, but clearly in the hope of meeting the woman in the bas-relief. The train to Rome is full of honeymooning couples, whom Hanold perceives as the interchangeable representatives of a subhuman species. He refers to all of the men as "August" and all of the women as "Grete,"[61] and imagines that they are all conducting the same conversation. Hanold eagerly awaits the moment when he will be able to escape from the "cage" he is forced to share with these lovebirds (22–23), but when he arrives in Rome, he encounters more Augusts and Gretes. He therefore continues his journey until he reaches Pompeii. While still on the train to Rome, Hanold dreams that he is once again in Pompeii on the day of its destruction, but this time he sees the Apollo Belvedere transport the Capitoline Venus to safety on a carriage or a cart (26–27). When he arrives in Pompeii, he has a series of mysterious encounters with a woman he believes to be Gradiva's ghost, but who turns out to be Zoë, his neighbor and childhood playmate.

It takes Hanold a long time to acknowledge that Zoë is a living woman (65). At the end of their third encounter, he still assumes that she lives in Hades, and earlier on the same day he gives her a cluster of asphodels. Zoë responds to his floral gift by drawing his attention to its funereal implications, and ours to the myth into which he is attempting to insert her. "One must adapt [oneself] to the inevitable," she wryly observes, "and I have long accustomed myself to being dead; but now my time is over for today; you have brought the grave-flower with you to conduct me back. . . . To those who are more fortunate one gives roses in spring, but for me the flower of oblivion is the right one from your hand" (71).

Jensen also refers to the story of Orpheus and Eurydice in a number of other ways. He writes that there is a "mythological-literary-historical-archaeological juggling in [Hanold's] head" (50), which makes it difficult for him to decide if Zoë is Greek (like Virgil's Eurydice) or Roman (like Ovid's). Although her "Hellenic ancestry" gradually becomes a "certainty" to him (8), three lines from Book VIII of *The Metamorphoses* subsequently occur to him: "her floating vest / a polished buckle clasped—her careless locks / In simple knot were gathered" (50).[62] As we have already seen, the verb "to clasp" also figures prominently in Book XI of *The Metamorphoses*. When Orpheus's "shade" arrives in the underworld, he searches through the "fields of the blessed" for Eurydice, and when he finds her, he "clasp[s] her tightly in his loving arms."[63] This word plays a pivotal role in Hanold's story. One of the first things the archaeologist notices about Gradiva is her golden clasp (54), and he later buys a clasp that was supposedly worn by a girl who died during the destruction of Pompeii. The vendor talks him into purchasing it by telling him that when the girl's body was uncovered, she and her lover were still "clasped" in a "firm embrace" (78).

Because the conversations Hanold overhears on the train to Rome are about the honeymooning couples' undying love and their desire to be constantly together, he dubs them the "inseparables" (24)[64]—and since he believes the couples to be interchangeable, he equates their inseparability with a loss of differentiation. However, after buying the brooch, Hanold is mysteriously drawn to a German man and woman with "youthful, attractive features" and "intellectual expressions." Although they resemble each other, they are not identical; the man has fair hair, but the woman "light brown tresses"(80). Hanold thinks they are a brother and sister, but later sees them "mutually embracing" and realizes that they, too, are a honeymooning couple. His eyes cling to this "*living* picture" more passionately than they have ever "clung" to the "most admired works of art" (86–87). Slowly, Zoë also comes to life, and eventually Hanold recognizes her as both his contemporary and his primal sibling. They stroll "hand in hand" through the streets of Pompeii, and—like Ovid's Eurydice—Jensen's heroine sometimes leads and sometimes follows.[65] In the last sentence of the novel, Hanold stays behind to look at her as she walks buoyantly "over the stepping-stones," to the "other side of the street" (117–18).

In his book about the novella, *Delusions and Dreams in Jensen's 'Gradiva,'* Freud aligns himself with Jensen, over and against men of science, because the two of them understand how repression works and they both believe in the importance of dreams.[66] He also declares there to be no better way of illustrating the mental process "by which something in the mind is at once made inaccessible and preserved" than through the "burial of the sort to which Pompeii fell a victim and from which it could emerge once more through the work of spades" (40).[67] There are even more striking similarities between the psychoanalyst and the protagonist of Jensen's story. Like Hanold, Freud collected antiquities and thought of himself as an archaeologist. The spectator in him was also capable of derailing the scholar; when he acquired a new antiquity, Jones recounts, he brought it to the dinner table so that he could look at it while eating.[68] He was especially attached to the "pieces" in his collection that were "perfectly preserved," because "they were beings that had lived for centuries, or else come back from the dead."[69] Like Hanold, Freud also purchased a plaster cast of "the famous Gradiva," and displayed it in his house.[70] Since there are no dream thoughts with which to analyze Hanold's dreams, Freud relies on his own "associations" (73) and justifies this astonishing substitution by observing that "the meaning that is intended for the patient's conscious" often "stirs up an understanding of the meaning that applies to [the psychoanalyst's] unconscious" (86).

His "associations" consist of a story about a doctor who lost one of his women patients to Graves' disease, and who worried that he might have contributed to her death through a "thoughtless prescription."[71] Several years later, a girl entered his consulting room who so closely resembled this patient that he "could only frame a single thought: 'So after all it's true that the dead can come back to life'" (72). The doctor was filled with "dread," which modulated into "shame" when the girl identified herself as the dead woman's sister and told him that she, too, was suffering from Graves' disease, which imparts a "marked facial resemblance" to everyone it afflicts. A few sentences later, Freud reveals that this doctor was "none other than [him]self" and that he therefore has "a personal reason for not disputing the clinical possibility of Norbert Hanold's temporary delusion that Gradiva has come back to life" (72).

Freud also identifies Hanold as the subject of the action he later attributes to the little girl: that of "permanently turning away from women." He provides the following description of this action in the third chapter of *Delusions and Dreams in Jensen's 'Gradiva'*: "The canary, whose singing sent Hanold off on his distant journey, belonged to Zoë, and its cage stood on her window diagonally across the street from Hanold's house. Hanold, who, according to the girl's accusation, had the gift of 'negative hallucination,' who possessed the art of not seeing and not recognizing people who were actually present, must from the first have had an unconscious knowledge of what we only learned later" (67). This is not the only time Freud speaks about negative hallucinations. In *Studies on Hysteria*, he uses the term to refer to the visual occlusions that can be induced through hypnosis.[72] Hippolyte Bernheim gave "a woman in a state of somnambulism a negative hallucination to the effect that he was no longer present, and . . . then endeavored to draw her attention to himself . . . ," Freud writes there. "He did not succeed" (103). The phrase also appears in *The Psychopathology of Everyday Life*, as a signifier for the foreclosed perceptions that create our sense of déjà vu.[73]

As we can see from the passage quoted above, negative hallucination is one of the psychic mechanisms through which the perceiving subject alters the world so as to bring it into conformity with his desires. Like disavowal, fetishism, and projection, it is epistemologically divisive; it splits the perceiver into two entities, one of whom "knows" and the other of whom "doesn't know." Otherwise, though, it is *hors classe*. Disavowal, fetishism, and projection reconstitute the world by *adding* something to the perceptual object, but a negative hallucination accomplishes its goal by *eliminating* the object. Although it falls by the wayside after *Delusions and Dreams in Jensen's 'Gradiva,'* it warrants a prominent place on the roster of egoic defenses.

Freud forged an even closer connection between negative hallucination and the Orpheus and Eurydice myth in a 1905 essay. He writes that when a person is removed from the perceptual world through a negative hallucination, this person is no longer able to "attract" the perceiver's attention; the latter looks through her, "as though [she] were 'thin air.'"[74] In the passage on which Freud bases his analysis of Hanold's negative hallucinations, Zoë uses a similar formulation. "When, occasionally, I met you at a party," she says to her childhood friend, "you did not look at me . . . to you, I was but air."[75] The first trope comes from *The Georgics*; when Orpheus looks back at Eurydice, Virgil writes, she vanishes from his "sight, like smoke mingling with thin air."[76] The second trope derives from *The Metamorphoses*; when Ovid's Orpheus looks back at Eurydice, he "seize[s] only empty air" (166).[77]

Finally, rather than turning away from Zoë by looking through her, the way Orpheus does with Eurydice, Freud compares himself to her, and this comparison works to *her* advantage. Like a psychoanalyst, he writes, Zoë makes what is repressed conscious, demonstrates the curative effects of explanation (89), and reawakens passion (90). But unlike the analyst, who was a "stranger" in the past and does not know how to help his patients "use their recovered capacity to love," Zoë is able to return the passion that she reawakens. Because it was toward her that the "liberated current of love" was originally directed, she also offers it "a desirable aim." For all of these reasons, she is the ideal physician (86, 90). By ceding this position to Jensen's Eurydice, Freud makes room within psychoanalysis for the act with which Salomé concludes her *Freud Journal*: that of turning around to face the "partner" who has been left behind.[78] And suddenly the sun dissolves the tomblike rigidity of the old stones, a glowing thrill passes through them, the dead awaken, and Pompeii begins to live again,[79] just as they do for the protagonist of Jensen's book.

NOW

All Things Shining

5

Cordelia: Nothing, my Lord.
King Lear: Nothing!
Cordelia: Nothing.
King Lear: Nothing will come of nothing; speak again.

—William Shakespeare

One man looks at a dying bird and thinks there's nothing but unanswered pain. And death's got the final word. It's laughing at him. Another man sees that same bird and feels the glory. Feels somethin' smilin' through it.

—Sergeant Welsh, *The Thin Red Line*

IN 1946 Heidegger presented an essay called "What Are Poets For?" to a small group of listeners. As he explains in the published version of the essay, this title reprises a line from Friedrich Hölderlin, which reads: "What are poets for in a destitute time?"[1] Since it would be hard to think of a more destitute time than the year after Hiroshima and Nagasaki were reduced to toxic rubble and the abominations of the camps exposed to Allied cameras, the question seems at first to be historically pointed. However, although Heidegger mentions the atomic bomb midway through the essay, he treats it as the manifestation of something larger. What "threatens" man "with death, and indeed with the death of his own nature," he writes, "is the unconditional character of mere willing in the sense of purposeful self-assertion in everything."[2] This fury began raging a long time ago—at the moment when no deity "any longer gather[ed] men and things unto himself, visibly and unequivocally, and by such gathering dispose[d] the world's history and man's sojourn in it"(91)—and it did not end with the war. It has lived on through the "peaceful" fantasy that "technological production" can put the world "in order" (116–117).

The problem is not that God has failed to arrive, Heidegger hastens to explain; it is, rather, that man has failed to see the "saving power" in his finitude.[3] He has turned away from the abyss revealed through God's "default" by making himself the foundation of his knowledge and his existence. He will eventually turn back and face his mortality, but not until the "world's time" becomes utterly destitute. When Western metaphysics completes itself, a poet will emerge whose language will permit man to "come into ownership" of his "own nature" (95).

Three years later, Heidegger presented an essay called "The Turning" to another group of listeners. This essay is also suffused with longing for the "turn" that will reveal the "saving power" of mortality to us, but man is no longer the actant. Turning is something that *Being* does—and what Being turns toward is *itself.* "When, in the turning of the danger, the truth of Being flashes," Heidegger writes, "the essence of Being clears and lights itself up. Then the truth of the essence, the coming to presence, of Being turns and enters in. Toward where does in-turning bring itself to pass? Toward nowhere except into Being itself."[4] All that man can do is hold himself open to the futural happening of this event.

Although Heidegger was speaking to his contemporaries when he wrote that Hölderlin's "time" is the era to which "we ourselves" still belong, these shifters have lost none of their interpellatory force; Abu Ghraib is as "desolate" as Buchenwald. But the darkness of our world cannot be attributed to God's "default"; we now have not merely *one* deity who "gathers men and things unto himself, visibly and unequivocally, and by such gathering disposes the world's history and man's sojourn into it," but *several.* It is also no longer possible to believe that Being will eventually reveal the saving power of our mortality to us by turning "into" itself. Turning is an emphatically human action, with profound consequences for other beings.

Surprisingly, given how remote it seems to be from Heidegger's concerns, the myth of Orpheus and Eurydice surfaces several times in "What Are Poets For?" The philosopher read the essay on the twentieth anniversary of Rilke's death, and he devotes most of it to the latter's poetry. He also suggests that it may be Rilke, rather than Hölderlin, who is the "poet for a destitute time." Finally, he quotes extensively from the *Sonnets to Orpheus* (97, 138–139), and although he spends most of his time talking about a later poem, he keeps circling back to it. Heidegger was clearly drawn to this work for the same reason I am: because he sensed that the "saving power" for which he was searching is hidden within the myth on which it is based.

Twenty-three years later, another interlocutor joined this conversation: the American filmmaker Terrence Malick. In 1969, Malick translated Heidegger's 1929 essay, "On the Essence of Ground,"[5] a text in which the philosopher attempts to provide what he calls "a more concrete interpretation of the phenomenon of world."[6] Malick also engages with the companion essay—"What Is Metaphysics?" (1929)—in *The Thin Red Line*, and the central event in this 1998 film is the one to which Heidegger devotes "The Turning" and "What Are Poets For?": the turn toward finitude.

There are also two other interlocutors in this conversation. One of them, Romain Rolland, makes his presence felt through a dense network of oceanic metaphors. The other, Lou Andreas-Salomé, enters the film through its primary event. Like the action Salomé describes in the final entry of her *Freud Journal*, the one staged by Malick is a turn toward other beings, and the first of these beings is Eurydice.

IN THE PUBLICITY STATEMENT with which it released *The Thin Red Line*, Fox 2000 Pictures describes Malick's third film as the story of the victory of an Army rifle company called " C-for-Charlie" over the Japanese during the Battle of Guadalcanal.[7] It "follows the journey [of the men]," we read there, "from the surprise of an unopposed landing, through the bloody and exhausting battles that follow, to the ultimate departure of those who survived."[8] Anticipating the popular reviews that would later excoriate Malick for his lack of interest in this story,[9] the Fox publicists acknowledge that *The Thin Red Line* is "more than a tale of men fighting a key battle"—it also "explores the intense bonds that develop between men under terrible stress, even evil" (1). Strangely, though, they then direct their attention away from the film to James Jones, the author of the novel on which it is based.[10] They also focus on the latter's life, rather than the story he recounts. "To Jones," they write, "who served with an army unit in Guadalcanal, the soldiers' feelings and emotions developed into nothing less than a sense of love . . . of family. The horrors of war helped them lose their idea of self and of the war around them. They were no longer fighting solely for patriotic reasons or the larger world and its issues which had brought them there; they were fighting for survival and for the men next to them."[11]

The Fox publicists were clearly in search of a marketing formula, and they gravitated for this purpose to one of the most frequently reiterated claims of the war film: the claim that the "army unit" is "like" a "family." They turn away from Jones's novel and Malick's film because there is no support in either of them for this cliché. As Stacy Peebles Power observes, the novel tells "a story about the dirty realities and physicalities of war" that "furiously resists the 'terrible lies' of film fictions."[12] The battle dramatized by *The Thin Red Line* also has none of the moral or political clarity that we are accustomed to impute to World War II, since it is impossible to establish a clear division between the aggressors and the aggressed.

From the Allied side, at least, this battle is necessary and "just." The Japanese have built an airfield on the island that gives them an enormous military advantage. If Charlie Company succeeds in wresting it away from them, it will weaken the Japanese and give the Allies airpower for a thousand miles in every direction.[13] But Malick shows the victory of Charlie Company to be driven by the most venal of motives. Lieutenant Colonel Tall (Nick Nolte), who presides over the Battle of Guadalcanal, knowingly confines his men to a "tomb" from which they cannot "lift the lid" when he orders them to proceed directly up the hill to the Japanese bunker at the top. He also forces his depleted platoon to continue fighting after the bunker has been taken, even though he knows that many troops will die from lack of water, because to have another officer finish off the Japanese on Guadalcanal would be "more than [he could] stand." As he tells a subordinate who persists in demanding water for the dehydrated men, "I've worked, slaved, eaten, done buckets of shit for this. . . . You don't know what it feels like to be passed over . . . [T]his is my first war!"[14] Shortly thereafter we see the men under his command beating and jeering at the Japanese soldiers they have captured, in another demonstration of American indifference to human life. Not surprisingly, given all of this, Malick refuses to treat Charlie Company as a family and criticizes the easy recourse of one commanding officer after another to the discourse of fatherhood. The last time an officer uses the language of patriarchy to naturalize his relationship to the soldiers serving under him, Sergeant Welsh (Sean Penn) responds in voice-over: "Everything a lie—everything you hear, everything you see . . . They just keep coming, one after another."

But it is not merely when the Fox publicists describe Charlie Company as a "family" that they appear to be talking past Malick's film. Nothing in their account prepares us for the singular affectivity of *The Thin Red Line*. By "affectivity" I mean both a darkness verging on total eclipse and a radiance brighter than the sun's return. To be present at a screening of Malick's third film is to be permeated to one's psychic core by an almost unbearable negativity—to live it, breathe it, and drink it. But it is also to participate in the search for a clearing in this black forest of the soul: a space opening onto illumination, affirmation, and joy. Although at the beginning of the film there appear to be many such clearings, each of them turns into a dense thicket. But it is while thrashing blindly through the undergrowth that we learn the crucial lesson the film has to teach us: the only way to reach the light is to plunge even deeper into the forest.

If I have not been able to describe the experience of watching *The Thin Red Line* without invoking Heideggerian metaphors, that is because Malick is more interested in Being than in character or story and because for him—as for the German philosopher—Being is "essentially finite."[15] There is no world beyond our own—no outside into which we could escape or expel other beings. And since there is nothing outside our world, there is also nothing that is not within it; everything is part of the same Whole—of "beings as a whole."[16] But although no force can undo this totality, it cannot be fully itself unless we assume our place within it—and since this requires us to face "the 'nothing' of the possible impossibility of our [*own*] existence,"[17] we are reluctant to do so.

It is through our affects rather than our cognitive faculties that our mortality is disclosed to us, and that we acknowledge or deny it. I say "affect" because it comes closer than any other English word to the one Heidegger uses: "*Stimmung*." As the philosopher explains in an important passage in *Being and Time*, a "*Stimmung*" is not an "inner condition which then reaches forth in an enigmatical way and puts its mark on [t]hings and persons." It is, rather, an attunement of the "inside" to the "outside" (176). The word "affect" also best describes the experience of watching *The Thin Red Line*; we are affected by the film in ways that make us feel our own mortality. However, Malick's account of mortality differs in important ways from Heidegger's.

For the author of *Being and Time* and "What Is Metaphysics?" death is utterly "non-relational"; it "lays claim" to us as an "individual" and turns us back upon our "ownmost potentiality-for-Being."[18] It does so through anxiety, which isolates us from others and orients us toward a threat that is "already 'there' and yet nowhere."[19] Since we do not want to acknowledge this threat, we often try to exteriorize it—to locate it in an outside agency. This changes our anxiety into fear. But if we remain within the space of finitude, our anxiety gradually modulates into a different affect: guilt. This guilt does not stem from something we have done or failed to do; it is ontological rather than psychological—a summons from our Being.[20] Although it turns us back upon our "self," our guilt attunes us to the "outside," because one of the defining attributes of this self is to be "alongside-things" and "with-Others," and because the "primordial totality" of its "structural whole" is "care."[21] For Malick, though, mortality is *pure relationality*; every time the central character in *The Thin Red Line* experiences his finitude, it is through the realization that he is part of a larger Whole. He consequently privileges wonder rather than anxiety—the most "opening" of affects instead of the most "closed." Malick's central character also assumes his finitude while living in the shadow of literal destruction.

The last of these differences might seem to explain the others. Although Heidegger is the greatest philosopher of mortality, he never spoke publicly about the "Final Solution." We do not need his biography to explain why. The death to which Hitler subjected his Jewish victims had none of the individuating possibilities about which Heidegger writes in *Being and Time*; by condemning those it deemed to be "non-human" to extinction, and by staging their annihilation as a mass event, the Nazis prevented them from achieving a redemptive Being-towards-death. They also attempted to expel their victims from the totality that Heidegger celebrates in "What Is Metaphysics?" Since warfare is another unwarranted intrusion into and "massification" of human mortality, what happened at Guadalcanal further challenges the claim that no one can take our death away from us.[22]

It is one thing to choose the destiny we cannot escape by becoming in advance of a transformative event the individual into which it will turn us, as Heidegger urges us to do, and another to be hurled by an external force into the mouth of a death machine. Malick makes us see this difference in *The Thin Red Line*. He shows us the clammy faces of the soldiers in the boats speeding toward the island of Guadalcanal; their frantic and spasmodic movements as they descend from the ship to the patrol boats and run from the patrol boats onto the beach; and their blind ascent of the hill at the top of which the Japanese gunners await them, protected by a concrete shell. He also makes us hear the protest of a soldier in the middle of the night against the demand that he subject himself all over again to a foe that he knows is there but that he cannot see. Since even death pales by comparison with this horror, he attempts to provoke his enemy to kill him immediately. Malick also exposes us to the terrifying sense of loss that afflicts those who live among the dead and dying. At the same time, though, he persists in demonstrating the complexity of mortality, even when it bears down upon his characters in the shape of an enemy cannon. In war, as in peacetime, it is through one's affective orientation to death—not through a bodily collapse—that one meets it or fails to meet it.

But it would be impossible to assume one's finitude in the way Heidegger describes even in the most advantageous of circumstances, since there is nothing primordial about anxiety and guilt; they are psychic states, not a summons to our Being. They are also what most prevent us from facing "the 'nothing' of the possible impossibility of our [own] existence," because they equate death with judgment and punishment. Finally, the self towards which they direct us is the ego, which is inimical to care, since it regards other beings either as foes or as extensions of itself. Malick's account of mortality differs from Heidegger's not only because he develops it within the context of a war film, and privileges wonder rather than anxiety and guilt, but also because he makes room within his phenomenology for the psyche. He shows us that every time we try to cheat death, we "other" it, and that this has fatal consequences for those around us. He also helps us to see how narcissistically wounding our finitude can be and how vulnerable this makes us to everything that promises to deliver us from our limits, whether it be religion, military conquest, love, or an ethnographic fantasy. Finally, Malick refuses to treat this desire for totality as a dangerous illusion. Like Salomé, Rilke, and Rolland his goal is not to dispel the oceanic feeling but rather to impute it to its proper source—to find the path leading out of our dreams of *individual* wholeness and into the "All."

THE THIN RED LINE begins with six shots of the flora and fauna of the Solomon Islands. Midway through the sequence, a male voice begins to speak over these images. "What's this war in the heart of nature?" it asks. "Why does nature vie with itself? The land contend with the sea? Is there an avengin' power in nature—not one power, but two?" This sequence modulates into another, devoted to human life on the Solomon Islands. We watch the members of a Melanesian tribe perform a wide range of group activities, all in utter harmony. Because the first sequence begins with an underlit shot of a crocodile slithering into water and the opening shots of the second sequence are accompanied by the last movement of Fauré's *Requiem*, "In Paradisum,"[23] we are momentarily seduced into believing that nature really is full of conflict and that human beings are inherently peaceful.

However, there are no signs of antagonism in the other images of this sequence, only trees rising up majestically before us and sunlight streaming through their leaves. Malick also begins the sound track before the image track,

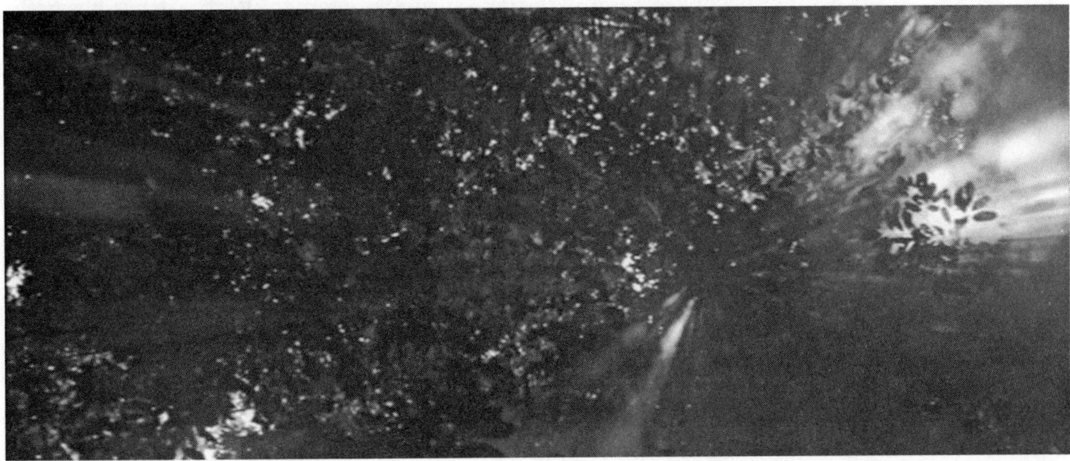

and isolates its diegetic components from Hans Zimmer's score. When the title credit appears on the screen, we hear a cacophony of forest sounds. After a few seconds an ominous chord from the opening musical theme breaks into this chatter, faintly at first but quickly building to a crescendo. It is because the crocodile crawls into this soundscape that it fills us such with dread. The fatal strains of the opening theme also die away before the male speaker poses his first question, and they are replaced by "In Paradisum." The last movement of Fauré's *Requiem* continues playing as the first sequence ends and the second begins, bridging the division between them.

As we soon learn, two AWOL soldiers from Charlie Company are living among the Melanesians. One of them—Private Witt (James Caviezel)—is the speaker to whom we have just been listening. Malick also attributes many shots in the second sequence to this character's look and establishes him as the source of its ethnographic idealizations. Midway through this sequence, which is much longer than the first and has many parts, Witt says to a Melanesian woman, "Kids around here never fight." She gently corrects him: "Sometimes . . . sometimes . . . when you see them playing . . . they always fight." She also reminds Witt that *he* is a fighter and confesses that because of this she is a little afraid of him.

His breezy response—"That don't matter"—explains why he sees an "avengin' power" when he looks at a tree. Appalled by the violence he has witnessed as a soldier, and unwilling to acknowledge that he has the same capacity to hurt, Witt goes looking for an unfallen world, one that will sustain his belief in his own goodness. Because the Solomon Islands have not yet been ravaged by civilization, he fantasizes that they *are* this world—and since this fantasy requires Melanesian society to be conflict-free, he conjures away all of its antagonisms. This leaves only one place where human violence can surface: the landscape.

Malick also emphasizes the infantile qualities of this Edenic fantasy. Shortly before his conversation with the Melanesian woman, Witt watches her bathe her child in the ocean. He immediately begins speaking about his own mother, indicating that *she* is what he really sees. However, rather than talking about the time when he was still in the paradise of her arms, he talks about her death—i.e., about the moment at which he was permanently expelled from this paradise. "I remember my mother when she was dying," he darkly observes. "She was all shrunk up and gray. I asked her if she was afraid. She just shook her head. I was afraid to touch the death I seen in her. Couldn't find nothin' beautiful or upliftin' about her goin' back to God. I've heard people talking about immortality—but I ain't seen it." Witt tries to recover what he has lost by projecting himself into the Melanesian woman's arms—by imagining himself bathing in the ocean of her love.

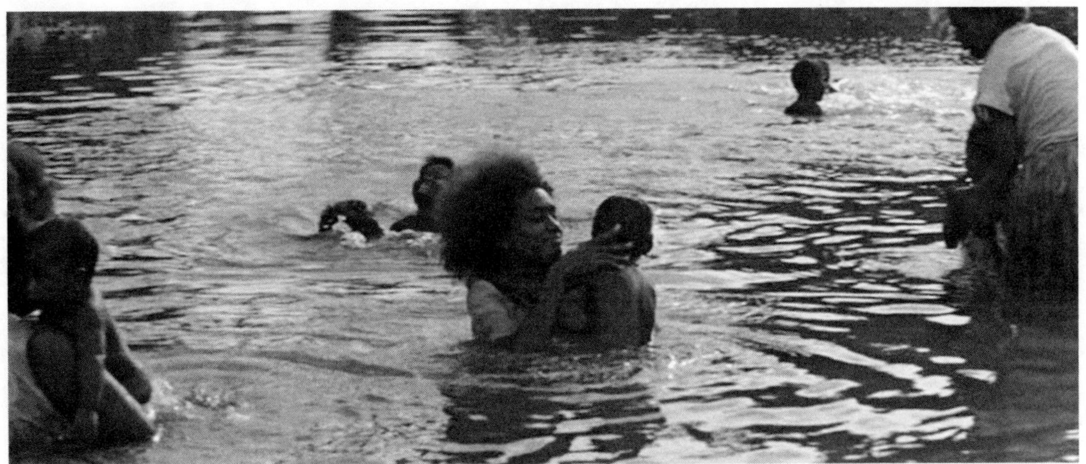

As we learn from this monologue, the death of Witt's mother also brought him face-to-face with his own mortality—and this was as intolerable as her disappearance. By turning back the clock, he gets rid of this unwanted burden. This forges a strong link between "innocence" and "immortality"; if he succeeds in being one of the boys who never fight, he imagines, he will live forever. When Witt says, "I was afraid to touch the death I seen in her," he speaks not merely for himself but for a vast number of other men. I have already spent many pages of this book attempting to explain why it is "in" women in general, and the mother in particular, that so many men "see" death, and what they do to avoid "touching" it. However, Witt differs from most of the figures I discussed earlier, because after looking away from his mother, he turns back to face her.

Malick draws our attention to this important difference in a number of subtle ways. At the beginning of this monologue, he uses the shot/reverse shot formation to distinguish Witt from what he sees. He also reinforces this distinction by having Witt speak "over" the image track rather than from "inside." However, Malick articulates these distinctions only in order to erase them. With a pan of his camera, he brings all three characters into the same frame. He also synchronizes the last sentence of Witt's speech with his lips and shows him delivering it to the other AWOL soldier. By embodying his voice, and localizing it in time and space, Malick renders it finite.[24]

After Witt finishes speaking, the camera cuts to a series of images of his mother during the last days of her life. These images contrast dramatically with his account of her death. Wordless, and illuminated by a golden light, they emphasize connection rather than separation; the dying woman strokes her son's hand lovingly and provides the welcome support against which her

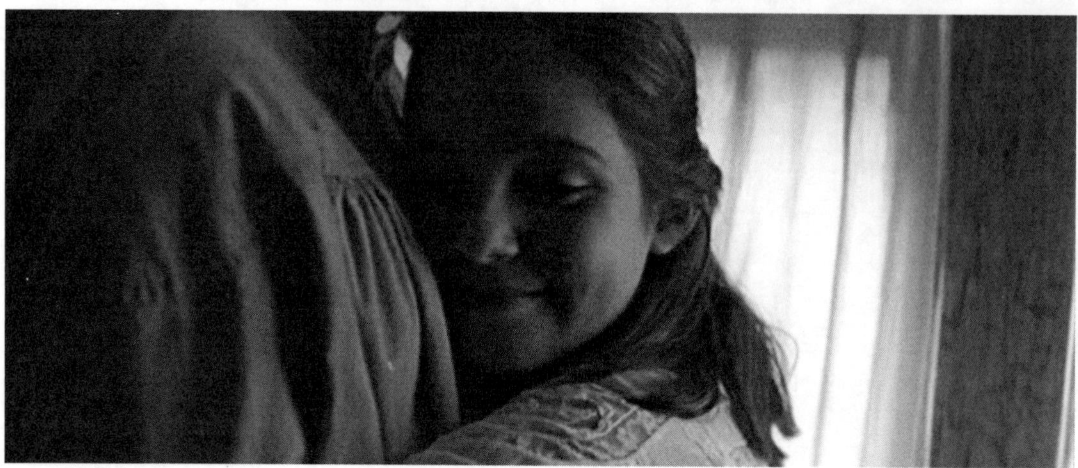

younger daughter leans. Her death is also enworlding; instead of transporting her to another domain, it gives her a bigger place within this one. In the last shot of this series, the camera pans away from the mother's bed and tilts upward, to the unobstructed blue of the sky. In a dissolve, the blue sky becomes part of the sea and land.

Over another montage of this sun-soaked environment, within which water also plays a central role, Witt meditates in voice-over upon his own death: "I wondered how it would be when I died—what it'd be like to know that this breath now was the last one you was ever gonna draw. I just hope I can meet it the same way she did—with the same calm. 'Cause that's where it's hidden—the immortality I hadn't seen." We now understand why the images of his mother's death do not mesh with his description. They depict not what *he saw*, but rather what *she felt* as she approached death: her calm. In the monologue that follows,

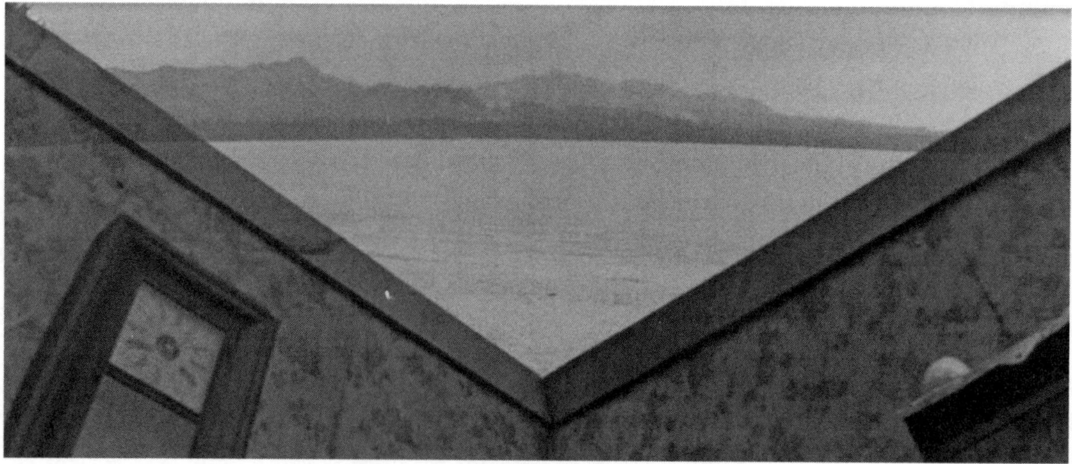

Witt turns around to face what he cannot yet see, and touch what he cannot yet feel. In so doing, he begins his own journey toward a similar tranquillity.

AT THE END OF THIS SEQUENCE of *The Thin Red Line*, an American patrol boat approaches the refuge where Witt and his comrade are hiding. Shortly thereafter we see Witt talking to his superior officer, Sergeant Welsh, aboard the ship transporting them to Guadalcanal. During this conversation, Welsh says, "In this world a man himself is *nothing*—and there ain't no world but this one." This is a message to which he will often return. And not only is there nothing beyond the world we inhabit, Welsh will later say; we ourselves *are* this "nothing." Welsh is not the only character in *The Thin Red Line* to express such views. Although they do not couch their invocations in conventionally Christian terms, both Captain Staros (Elias Koteas) and Private Bell (Ben Chaplin) appeal to an extraterrestrial principle—and both come to see that they are calling into the void.

On the night before the first part of the Battle of Guadalcanal, Staros prays to an unidentified power while looking at the flame of a candle. "Let me not betray you. Let me not betray my men," he says. A night later he utters a similar but even vaguer appeal in voice-over, as the camera focuses on a luminous moon: "You're my light—my guide." On the intervening day, Malick shows Staros adhering to a strict Judeo-Christian code of ethics in his relation to his men, refusing to obey his superior's command to send his remaining soldiers forward into a battle situation that would mean death for many of them. Later, though, he seems to abandon all belief in a law higher than the one operative on the battlefield. He acknowledges to Tall that the latter is "right about everything [he has] said" and does not protest when Tall responds: "It's not necessary for you to ever tell me that you think I'm right—ever! We'll assume it." Surprisingly, Malick also imputes greater authority to the lieutenant colonel than to the morally upright captain. The other soldiers obey Tall's commands, and they win the Battle of Guadalcanal.

The weaning of Captain Bell away from his belief in another world is a much more protracted and painful affair, and one whose affective permutations Malick makes fully available to us. During the boat trip to Guadalcanal, another soldier asks Bell why he, having earlier been an officer, is now an enlisted man. Bell explains that he missed his wife so much during an earlier tour of duty that he resigned his commission. Through a series of extraordinary flashbacks that reprise the primary colors of the Solomon Island sequences, Malick does two seemingly contradictory things: he affirms Bell's love for his wife and shows Bell using this love as a refuge from his mortality.

The first of these flashbacks begins while Charlie Company is still en route to Guadalcanal. It consists of three shots, in all of which blue predominates: one of Bell's wife alone on the green lawn of the air force base, and one showing the two of them together at dusk on a beach. In the last shot, she strokes his back through his Hawaiian shirt. As the camera focuses on the fabric of this shirt, which reiterates the blue of the ocean and the darkening sky, Bell asks: "Why should I be afraid to die? I belong to you." He continues speaking over images of terrified soldiers feverishly preparing to leave the ship: "If I go first, I'll wait for you there, on the other side of the dark waters. Be with me now." "Dark waters" is Bell's name for death, both here and elsewhere, but the way he relates to them is constantly shifting. In this flashback he attempts to overcome his finitude by imagining that there is another shore—one to which he and his wife can simply swim.

Bell's third flashback occurs as he makes his way alone to the top of the hill on which so many soldiers have already died on a reconnaissance mission.[25] It begins with a series of images of him making love to his wife, all lit with a golden light. They are clearly his attempt to hold the darkness at bay. However, a funeral bell tolls ominously throughout this flashback, and in the last three shots Bell faces the cold blue expanse of a nocturnal ocean. No shore can be seen on the other side, but there is another kind of eternity: the eternity of love. Bell's wife stands in the dark waters, wearing a yellow sundress. "Come out," she says reassuringly. "Come out to where I am."

At the beginning of Bell's fourth flashback, he and his wife are back in their gold-lit bedroom. Now they no longer need to worry about the ocean because they have become it—and since they are liquid, nothing will ever be able to separate them from each other. "We . . . we together . . . one being . . . flow to-

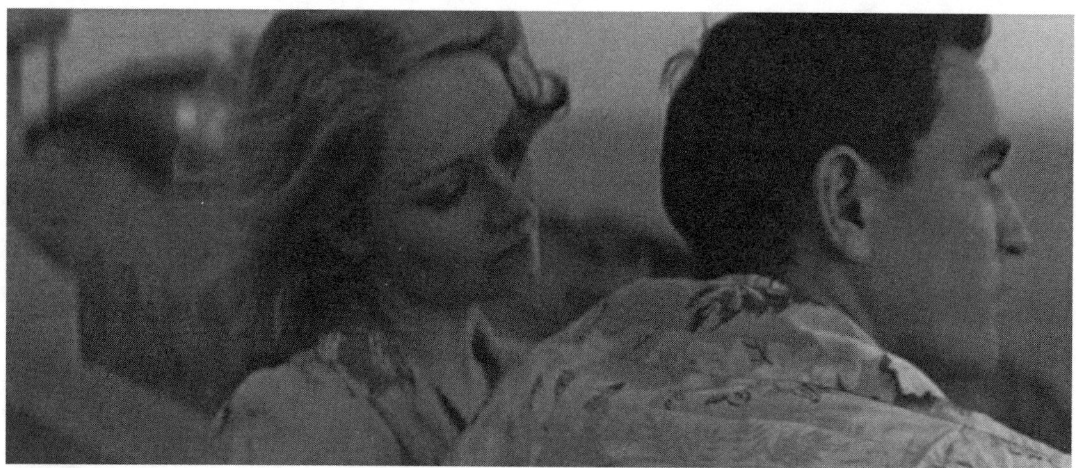

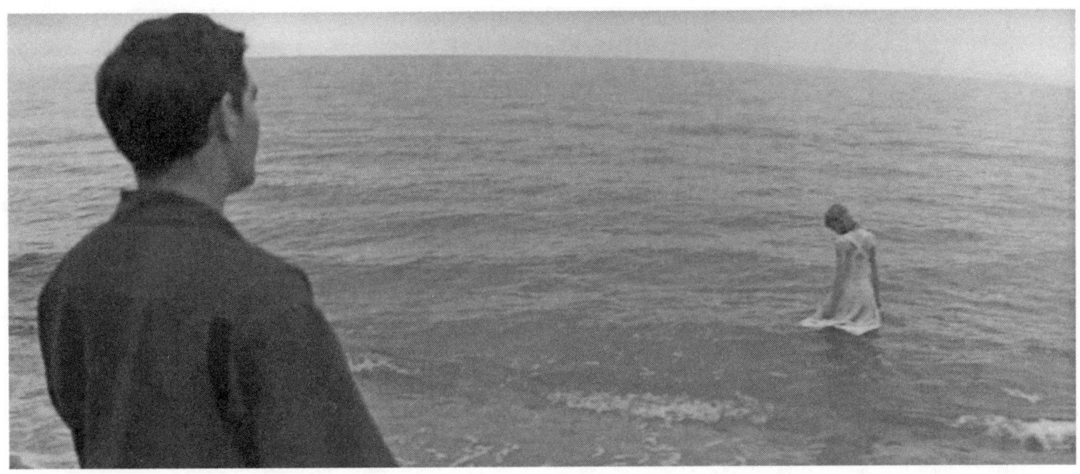

See also Plate 5 in color insert.

gether like water, till I can't tell you from me," he says over the images of their lovemaking. But Malick interrupts this dream of wholeness with a shot of the hill on which American soldiers are bleeding to death. We then hear the sound of waves, and the ocean reasserts its separateness from the lovers. Bell makes two more attempts to recuperate the dark waters, first by reconstituting them as the bathwater in which he washes his wife and then as the glass of water his wife might be said to represent. "I drink you," he says to her, "now." But only in the last seconds of this flashback do the ominous sounds of the waves fade away.

Bell's fifth flashback comes near the end of the film, after a number of battle scenes and sequences of mind-numbing cruelty and suffering. Initially we see him walking among the palm trees on the island where Charlie Company is spending a recreational week. This time his voice-over exteriorizes what appears to be a mental letter: "My dear wife, you get something twisted out of your

See also Plate 6 in color insert.

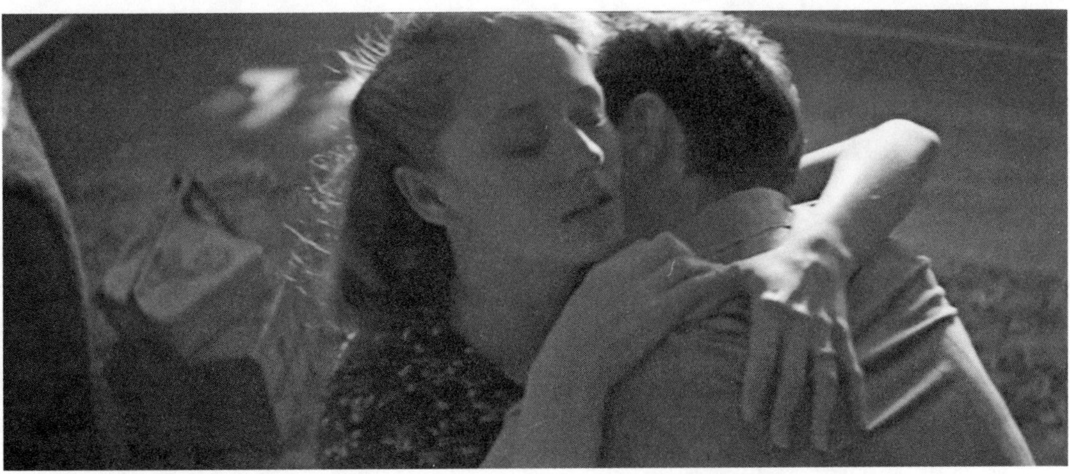

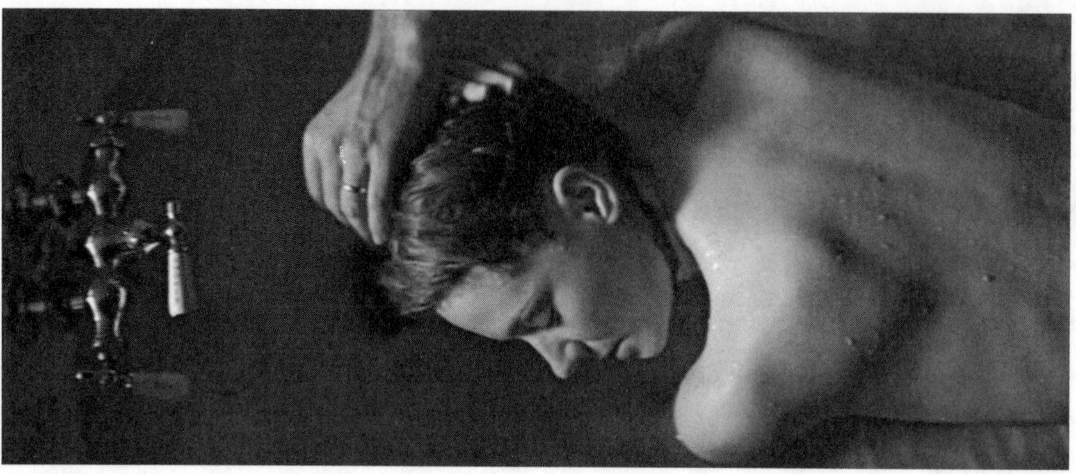

See also Plate 7 in color insert.

insides by this blood, filth and noise." Bell's interior monologue continues as he looks out at the Pacific Ocean: "I want to stay changeless for you," he exclaims, again as if he were speaking to his wife. But the images that follow emphasize their isolation. We see Bell gazing out at the Pacific Ocean from a remote and lonely perspective; his wife lying alone on their marital bed, in a semi-fetal position; a shot of a canoe on the water from his side of the Pacific Ocean; and then a shot of her looking at the same ocean from the other side. What Bell says as we look at her recumbent form—"I want to come back to you the man I was before" also attests to the impossibility of his wish to remain changeless for her; that man, he admits, no longer exists.

A moment later, Bell also acknowledges the untraversability of the dark waters he earlier imagined himself swimming effortlessly across. As we look first at him and then at his wife gazing out at the immensity of the sea that divides

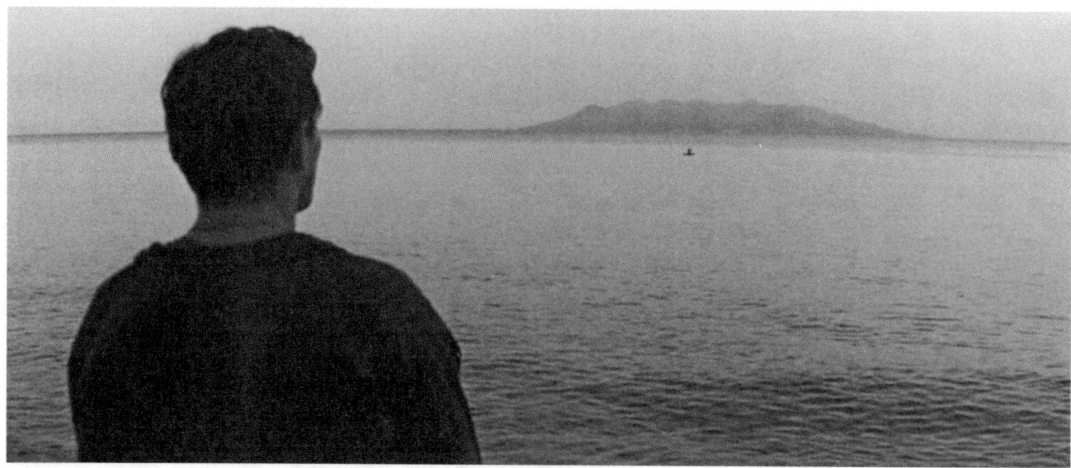

them, he asks, poignantly: "How do we get to those other shores?" Although this question now has a literal as well as a metaphoric meaning, the answer is still the same: *we do not get to those other shores.* The shots of Bell and his wife looking at the Pacific Ocean from opposite sides are followed by one of waves crashing against rocks.

IN THE FIRST SCENE on the ship carrying Charlie Company to Guadalcanal, Tall thinks about what it has cost him to hold the darkness at bay. Rather than being open to a potentially transformative future, he relates to his own life according to the temporal logic of the "already over" and the thematic logic of "waste." Tall once had gifts to give, but they were never bestowed. As the tortuous ascent of Charlie Company up the hill to the well-protected enemy will later make clear, Tall is not the only one who is forced to pay for his repudiation of mortality. His will-to-mastery in the face of death means mass destruction for his own soldiers as well as the enemy. Ironically, Tall already knows before the Battle of Guadalcanal even begins that whatever its outcome, his own internal war will be impossible to win. Far from neutralizing his fear of death, the exorbitant demands that he is about to make on his men are only likely to increase it. "Worked my ass off," he muses bitterly. "[B]rownnosed the generals, degraded myself—for them, my family, my home. . . . [A]ll they sacrificed for me—poured out like water on the ground. All I might have given for love's sake. Too late. Dyin' slow as a tree. The closer you are to Caesar, the greater the fear."

But the most chilling dramatization of what happens to others when we refuse to face "the 'nothing' of the possible impossibility of our existence" occurs after the storming of the bunker. An American soldier pulls two Japanese soldiers out of their hiding place at the top of the hill, shouts obscenities at

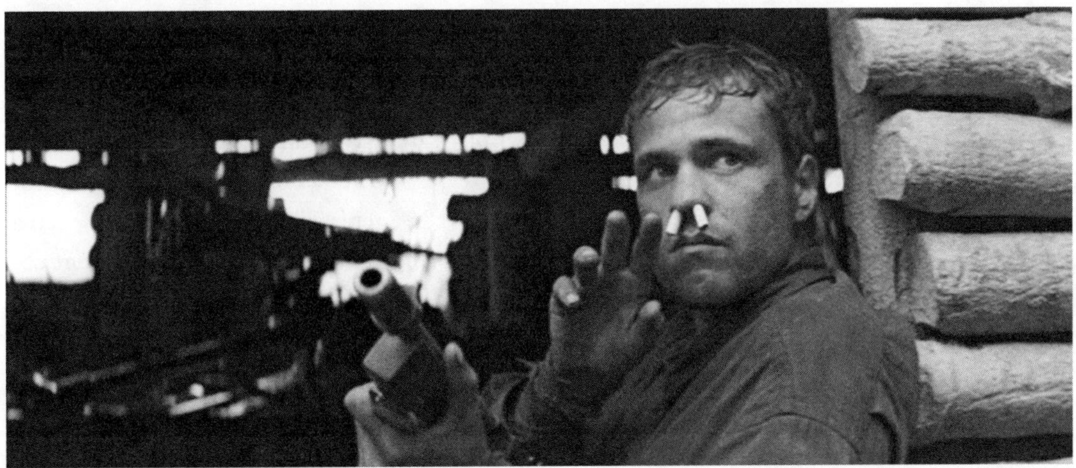

them, beats them, kicks them, and kills one of them. As he makes painfully evident both to the Japanese soldiers and to us, he sees them as a radically different species from himself. In a closely adjacent scene, several members of Charlie Company gather their prisoners in a hut. One of them—Private First Class Don Doll (Dash Mihok)—spits at a prisoner and puts two cigarettes in his nostrils to block out the smell of Japanese corpses. Mortality, he thereby proclaims, is an alien and unwelcome odor.

After much additional fighting, the American soldiers once again herd their prisoners together. One of these soldiers, Private First Class Charlie Dale (Arie Verveen), crouches down beside a dying Japanese soldier and taunts him with his imminent death. He does not hesitate to induce in the other the thought that is unthinkable for him: "Where you're going, you're not coming back from." As the Japanese man stands, looking at the vultures gathering in the sky above him, Dale inserts cigarettes in his nostrils, and plays with the gold teeth he has ripped out of enemy mouths. When the dying man returns to the ground, the American soldier turns away from him, while once again locating his own mortality elsewhere. As he does so, he says over the image: "'What are you to me? Nothin.'" He then pulls the body of another dying Japanese man toward him, his pliers at the ready.

In these three scenes, it is the enemy who is stripped of all possible value and reduced to "a piece of shit." Since this enemy is responsible for the loss of countless American lives, his devaluation might seem an understandable and unavoidable revenge. However, as Dale mocks the dying soldier, the latter says, "*Kisamawa shinundaya*" ("you will also die someday"), over and over again. These words come back to haunt Dale later, as he sits alone in the rain, clutching a rosary. He flings the rosary away as soon as he hears the dead man's voice and begins sobbing uncontrollably. Malick also distinguishes the process of affectively negating another being from the process of defeating that same being in battle by showing Witt later giving water to a Japanese captive, and he reminds us that once we succumb to indifference in relation to one part of the world, it is only a matter of time before it invades even our most intimate relations. In a scene late in *The Thin Red Line*, Welsh and another American soldier sit together in a tent, talking about their respective states of mind. Gesturing toward a dying comrade lying on an adjacent cot, the other soldier says, "I look at that boy dyin', I don't feel nothin'. I don't care about nothin' anymore."

Malick also refuses to characterize this affective indifference as the inevitable outcome of the brutalizing experiences undergone by Charlie Company. Welsh, who has inhabited the eye of the Guadalcanal storm, responds: "I don't have that feeling yet—that numbness. Not like the rest of you guys." Malick also shows us why Welsh is still able to manifest concern for someone like Witt and why he stands apart from the desecration to which some of his men subject the Japanese. In opposition to the soldiers for whom death is a foreign smell, to be blocked out with cigarettes, Welsh is used to looking his mortality in the face. At the very beginning of this scene, he says in voice-over: "No matter how much training you got, how careful you are, it's a matter of luck whether or not you get killed. Make no difference who you are, or how tough a guy you might be. You're in the wrong spot at the wrong time, you're gonna get it."

But although Welsh is conscious of his mortality and continues to care for his men after others have succumbed to numbness, the scenes in which he appears are saturated with melancholy. Nothing emerges from the "nothing"; ashes are merely ashes, and dust, dust. Welsh is blind to the "glory" shining through death because he does not understand that finitude is relational. He equates death with the destructive forces unleashed by the war—with disintegration and atomization—and he responds to it in the same way: by going into solitary confinement. "We're living in a world that's blowing itself to hell as fast as everyone can arrange it," Welsh tells Witt while they are still aboard the ship transporting them to Guadalcanal. "In a situation like that all a man can do is shut his eyes." "This army's gonna kill you," he adds later, after the first day of fighting. "If you're smart, you'll take care of yourself. There's nothing you can do for anybody else. . . . [I]f you die, it's gonna be for nothing."

Near the end of *The Thin Red Line*, Welsh observes that there is only one alternative to a life of absolute negation, and that is to find something of one's own and make an island out of it. However, he still cannot imagine himself being connected in this way to another person; all he can do is mourn the loss

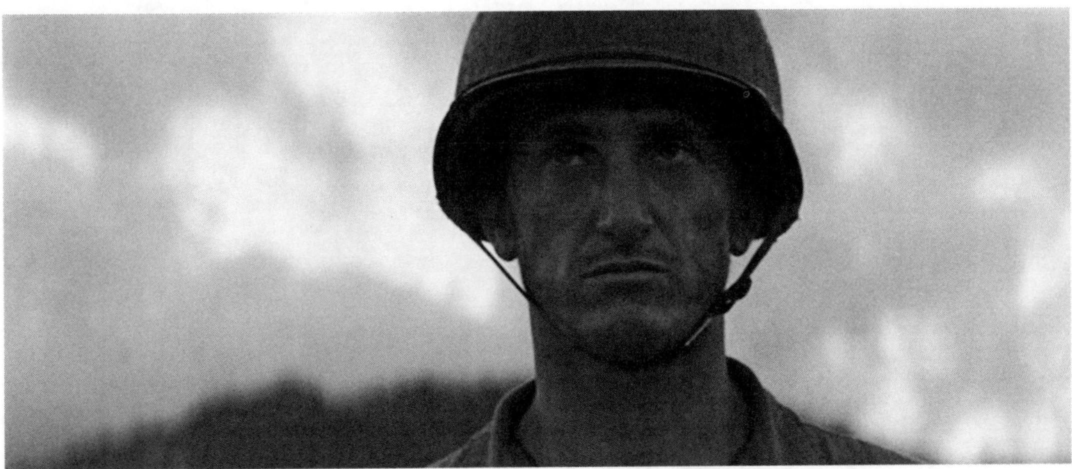

of what he will never possess. "If I never meet you in this life," Welsh says in voice-over as he and his new platoon march pass a military cemetery, "let me feel the lack. A glance from your eyes and my life will be yours." A woman is standing in the cemetery, and although she has no place in the story, it is impossible to keep her out of the picture he paints, because his yearning is as palpable as his despair; she stands for all the women whose look he will never meet.[26]

It might seem startling to find Malick treating the heterosexual couple as something tragically foreclosed for Welsh, since he spends so much time weaning Bell and Witt away from their island fantasies. But although he discredits the fantasies themselves, he affirms the "oceanic feelings" they awaken in these two characters. Bell's fifth flashback ends not with the image of waves crashing against rocks but rather with a series of gravity-defying shots of his wife swinging in slow motion, clad in her yellow dress.

The last of these shots hovers as an after-image over a blue sky, which yields to images of carnage and destruction, and—finally—the beam of a flashlight playing across the mosquito nets under which some American soldiers are sleeping. "Where does [love] come from?" asks Bell over these images. "Who lit this flame in us? No war can put it out, conquer it. I was a prisoner—you set me free." What Witt feels when he projects himself into the Melanesian woman's arms is also surprisingly congruent with what his mother feels at the moment of her death, and he assumes his finitude not by surrendering this feeling but rather by attributing it to its proper source.

As we have already seen, the concept of the "oceanic feeling" comes from Romain Rolland, a French writer and political activist with whom Freud corresponded from 1923 to 1936. In a 1927 letter to the psychoanalyst, Rolland describes this feeling as the "sentiment" or "sensation" that discloses to us that

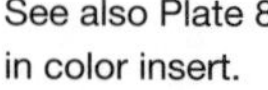
See also Plate 8 in color insert.

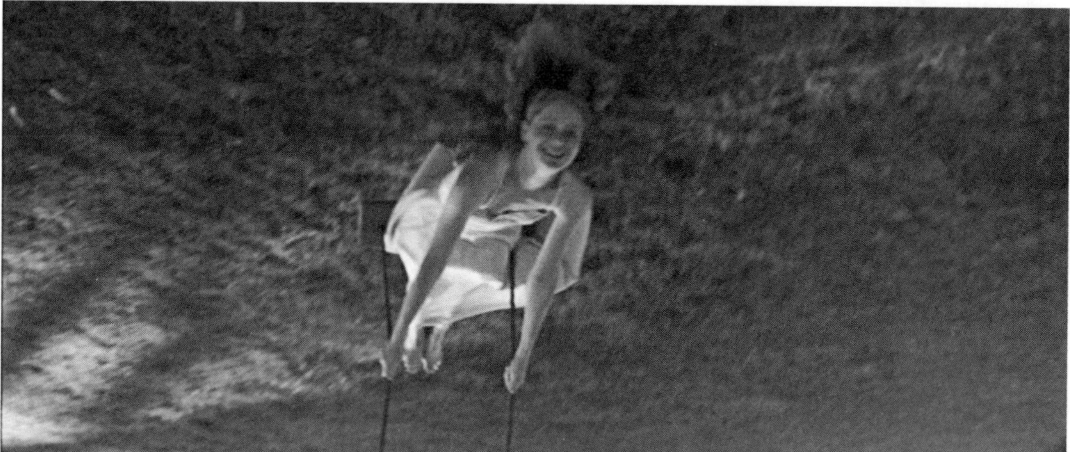

we are part of a limitless Whole.[27] He characterizes it as "a *contact*," suggesting that it is through our connections with other beings that we access it (174).[28] The sea is also Malick's primary metaphor both for the totality to which we all belong and the experiences through which it is revealed to us, and the common denominator of all of these experiences is *touch.* Witt is unable to see his mother's calm because he is afraid to "touch" the death "in" her, and Welsh is blind to the glory shining through mortality because he won't "let nothin' touch him." Tactility is also the dominant trope in Bell's happy memories and the shots of the Melanesian child in her mother's arms, and although it is freighted in both cases with a meaning it cannot sustain, it has a disclosive force because it connects us to what is outside of ourselves.

Malick thematizes Welsh's solitude as the failure to meet a woman's look not because heterosexuality is the gateway to relationality but rather because it is through the sweet pressure of a mother's embrace that most children first sense that they are part of a larger Whole. Many of us also cling to the fantasy that if we are united with her—or one of her surrogates—we can *be* this Whole. As Salomé puts it in a striking passage from her memoir, "Our love for one another is a life jacket which allows both partners to learn to swim, yet we behave as if the other person is instead the sea that carries us both."[29] Because of this, love can be "as misleading and confusing as infinity." The remedy, however, is not to climb out of the water, as Welsh attempts to do, but rather to find the point at which this inlet connects with the ocean. I take the last metaphor from Malick himself, who not only stages the bathing scene in an inlet but also shows the Melanesian woman walking afterward toward the open sea, her child still in her arms. When Witt utters the words "I just hope I can meet it in the same way she did—with the same calm. 'Cause that's where it's hidden—the immortality I hadn't seen," he, too, faces the ocean.

MALICK DRAMATIZES the stages in Witt's journey toward finitude through a series of other voice-over monologues. The first occurs as the soldiers in Charlie Company are slogging through an inhospitable forest on Guadalcanal. Like Witt's opening meditation, it begins with a question spoken over a low-angle shot of light streaming through trees, and this shot is linked to several other nature shots. However, in the last of these shots the camera tilts down from the top of a thicket of trees to the soldiers below, and for most of the rest of the monologue the emphasis is on the inextricability of the human figures and the landscape. In his monologue, Witt extends this same principle to everything; he uses the word "all" three times in the first two sentences, always with the aim of overriding the divisions separating one being from another. I say "divisions" rather than "distinctions" because the "all" is not homogenizing; although Witt emphasizes the ontological bonds linking even the most antithetical of things, he also emphasizes the non-totalizable nature of this totality by pointing to the infinite variety of finite forms. "Who [are you] to live in all these many forms?" he asks. "You're death that captures all, and you too are the source of all that's gonna be born."

When Witt says, "You're death that captures all," Malick focuses on Doll, the first of the two soldiers who later attempt to block out the smell of Japanese corpses. In so doing, he not only emphasizes the inescapability of death, he also distinguishes it from the violence of war. When Witt utters the second part of this sentence—"and you too are the source of all that's gonna be born"—the camera holds on Dale, the soldier who rips gold out of Japanese mouths. Since new beings are constantly emerging out of the dust into which dead ones decay, mortality is literally "the source of all that's born." It is also the metaphoric soil in which the affirmative affects grow; it "gives," as Witt goes on to say, "glory, mercy, peace, truth . . . calm of spirit, understandin', courage, [and] the contented heart." By turning away from the dying soldier, Dale not only "outsources" death but also deprives himself of the possibility of experiencing these affects—a loss to which his uncontrollable sobs will later attest. Malick ends this sequence with a series of images of Bell and his wife touching each other in their bedroom, illuminated in the usual way. The combination of one man's meditation on mortality with another man's memories of his beloved wife is a powerful evocation both of the relational nature of finitude and of beings as a whole.

Later in the film, Witt walks amid the carnage wrought by Japanese land mines on the members of Charlie Company. Initially he and the injured soldiers seem to occupy separate strata of existence; the injured lie on stretchers on

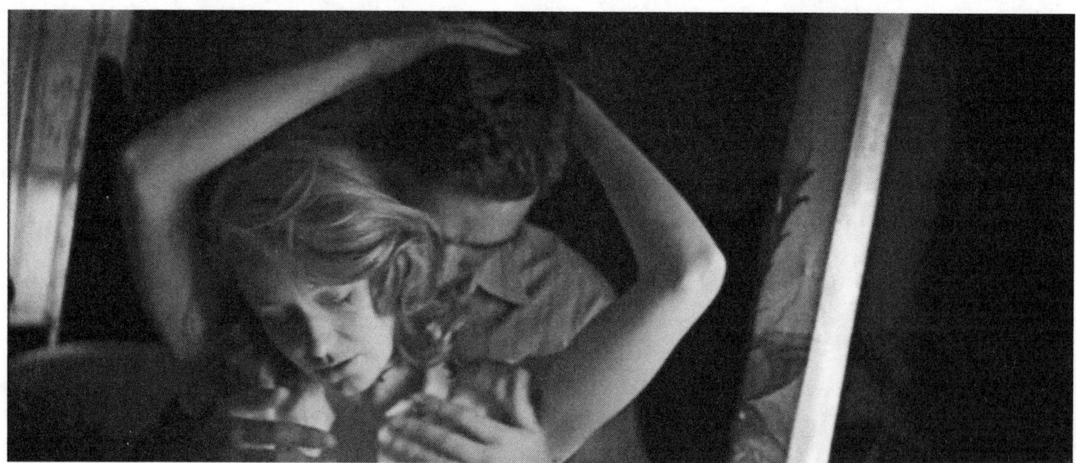

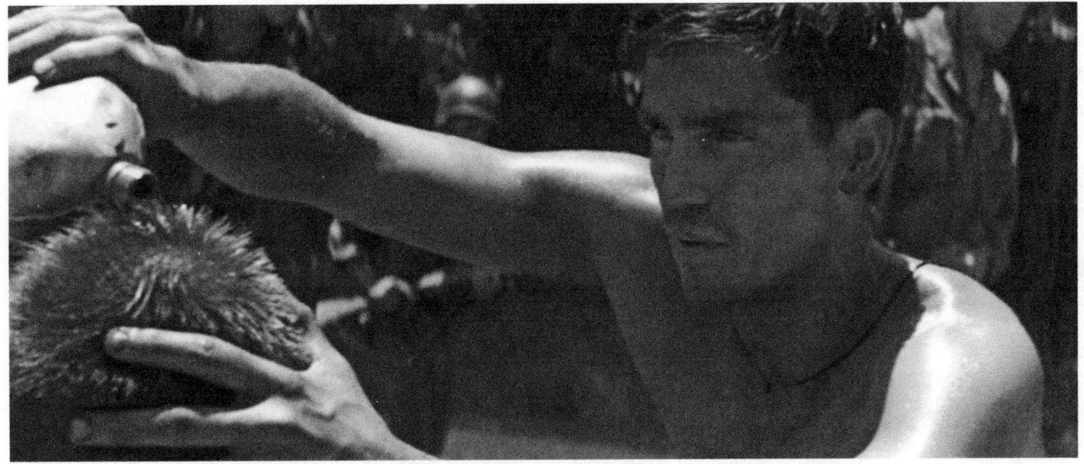

See also Plate 9 in color insert.

the ground, near a stream of water, but he is dramatically erect. As a result of the low angle of the shot, his bare head and shoulders also seem to reach almost to the tops of the highest trees. But Witt's words undo this separation; they suggest that if he appears larger than life, it is because he represents more than himself. "Maybe all men got one big soul that everybody's part of," he says in voice-over as he moves among the wounded. "All faces of the same man—one big self."

A moment later Malick gives us a medium close-up of the stream, red with the blood of the injured, and then a medium shot of Witt pouring water on the head of an injured man. In the hands of most filmmakers, this juxtaposition would be ironic in nature. "How can we be one big self," we would be encouraged to think, "when we kill each other like this?" But Malick does not let us off the hook in this way. He shows us that we kill each other because we do not want to belong to this totality—to be subject to the limits that are the basis of its limitlessness. He also reminds us that we have other ways of asserting our autonomy by having Witt reflect on the one he has chosen: the fantasy of a personal redemption. While pouring cooling water on the wounded man's head, Witt says in voice-over: "Everyone lookin' for salvation by himself—each like a coal thrown from the fire." Malick then cuts again to the stream, exchanging the metaphor of fire for that of water. What a moment ago was red with blood now flows clear and pure.

But although Witt entertains the possibility that we may all be "faces" of the "same man" in this early scene, he continues for a long time thereafter to believe that he will be one of the coals that return to the fire. It is not until he is able to see himself in the Other, and the Other in himself, that he abandons this fantasy. Since Witt defines "Otherness" in moral rather than racial terms, this means acknowledging that there are soldiers on both sides of the Pacific war who are as "good" as he is, and that he has the same capacity for violence as the most vicious members of Charlie Company. The first stage in this process occurs shortly after the storming of the bunker. Standing outside the enclosure in which the American soldiers have gathered their military prisoners, Witt looks down at the almost-buried face of a dead Japanese soldier. The dead soldier addresses him through the voice of the most virtuous member of his platoon: Captain Staros. "Are you righteous, kind?" he asks. "Does your confidence lie in this? Are you loved by all? Know that I was, too. Do you imagine your sufferings will be less because you loved goodness, truth?"

Witt's fantasmatic encounter with this soldier comes immediately after an off-screen exchange between himself and Welsh. "Have you seen many dead people?" he asks Welsh, and the latter responds: "Plenty. They're no different than dead dogs, once you get used to the idea. You're meat, kid." This sudden confrontation with the equalizing materiality of death makes Witt aware in a new way of what it means to be mortal. From the site of the void toward which each of us is headed, a man is no different than a dog.

The words that Witt imagines the Japanese soldier to be uttering constitute in part a variation on this same theme: once dead, all men are the same. However, these words also suggest that the ontological distinctions he has assumed to obtain between one *living* man and another may also be nonexistent. Malick underscores this point by having the Japanese soldier speak in Staros's voice. Finally, with the words Witt imputes to his ostensible enemy, Malick dramatizes his realization that morality can provide no refuge against mortality. No one gains an exemption from death through the virtue of his life.

Witt's first encounter with the Other within himself occurs after a painfully long and detailed sequence of the atrocities committed by Charlie Company after it wrests the bunker away from its foe. A manifestly superior force, the American soldiers shoot the Japanese, bayonet them, burn down their huts, and herd them into abject groups of prisoners. During a lull in the fighting, in which he has fully participated, Witt stops to think about what he has been doing. At first he conceives of this violence in almost Christian terms, as an extraneous evil that has stolen into a previously blameless world. He then attempts to locate it once again in the natural domain. Finally, he acknowledges that the ground in which it grows is not material, but, rather, psychic. "This great evil, where's it come from?" he asks. "How'd it steal into the world? What seed, what root did it grow from? Who's doin' this? Who's killin' us? Robbin' us of life and light? Mockin' us with the sight of what we might have known? Does our ruin benefit the earth? Does it help the grass to grow, the sun to shine? Is this darkness in you, too? Have you passed through this night?"

Even now, Witt does not employ the first-person pronoun, but when Charlie Company is sent to the Solomon Islands for a week of rest and recreation, he finally locates the war where it belongs: in "us." He looks again at his beloved Melanesian society and sees the aggression and suffering he earlier conjured away so that he could believe in his *own* goodness: quarreling adults, crying children, scars left on young bodies by a ravaging disease, masses of human skulls, and—finally—a chicken with her brood. When the last of these images appears on the screen, Witt begins to speak, once again in voice-over. "We were a family," he muses. "Had to break up and come apart so that now we're turned against each other, each standing in the other's light. How'd we lose the good that was given to us—let it slip away, scattered, careless?"

This is a radically different understanding of "family" than that espoused by Staros's replacement (George Clooney) at the end of the film. Unlike the one described by the latter, whose membership is limited to the soldiers in Charlie Company and governed by an authoritarian father, this one is fatherless and encompasses not just all *human* beings but *every* kind of being. And although Witt's monologue begins with an invocation of the fall or—better yet—the conflict of Cain and Abel, he refuses to situate what he invokes within Christian coordinates. He ends his monologue not with another lamentation about all that we have lost but rather with the invocation of what awaits us. "What's keeping us from reaching out, touching the glory?" he asks. The question contains an implicit declarative: "There is nothing keeping us from reaching out, touching the glory."

In a closely adjacent scene, Malick also rearticulates the temporality of the fall. Over a montage that begins with a shot of American soldiers leaping with boyish abandon into the ocean and ends with the lacerating image of Dale sobbing in the rain, Doll says, "Cain't nothing make you forget it. . . . [W]ar don't

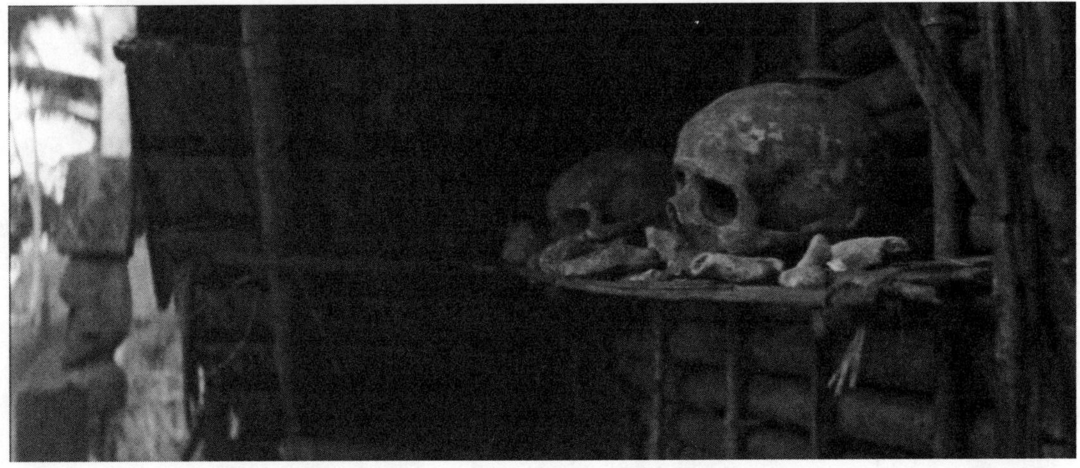

ennoble men. Turns 'em into dogs. Poisons the soul." At the same time, though, no battle either predetermines the next one or provides an alibi for fighting it. Instead, "each time [one] start[s] from scratch." For Malick, it seems, as for Heidegger, human beings have a propensity for "falling."[30] There is, however, no more an action that could render us forever "lost" than one that could render us eternally "saved." We are "fallen" only if we keep "falling."

IN THE CLIMACTIC SEQUENCE of *The Thin Red Line*, we see the surviving members of Charlie Company wading up a river framed on both sides by forest. It soon becomes apparent that they are metaphorically as well as literally up to their knees in dark waters. The enemy is close at hand, and the Americans' position could not be more exposed. When the commanding officer orders two inexperienced recruits to track down the enemy, Witt decides to accompany them, and—after finding the Japanese perilously near—sends them back to warn the others. He then precipitates his own death by diverting the attention of the Japanese soldiers away from the younger men to himself. While fleeing them, he finds time to affirm the beauty of the natural world, and he is even more absorbed in the landscape as he waits for them to shoot him. Malick cuts with the gunshot that kills him to what he sees: sunlight streaming through the green leaves of a tree. It is a variation on one of the opening shots of the film, now free from the burden of representing human violence.

Although already dead, Witt utters the words with which *The Thin Red Line* ends. As the camera scans the faces of the surviving members of Charlie Company, who are leaving Guadalcanal aboard a military ship, he asks: "Where is it that we were together? Who were you that I lived with . . . walked with? The brother . . . the friend . . . darkness, light, strife, and love, are they the workings

See also Plate 10 in color insert.

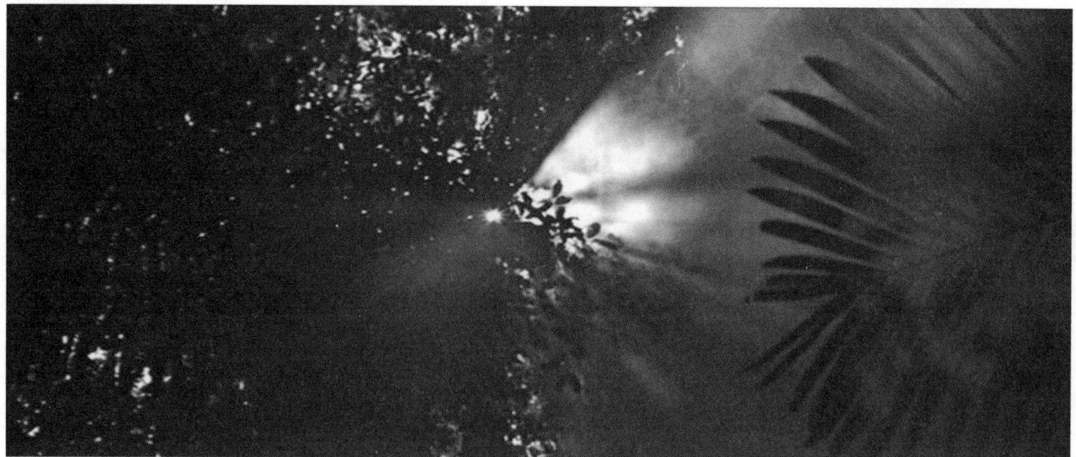

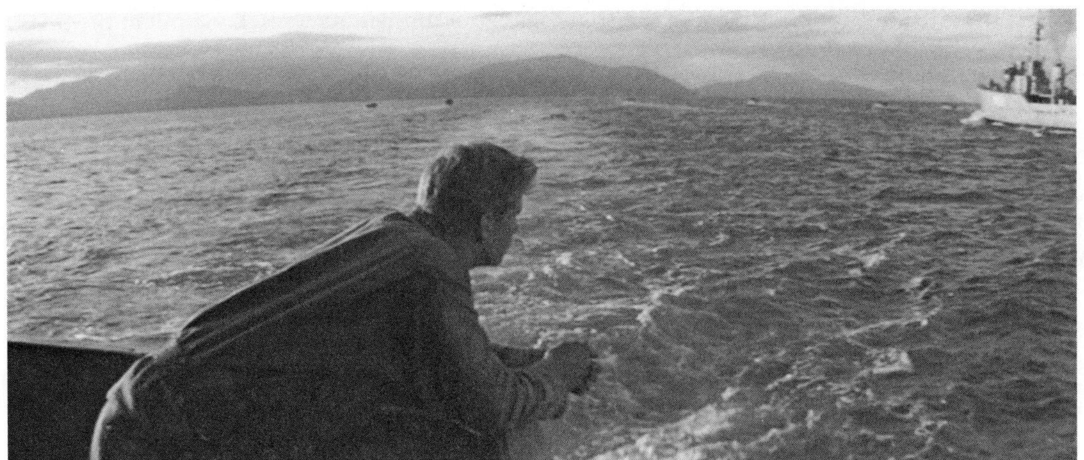

of one mind, the features of the same face?"[31] We are not surprised either by Witt's capacity to speak beyond the grave, or by the wonder with which he addresses his former comrades. Since there is nothing outside the totality to which we all belong, there is also nowhere else to "go"; what "is" includes what "was." And since there is no "outside" from which to look at this totality, it is as mysterious to the dead as to the living.

Toward the end of this monologue, the camera cuts to a solitary figure looking out at the ocean from the prow of the ship, and finally to the vast expanse of the sea. It is Doll, whose place among us Malick once again secures.[32] Query now gives way to apostrophe, and as a result of an astonishing pronominal chiasmus, the "you" to whom it is addressed refers simultaneously to Witt's soul, the soldiers on the ship, and beings as a whole. "O my soul, let me be in you now," exclaims Witt in voice-over, as we look at the waves produced by

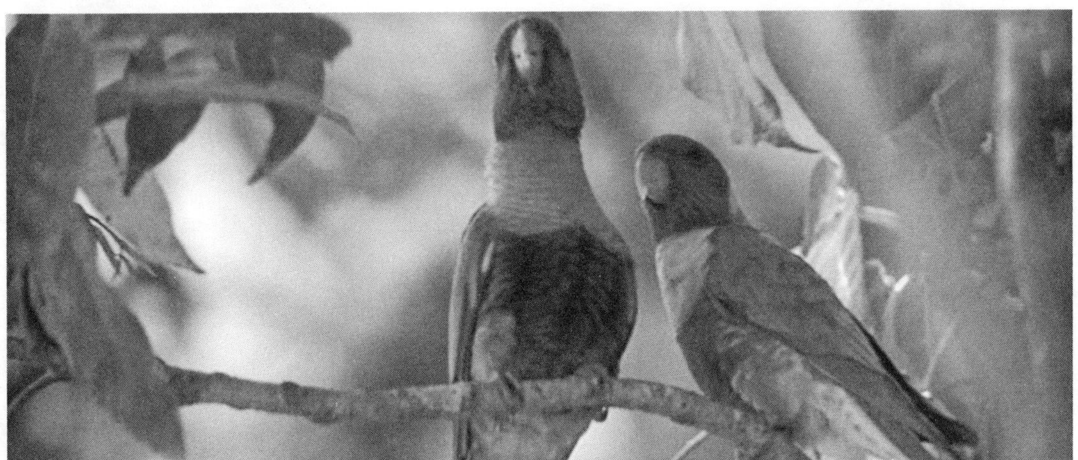

the movement of the ship. "Look out through my eyes. Look out at the things you made. All things shining." With these last words, Malick returns us to the finite world. He reminds us that when we affirm Being, it is always through phenomenal forms; the "All" could not be more earthly or more diverse. He also teaches us another crucial lesson: although we can apprehend what we are only by thinking beyond ourselves, we can affirm the world only through a very particular pair of eyes.[33]

When Witt stops speaking, the sea gives way to a series of shining things: Melanesian children in two small canoes floating on a forest green river, two multicolored parrots, and a plant growing on a tiny island. With these images Malick discloses a few of the countless features that constitute the visage of Being. Through the radiance that he imparts to them, he also proves the truth of an axiom once invoked by Walter Benjamin; he shows us that things really do retain something of the looks that have rested on them.[34] It is in this way that they become, or fail to become, *themselves.*

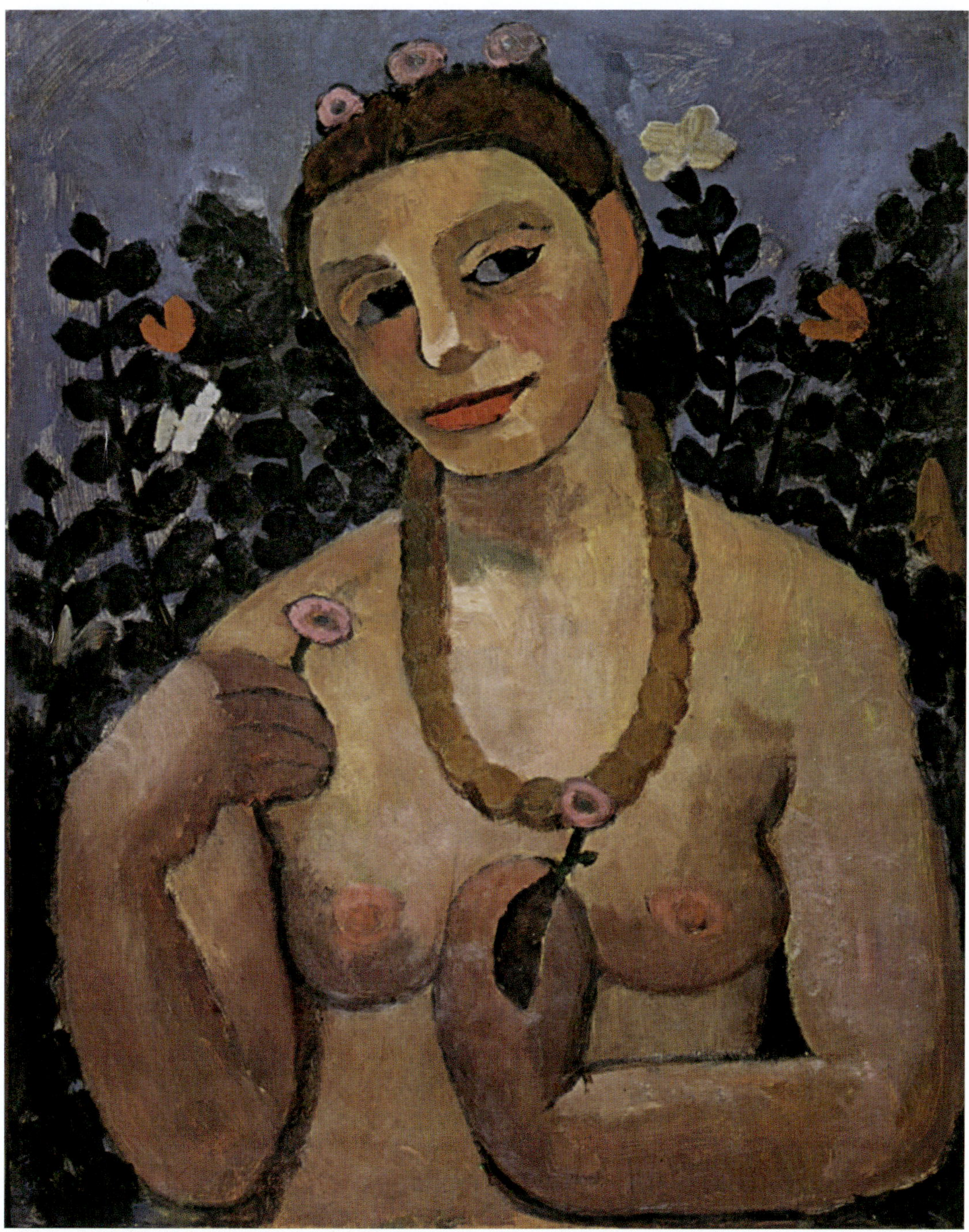

Plate 1

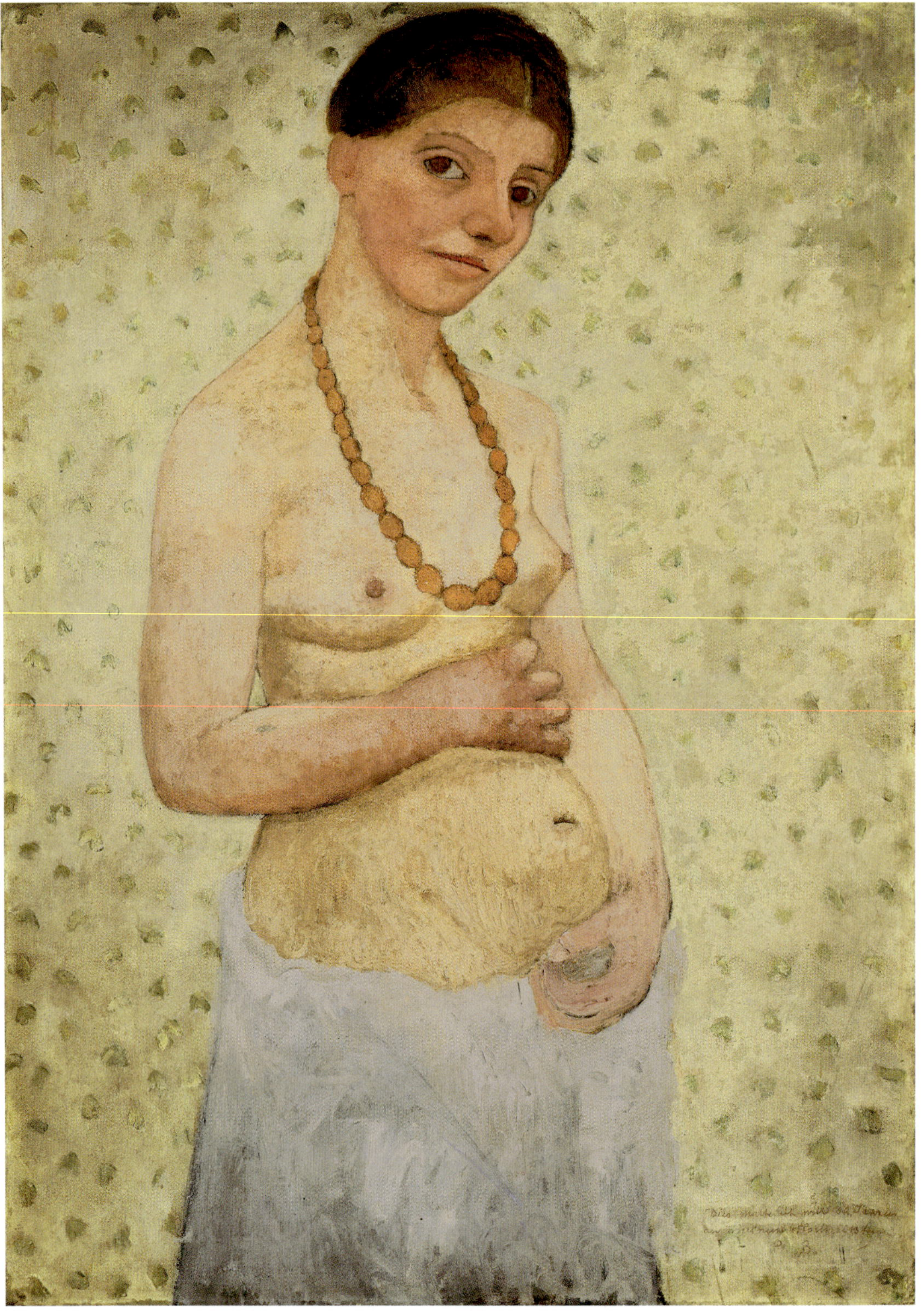

Plate 2

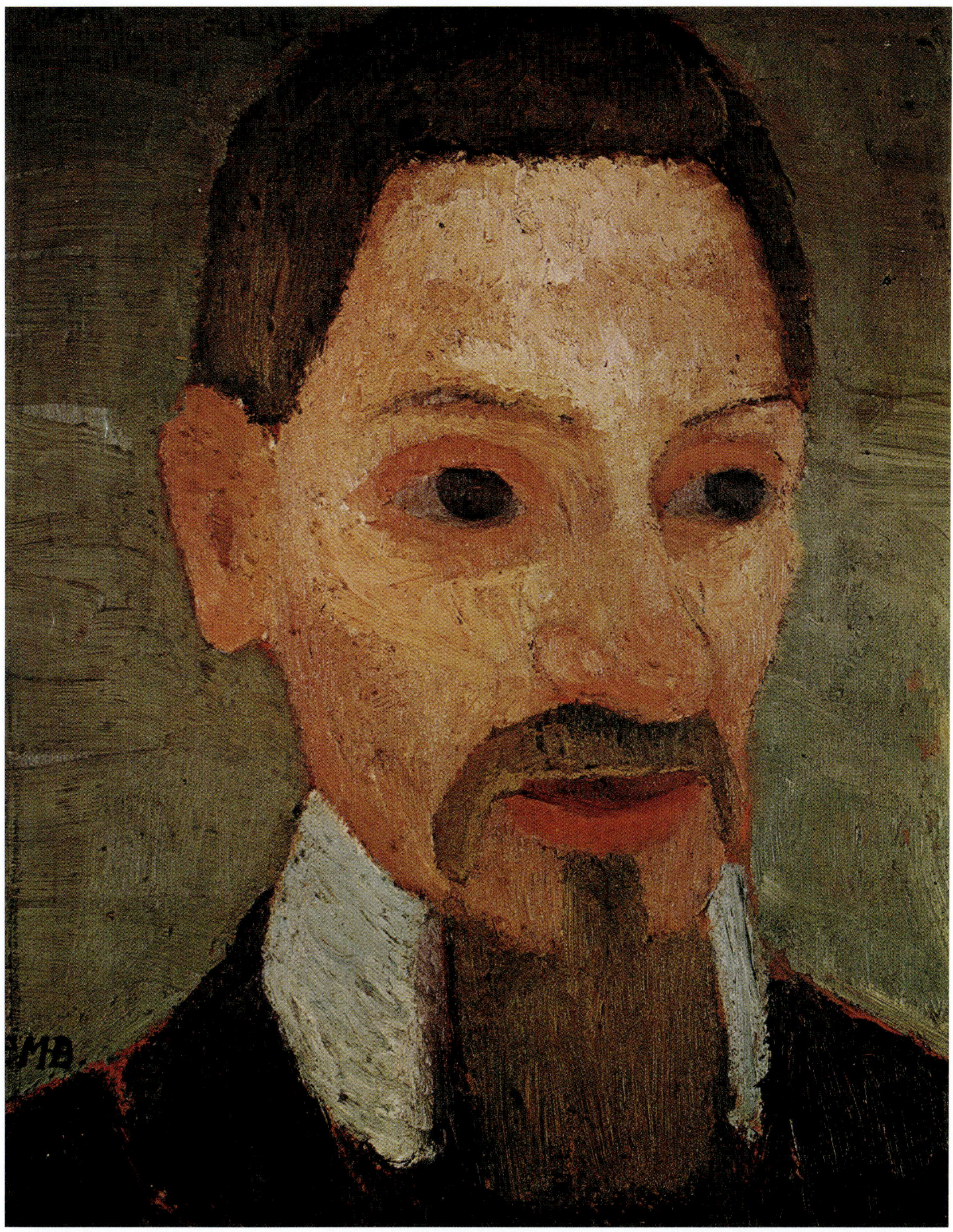

Plate 3

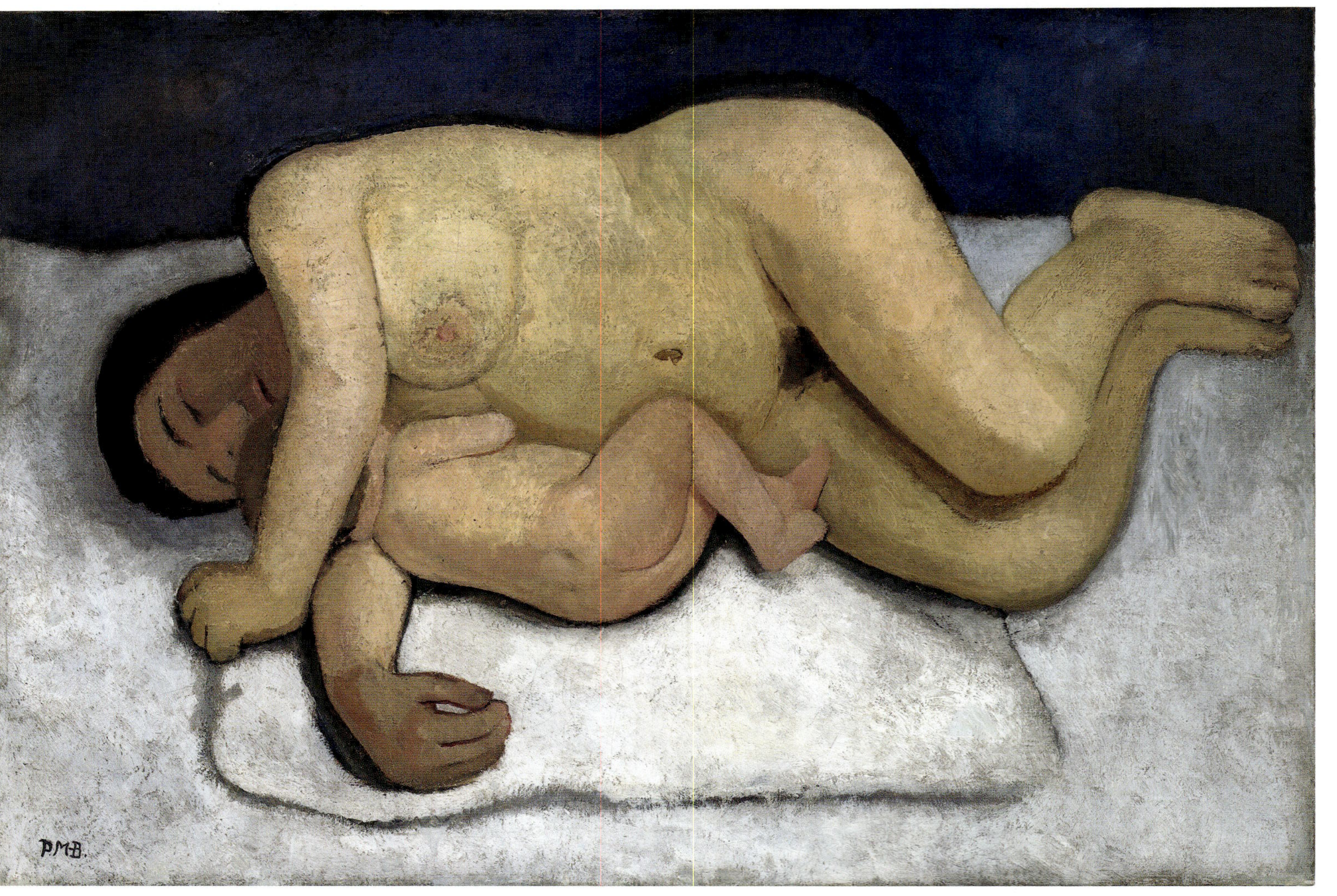

Plate 4

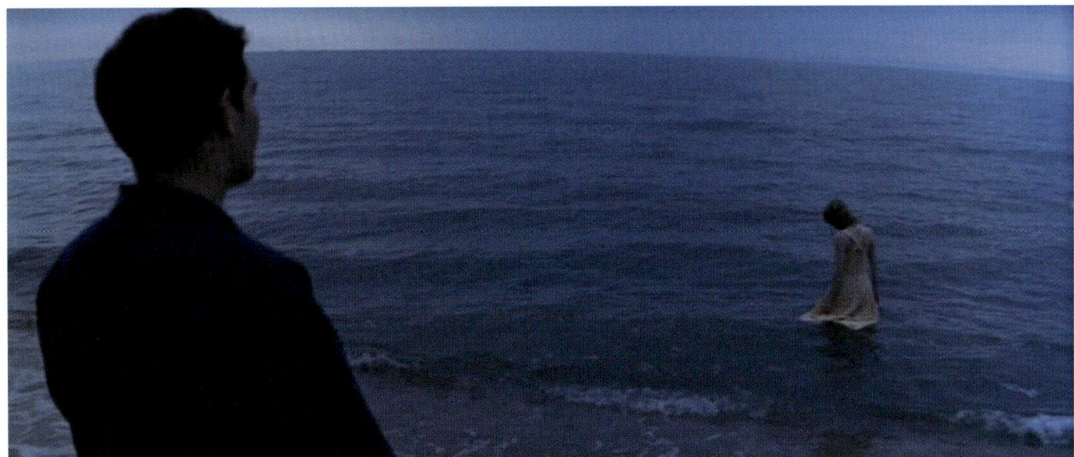

Plate 5

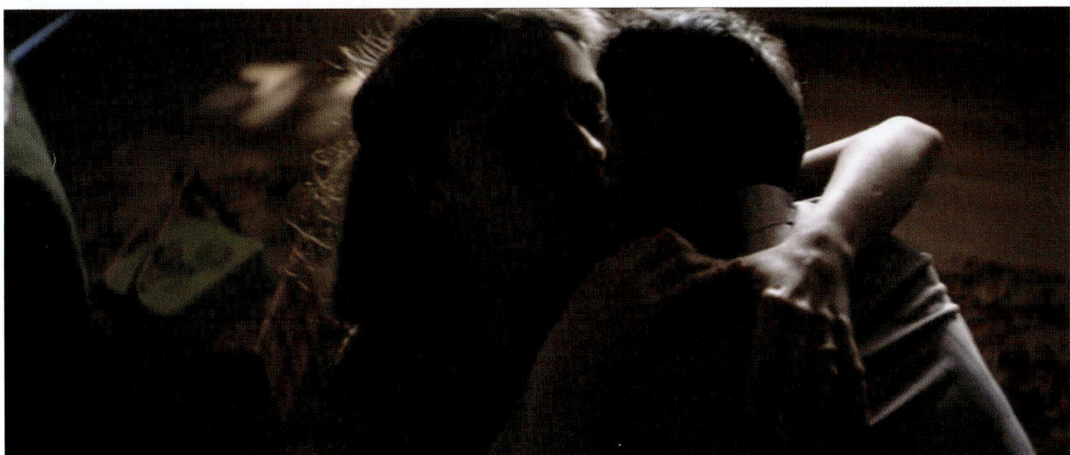

Plate 6

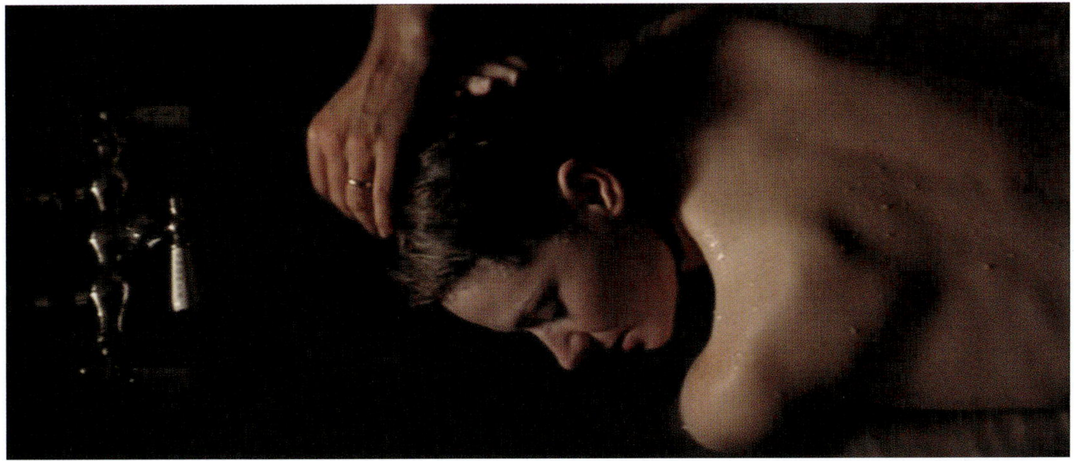

Plate 7

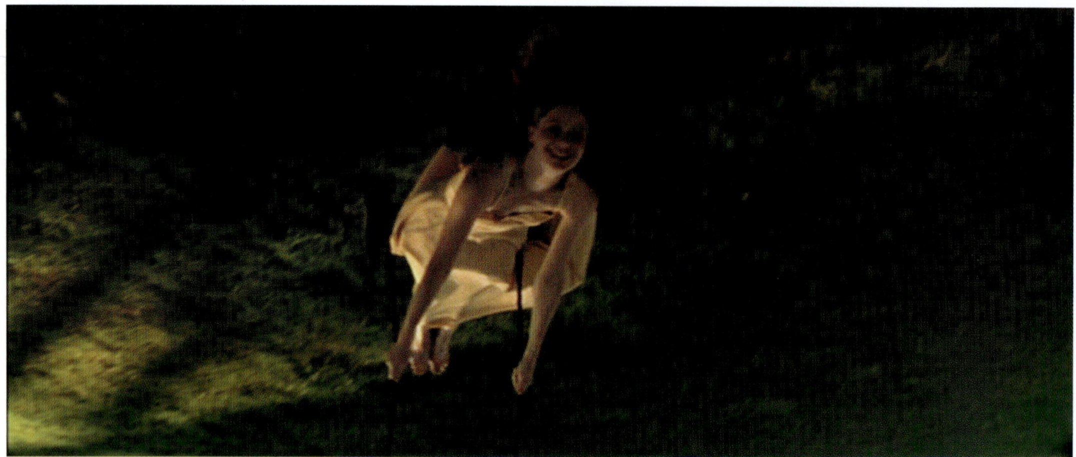

Plate 8

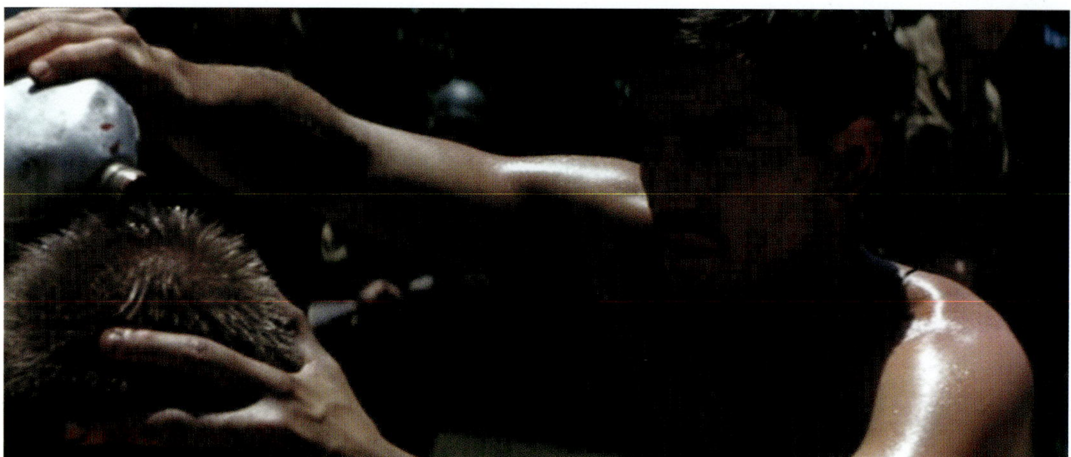

Plate 9

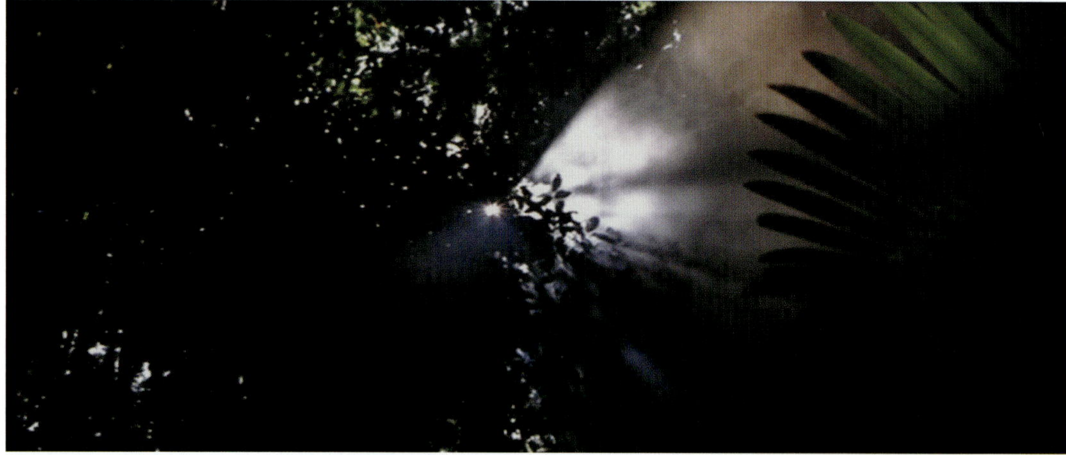

Plate 10

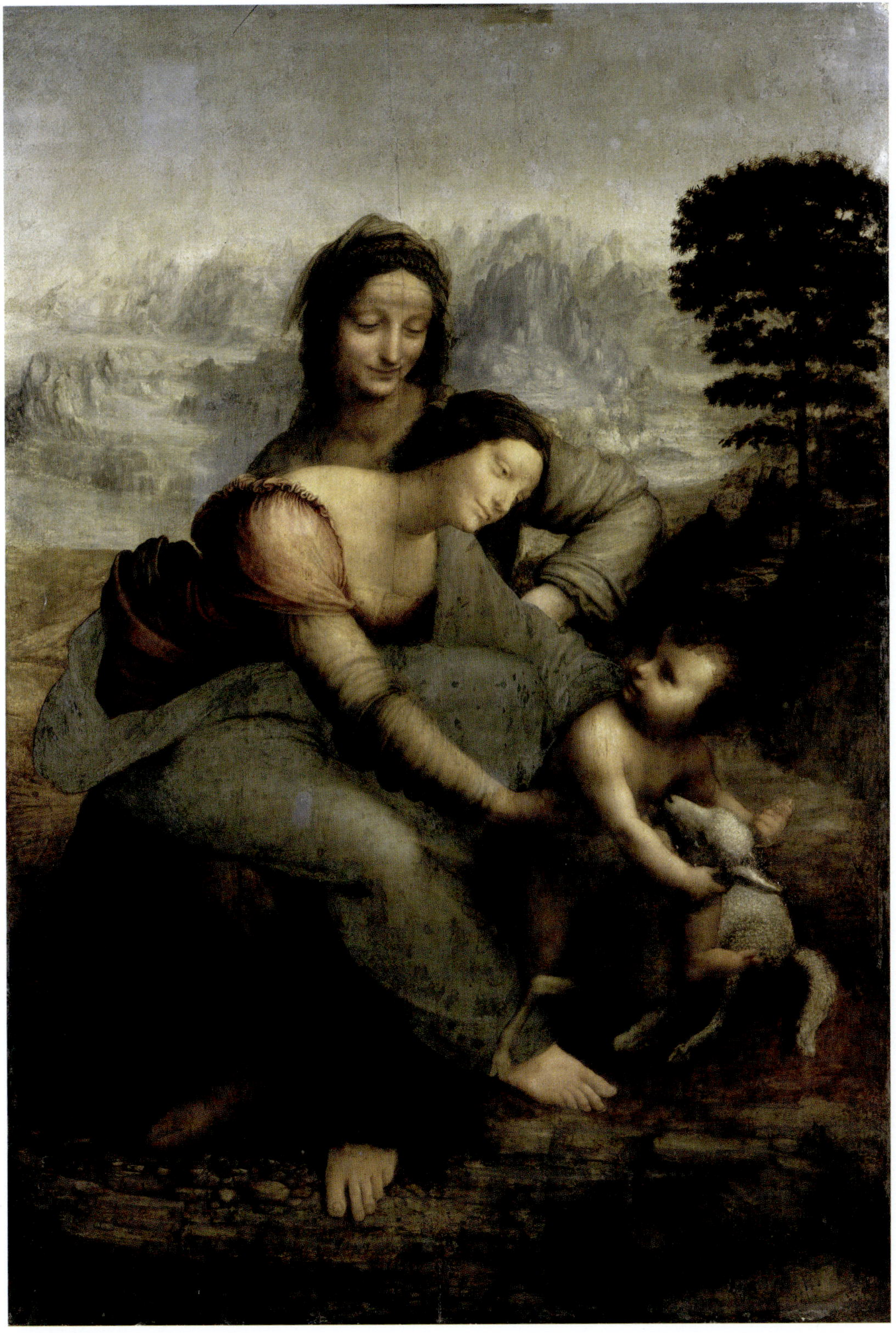

Plate 11

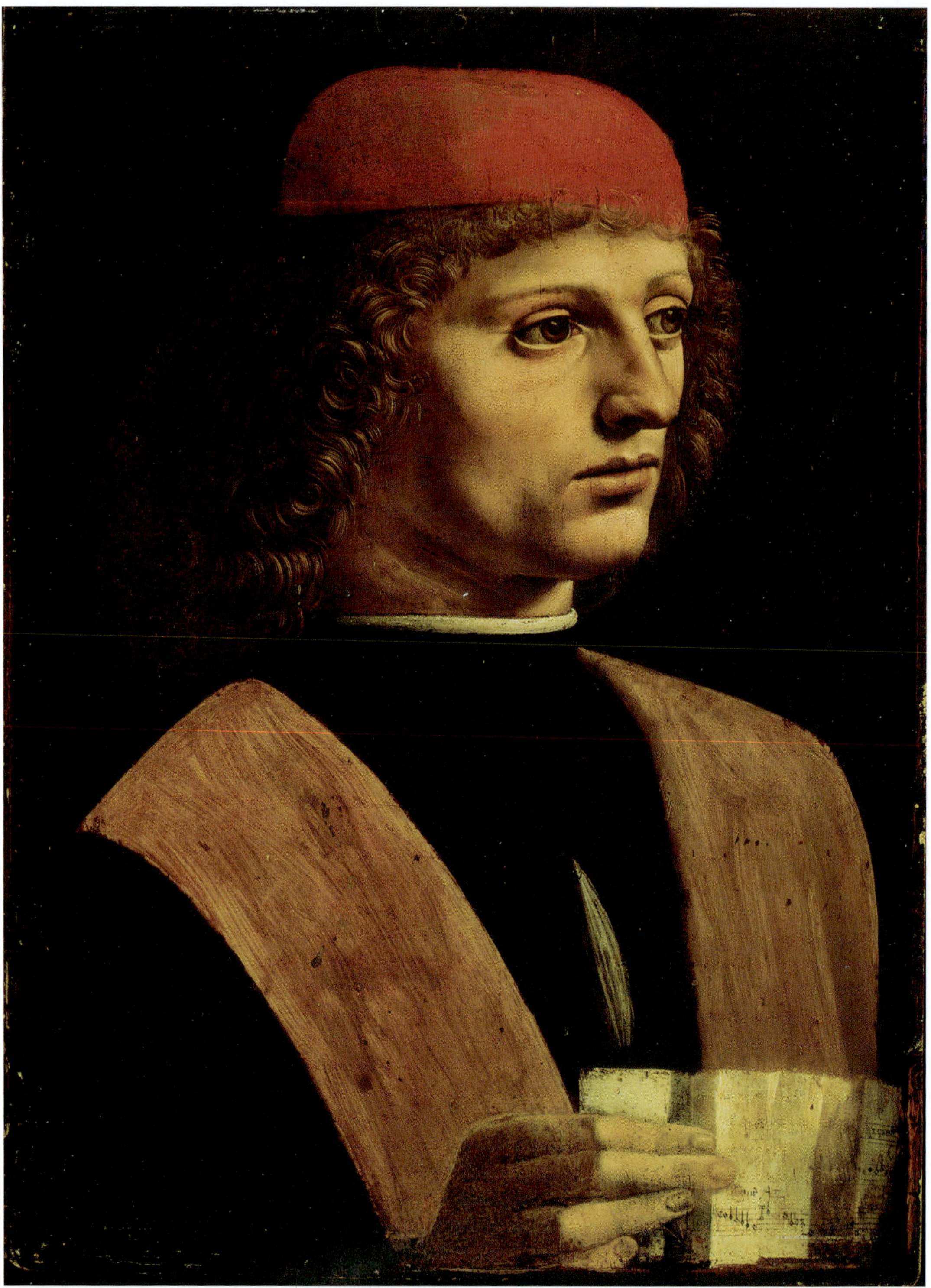

Plate 12

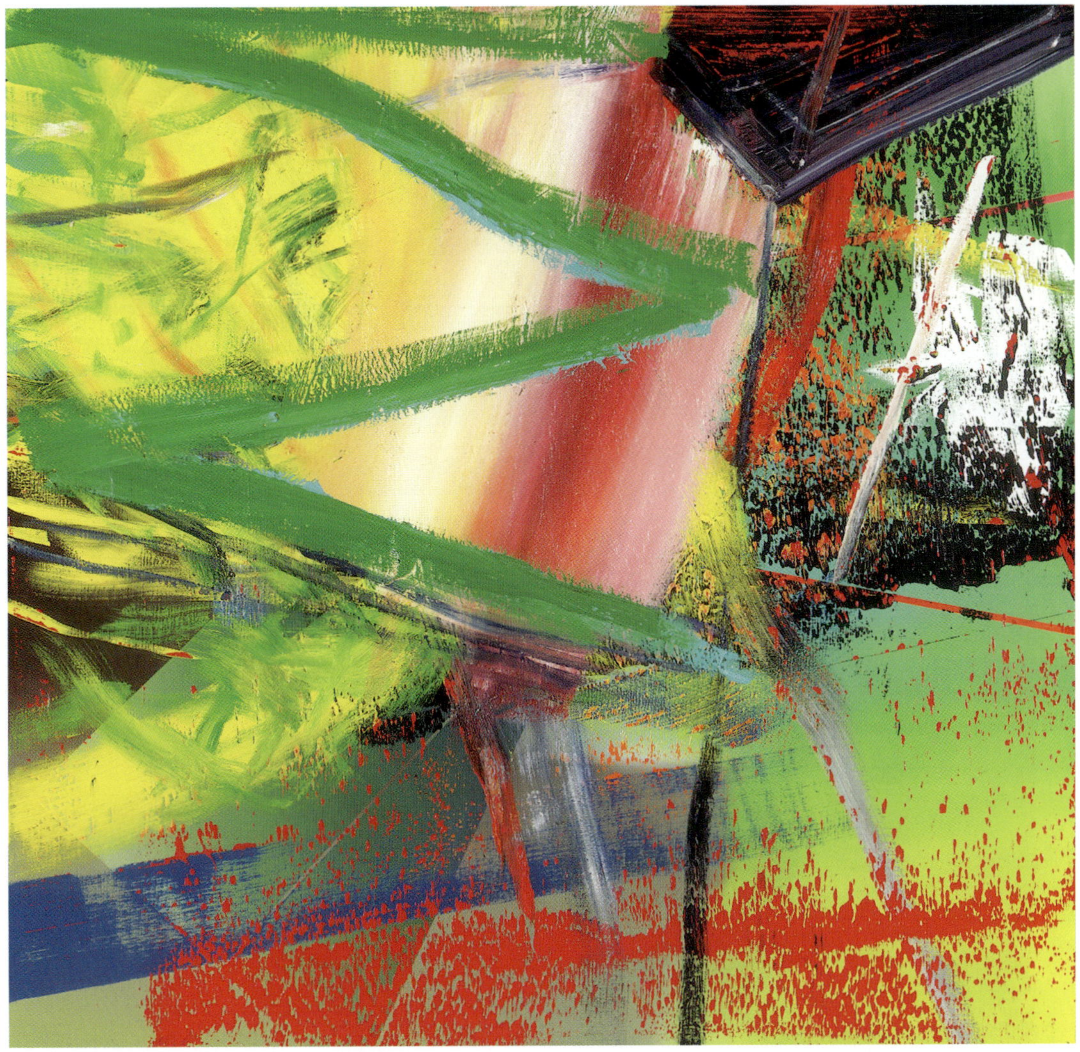

Plate 13

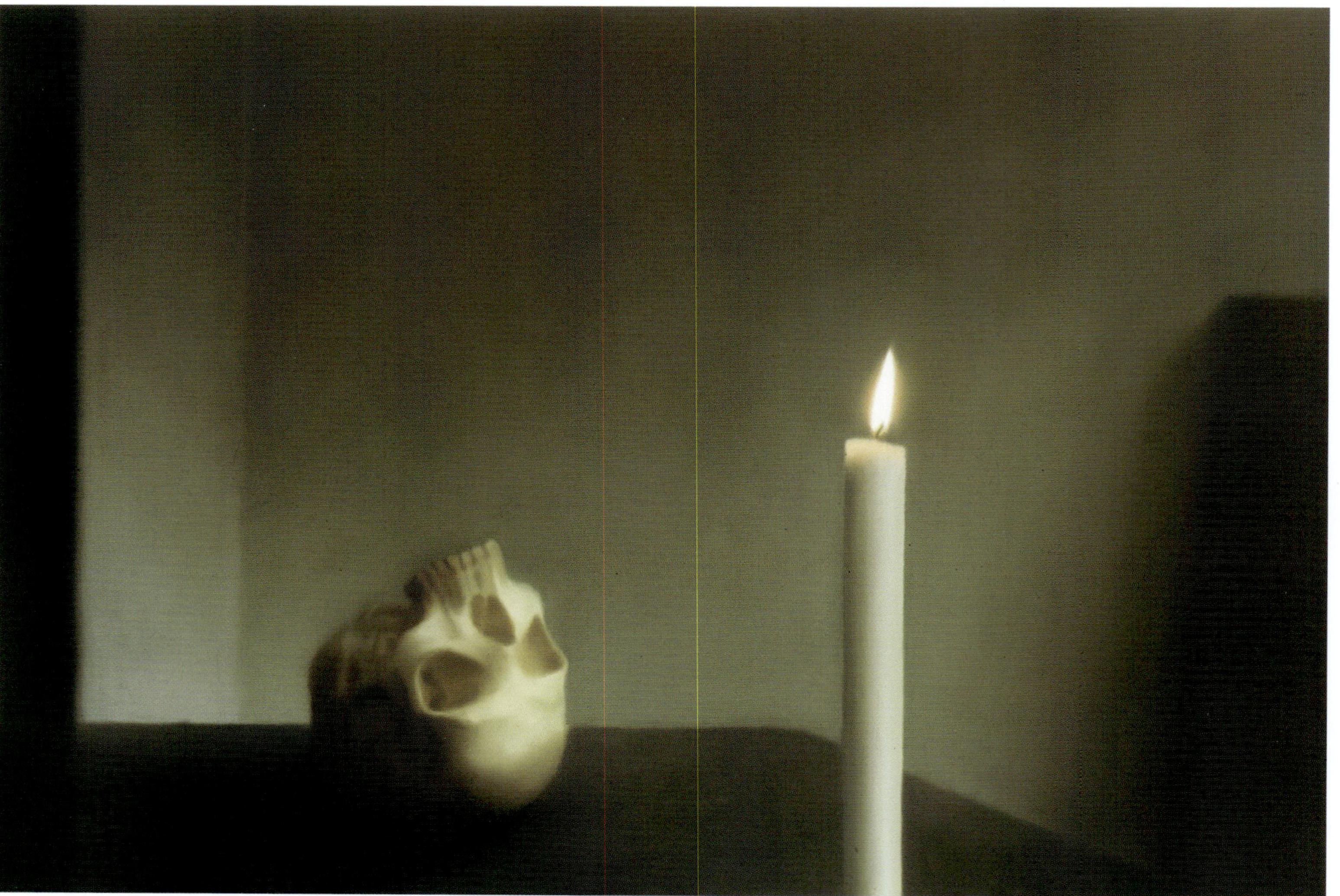

Plate 14

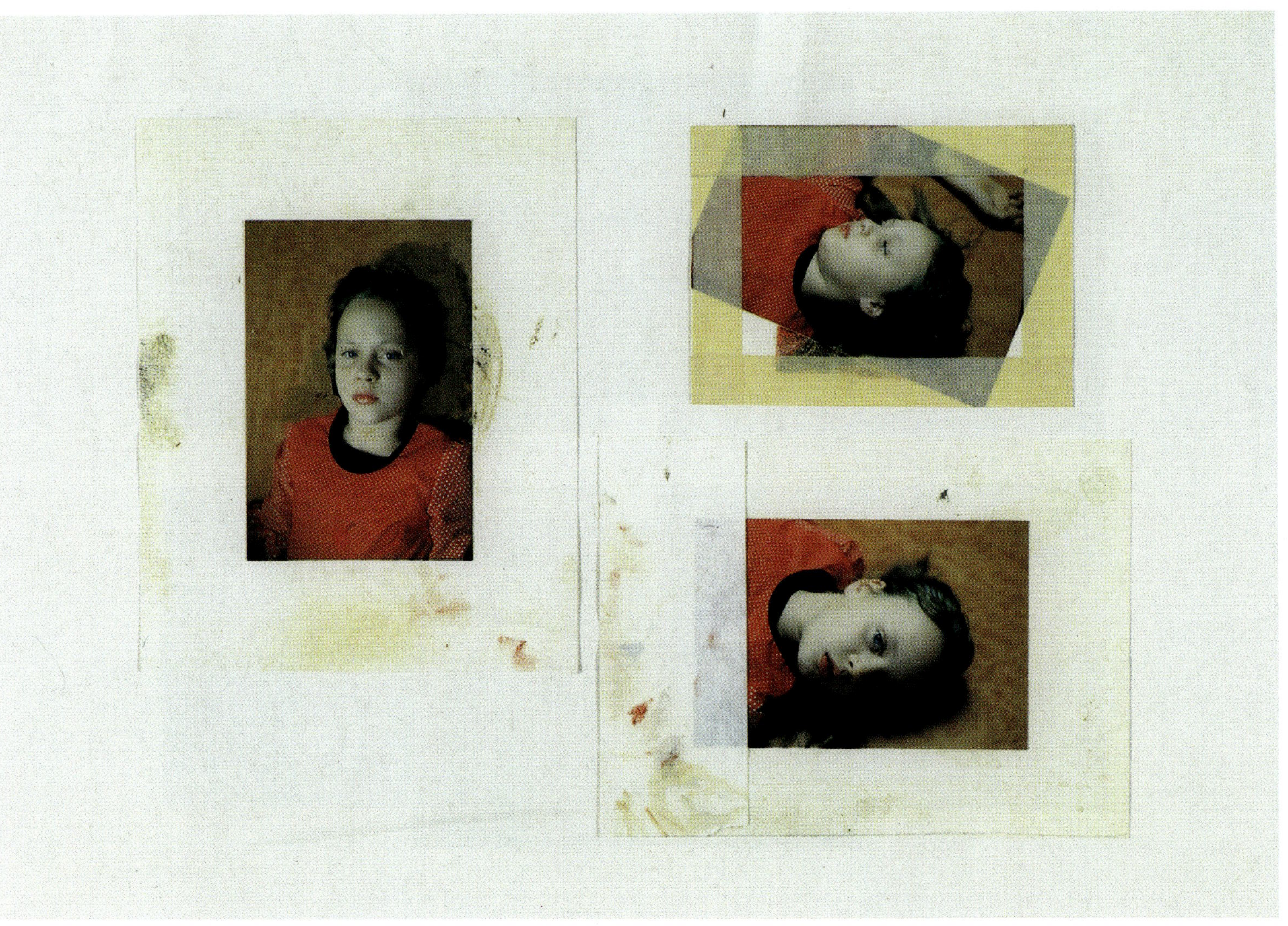

Plate 15

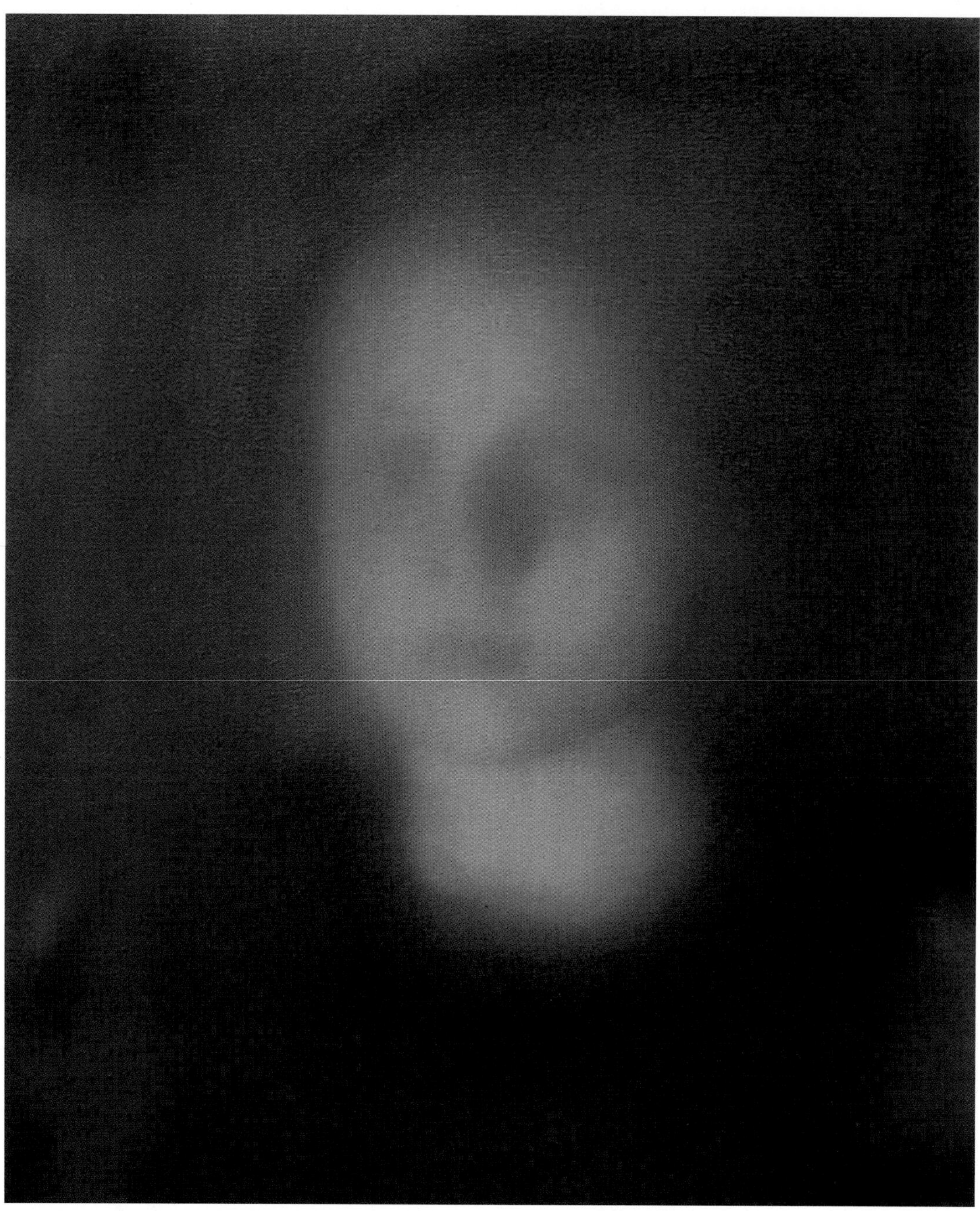

Plate 16

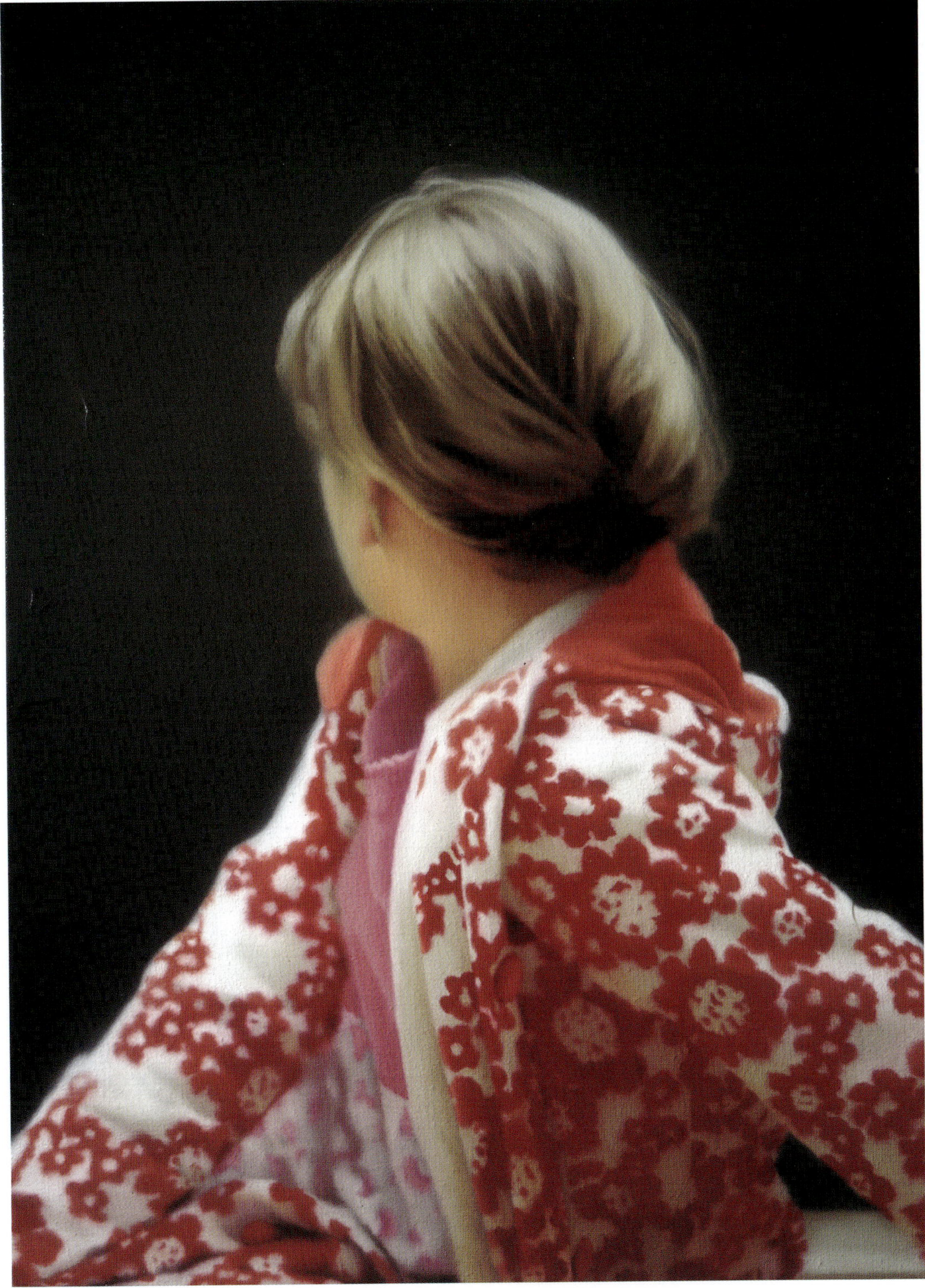

Plate 17

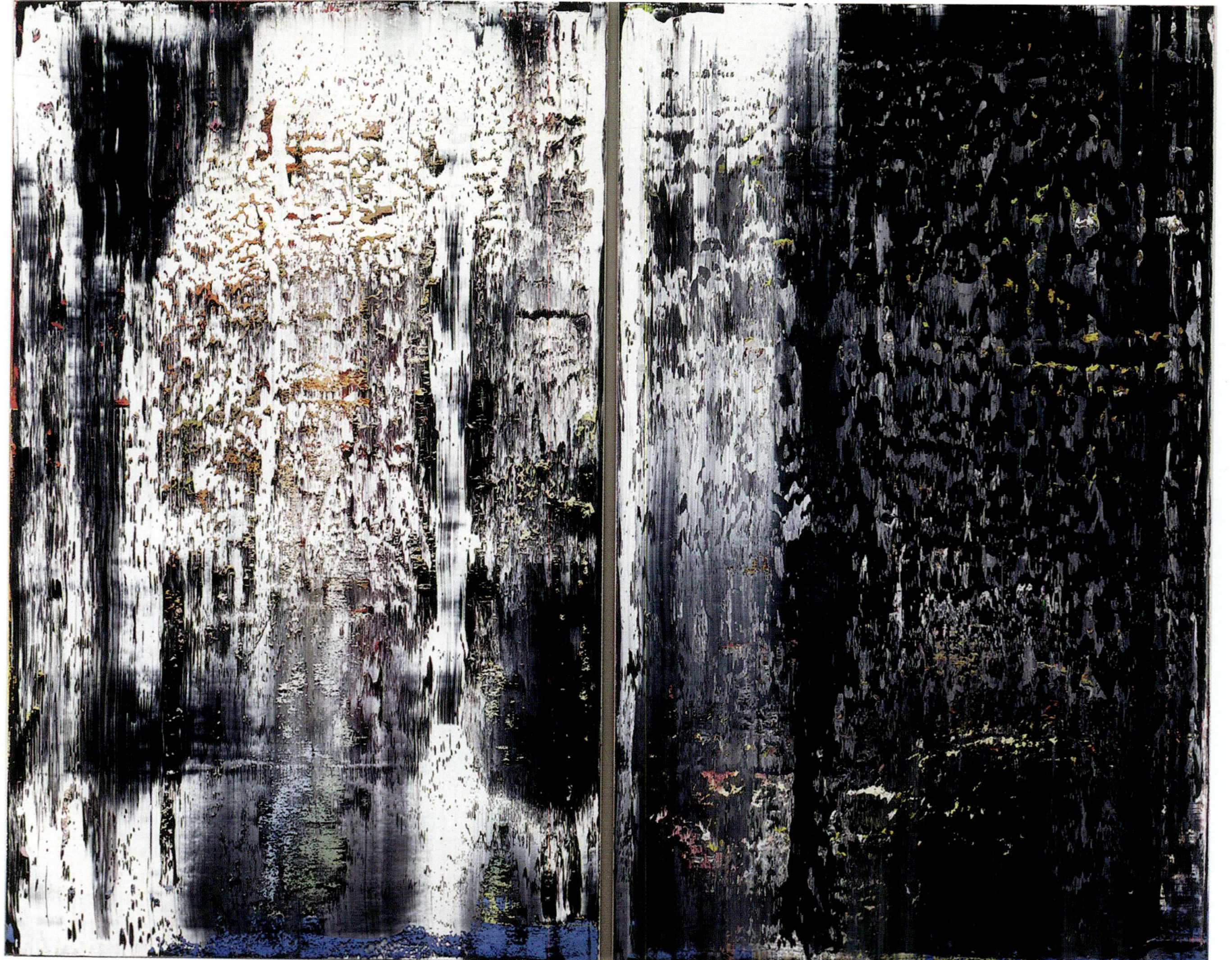

Plate 18

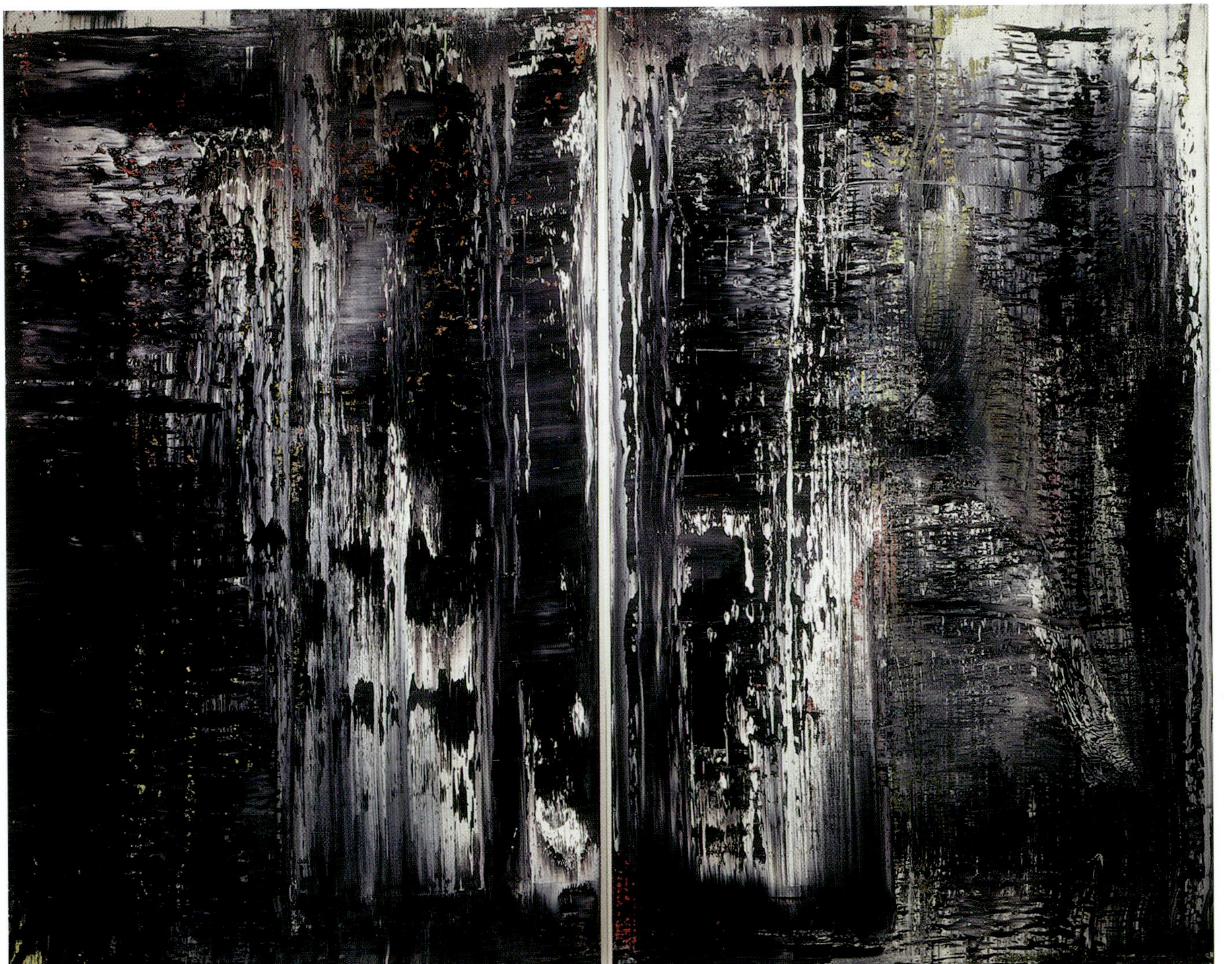

Plate 19

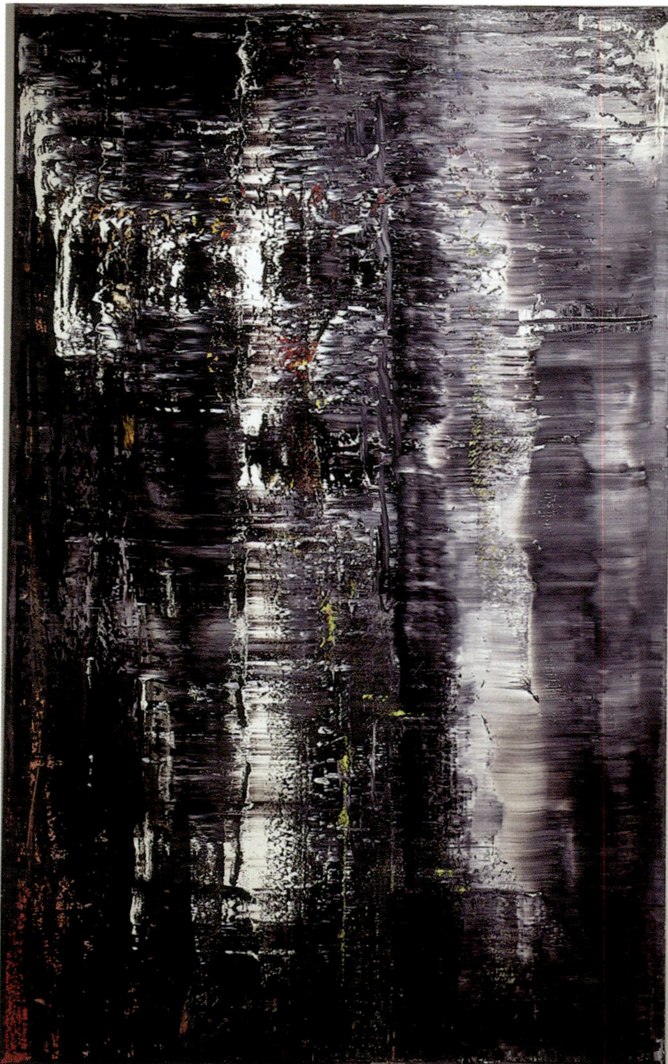

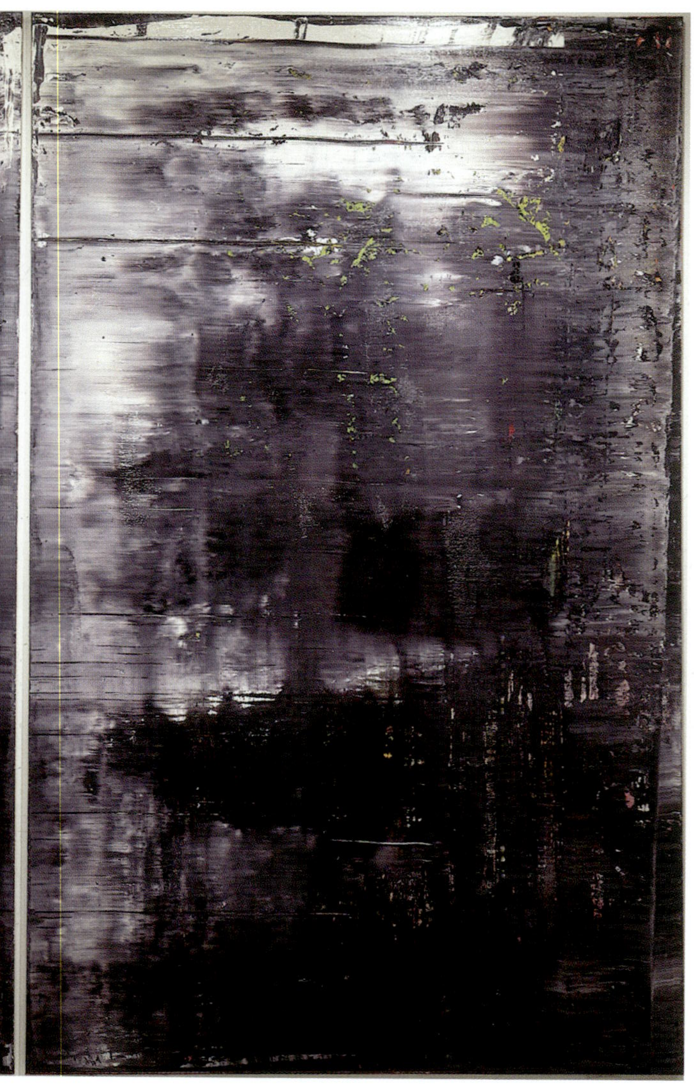

Plate 20

The Twilight of Posterity

6

[A] work is never completed except by some accidents such as weariness, satisfaction, the need to deliver, or death: for, in relation to who or what is making it, it can only be one stage in a series of inner transformations.

—Paul Valéry

The productions of the past . . . once went beyond yet earlier productions towards a future which we are, and in this sense called for . . . the metamorphoses which we impose on them.

—Maurice Merleau-Ponty

IN 1887, the year Nietzsche published the final version of *The Gay Science*, Paul Valéry wrote a first-person poem called "Solitude."[1] The narrator of this poem is more solipsistic than any of the writers discussed in the first half of this book. He lives all alone, "far from the world," and derives "endless joy" from his own mind; when a desire "stirs" him, he satisfies it with "marvelous hallucinations." Since this figure dispenses with nature as well as with other people, he doesn't seem at first to have an Orphic pedigree. However, in the third stanza we feel a blast of cold air and realize that we are in a familiar venue: on the slope leading from Hades to earth. "I scorn the senses, the vices, and women," the narrator announces there. "I who in the depth of my soul can evoke / Light . . . sound, beauty in its complexity!"

In 1891 Valéry published an essay called "Paradoxe sur l'architecte" that included a passage on Orpheus. Pierre Louÿs, to whom the essay was dedicated, urged him to rewrite it as a poem. Valéry modified the passage slightly, rearranged it as a sonnet, titled it "Orpheus," and published it later the same year.[2] This poem focuses on another scene from the same myth: the one in which Orpheus performs for a nonhuman audience. Seated at the "edge" of the "munificent sky," the musician plays his lyre, and the "fabulous rocks" respond to the "omnipotent rhythm" of his song by arising in the sun. The "immense soul" of Orpheus's "grand hymn" also fills "the sacred wood" with light, creates a golden "sanctuary," and "enchants the stones of porphyry."[3]

In 1926 Valéry revisited the figure who appears in his 1887 poem, but without the same enthusiasm. In an open letter to Rilke, he recalls his journey to Muzot, the last of the poet's retreats. "A minute castle terribly isolated in the midst of a vast expanse of rather somber mountains," he writes, "ancient, dreamy rooms with dark furniture and narrow windows—all this made my heart ache. . . . I could not conceive a life of such isolation."[4] Valéry also published a new version of "Orpheus." The musician still overwhelms the landscape with his eloquence, but now his power is destructive; he "breaks the all-powerful site" of the mountain where he sings, and forces the rock to "walk" and "stumble." Valéry also underscores the egotism of this kind of art-making. As the sun looks on in "horror," Orpheus "gathers and organizes himself in gold."[5]

Although he is never identified as such, the 1891 Orpheus reappears in the three essays Valéry wrote about Leonardo: "Introduction to the Method of Leonardo" (1894), "Note and Digression" (1919), and "Leonardo and the Philosophers" (1929).[6] The Florentine artist descended "into the depths of that which exists for all men," Valéry asserts in the first of these essays, but unlike other men, he penetrated "the habits and structures of nature," worked on them "from every angle," and constructed them, enumerated them, and set them "in motion" (6). This "master of faces, anatomies [and] machines" also succeeded where Zarathustra failed; he was the "ever more admirable riding master of his own nature" (33, 80).

However, these claims are assailed from many different directions. The first challenge comes from the Book of Nature. There is a "pattern" to the world, Valéry acknowledges in "Note and Digression," and this pattern "belongs to a family of patterns." Invention is possible only because "without knowing it, we possess all of the elements of the infinite group" (93). The artist is consequently not a creator, but rather someone who perceives, "voluntarily or involuntarily," the connections in this larger "structure." But it is not just that the artist is *able* to correspond with the external world; he is *compelled* to do so. "The secret," Valéry observes in the first essay, "—whether of Leonardo, or of Bonaparte, or that of the highest intelligence at a given time—lies and can only lie in the relations they found—and were compelled to find—*among things of which we cannot grasp the law of continuity*" (12–13).

And this reckoning of Leonardo's knowledge is still too generous, because analogy is an internal as well as an external principle. Since everything perdures by ceaselessly generating fresh variants of itself, even apparently inanimate objects move faster than the eye can see. "The armchair decays in its place, the table asserts itself so fast that it is motionless, and the curtains flow endlessly away," Valéry writes in an important passage from "Introduction to the Method of Leonardo." The only way we are able to regain our "control" in the "midst of the moving bodies, the circulation of their contours, the jumble of knots, the paths, the falls, the whirlpools, [and] the confusion of velocities" is by resorting to our "grand capacity for deliberately forgetting" (25–26).

Time assails Valéry's fantasy of aesthetic mastery from another direction as well. The author is a retroactive construction, rather than a real person, which means that Leonardo is the "effect" of his works, instead of their "cause" (105). And not even this retroactive construction is a secure legacy, because what an artist leaves behind when he dies are "the dreams that his name inspires and the works that make his name a symbol of admiration, hate, or indifference." Those who come later constantly "refashion this thought" so that it meshes with their own (3). This process never ends; there is no thought that concludes "the power of thinking . . . no position of the bolt that closes the lock forever" (90–91).

Valéry tries to neutralize these challenges to Leonardo's sovereignty by appealing to one of the privileged values of high modernism: impersonality.[7] Leonardo renounced his personality by making it the object of his thought, and by installing an "unqualifiable *I*" in "the place of *subject*." What "raises" him to such a "high degree" is therefore not "his precious personal *self*" but rather a "universal" self—one that includes the pattern of the world, the larger pattern to which this pattern belongs, all of the dreams that his name will ever inspire, and all of those who will ever refashion his thought—in short, the Whole (102–104). The only "particularity" Leonardo retains is the one that comes from having assimilated everything that could threaten his authority: that of being "master and center of himself" (38). But as Valéry clearly sees, this is an untenable solution. Not only is there no room here for another person, there is also no room for any *other* kind of audience, or even for works of art. This impersonal Leonardo "[goes] beyond all creations, all works, and even beyond his lofty designs" (103). Like the male recluse in "Solitude," he is "locked inside [his] heart more than in a tomb."[8]

Since Leonardo can be "universal" only if he has neither a history nor a body, Valéry denounces biographical interpretations of his work (104–106). This denunciation is a veiled reference to Freud's 1912 essay, "Leonardo da Vinci and a Memory of His Childhood," which explores the connections between Leonardo's mother and the female figures in *Virgin and Child with Saint Anne*.[9] From time to time, though, Valéry invokes another Leonardo—one who relates to the world the way the retina relates to light—and this Leonardo, who is a receiver and a giver, instead of a "pure consciousness" (104), is closely linked to the painting discussed by Freud.

In "Cézanne's Doubt," Maurice Merleau-Ponty criticizes Valéry for refusing to take Leonardo's biography into account. Although "it is certain that a person's life does not *explain* his work," he writes there, "it is equally certain that the two are connected. The truth is that the *work to be done called for that life*."[10] He supports this claim by summarizing Freud's interpretation of *Virgin and Child with Saint Anne* (72–75). At the same time that Merleau-Ponty narrows the distance between Leonardo's paintings and his life, though, he drastically expands the number of people who could be said to "author" Leonardo's art. "The painter can do no more than construct an image; he must wait for this image to come to life for other people," he writes earlier in the same essay, "When it does, the work of art will have united these separate lives. . . . It will dwell undivided in several minds, with a claim on every possible mind like a perennial acquisition" (70). Merleau-Ponty thus encourages us to think of Leonardo's life the way Rilke thinks of his: as "more than just a private event."[11] The same is true of us. Each of us has a biography that is distinctly our own but does not *belong* to us.

IN JUNE 2003, the Louvre mounted a major exhibition of Leonardo's work. It included many of the artist's drawings and manuscripts; sketches from the Verrocchio workshop, where Leonardo apprenticed; drawings from a number of his followers, the "Léonardesques";[12] an "intervention" by the contemporary Irish artist James Coleman; and the painting discussed by Freud and Merleau-Ponty—*Virgin and Child with Saint Anne.* Coleman's intervention had six components, which were dispersed through the exhibition space—a wall text, four small sets of black-and-white video-editing monitors, and a large-screen digital projection of *The Last Supper.* The images on these five screens corresponded in complex ways both with the rest of the exhibition and with Valéry, Freud, and Merleau-Ponty. Coleman used them to show that the myth of Orpheus and Eurydice is central to Leonardo's work—but that unlike the figure in Valéry's "Orpheus" poems, Leonardo's Orpheus is not alone, because he never turned away from Eurydice.

Inconspicuous, and lacking a room of their own, the four sets of editing monitors appeared to be "informational" rather than aesthetic. Few visitors stopped to look at them. They displayed ghostly renditions of several works by Leonardo that did not appear elsewhere in the exhibition. The color projection, on the other hand, was impossible to miss. In sumptuous color, one image after another of Leonardo's painting *The Last Supper* filled an enormous screen.

Sometimes this image was a "shot" of the whole painting, taken via what appeared to be a stationary camera setup. At other times, the "camera" focused on the left or right side of the painting, before slowly panning to the other side. On yet other occasions, it zeroed in on a detail of the painting, sometimes through so extreme a close-up that figuration gave way to pure abstraction. Each of these images occupied the screen for long enough to outgrow its status as a detail and become a painting in its own right. But then another with an equal claim to be *The Last Supper* would fill the screen.

There were zooms as well as pans in the large-screen projection, reinforcing my initial impression that a camera was responsible for the images at which I was looking. However, there was a large projector in the viewing area, and a computer at the back of the room, in an illuminated, glass-enclosed space. An ever-increasing number ran along the lower left side of each image, indicating the size of the file that was being assembled, and therefore how close the computer was to producing the next image. I soon realized that this apparatus was not just the source of the images projected onto the screen but also the "factory" within which they were fabricated. But I am moving far too quickly. Let us start at the beginning, in the many-sided room with which the exhibition began.

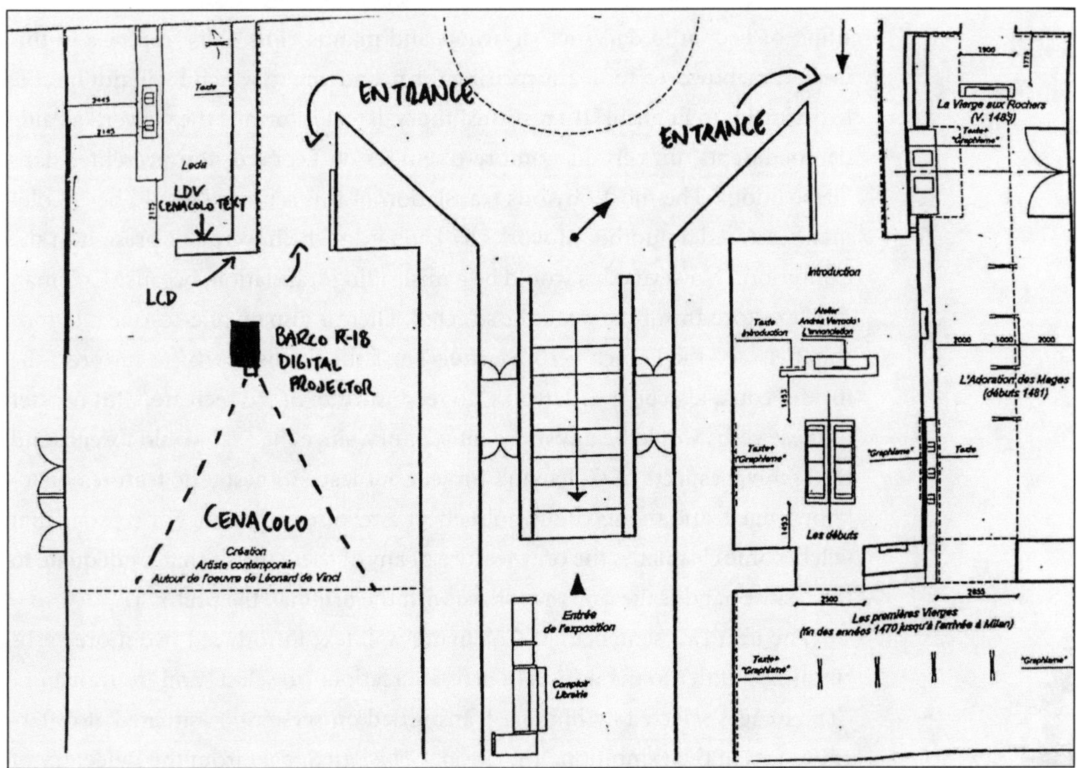

As can be seen from part 1 of the exhibition blueprint, whereas a single door led into this room, two led from it to the rest of the exhibition: one on the right and one on the left. The right door opened onto the first room of Leonardo drawings, and the left door to the large-screen projection of *The Last Supper*. There were no instructions indicating where the viewer was to begin, but regardless which door she chose, she was destined to conclude her visit where she had started it: in the entryway. A text was printed on the wall next to each door. The one on the left was written by Coleman, but modified somewhat during the production process:

> Invité à concevoir un projet pour le musée du Louvre à l'occasion de l'exposition *Léonard de Vinci, dessins et manuscrits*, James Coleman a restitué, à l'aide de documents, un certain nombre d'œuvres de Léonard non présentes dans l'exposition. Les images qu'il a sélectionnées sont diffusées sur des écrans situés en différents points du parcours de l'exposition. *La Cène* du Réfectoire de Sainte Marie des Grâces à Milan dispose d'un espace à elle seule et est présentée par une projection numérique. Les œuvres montrées constituent une sorte d'archivage ou de mémoire éphémère et leur réception est indissociable du contenu de l'exposition.

This text began conventionally enough, with the mention of the Louvre's invitation to Coleman to "conceive a project . . . on the occasion of [its] exposition of Leonardo da Vinci, drawings and manuscripts." His response to this invitation, however, took a surprising form, and one to which I will not be able to do justice in English. "Il a restitué," the wall text informed the viewer, "à l'aide de documents, un certain nombre d'œuvres de Léonard non présentes dans l'exposition." The most obvious translation of this sentence would be "[Coleman] restored a number of works by Leonardo which were not present in the exhibition." However, this would be a misleading translation, because Coleman didn't restore any of the works he selected. There is also no one-to-one relationship between the French verb "*restituer*" and the English verb "to restore"; the former could also be translated as "to reconstitute" or "to recreate." But neither of these verbs would be any more satisfactory, since the first would foreground the archival aspects of Coleman's project but leave its aesthetic features unacknowledged, and the second would effect a reverse exclusion. For reasons that will become clear later, the only feature of any of these words that is adequate to the task at hand is the one they share with the original: the prefix "re."

The next two sentences of Coleman's wall text introduced two more verbs running counter to the notion of artistic creation: "to select" and "to transmit." "The images selected by him are transmitted on screens . . . situated at different points in the exhibition," they read. "*The Last Supper* from the Refectory of

Santa Maria in Milan has at its disposal a space of its own and is presented by a numerical projection." Albeit a far cry from the generative powers so often associated with the artist, the first of the activities identified by Coleman at least had him as its agent; he chose which Leonardo works to use as the basis of his intervention. With the verb "to transmit," though, he disappeared, never to return. He ceded pride of place to the images he chose, and his agency to the numerical projection and video monitors. In the final sentence of Coleman's wall text, he declared his contribution to the Leonardo exhibition to be "indissociable from the contents of the [larger] exposition." He thereby stripped it of all autonomy. This would seem the moment to note that it did not have a name, and that since it was not really a "work," it is difficult to know how to refer to it. (The word "intervention," which I have been using, derives from the artist himself, who supplied it when I indicated my need for a designator.)

In his wall text, Coleman suggested that his digital images provided "a kind of archive or ephemeral memorial" for Leonardo's work. "Ephemeral memorial" is an oxymoron; it combines the notion of transitoriness with that of a lasting testimony. Coleman used the word "ephemeral" in part because his intervention was site-specific, like Robert Smithson's *Spiral Jetty*. He also emphasized the ephemeral nature of his images because they constituted a process rather than a product. The French word that I have translated as "archive" is "*archivage*," a neologism created to underscore the difference between his intervention and a more conventional archive. Most archives work by lifting things out of time and making them part of a synchronic system. Coleman's did the opposite; it provided the space within which a series of images could emerge and then disappear. Finally, with the word "ephemeral," Coleman served notice that he would not allow his intervention to be documented. When the exhibition closed, there was nothing to testify to its having been there—no photographic or video record of the sort that permitted us to visualize *Spiral Jetty* while it was still submerged in water.[13]

Coleman submitted both Leonardo's painting and his own intervention to the exigencies of the computer. It was not he who determined in which order the digital images of *The Last Supper* would appear, but rather the software he had designed for this occasion. This software also generated the pans and zooms, again "on the spot." Since it did so in an absolutely random fashion, no two viewings of the projection were the same, nor did their assemblage ever achieve the "finish" that we associate with a work of art. What makes this project all the more remarkable is that when the curators of the Louvre approached Coleman about working with them, they gave him absolute carte blanche. He decided to contribute to the Leonardo exhibition, instead of making something of his own.

But I have not yet acknowledged the full complexity of the last sentence of Coleman's wall text. In it, he did not say that his images were "indissociable from the contents of the exhibition"; he said, rather, that their "reception" was. The word "reception" has a technological meaning; we use it when speaking about the transmission of audio, visual, or audiovisual information. In this context, it refers to the amount of information that is likely to arrive at a given destination; in some places radio or television reception is "good," and in others "bad." Because Coleman used the word "transmission" in the first sentence of his wall text, in connection with the editing monitors, "reception" communicated this technological meaning when it emerged in the final sentence.

But "reception" can also index what happens to a broadcast when it arrives at its destination. And whereas radio or television reception tends to be the same for everyone living on a particular block, an audio or audiovisual transmission will not be received by all of them in the same way. What such a broadcast represents to an individual viewer can also change dramatically over time. When the word "reception" appeared in the last sentence of the wall text, it also conveyed this meaning, since it rubbed shoulders both with "exhibition" and with another word that cannot be adequately translated into English: "*mémoire*." In addition to "memorial," this last word can mean "human memory" and "computer RAM or ROM." With it, Coleman challenged the notion that a computer is a storage system that preserves what we put on it. He also reminded us that our memories are as provisional as the digital images of *The Last Supper*. Finally, he expressed his hope that the viewers of the Louvre exhibition would do for his images what he did for Leonardo's—provide them with an ephemeral memorial. It is in the spirit of this hope, and not as a documentation of Coleman's intervention, that this chapter should be read.

THE MEANING ACTIVATED by Coleman through the verb "*diffuser*" has been available for only a hundred years or so. The same is true of its English equivalent, "to transmit." During the nineteenth century, "transmission" functioned primarily as a signifier for "hereditary conveyance." The values handed down from one generation to another throughout history have been heavily patriarchal, regardless of the agency of their transmission. Wealth and property have also passed from father to son, and even in cultures where women are allowed to inherit these things, men remain the only "legal" recipients of another kind of legacy—that implied by the Name-of-the-Father.[14] Transmission is also a crucial component within the system of exchange upon which patriarchal cultures are based, a system within which men are the subjects and women are the objects.[15]

Art has traditionally served as one of the most important vehicles for generational transmission. As Gregg Horowitz puts it, "In all past art, we can locate an implicit conception of generations bound together through representational and affective practices. Succeeding generations were conceived as the bearers of a past in which the past imagined itself overcoming its finitude, and art was the sensuous vehicle of this transmission."[16] Horowitz argues that since Kant, art has no longer been able to perform this function, but in making this claim he overlooks a crucial institution: the museum. Modernist art and aesthetics may, indeed, be "born of a perception of the finitude of sensuous life" (3), but this is not a perception available to most viewers, since museums treat contemporary paintings, drawings, and sculptures in the same way they treat earlier ones: they preserve them for the future, and at the first sign of wear and tear they restore them. When a museum commissions a work of art, it is generally with the expectation that the artist will create something precious that can be added to its holdings and transmitted—like the *Mona Lisa*—to posterity.

By characterizing this commission as an invitation to "conceive" something, Coleman drew attention to the intimate connection between aesthetic transmission and paternal transmission. He himself, though, refused to step into the symbolic position of a "father." He also effaced himself as author, thereby removing one of the primary sources of aesthetic value; built an expiration date into his images; and prevented them from cohering into an independent work of art even during the brief tenure of their existence. Finally, he protected his images from a posthumous entification by making the human psyche the only possible agency of their memorialization.[17]

Although Coleman himself "confused" the "generations," as Lacan would say, the exhibition in which he participated seemed on a first viewing determined to "knot and braid" the "thread of lineage."[18] As I have already mentioned, the Louvre displayed works from three different generations of artists, the first of whom transmitted a certain "know-how" to the second, and the second of whom constituted a model for the third. The passage printed on the wall beside the door leading to Leonardo's early work also provided a classic instantiation of Oedipal revolt; in it, the artist imputes to himself the capacity to create ex nihilo, thereby usurping the prerogatives of his heavenly as well as his earthly father. "If the painter wishes to see beauties capable of inspiring love," this passage reads, "he has the ability [to create] them, and if he wishes to see monstrous things that frighten, or jests that cause laughter, or things that inspire piety, he is their lord and master. If he wishes to create landscapes, or deserts, or fresh and shady places in warm weather, he depicts them. . . . If he wishes valleys, if he wishes to disclose great sweeps of land from the high peaks of mountains . . . he has the power to do so. . . . [A]ll that exists in the universe

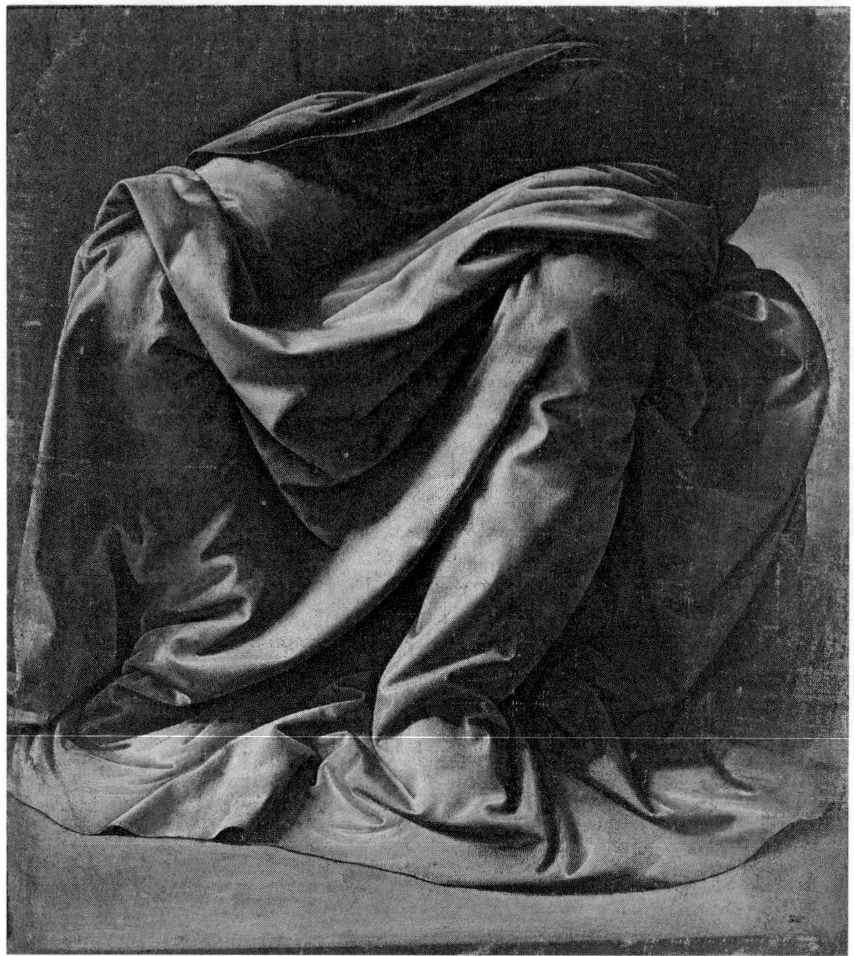

through essence, real or imaginary, he has it first in his mind and then in his hands. And these are of such excellence that at a given moment they create a proportioned harmony taken in by the eye as the reality itself."[19]

But in the first room of the exhibition, the yarn of lineage began to unravel. This room was divided into two parts: one devoted to drawings by Verrocchio and the artists in his atelier, and the other to a series of drapery studies. Although the Louvre identified Leonardo as the source of the drapery studies and indicated that he produced them while he was Verrocchio's apprentice, their provenance remains unclear. Françoise Viatte suggests in "The Early Drapery Studies" that many hands may have been involved in their original production, that other artists may have worked them over later, and that their apparent unity may be a retroactive construction, conferred upon them by a seventeenth-century collector. In an attempt to make theoretical sense of these attribution difficulties, Viatte says something that is highly germane to the present discussion: “Perfection is anonymous. . . . [A]ll we do is grant it its place without claiming to retrace its generation.”[20]

And these are not the only ways in which the drapery studies refused to assume their pre-assigned place within the Oedipal narrative. It is unclear whether they are freestanding works or preliminary sketches for another work, and since the bodies that appear in them are headless and devoid of the usual markers of

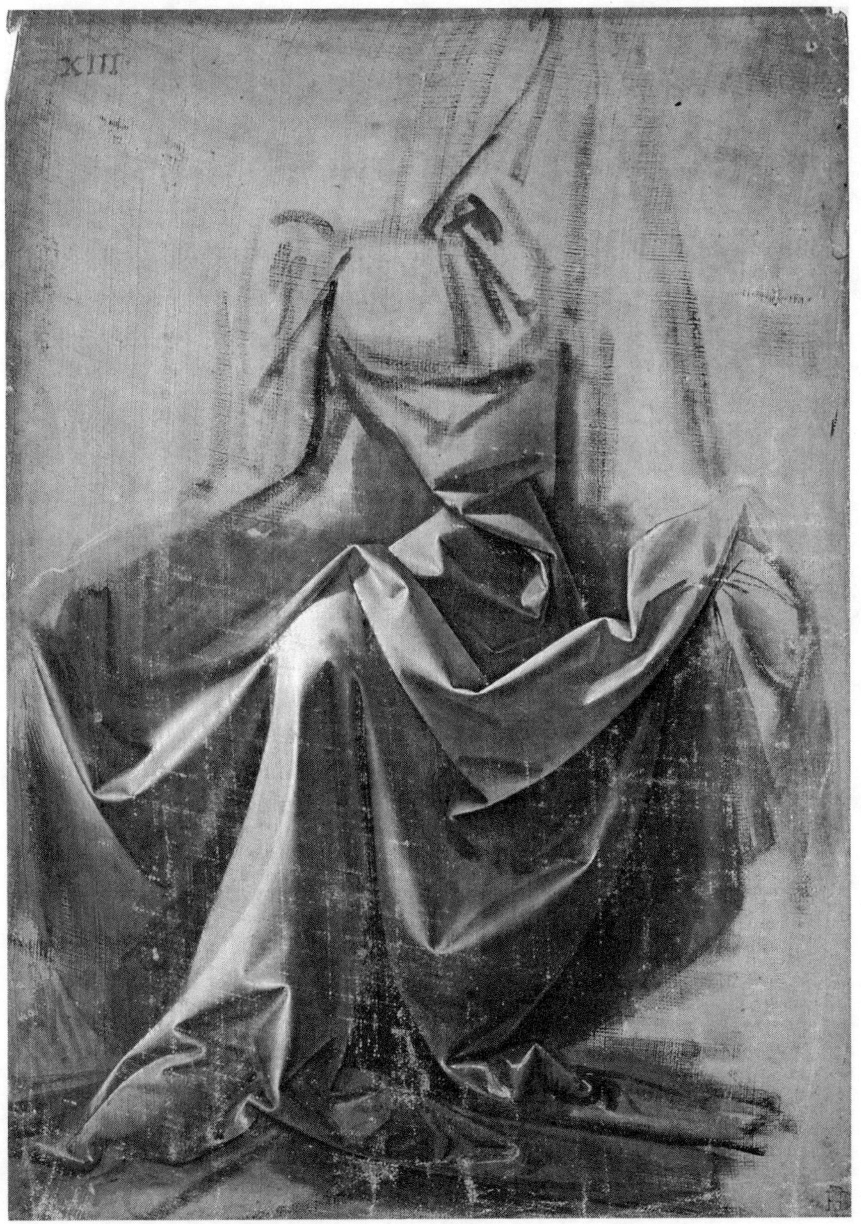

age, sexual difference, or socioeconomic status, we can say nothing whatever about the historical personages who served as their models. But although the father of these drawings cannot be named, the bodies in five of them are emphatically maternal. Three are seated, a position that was presumably chosen because it dramatically increases the number of folds in the fabric, but that also creates something that would not otherwise exist: a lap. The legs of two of the seated women are widely spread, making their laps unusually capacious and inviting, and—at least to a contemporary eye—one appears to be pregnant.[21] The drawing in which this figure appears also breaks off just above her rounded belly, leaving nothing but dead space in the upper portion of the frame.

Motherhood emerged as an explicit topic in the next two rooms of Leonardo's works, the first of which was devoted to early sketches of the Madonna and Child and the second to studies of a related subject, the Adoration of the Magi. Because in almost every drawing in which the Virgin Mary appeared, she was also seated, the mother also continued to be defined through her lap. The image of a seated Virgin was of course a common one in medieval and Renaissance art. It is also ideally suited to the depiction of the Madonna as a physical support and aesthetic frame for the Christ child. It therefore might not seem particularly surprising that the Florentine artist should privilege it. However, Leonardo refused to be bound by convention when working with this theme.

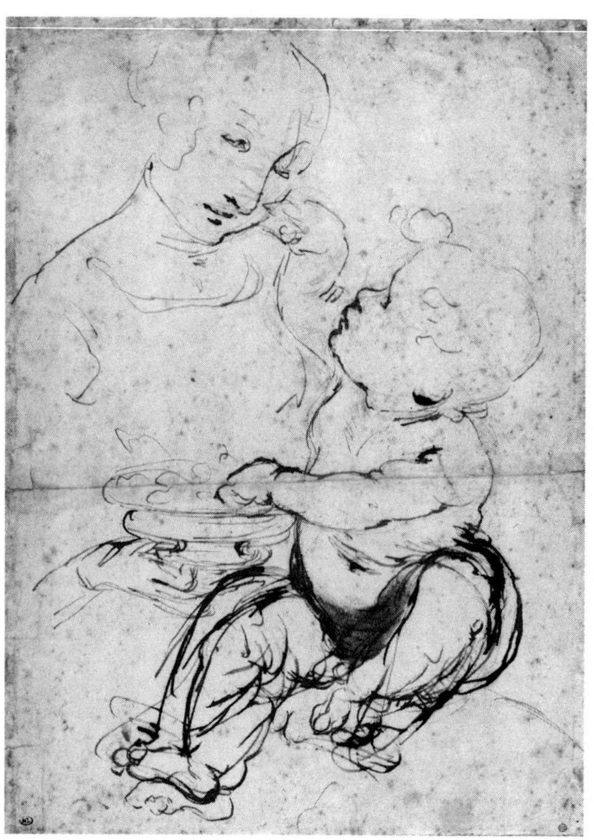

In the *Virgin and Child with Saint Anne and John the Baptist*, he places the infant Jesus on his mother's lap and Mary herself on her mother's lap. In a closely related painting, the *Virgin and Child with Saint Anne*, he again situates the Madonna on Saint Anne's lap. He also makes her own lap unusually generous, and gives it pride of place. Rather than placing the Christ child on his mother's lap, Leonardo locates him near the ground. Finally, instead of treating the Virgin Mary as a supporting player in a narrative that will soon transcend her, Leonardo connects her to her son in the same way he connects

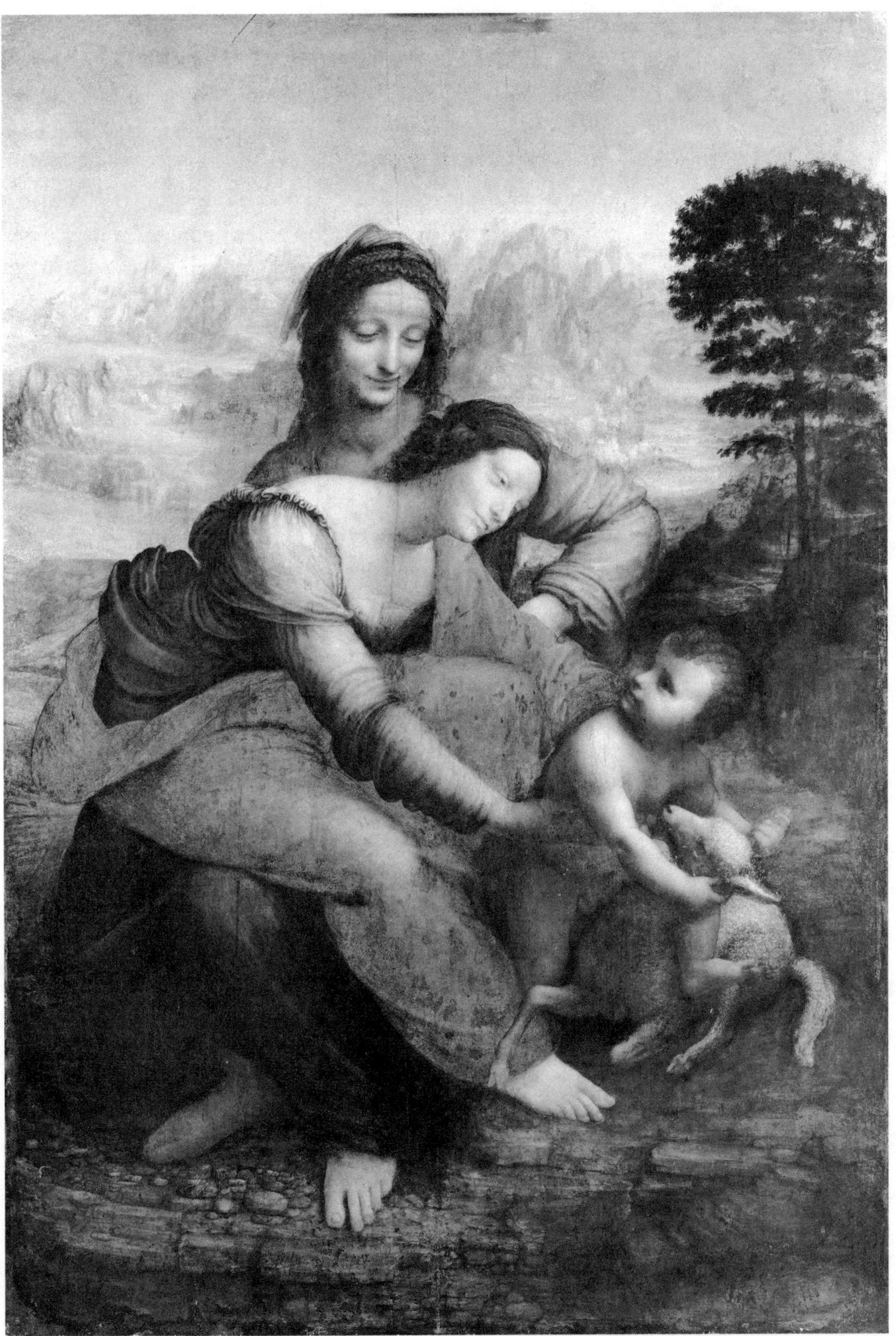

See also Plate 11 in color insert.

her to her mother: through a visual correspondence. She reaches out to hold the Christ child, who repeats this gesture with a lamb.

And it is impossible to keep these two works out of the present discussion, since they are linked in several other important ways to the drapery studies. First, the torque of Mary's body in *Virgin and Child with Saint Anne and John the Baptist* echoes that of the figures in several of these studies. Second, the Virgin's lap is empty in *Virgin and Child with Saint Anne*, just as the laps in the drapery drawings are, and although the Louvre exhibition was devoted to Leonardo's drawings and manuscripts, the curators included this painting in it. When we allow these works to communicate in this way, we realize how much they need each other. By placing Mary on Saint Anne's lap in *Virgin and Child with Saint Anne*, but having her reach out to a child who has either just climbed down from her own lap or is about to return to it, Leonardo underscores the receptive aspects of motherhood. However, because there is still a tenuous connection between this tableau and the Christian narrative, it is possible to mistake this receptivity for that traditionally associated with the Virgin Mary. The drapery studies disable this reading. They liberate the mother from her role as the "vessel" of God, allowing her to become the representative of a much more radical openness.

THE ROOM DEVOTED to the "Léonardesques" provided the opportunity to think further about the issues raised in the first two spaces. "Room" might seem an odd word to use in this context, since the space in question was vast; it extended across the entire width of the exhibition. It was also divided into five smaller areas by walls. The symmetry of the room, though, overrode these divisions. Its two sides were architecturally identical, as were the smaller rooms onto which they opened. In both of these areas the names of Leonardo's imitators were also emblazoned on the floor. Finally, facing mirrors were attached to parallel walls at each end. The facing mirrors and the exaggerated symmetry of the room were obvious metaphors for the Léonardesques, who reprised the Florentine artist's style and themes, and even some of his works. Although imitation is often assumed to be the sincerest form of flattery, it is as fraught with potential violence as transmission. It is also informed by the same logic.

During the many centuries of Western history when the Christian narrative remained largely unchallenged, human beings were able to find refuge from their own finitude in the notion of a heavenly afterlife. But with the increasing secularization of Europe, this refuge became less secure, and transmission became the primary vehicle for self-perpetuation. Shakespeare's writings are massively concerned with this issue, and in his *Sonnets* he identifies the two primary agencies through which the early modern subject sought to extend his life:

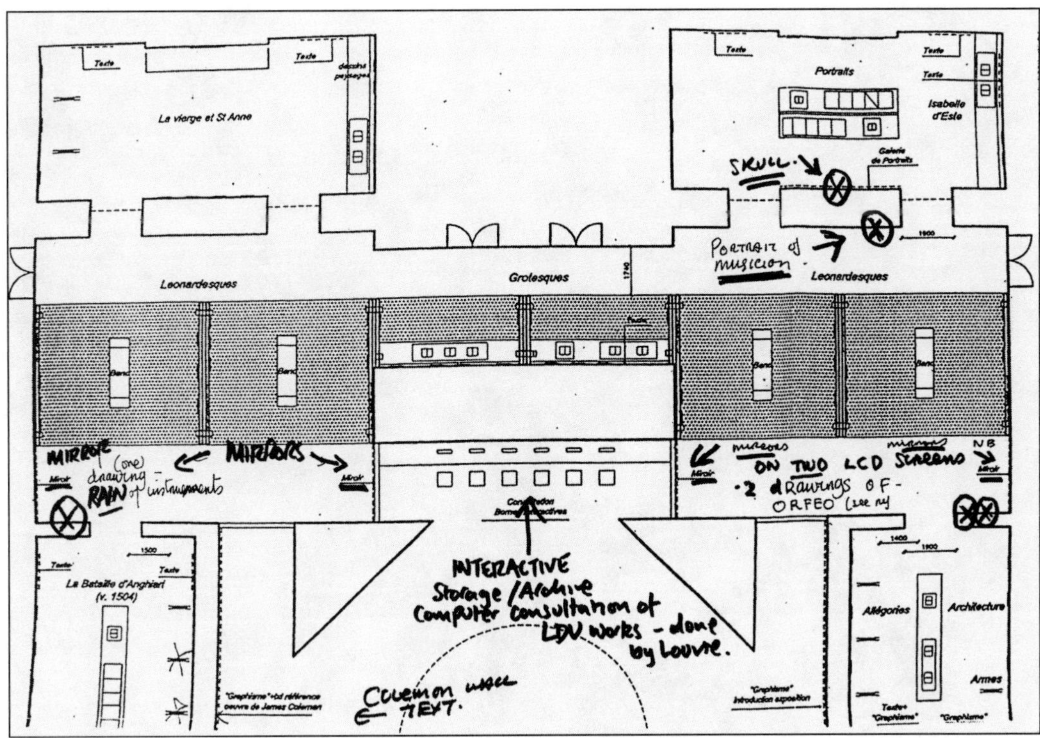

fatherhood and artistic creation. In Sonnet 1, he urges the young man who is the object of his desire to tend to his posthumous future by propagating a son. When the young man fails to do so, the poet offers to immortalize him through verse.

Shakespeare also acknowledges that the conveyance of the paternal legacy from the father to the son is not sufficient in and of itself to "conquer" death. If the father wants to triumph over his mortality, he must also induce the son to be his surrogate. In Sonnet 6, the poet urges the young man to "breed another thee," in Sonnet 11 to "print" another "copy" of himself, and in Sonnet 3 to create a facsimile of his face, so that when he is old he will still be able to see his youthful self. To "stop posterity," Shakespeare suggests in the last of these poems, would be to become the "tomb" of one's "self-love."[22] When a son starts to imitate his father, it is often in response to precisely this kind of paternal solicitation. Sooner or later, though, he will begin to dream of beating the father at his own game, and imitation will become a clandestine way of eradicating the paternal image, and disseminating his own.

Leonardo, though, did nothing to secure himself a posthumous existence. He did not have any children, and he chose his apprentices for their beauty, rather than their talent or their eagerness to mimic him. Not surprisingly, given this, none of them became a disciple.[23] The Florentine artist also spent far more

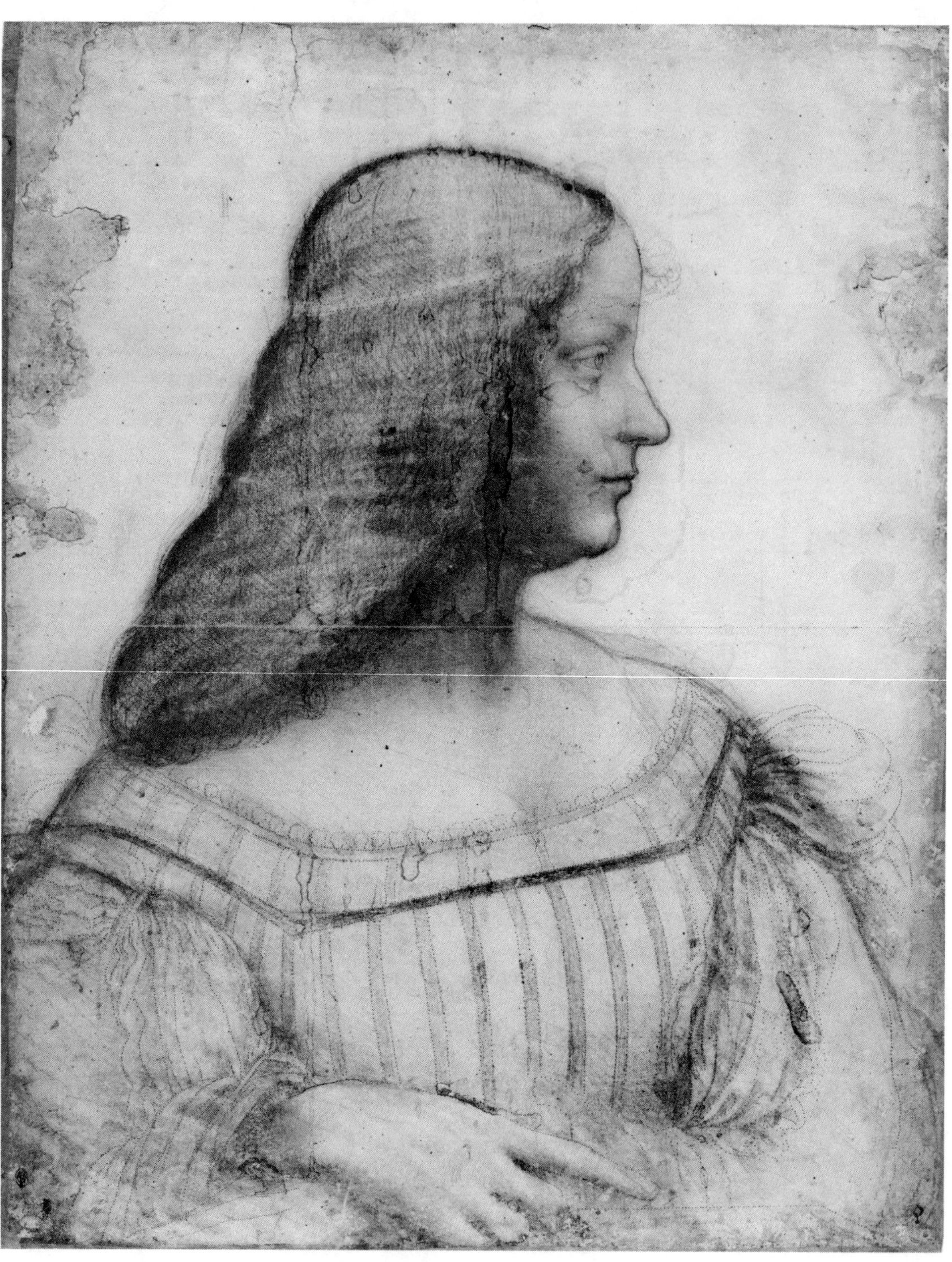

time on preliminary drawings than on the paintings to which they were supposed to lead, and he was notorious for leaving works half finished. He even neglected to determine in advance whether the experimental technique he deployed when painting an important fresco would result in a lasting painting. In the *Codex Atlanticus*, Leonardo also advises artists not to imitate each other,[24] warning that "the art of painting declines from age to age and is lost if painters have no other guide than what was done before them."[25] Elsewhere, he inveighs against painters who do what Shakespeare urges his lover to do—make copies of themselves. "It is the greatest defect in painters to repeat the same movements and the same faces and draperies in a composition and to make most of the faces resemble their author."[26]

Leonardo's ideal artist is neither an imitator nor a transmitter. He is, rather, a receiver. This is to some degree a given, because to perceive is to receive external images. "If you look at the sun or another luminous body, and then close your eyes, you will see it again inside the eye for a long time. This is proof that the image entered it," Leonardo writes in the *Codex Atlanticus.*[27] However, the ideal artist receives the world, instead of the work of his predecessors. He also takes on the "colors" of what he perceives—and because his psyche is as capacious as the maternal laps in the drapery studies, there is no limit to the number of things he can embrace in this way. "The mind of the painter should liken itself to a mirror which always takes on the color of the thing it reflects and be filled by as many images as there are objects before it," Leonardo writes in a famous passage in *Codex Ashburnham 1.*[28]

A different kind of relationality emerged as one stepped into the first room of Leonardo's drawings, not just because of the attribution difficulties posed by the drapery studies, and their emphasis on maternal laps, but also because the figures in them were headless, and therefore incapable of establishing their existence through thought.[29] The room reserved for Leonardo's "portraits"[30] posed an even more explicit challenge to the notion of individuality. Portraiture was born along with the individual, and has traditionally served as one of its primary supports.[31] All but one of the works in this exhibition area, though, had generic titles, like *Head of a Young Woman*, and the one that did identify its model—*Portrait of Isabelle d'Este*—constitutes the preliminary sketch for a portrait, rather than an actual one. This latter also has the ghostliness—and flatness—of the images that appeared on Coleman's editing monitors, and it communicates the rank rather than the subjectivity of its model. Through both its refusal to interiorize and its adherence to what Daniel Arasse calls "the traditional, fixed pose in profile" (399), *Isabelle d'Este* points backward in time, to the princely portrait, rather than forward, to psychological portraiture.

Leonardo was as resolute in his refusal to articulate the human form as he was to psychologize it. In a passage printed on one of the walls in the room devoted to the *Madonna of the Rocks*, he cautions young artists against beginning their paintings with clearly delineated drawings: "Avoid profiles or sharp edges for objects," he writes. "Do not make the contours of your forms of a different color than that of the background itself against which they are set; that is, do not detach your figure from the background by means of a dark outline."[32] Leonardo adhered rigorously to his own advice. "In the mid-1490's," Pietro C. Marani writes, he "used the Florentine metalpoint technique of drawing on prepared pink or blue paper less and less often," and eventually "abandoned it almost entirely in favor of black or red chalks, which allowed him to achieve greater softness and chiaroscuro effects with heightened atmospheric qualities and *sfumato*."[33] Leonardo also frequently covered a sheet of paper with competing versions of the same figure, drew on the recto and verso of the same sheet of paper, and positioned forms so close to the edges of his drawing surface that they seemed to spill over into the surrounding space, thereby affirming the boundlessness of the world over and against the narrow confines of the frame. As Carlo Vecce suggests, leaving things unfinished was another way of denying the boundary between "life" and "art."[34]

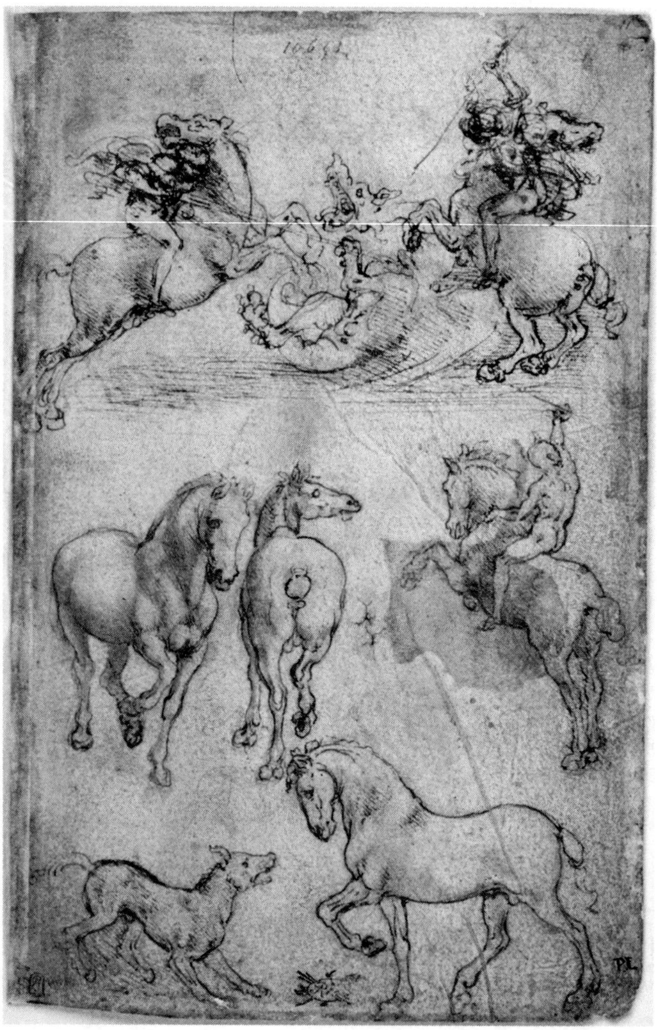

Leonardo carried over the same principles into his paintings. He smudged the outlines of his figures, so that it was impossible to say where they ended and their surroundings began; used sketches he had produced in preparation for one painting as the basis for others; and generated two different versions of several of his most famous paintings. He also pulled the rug out from underneath Albertian perspective by pointing out how different the same thing can look in the morning and at night, or when the weather is good and when it is bad, and by suggesting that objects transmit light rays not in one direction but rather in a dizzying number of different directions. The passage in which Leonardo advances the last of these propositions provides a startling contrast to the one used as the Louvre wall text. Far from being the "lord" and "master" of the universe, the painter is emphatically in the world. He can look in only one direction at a time, and see only one side of a phenomenal form—the side it turns toward him. He must also wait for a ray of light to carry this image to him. "Any opaque body will fill the surrounding air with an infinite number of images representing it completely everywhere and at each point by virtue of the infinite number of pyramids filling this air," Leonardo writes, "[and] each pyramid, formed by long rays, encloses an infinite number of pyramids, and each one contains all of them in its power."[35]

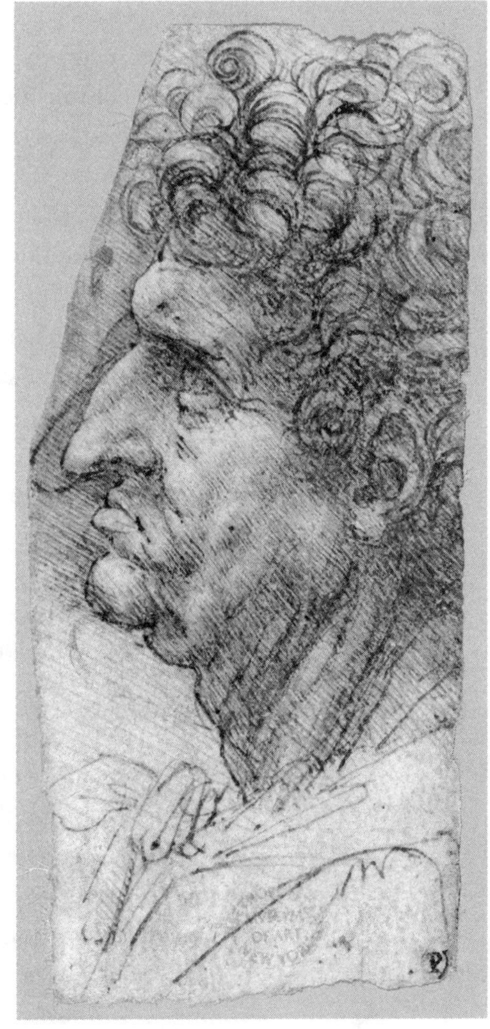

The group of drawings that the curators of the Louvre exhibition called the "grotesques" posed a further challenge to the notion of individuality, both because they constitute "types" and because they insist upon aspects of human existence that are inimical to the self. The latter aspires to ideality, as well as uniqueness and autonomy, and whenever it believes that it has realized this goal, it attempts to maintain the desired form by halting movement and stopping time. In his caricatures, Leonardo does the opposite; he focuses on what escapes ideality (exaggerated features) and destabilizes form (human emotions, the aging process).

The curators mitigated this challenge to identity by hanging Leonardo's "grotesques" in a corridor-like space in the middle of the room devoted to the imitators, and his "portraits" in one of the two exhibition areas onto which the same room opened. However, they also devoted the second of the two adjoining exhibition areas to the painting whose spirit could already be felt in the drapery studies: the *Virgin and Child with Saint Anne*. In so doing, they helped to clarify both why Leonardo privileged reception over creation and why he never really succumbed to the dream of a unique and autonomous "self." They also offered an implicit critique of, and suggested an alternative to, paternal transmission

LIKE THE LARGER EXHIBITION, the *Virgin and Child with Saint Anne* brings together three generations of the same "family." However, it does not do so in order to secure power and privilege on one side of the gender divide; indeed, it does not even acknowledge that there *is* a gender divide. Nor does it convene Mary, her mother, and her child in order to demonstrate the influence exercised by an earlier generation over later ones, or the triumph of innovation over precedent. The three generations in the *Virgin and Child with Saint Anne* are contemporary with each other; Saint Anne is only a little older than her daughter, and the Virgin Mary occupies the position simultaneously of a small child and a mother.

Even more surprisingly, although each of the human figures in the painting constitutes a distinct person, none of them is an individual. The outstretched arms and spread legs of the child echo those of his mother; the position of the lamb, that of the child; and the Virgin Mary's lap, the one on which she is sitting. The Madonna and Saint Anne are also literally joined at the hip, and although Jesus is positioned at a distance from his mother, he remains connected to her, just as the lamb is to him. It is impossible to say whether he has just climbed down from her lap or is about to return to it, but this poses no crisis of interpretation, since each of these actions is so clearly the prelude to the other.

As the Louvre exhibition made clear, Leonardo saw these kinds of family resemblances everywhere he looked. I say "family resemblances" because similarity signified "ontological connectedness" for the Florentine artist; if two things shared only one trait, they belonged to each other at the most profound level of their being. Every phenomenal form corresponded in this way with many others, and those with yet others. As a result of this vast latticework of resemblances, the world was one single, throbbing organism. "Feathers grow upon birds and change every year; hair grows upon animals and changes every year, except some parts, such as the hair of the whiskers of lions and cats, and others," Leonardo writes in an extraordinary passage in the *Codex Leicester*. "[G]rass grows in the fields and leaves on the trees and in large part are renewed each year; therefore, we may say that the earth has a germinating soul, and that its flesh is the soil; its bones are the successive strata of rocks of which the mountains are made up, its cartilage is the tufa stone, and its blood the running water; the lake of blood that surrounds the heart is the ocean, and its breathing . . . is the ebb and flow of the sea."[36]

But if everything is already part of a single great organism, why should it be necessary for the painter to "take on" the "colors of the world"? And with what mental faculty would he do so, given that "self" and "analogy" are opposed categories? We have arrived at the richest—albeit the most seemingly paradoxical—aspect of Leonardo's thought. Although the resemblances that link one thing to another predate us, will remain in place long after we have departed, and override the category of the individual, it is only within the human psyche that they can grow into analogies. We do not create the world, but we are the site of its realization.

The idea that phenomenal forms address something within us that they need in order to live has surfaced over and over again in the centuries separating us from Leonardo. Two of its most articulate spokesmen—Valéry and Merleau-Ponty—also developed their own accounts of this exchange in dialogue with the Florentine artist. As we have already seen, in an important passage in "Introduction to the Method of Leonardo," Valéry attributes the brilliance of the latter's drawings and paintings to his extraordinary sensitivity to the affinities linking one thing to another, rather than to his encyclopedic knowledge or his aesthetic virtuosity, and Merleau-Ponty endorses this part of Valéry's argument in "Cézanne's Doubt."

Valéry offers two different explanations for why Leonardo was so sensitive to the resemblances between things. The first is that there is an ideational counterpart for every phenomenal form within the human mind. Some people, like Leonardo and Bonaparte, are able to activate these mental images, but in others they lie dormant. The more available a given psyche is for this purpose, the more impersonal it becomes. Leonardo's psyche was so open to the world that it lacked all "particularity."[37] In "Notes and Digression," he imputes a similar impersonality to himself. "I have wandered so far into Leonardo that for the moment I do not know how to come back to myself," he writes there. ". . . Well! Any road will lead me there; that is the definition of the self."[38]

In several other passages, though, Valéry suggests that the world attempts to "think itself"[39] in us, and that what it seeks to mobilize for this purpose is the specificity of the psyche, not universal archetypes. It initiates this thought process by conveying an image of itself to us, and we respond by linking the image to similar images from our mnemonic reserve, thereby expanding its semantic range and animating it affectively. The exchange I have just described, which allows us to hear the prefix "co" in the word "correspondence," has an energizing effect upon both us and the world.

In the passage in which Valéry valorizes impersonality, he suggests that the artist communicates with the world by vanishing into it, but in the passage in which he stresses the importance of psychic particularity, he conceptualizes the human mind as a receptacle, just as Leonardo does in his advice to the painter. Valéry also provides a detailed description of the mental operations through which we receive, think, and finally energize the world. "At first the process is undergone passively, almost unconsciously, as a vessel lets itself be filled: there is a feeling of slow and pleasurable circulation. Later, one's interest being awakened, one assigns new values to things that had seemed closed and irreducible; one adds to them, takes more pleasure in particular features, finds expression for these; and what happens is like the restitution of an energy that our senses had received. Soon the energy will alter the environment in its turn, employing to this end the conscious thought of a person."[40]

Valéry never commits himself fully to either account of analogy, but as Merleau-Ponty points put, Leonardo did not suffer from the same indecisiveness. His analogies always had their origin in "the situation into which his birth and childhood had put him."[41] Merleau-Ponty also suggests that there is, finally, no other way in which the psyche can communicate with the world: "Becoming a pure consciousness is just another way of taking a stand in relation to the world and other people. . . . There can be no consciousness that is not sustained by its primordial involvement in life and by the manner of this involvement."[42] But although each of us leads a singular life, not all of us put our psychic particularity at the disposal of the world. If we want to provide the soil within which its analogies can bloom, we must do more than live; we must assume our history. It was because of his readiness to do this that Leonardo was able to "take on" the "colors" of the world.

Merleau-Ponty bases these claims on Freud's essay "Leonardo da Vinci and a Memory of His Childhood." His reliance on this text is startling, not just because of its historical errors,[43] but also because it pathologizes Leonardo's relationship with his mother. Freud's argument goes something like this: Leonardo was the bastard son of a notary (Ser Piero) and a peasant woman (Caterina). Although he was eventually taken into his father's house, and raised by his father's wife, he spent the early years of his life with Caterina. Because Leonardo was fatherless during this formative period, he became passionately attached to his mother (90–92). This relationship did not diminish in intensity when he moved into Ser Piero's house, because his separation from Caterina awakened a deep yearning in him. Leonardo's new living arrangement also strengthened his attachment to the mother in another way: it provided him with a second source of maternal approbation—that offered by Ser Piero's wife (113).

Leonardo's love for Caterina survived the castration crisis as well, Freud argues, because he devised an ingenious way of covering over her anatomical "lack." By tenderly nurturing a series of boys, just as she had earlier nurtured him, he refashioned her in his own image, thereby equipping her with the missing appendage. The smiles on the faces of the *Mona Lisa* and the two women in *Virgin and Child with Saint Anne* attest to the longevity of Leonardo's attachment to his mother, which stunted his sexual development and inhibited him as an artist (63–107).

But although "Leonardo da Vinci and a Memory of His Childhood" is incompatible at the level of its larger argument with the one presented in "Cézanne's Doubt," Freud does indeed lay the groundwork for the claims Merleau-Ponty will later make about the artist. He devotes a whole chapter to the *Virgin and Child with Saint Anne*, and he spends most of it exploring the similarities between the painting and Leonardo's life. "Leonardo's childhood was remarkable in precisely the same way as this picture," Freud writes. "He had had two mothers: first, his true mother, Caterina . . . and then a young and tender stepmother, his father's wife, Donna Albiera. . . . [By condensing these two figures] into a composite unity, the design of 'St. Anne with Two Others' took shape for him. The maternal figure that is farther away from the boy—the grandmother—corresponds to the earlier and true mother, Caterina, in its appearance and special relation to the boy" (113). This passage helps us understand what Merleau-Ponty means when he says that Leonardo assumed "the situation into which his birth and childhood had put him" (73–74).

Freud's interpretation of *Virgin and Child with Saint Anne* is also an important corrective to the story he recounts in *Beyond the Pleasure Principle*.[44] The boy in the painting is approximately the same age as little Ernst was when he began playing the game with the spool, and like the latter, he is in the process of distinguishing himself from the mother. But instead of turning this distinction into a repudiation, he does what we all should do when we are separated from someone we love: he corresponds with her. Because he remains connected to her through the lifeline of analogy, every step away from her is also a step toward her, and every "*fort*" a joyful "*da*."[45] And rather than focusing his affections on a single object, these affinities point outward, to the world; the blue of the Madonna's tunic finds its echo in the sky, the mountains, and even the lamb, and the reds and browns in her dress are repeated in the cliff on which she and her mother sit.

Unlike paternal transmission, which plays out in linear time, the analogies that connect everything to everything else in *Virgin and Child with Saint Anne* are reversible. The mother gives birth to her son, both formally and biologically, and he revitalizes the gestures he receives from her by rhyming with them instead of repeating them. And rather than killing off the good-for-everything mother, and replacing her with one who is good for nothing, the son leaves her in her exalted position in the background but directs his attention downward, to her earthly analogue. Although this second mother bears a strong resemblance to the first, from whom she "descends," she differs in one crucial respect: she is emphatically embodied.

This would seem the moment to note how central the principle of gravity is to the organization of *Virgin and Child with Saint Anne.* Because the horizon is so high, only the upper third of the painting is devoted to the "celestial," and even here the earth intrudes, through the tree on the right. The reiterative logic of the painting also unfolds from the upper left to the lower right, i.e., via a falling motion. It could of course be argued that this downward movement is internal to Christianity itself, which recuperates it; Jesus descends to earth, but only to return to heaven and make this ascent possible for mankind as well. But nothing in the painting speaks to the second half of this narrative. Both Saint Anne and the Madonna look downward, rather than upward, and the final term in the painting's unfolding is not even human. The infant Jesus and his two mothers also form a trinity—one that challenges both the primacy and the generative powers of God the Father.

If we were reading a book by D. W. Winnicott, instead of looking at a painting by Leonardo, the figure who initiates the fall into finitude would be the "good-enough-mother."[46] But the *Virgin and Child with Saint Anne* is concerned less with the limits to which we need to accommodate ourselves than with the opening that these limits create. Because we are finite, this extraordinary painting shows us, our capacity for relationality is infinite. Few subjects ever manage to forgive the mother for not satisfying their infantile demands, and far fewer to see what a gift that was. But for those who do understand their limits to be the doorway to relationality, the mother ceases to be "good enough," and becomes, quite simply, "human."

AT FIRST GLANCE, Coleman—like Valéry—appeared to have wandered so far into Leonardo as to have lost all particularity. Not only did he make his intervention indissociable from the larger exhibition, but he also based every one of its components on photographs of Leonardo's work. But the images that appeared on Coleman's screens were not reproductions of an original; they related to Leonardo's drawings and paintings in the same way in which Leonardo related to the world—through reversible and potentially transformative analogies.

These analogies also extended from one end of the exhibition to the other. Directly across from the door leading into the entryway was an area partitioned off for an interactive viewing of Leonardo's notebooks. Museumgoers could sit in front of video monitors and "read" the artist's notebooks, turning the pages with a click of the mouse. The Louvre architect created this area by carving a section out of the rectangular space devoted to the Léonardesques, thereby making it a strange, liminal zone—exterior to the aesthetic but interior to the exhibition. By displaying Leonardo's notebooks on high-tech computer screens and placing them in this liminal space, the curators of the exhibition invited the viewer to return to a moment prior to the division of art from science, education, warfare, or even life itself—to the moment when the universe still pulsed with family resemblances. The images on Coleman's editing monitors had the same hybrid status as the drawings in Leonardo's notebooks, and corresponded with the computers on which the latter were displayed and the space in which they were housed.

During one of my visits to the room with the large-screen projection, I sat down behind the huge projector. Its boxlike structure removed a piece of Coleman's *Last Supper* from my field of vision that was reminiscent of the one earlier cut out of Leonardo's mural. And this analogy linked the two-dimensional space of the digital *Last Supper* to the three-dimensional space in which I was sitting, like the one connecting the painting to the refectory. (Since no one eats in this room anymore, the last of these analogies has lapsed, but Goethe revives it for us in a review of Giuseppe Bossi's study of *The Last Supper*: "It must, at the hour of the meal, have been an interesting sight, to view the tables of the prior and Christ, thus facing each other, as two counterparts, and the monks at their heads, enclosed between them. For this reason it was consonant with the judgment of the painter to take the tables of the monks as models; and there is no doubt that the table-cloth, with its pleated folds, its stripes and figures, and even the knots, at the corners, was borrowed from the laundry of the convent. Dishes, plates, cups, and other utensils were probably likewise copied from those, which the monks made use of.")[47]

The four sets of editing monitors corresponded in a similar way both with each other and with the larger exhibition. Three hung in the room devoted to the Léonardesques—one on a wall between two of the facing mirrors, just inside the door on the right; another in a more or less equivalent position on the other side of the room; and the last on the facing wall. The first set of editing monitors displayed digital renditions of the sketches Leonardo made for a machine to be used in the staging of Poliziano's play, *Orfeo*; the second showed comparable images of the recto and verso of an extraordinary drawing, *A Cloudburst of Material Possessions*; and the third analogous images of a Leonardo painting, *The Musician*. The fourth set of editing monitors was situated in the "Portraits" room, and showed digital versions of two other Leonardo drawings, *Interior of a Skull* and *Divided Skull*.

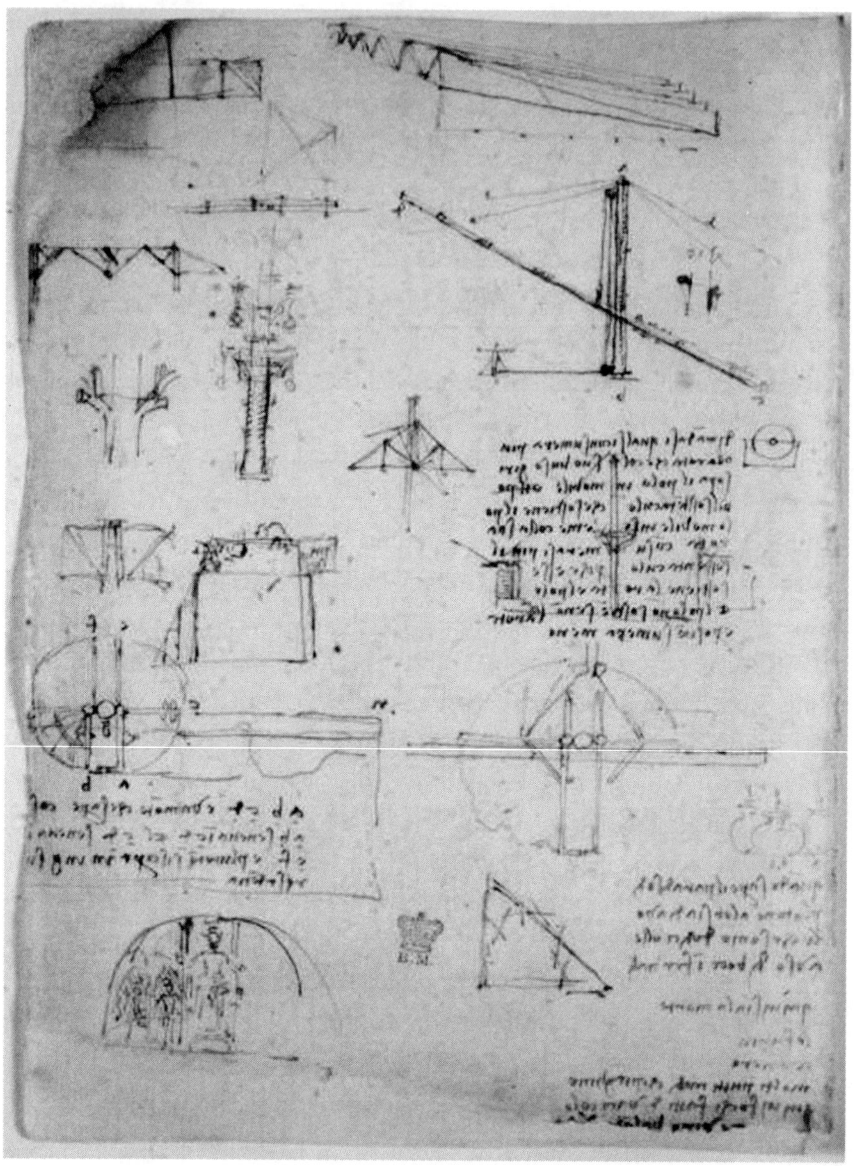

A dizzying series of associations linked the monitors referencing the Orpheus machine to those referencing *The Musician.* When Leonardo moved from Florence to Milan, the city where he painted *The Musician,* he brought with him a lute, which he presented to Ludovico Sforzo on behalf of Lorenzo the Magnificent. He played the instrument for its new owner, who was enchanted by his skill. A young friend accompanied Leonardo during this performance, and later played the part of the eponymous musician in a production of Poliziano's *Orfeo.* This friend—Atalante Miglioretti—may also have been the model for *The Musician.*[48]

As we have already seen, although Poliziano de-Christianizes the myth of Orpheus and Eurydice, he feminizes death and cordons off Hades from the earth. The machine Leonardo designed for the staging of the play undoes both of these things, since instead of lowering Orpheus to Hades and then returning him to earth, it elevates Hades to the earth. Coleman foregrounded this dimension of Leonardo's machine by devoting the third set of editing monitors to drawings whose primary subject is mortality: *Interior of a Skull* and *Divided*

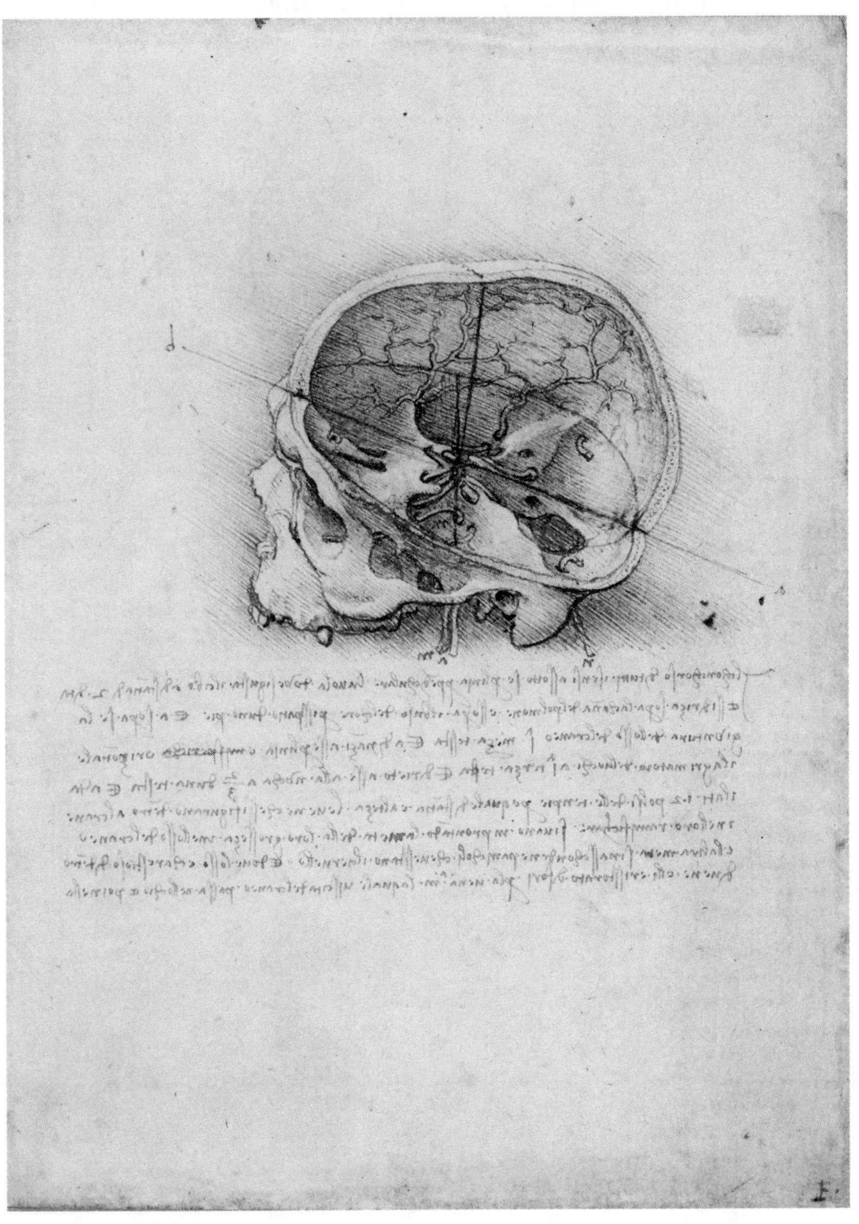

Skull. In the first, the Florentine artist slices open a human skull in order to locate the *sensus communis*—the point at which all of the senses were assumed to converge. He identifies this site by means of two intersecting lines. In the second drawing, which occupies the other side of the same sheet of paper, Leonardo again slices a human skull in half, this time vertically rather than horizontally.

Although *Interior of a Skull* and *Divided Skull* are two of the most beautiful and philosophically resonant drawings Leonardo ever produced, they are not topically remarkable. The Florentine artist dissected many corpses, and produced detailed anatomical drawings of them. He also accompanied some of their beneficiaries to their place of execution, in a spirit of collaboration

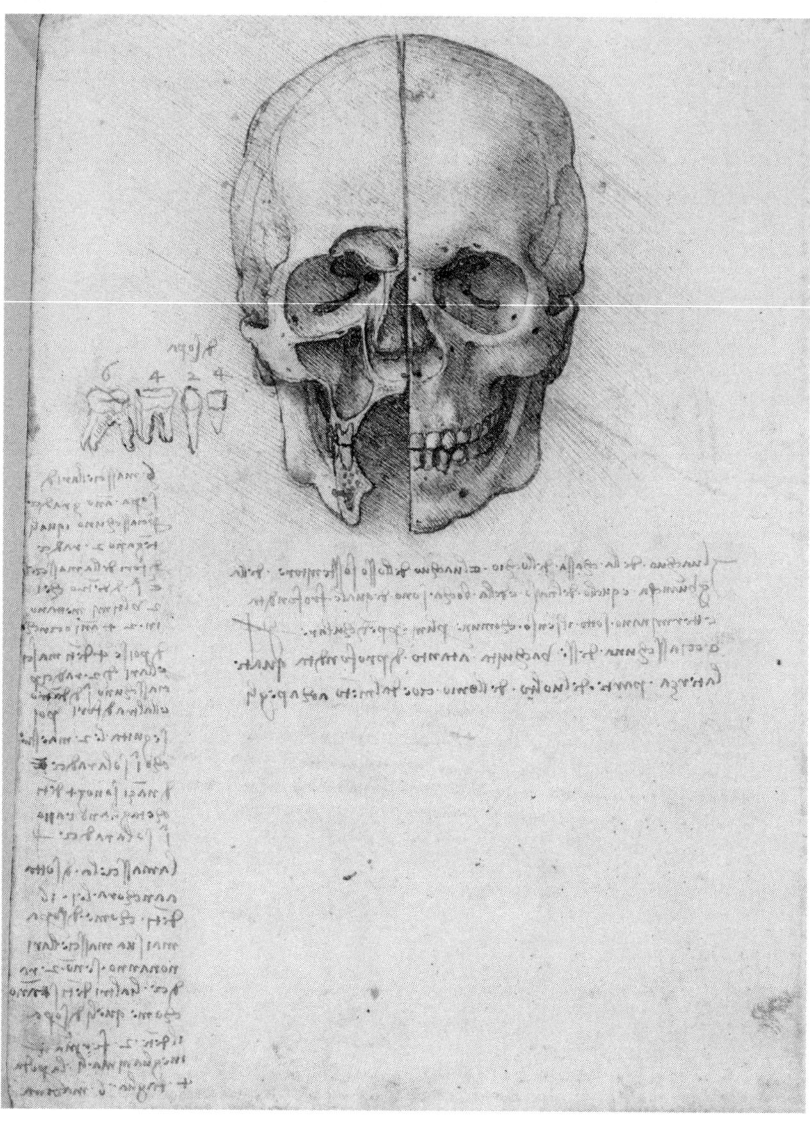

that would be unthinkable for us today. Leonardo was fascinated by the aging process, and what it did to the human body. Like Shakespeare, he also had a keen sense of its leveling force. "Even if he was as big as our world," he writes in *Manuscript F*, "[man] would only be a dot in the universe . . . [since] men are mortal, putrescible and corruptible in their graves."[49]

By placing his digital renditions of *Interior of a Skull* and *Divided Skull* in the "Portraits" room, Coleman helped the viewer to see that mortality is as inimical to the notion of the individual as it is to social distinctions. He drove this point home by attaching his versions of these drawings and his digital *Musician* to opposite sides of the same wall—by making them the recto and verso of the same subjectivity. But the spectator did not even have to enter the "Portraits" room to see the bone beneath the flesh, because it was already visible on the monitors devoted to *The Musician*. The figure in Leonardo's painting wears a red cap and a brown stole, both of which have a blocklike solidity. He also holds two other objects that stake out a place for themselves within the physical world: a white quill and a cream-colored sheet of music. However, his tunic is black, and all that prevents his torso from disappearing into the black background are the two panels of his brown stole. Parts of the quill and the sheet of music are also diaphanous.

Coleman heightened this figure's spectral qualities by making his digital version of the painting black and white. His work also occupied only part of the screen on which it appeared; hovering in the nowhere of virtual space, it was more a "phantom" than a "real" image. The fourth monitor in this little cluster of editing screens was completely blank, and when I returned from it to the digital painting, the musician seemed to melt away. This created the space within which a different kind of image could emerge: that represented by the *Virgin and Child with Saint Anne.*

Since each time I visited the Leonardo exhibition, I entered it through the door on the right, I always encountered the three sets of editing monitors I have just described prior to seeing this extraordinary painting. But in order to complete my viewing of the show, I had to return to the room devoted to the imitators and proceed from it to the room with Leonardo's sketches of the Battle of Anghiari and then to the space reserved for Coleman's large-screen projection of *The Last Supper*. Just before leaving the room devoted to the Léonardesques, I encountered the fourth set of editing monitors, which hung to the right of the door. The drawing that they digitally reprised, *A Cloudburst of Material Possessions*, shows a cascade of objects falling like water from the heavens, many of which are military in nature. It therefore seemed to presage the contents of the next room, and so to mark the resumption of the Oedipal battle. An adjacent

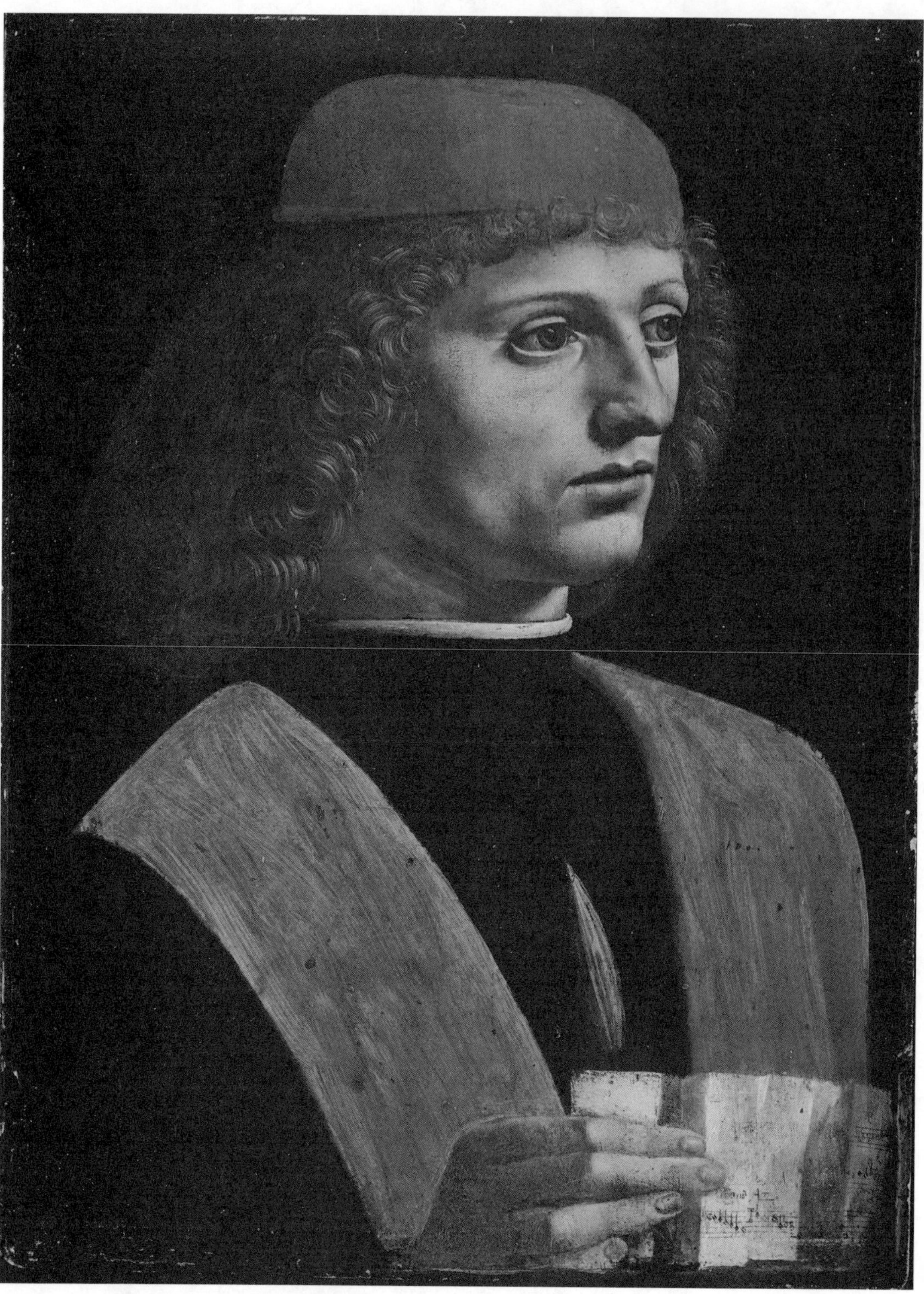

See also Plate 12 in color insert.

screen displayed a digital image of the reverse side of this drawing, onto which Leonardo had jotted a shopping list. Juxtaposing the recto and verso of *A Cloudburst of Material Possessions* seemed to be Coleman's way of underscoring the intimate relationship between warfare and commerce.

The large-screen projection offered more grist for this reading. Mary is conspicuously absent from the scene depicted in *The Last Supper*, and this farewell meal anticipates the moment in which she is most dramatically written out of the biblical narrative: the Crucifixion. John is the only one of the four Gospels even to situate her in the crowd that gathers at the foot of the cross, and it places her there in order to strip her of her status as the mother of God. "When Jesus saw his mother and the disciple whom he loved standing next to her," this passage reads, "he said to his mother, 'Woman, here is your son.' Then he said to the disciple, 'Here is your mother.'"[50]

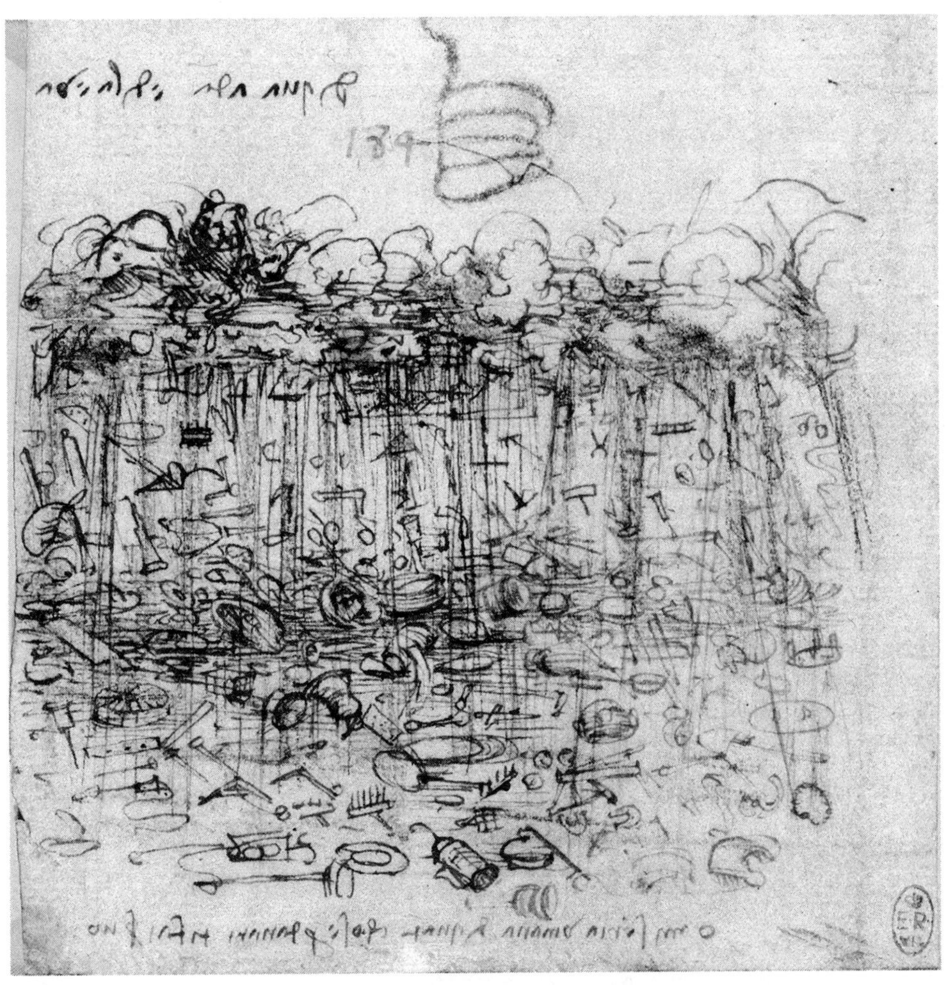

But when I returned to *A Cloudburst of Material Possessions* in the hope of finding out why the father should once again have gained the upper hand, I noticed that although the cascade of objects does indeed contain weapons, it also contains many domestic implements. Like the other works reprised by Coleman, it therefore opens up a place for death within everyday life. The primary subject of this sketch is *motion*, not warfare or domestic existence. The same is true of Leonardo's drawings of the Battle of Anghiari; they are studies of bodies convulsed with movement, not violence. The curators drew attention to this aspect of the drawings by hanging them in the same exhibition space as Leonardo's drawings of windstorms, and *Leda and the Swan*.

IN ONE OF HIS PRELIMINARY SKETCHES for *The Last Supper*, Leonardo recapitulates the downward arc of the *Virgin and Child with Saint Anne*. This arc did not find its way into the actual painting, but the force it represented did, both thematically and formally. There is an air of finality about the title, which evokes the meal served to a prisoner before his execution. The painting itself is also under the sign of mortality. Because working with the fast-drying paint conventionally used in frescoes would have forced him to make quick, irrevocable decisions, Leonardo relied on an experimental technique when painting *The Last Supper*: tempura on two layers of dry preparatory ground. The materials did not adhere properly to the wall, and the painting began almost immediately to decompose.[51]

Over the years, there have been many attempts to halt this process, either by cleaning, restoring, or repainting it, or by reproducing it in other, less perishable materials, like ceramic.[52] This preservation frenzy has continued unabated to the present. *The Last Supper* was recently restored yet again, and a high-tech laser system has now been installed to prevent it from disintegrating further. This system monitors the activity of the ground on which the Church of Santa Maria della Grazie stands, and immobilizes the mural wall at the first sign of a tremor.[53] But in spite of all of the efforts that have been made to arrest its decomposition, *The Last Supper* has continued to crumble.

The assumption on the part of the painting's restorers has always been that there is a "true" version of *The Last Supper*, and that is the one that sprang to life when Leonardo applied his last dab of paint to the refectory wall. The Florentine artist also intended the painting to *last*—to survive the vicissitudes of time, like every other masterpiece. Each one of the changes it has subsequently undergone has therefore been both accidental and a corruption of its essence. The goal of the restorer should be to undo these corruptions and recover as much of the original painting as possible. But although each new restoration initially seems to achieve this goal, it subsequently becomes yet another of the corruptions from which the painting must be liberated.

Bernard Berenson praised Mauro Pellicioli's 1953 restoration by saying: "I felt that many centuries of restorations had been stripped away in the end, and that I was engrossed in looking at Leonardo's true painting, deteriorated for centuries, but no longer disfigured by incompetent hands."[54] Marani exposes the

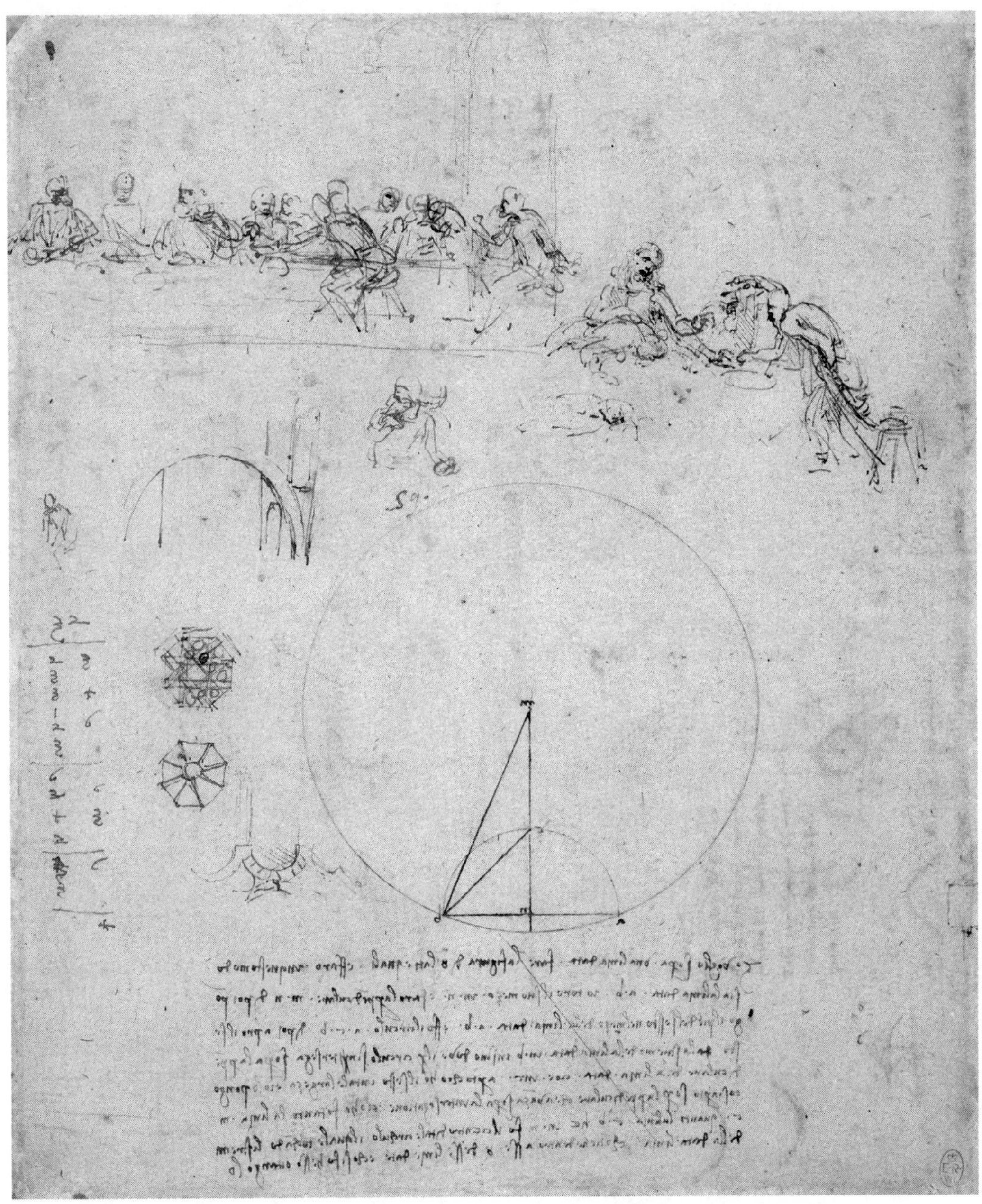

absurdity of this logic in "Leonardo's *Last Supper*,"[55] but he also participates in it. "Today we know that Pellicioli's restoration, although admirable, was not . . . definitive . . . because Pellicioli did not remove all of the old repaint," he writes near the end of his essay. "[Now, though, with the completion of the Pinin Brambilla Barcilon restoration,] the shadowy crevices, the luminous drapery, the plastic power of the faces, the suspended arms and the expressiveness of the hands have been unveiled before our eyes, as if immersed in an atmospheric continuum" (52). Marani also imputes to the newly unveiled painting a similar capacity for disclosing the real. "We again see the gestures, the gazes, and almost hear the words of Christ resonating in the air," he exclaims later in the same passage.

This might seem the moment to point out that *The Last Supper* is only a representation, and its restorations mere representations of this representation. However, the fresco doesn't function like a representation—not only because it corresponds with the space in which it is situated but also because of its instability. Leo Steinberg observes that the energy of the painting "expands into the space we ourselves occupy" and that "perspective . . . seems to reverse itself."[56] Both he and Arasse also comment on the compositional agitation caused by all of the pointing fingers, and the "temporal sfumata" created through multiple durations, and the co-presence of different moments in the Christian narrative.[57] Leonardo's mural is also *ontologically* unstable; it is constantly dying and being reborn in a slightly different guise, and its many variants relate to each other the same way the Madonna relates to Saint Anne and her son, and *The Musician* to the artist's sketches for the Orpheus machine—through analogy.

Leonardo was not the first to take an interest in the comings and goings of the phenomenal world. Ovid pursues the thesis that "every form takes visible shape as it wanders" from one end of *The Metamorphoses* to the other.[58] However, it was not until analogy ceased to be regarded as a divine prerogative that it was possible to see this wandering as something other than a corruption or degradation. Few modern subjects have been willing to exercise this new capacity, because it is so threatening to identity. If things are constantly falling into bits and pieces, and being put back together in a slightly different way, then the same must be true of human beings, because the ego is "first and foremost a bodily ego."[59] Leonardo opened his ears to the lesson that his age had to teach him because he saw that death is not the enemy of form but rather what animates it. He also knew this to be as true of us as it is of the phenomenal world; all vital subjects are constantly emerging out of the ashes of their own extinction—the same, yet different.

Coleman corresponded with this aspect of Leonardo's work by constantly changing the images in his large-screen projection and by using computation to absolutize the concepts of absence and presence.[60] When the Louvre exhibition ended, most of Leonardo's work was removed from the walls of the museum, but it did not vanish. It was absent there, but present elsewhere—in a private collection, another museum, or a vault in the Louvre. However, when the Louvre stopped showing the digital *Last Supper*, the projection ceased to exist—and this was also true of each image as soon as it left the screen. If we had cut open the computer at any point during the exhibition, we would have been unable to locate anything it permitted us to see, because when a digital image disappears, it decays into the "dust" of numerical data. The data could of course be used to create a computationally identical image, but that image would still be *new*.

The ever-changing numbers at the bottom of each image in the large-screen projection indicated how close the computer was to completing the next image. This process was live; it happened in real time, before our very eyes. But the escalating numbers also helped us to see that until this image-in-the-making was visible, it would not exist—that its life would begin only when it appeared on the screen, and last only as long as it remained there. Since Coleman laid his digital *Last Supper* to rest when the Leonardo exhibition ended, he might seem to have concluded this *fort/da* game with a resounding "gone." It will not be long, though, before an analogous work emerges, and when it does, so will its human partner. Her name will be Caterina, Mary, or perhaps Eurydice.

7 Photography by Other Means

Our life, it can be said, is a muscle strong enough to contract the whole of historical time. Or, to put it differently, the genuine conception of historical time rests entirely on the image of redemption.

—Walter Benjamin

The past has left images of itself in literary texts, images comparable to those which are imprinted by light on a photosensitive page. The future alone possesses developers strong enough to reveal the image in all its details.

—André Monglond

IN A 1986 CONVERSATION with Gerhard Richter, Benjamin Buchloh suggested that there is something contradictory about the fact that Richter produces figurative as well as abstract paintings. The artist responded: "I don't really know what you mean by the contradiction between figurative and abstract painting."[1] This is an astonishing claim, particularly given the fact that Richter bases his figurative paintings on photographs. What is abstraction, if not one long assault on figuration? And what is photography, if not the primary medium through which figuration has fought back?

An abstract painting, we have been taught, is autonomous. It does not stand for something else; it is, rather, a thing unto itself. Its essence also resides in its material properties. It helps us to locate this essence by turning insistently back upon itself—by being reflexive, or self-conscious. Finally, an abstract painting is flat; it abolishes the perspectival illusion of three-dimensional space. The photographic image, on the other hand, offers a representation of something else. It generally does so iconically—by providing a "likeness" of the latter. But even when a photograph does not offer an intelligible image, it points stubbornly outward, since it depends for its existence on the transmission of light between a material form and the camera. Last, but not least, the photographic image draws on the system of perspective in order to project a three-dimensional space. As a result, it often seems to be "transparent"—to open directly onto the world.

Because of the radicality of these divergences, one is inclined to dismiss Richter's claim as a simple provocation. But the painter is not sparring with the critic; as his artistic practice consistently shows, he really doesn't see abstract painting and photographic figuration as contradictory forms. This is not because he is blind to what distinguishes them from each other, or ignorant of the battles that have been fought on their behalf. It is, rather, because differences do not translate into oppositions for Richter. He has a profound aversion to binary formulations, both within the domain of politics and within that of art, and he cannot encounter one without attempting to dismantle it. In 1961 he crossed the boundary separating one half of a bitterly divided country from the other—a boundary that in the same year hardened into a wall. And in the early sixties, he began bridging another divide: that separating abstract painting from photographic figuration. He did so by painting canvases based on photographs, and then—while the pigment was still wet—working over their surfaces with a squeegee.

The works that resulted from this two-step process, which Richter calls his "photo pictures," are often experienced by their viewers as "blurs." This is in part because they soften outlines and eliminate many of the details available in the original image. But the indeterminacy of many of Richter's photo pictures also has another source. They bring together abstract painting and photographic figuration without abolishing the distinction between them. They are consequently invitations to see double. Unholy as this alliance may seem, Richter was not the first to bless it. Warhol married abstract painting to photographic figuration one year before the German artist painted the first of his photo pictures.[2] The double vision for which Warhol is most famous, however, is ironic in nature.[3] In early silk screens like *192 One Dollar Bills* (1962) and *Thirty Are Better Than One* (1963), the American artist uses painting to establish a bemused distance from photography, and photography to do the same with painting. And although this is a reversible relationship, and one in which the partners can switch positions at a dizzying speed, it is not democratic; one term always passes ironic judgment on the other. Richter went through a brief phase as a pop artist, but he was always a reluctant ironist, and he soon stopped passing this—or any other kind—of judgment. The duality at the heart of most of his photo pictures is of a completely different order. It is non-hierarchical—a relationship between equals. Each also points toward, and finds itself within, the other.

Richter describes how this relationship works in his photo pictures in a note from 1965: "Like the photograph I make a statement about real space, but when I do so I am painting; and this gives rise to a special kind of space that arises from the interpenetration and tension between the thing represented and the pictorial space."[4] The first version of *Motor Boat*, a photo picture from the same year, provides a particularly striking example of this "interpenetration" and "tension." The source photograph shows three women and one man speeding across a lake in a motorboat. Their clothing indicates that they are wealthy and on holiday, and their gestures and smiles show how delighted they are to be rich vacationers. But their emotional display is so theatrical that it is ripe for parody, and Richter does not fail to take advantage of this in the painting he produces from it. With his blurring utensil, he broadens the smiles on the faces of the human figures, transforming them into caricatures of themselves.[5]

The attentive viewer is likely to remain standing in front of this canvas for a long time after she "gets" this "joke," though, because irony is not its main order of business. In the photograph with which the painting is in dialogue,

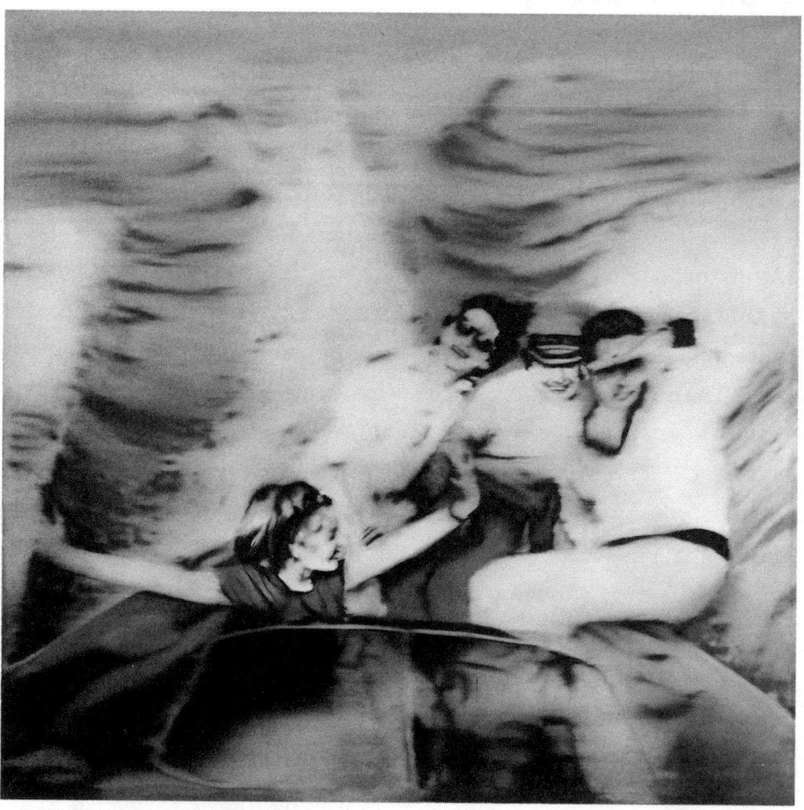

the choppy waves produced by the boat stretch out behind it, as a kind of receding prospect. They thus convey a powerful sense of three-dimensionality. The waves also have a prominent place in *Motor Boat*, but they are no longer individually delineated, and they vie for our attention with the paint. This has a flattening effect on the aquatic prospect. The artist also softens the outlines and details of three of the human figures. However, he leaves the head and torso of the woman in the foreground of the photograph largely untouched, so that she continues to seem closer to us than the other figures. As a result, *Motor Boat* does not abolish depth of field. Instead, it makes room within the same canvas for two-dimensionality, and three-dimensionality. The waves are simultaneously "behind" and "above" the speeding boat and its human occupants, something that makes for an unsettling—but also a highly pleasurable—viewing experience.

It is not only in his photo pictures that Richter suspends the opposition between abstract painting and photographic figuration; he also produced a number of early abstractions by painting over a photo picture. Whereas in some of these works, bits of the image remain visible, in others it is completely obscured.

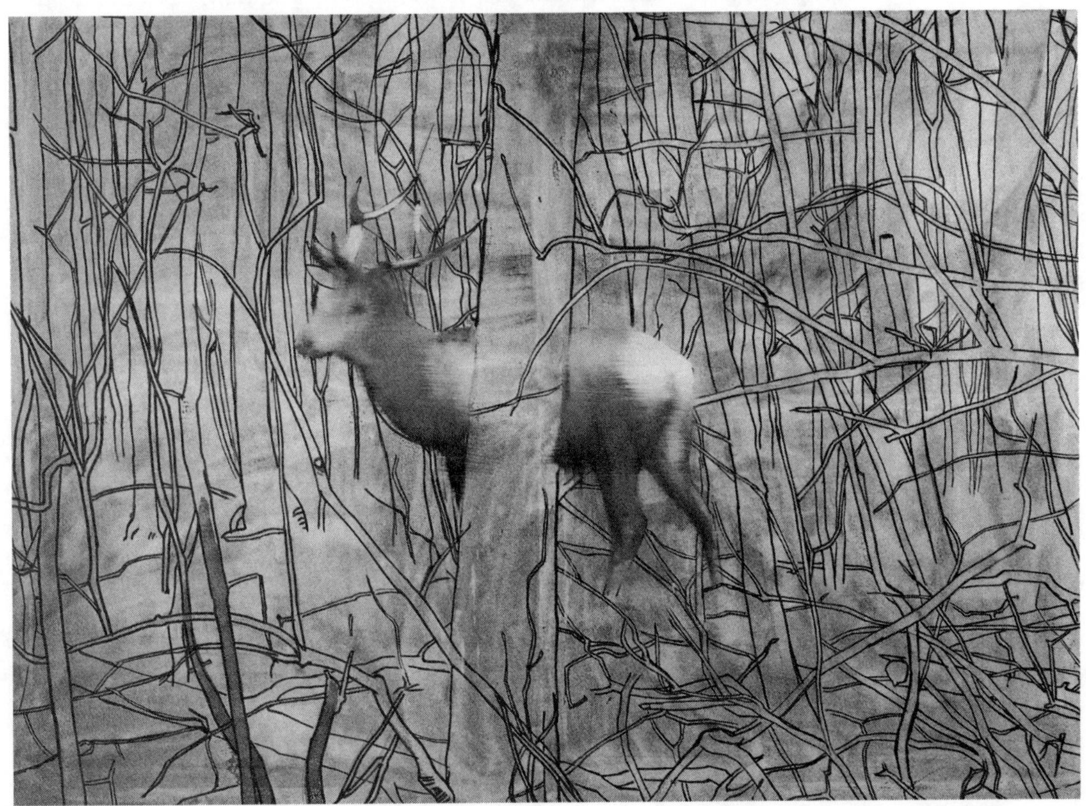

But as he helps us to understand in an important work from the early sixties, even when the latter is completely eclipsed, it does not go away; it hovers in the background, waiting to be recognized.[6] The work in question—*Stag* (1963)—is predominantly abstract; most of it consists of a forest of two-dimensional and heavily stylized trees, rendered in a graphic rather than a painterly mode. But in the middle of the painting there is a "swatch" of a photo picture, which derives from a photograph of a stag.

At first glance, this work seems very different from Richter's abstract painting. It does not pose as radical a challenge to figuration, and it appears to position the stag in front of the forest, rather than behind, suggesting that the artist painted the photographic component last, instead of first. Almost immediately, however, one notes that a "strip" of the forest runs down the middle of the painting, like a piece of wallpaper, covering the front legs and belly of the stag. And if this sudden assertion on the part of the forest to constitute the foreground as well as the background of the painting were not already sufficiently disconcerting, Richter extends some of the branches from the background across the strip of forest, which cuts the stag into two pieces, and continues them onto the other side. The stag's feet also seem to be dissolving into the forest, and his body appears upon closer inspection to have been shaped as much by a squeegee as a paintbrush. Finally, although Richter will not produce any of his gray paintings for another five years, one appears to be lying in wait, behind the graphic forest.

But by this point in our viewing, we can no longer place any credence in temporal or spatial demarcations. Richter renders these demarcations even more unstable in a 1990 interview with Sabine Schütz. He tells us that he shot the photograph on which he based *Stag* when he was a boy, i.e., in the distant past. He also draws attention to the age-old preoccupation of Germans with forests and stags. Finally, he intimates that he began the painting in the usual way: with a photo picture.[7] When describing the sudden appearance of an animal in a forest, we often say that it "broke" through the thicket. In a similar way, Richter's photographic stag breaks through the forest of abstraction, moving the background to the foreground, and the past into the present.

In the period extending from 1968 to the present, Richter has produced more abstract than figurative paintings, and it has become unusual for him to start them with a photo picture. It might therefore seem that the tension between abstract painting and photographic figuration was finally resolved in favor of the first of these forms. But this "authentically abstract oeuvre," as Martin Hentschel puts it,[8] began with a series of black-and-white photographs of details from an abstract painting,[9] and Richter has also created a number of abstract paintings based on photographs of paint strokes or splotches of paint.[10] In some of Richter's most important abstractions, the paint assumes an almost photographic consistency,[11] and four of them—*Blanket* (1988), *January* (1989), *November* (1989), and *December* (1989)—function in a way that is uncannily close to *Stag.*

In the past few years, the artist has begun to smear and splatter paint onto actual photographs.[12] For a long time now, he has also been an assiduous photographer, almost always producing the images from which his paintings derive. At documenta 10, Richter exhibited the *Atlas*, his vast compendium of found and "authored" photographs, both as the source of his figurative paintings and as a work in its own right.[13] He also claims to paint "like a camera," even when no photograph figures in the production of his work. "I'm not trying to imitate a photograph," he told an interviewer in 1972. "I'm trying to make one. And if I disregard the assumption that a photograph is a piece of paper exposed to light, then I am practicing photography by other means. . . . [T]hose of my paintings that have no photographic source (the abstracts, etc.) are also photographs."[14]

RICHTER DOES MORE than dismantle the opposition between abstract painting and photographic figuration; he also bridges the gap separating art from the world. He accomplishes both of these undertakings in the same way: by creating analogies. I take the word "analogy" from Richter himself, who uses it often in his interviews and writings.[15] It is his name for a special kind of relationship, one that has become more capacious with each new development in his art-making. An analogy brings two or more things together on the basis of their lesser or greater resemblance. I say "lesser or greater" because although in some of Richter's analogies similarity and difference are evenly balanced, in others similarity outweighs difference, or difference, similarity. But regardless of the form they take, these couplings neutralize the two principles by means of which we are accustomed to think: identity and antithesis.

As Richter helps us to understand, an analogy is a very different thing from a metaphor. A metaphor entails the substitution of one thing for another. This is a profoundly undemocratic relationship, because the former is a temporary stand-in for the latter and because it has only a provisional reality. In an analogy, on the other hand, both terms are on an equal footing, ontologically and semiotically. They also belong to each other at the most profound level of their being. Richter does not produce them; rather, he waits for them to emerge. "Letting a thing come, rather than creating it," he writes in a note from 1985. "[N]o assertions, constructions, formulations, inventions, ideologies—in order to gain access to all that is genuine, richer, more alive: to what is beyond my understanding."[16] "Painting as change, becoming, emerging, being-there, thusness," he observes in another note from the same year (121).

Richter grew up in a world of stark oppositions.[17] Shortly after crossing the border separating the German Democratic Republic from the Federal Republic of Germany, he was confronted with another set of polarities. The antinomies that were his daily bread in the GDR were of course those that distinguished the latter country from the FRG: communism versus capitalism, and Eastern Europe versus Western Europe. Those that he was asked to digest after settling in the West were internal to the FRG; they pitted the generation who grew up after World War II against those responsible for it, and leftists of all stripes against the state, the military, and the social and economic establishment. Richter's response to this "either/or" thinking, which he calls "ideology," was to debinarize difference. He turned for this purpose to a particular kind of analogy: one in which there is the smallest possible difference. He found the prototype for this analogy in photography.

This might seem a baffling claim. The "logos" in "analogy" links the latter firmly to language and reason. Everyday usage does the same; we turn to analogy when we want to clarify an obscure point or establish the structural equivalence of two or more things. Photography, on the other hand, is a visual form, and it appeals more to belief than to reason. The ways in which this medium has been theorized also make it difficult to see how it could perform the role Richter attributes to it. For "realists," like André Bazin, and the late Roland Barthes, a photographic image is a trace of, and perhaps even ontologically identical with, what it depicts; there is consequently insufficient distance between the two for them to constitute an analogy.[18] Those who distinguish between the two, on the other hand, generally do so absolutely. No matter how closely a photograph approximates its referent, it is—finally—"no cigar"; whereas the second of these terms is real, the first is "only" a representation. And the more striking the resemblances between a photograph and its referent, the more emphatically we must distinguish between them, because there is no more powerful form of ideological mystification than similarity.[19]

In Richter's view, however, the photograph inhabits the same world as its referent—the world of forms. Neither takes priority over, or constitutes a replacement for, the other; instead, the two relate the same way all other forms do: by corresponding with each other. The correspondences between a photograph and its referent are extraordinarily abundant—so much so that one can be seduced into believing that if the former were enlarged, it would match up point for point with the latter. This does not mean, however, that the photograph is a false pretender. It means that it is photography's essence to be "*almost nature*" [my emphasis]. The small but decisive difference that separates it from the referent is also not a defect, but rather the precondition for relationality. Although it is through their resemblances that the two correspond, it is only because they are at the same time distinct from each other that they are able to do so. It is also only by turning to one that we can approach the other. "I would like to try to understand what *is*," Richter told an interviewer in 1970. "We know very little, and I am trying to do it by creating analogies."[20]

Part of what drives the artist to paint his photo pictures is his desire to show us the marginal difference that separates a photograph from its referent. "Perhaps because I'm sorry for the photograph, because it has such a miserable existence even though it is such a perfect picture," he wrote in the mid-sixties, "I would like to make it valid, make it visible—just *make* it."[21] But by rendering visible the special kind of analogy that links a photograph to its referent, Richter also teaches us to think differently about other kinds of difference.

As should be evident by now, it is through an implicitly photographic analogy that the artist brings together abstract painting and photographic figuration. He begins his photo pictures by painting a figurative analogue of a photograph. He then uses a blurring device to produce an abstract analogue of this figurative analogue. The analogy between the figurative painting and the abstract painting operates within the frame of the photo picture, but the analogy between the figurative painting and the photograph "behaves" like the analogy between a photograph and its referent: it links the photo picture to something external. The resulting canvases consequently do even more than analogize abstract painting and photographic figuration; they also analogize photography's own way of analogizing. It is for this reason, I believe, that Richter claims to paint like a camera.

As the artist's notes indicate, he felt under increasing pressure during the 1960s to take sides in the cultural battle that was raging around him.[22] His immediate response was to negate even the small distinctions upon which photographic analogy depends. "All that interests me [are] the gray areas," Richter observes in an oft-quoted passage. "[T]he passages and tonal sequences, the pictorial spaces, overlaps and interlockings. If I had any way of abandoning the object as the bearer of this structure, I would immediately start painting abstracts."[23] The logical end point of this experimentation was of course the monochrome.[24] In his notes from this period, Richter celebrates the leveling effect of gray,[25] but by the mid-1970s he had ceased to regard it as an agency for debinarizing difference and had come to equate it with *indifference.* "Gray, to me," he told an interviewer in 1975, "was absence of opinion, nothing, neither/nor."[26]

Richter did not stop painting gray monochromes,[27] but he did start attending to the particularities that distinguished each of them from the others. Looking closely at the paintings, he discovered that he had unconsciously introduced a second term into the equation: sculpture.[28] As Michael Edward Shapiro elegantly puts it, he had been "manipulating the surfaces and structures of the paintings: using horizontal strokes of thick paint, leaving a galaxy of points and peaks; using flat matte paints to make gray paintings, whose surface patterns are elusive to the eye."[29]

Richter also came back to analogy through a new kind of abstract painting—one built up from multiple layers of paint and "random [and] illogical colors and forms."[30] Whereas many of the gray paintings evolved out of photo pictures, these new works did not; they are abstract through and through. But although they do not make any concessions to figuration, one cannot stand for very long in front of them without beginning to see things; like cumulus clouds in a blue sky, they invite us to search within them for phenomenal forms. Richter manifests no embarrassment whatever when questioned about this dimension of his color abstractions. On the contrary, he tells Robert Storr that he, too, apprehends "lake[s]," "red rain," and "broken cliffs" when he looks at them.[31]

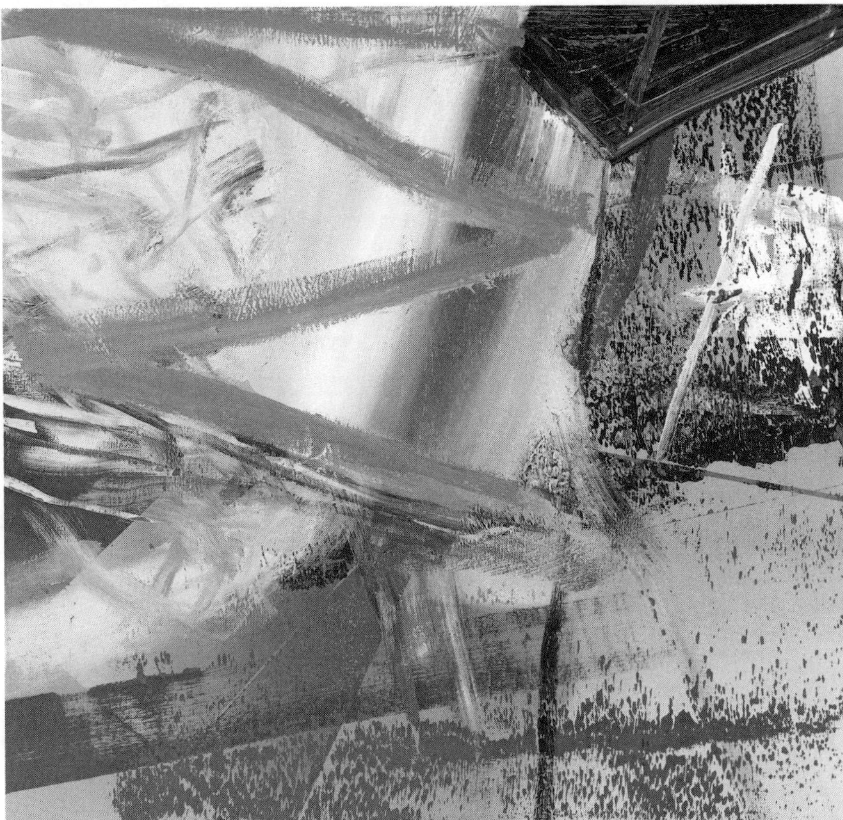

See also Plate 13 in color insert.

He also maintains that this kind of recognition is at the heart of all aesthetic experience—even the most seemingly non-referential. "We only find paintings interesting because we always search for something that looks familiar to us," he says in the same interview. "I see something and in my head I compare it and try to find what it relates to. And usually we do find those similarities, and name them: table, blanket, and so on" (304).[32]

Richter made these observations shortly before MoMA's 2002 retrospective of his work, but he started thinking along these lines much earlier. In 1980 he remarked that abstract painting "draws its life from analogies with the appearance of nature,"[33] and from 1970 to 1973 he engaged in an astonishing aesthetic experiment. He shot a number of photographs of brushstrokes and details of brushstrokes from abstract paintings and used them as the basis for a series of photo pictures.[34] One would expect the resulting canvases to cancel photography's contract with the real, either by making painting its referent or by breaking down its referentiality altogether. However, they point insistently outward. What they point toward, moreover, is not just painting but the natural world as well. They invoke the latter associatively—by activating our memories of similar forms.

But although these abstract paintings refer beyond themselves every bit as emphatically as the photo pictures do, they do not tell us what they are referring to. It is we who must provide the missing term. And since the image or set of images that an abstract painting precipitates in one psyche are never the same as those it precipitates in another, this term is constantly changing. The analogies we create when looking at Richter's color abstractions are also impermanent because the paintings themselves do not ratify them. No matter what connections we make, they go on pointing outward, suggesting that we have not yet located what they are tending toward. Because of this, these works eventually become extra-referential in a second way as well: they direct us toward what we are accustomed to thinking of as "the ineffable." As usual, Richter himself was the first to see this. "Painting is the making of an analogy for something nonvisual and incomprehensible: giving it form and bringing it within reach," he wrote in 1981. "And that is why good paintings are incomprehensible."[35]

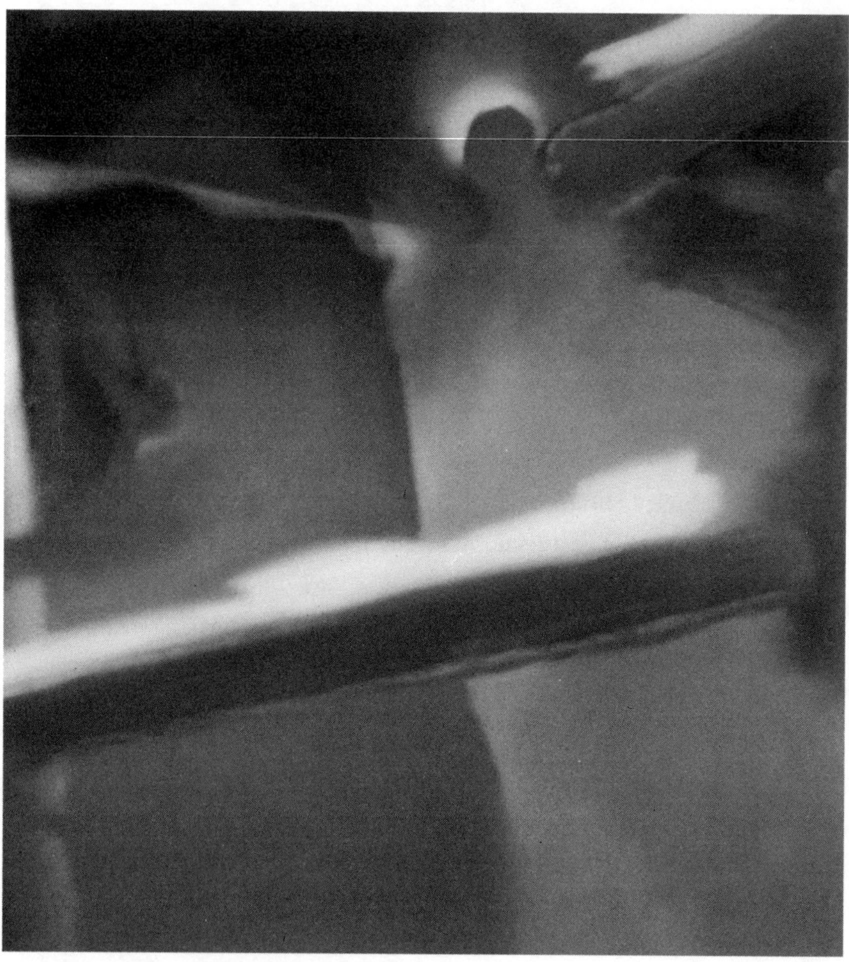

Those who—like me—are unable to subscribe to the notion that there is another domain "higher" than our own are likely to respond to this aspect of Richter's aesthetic with not just skepticism but downright suspicion. However, in the text he wrote for the 1982 documenta, which provides the next entry in *The Daily Practice of Painting*, the artist points out that this kind of analogy has nothing to do with religion, or even the sublime.[36] What theologians call "the unknown," "the invisible," and "the infinite" is simply what falls outside our conceptual universe—what our thought does not allow us to think, or our eyes to see. Abstract painting helps us to expand what we can think and see by referring insistently beyond it. In the sixteen years since Richter made this claim, he has used it to transcend all kinds of limits—aesthetic, political, historical, and even geographical.

SURPRISINGLY, the artist attributes the same potential to photography. The analogical value of the photographic image is not exhausted once we have explored its relationship to its referent. It moves through time, in search of its "*semblables*" and "*frères*."[37] The analogy that comes into existence when a photograph locates one of its relatives is historical in nature; it links the past to the present. It remains in a state of latency, though, until we recognize it.[38] Fortunately for us, photographs do not passively await this recognition; instead, they actively solicit it by "dropping" on the "doormat," like advertising flyers.[39] This is another of the reasons why they are so important to Richter, and why he so frequently emphasizes their agency and authorlessness.

The kinds of analogies I have just described closely resemble what Walter Benjamin calls "dialectical images."[40] They connect our present to specific moments from the past. They also do so in the face of powerful opposition; we do not want to acknowledge the affinities upon which they insist. Our resistance strengthens the link between us and our predecessors, since what we call "history" has been one long refusal to open the Book of Life.[41] Over the centuries, the pile of unacknowledged analogies has grown ever higher, impeding our vision, and our capacity to change. But although the past prefigures the present, it does not predetermine it. It shows us not who we are, or who we will be, but rather who we are in the process of becoming. It does so in the hope that we will prevent this particular analogy from being realized. If we succeed, we will not just free ourselves from the repetition compulsion of history but also change the "specific character" of the past by generating an altogether different analogy.[42] It is to this mysterious reciprocity between what is and what has been that Benjamin refers when he writes: "The past carries with it a secret index by which it is referred to redemption. . . . There is a secret agreement between past generations and the present one.... Our coming was expected on earth.... Like every generation that preceded us, we have been endowed with a *weak* messianic power, a power to which the past has a claim."[43]

There are, though, some important differences between Richter's account of redemption and Benjamin's. Benjamin wrote the words I have just quoted in the mid-thirties, when it was still possible to think of a generation as a possible engine for social redemption. By 1988, when Richter produced the first of his "history paintings," this illusion had been utterly dissipated—as much by the events of the 1960s and 1970s, as by those of the 1930s and 1940s. It had become painfully evident to him that the force from which the past needs to be rescued is not social or economic but psychic in nature. This force is what Freud calls the "death drive," and it threatens us from the inside as well as the outside.[44] "Crime fills the world, so absolutely that we could go insane out of sheer despair," Richter wrote in 1986, in a passage that could have been lifted directly out of *Civilization and Its Discontents.* "(Not only in systems based on torture, and in concentration camps: in civilized countries, too, it is a constant reality. . . . Every day, people are maltreated, raped, beaten, humiliated, tormented and murdered—cruel, inhuman, inconceivable.) Our horror, which we feel every time we succumb or are forced to succumb to the perception of atrocity . . . feeds not only on the fear that it might affect ourselves but on the certainty that the same murderous cruelty operates and lies ready to act within every one of us."[45] As Richter intimates, the second of these fears is even greater than the first; most of us will go to far greater lengths to avoid thinking about our capacity to injure others than theirs to injure us. But this fear protects us from something even more unthinkable: our own mortality.

For Richter, as for most of the other figures in this book, mortality constitutes the basis of human existence.[46] Only at the moment of our death will a period be inserted into the sentence of our life, thereby fixing its meaning. Since until that moment we will remain in a state of perpetual becoming, this futural relationship to ourselves makes it possible for us to change. It also makes room in the world for others. The fact that we will not live forever provides the guarantee that there will be air for future generations to breathe and water for them to drink. Our finitude also links us while we are alive to every other living creature or thing, ranging from those who most closely resemble us to those who seem most alien. It is consequently the most capacious and enabling of all analogies.

What Freud calls the "death drive" is the powerful force within us that seeks to override this limit. Until we learn to live in a way that takes cognizance of our mortality—to be oriented "towards death"—all of our attempts to devise a more equitable society will end in failure. But what makes this task even more Herculean is that there are no collective ways of accomplishing it; each of us must pursue her own path to death. It is not just by opening the Book of Life but also by turning to the chapter that constitutes our existence that we find our way to finitude and to the world.

MOST OF THE PHOTOGRAPHS in the *Atlas* that were not shot by Richter himself belong to the category of the "found image." A number of them, however, could more properly be said to have found him. Some of the earliest to seek him out were a group of concentration camp photographs.[47] Richter responded to their solicitation by attempting to paint them, but he was unable to do so. Since in the view of many artists and scholars the Holocaust is essentially unrepresentable, this might not seem to warrant further discussion.[48] Richter, however, was unable to leave the camp photographs alone. He arranged and rearranged them. He also colored some of them. Finally, he positioned them side by side in the *Atlas* with a cluster of pornographic photographs and marked this juxtaposition as an analogy rather than a random coupling by imparting to representative images in each group his signature "blur."[49]

This is a startling analogy, to say the least. Even if we were prepared to view pornography as a violation of the human body, most of us would balk at the notion that it could be compared in any way to what happened in the camps. And Richter himself clearly did not subscribe to this moralistic account of pornography when he created the analogy, because he based a contemporaneous series of photo pictures on pornographic photographs. Many years later, in a conversation with Jan Thorn Prikker, he characterized the analogy as "weird and seemingly cynical."[50] He also effectively nullified it by detaching the concentration camp photographs from the pornographic photographs and connecting them to a very different set of photographs: those documenting the arrest, imprisonment, death, and burial of four members of the Red Army Brigade: Ulrike Meinhof, Gudrun Ensslin, Andreas Baader, and Holger Meins.

The RAF, also known as the Baader-Meinhof group, came into existence during the Vietnam War, as a protest against it, against the FRG's failure to break with its past, and against that country's social, economic, and military alignment with the United States. It was founded on the belief that the only way to counter the violence of the state was with violence of one's own. The FRG responded to the violence of the terrorists through an intensification of its own, which of course upped the ante on the other side. But since this was, as Heinrich Böll put it, a battle of six against sixty million,[51] it had only one possible ending: the eradication of the terrorists. Drawing on all the resources at

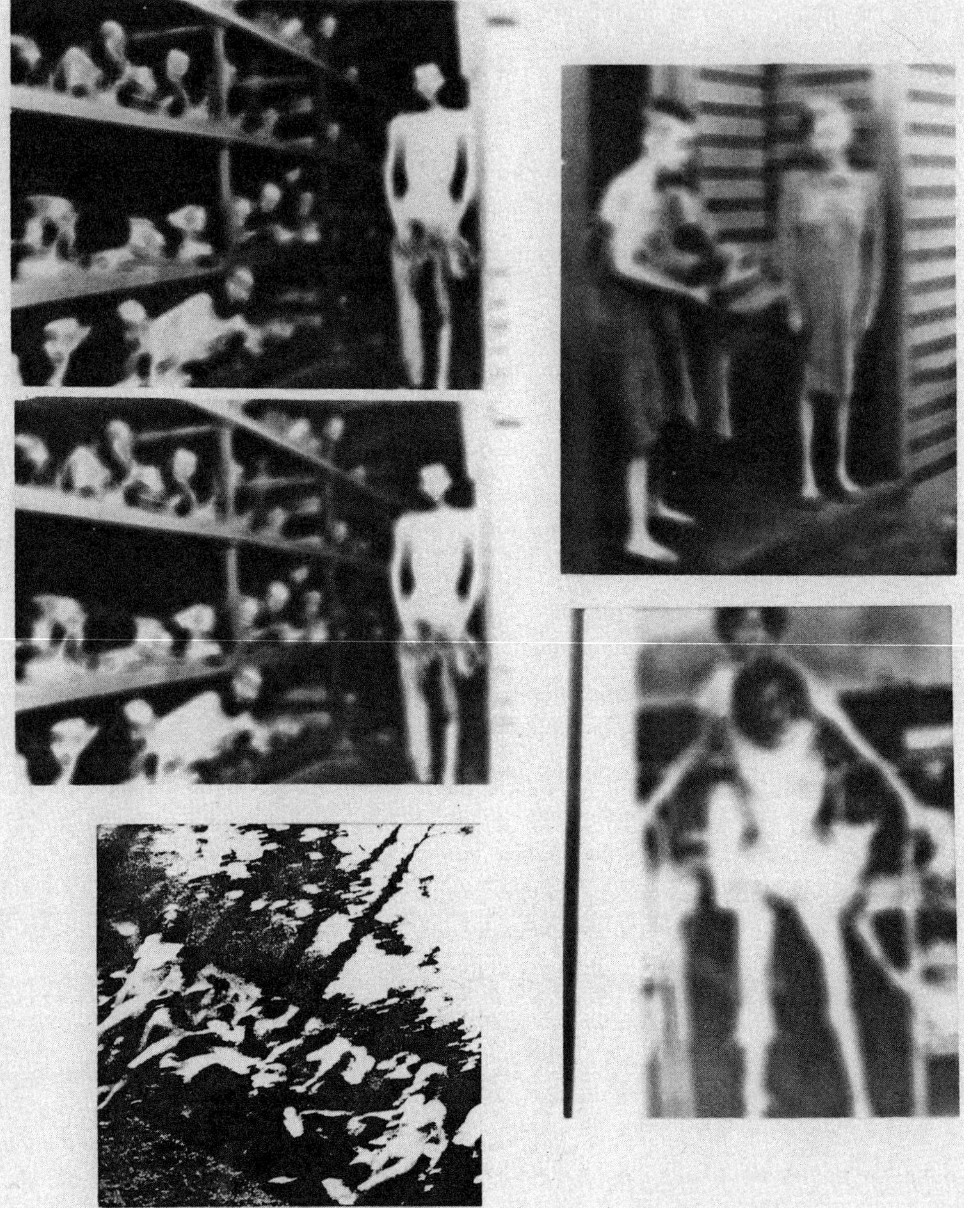

its disposal, some of which were constitutional but most of which were grossly unconstitutional, the FRG apprehended, tried, convicted, and imprisoned Meinhof, Baader, and Ensslin, along with a number of other members of the RAF. It kept Meinhof in the "dead zone" of a Cologne jail for a year, and later confined all three terrorists to a high-security wing of Stammheim, a prison in Stuttgart.

On May 9, 1976, Meinhof's lifeless body was found hanging in her cell. Sometime during the night of October 17, 1977, Baader and Ensslin also died in their cells—Baader as a result of a gunshot and Ensslin by hanging. Many on the left accused the state of murdering all three of them. Prison officials, on the other hand, claimed that the terrorists had committed suicide. But as Stefan Aust shows in his brilliant study of this period of German history, to which the present discussion is profoundly indebted, even if Meinhof, Ensslin, and Baader did kill themselves, it was in response to external pressure, since the conditions under which they were living were unendurable.[52] Suicide was also the only means left to them for protesting against the treatment to which they were subjected. This was the course of action chosen by Holger Meins, who died on the fifty-third day of a hunger strike in the Wittlich jail.[53]

This new analogy is clearly very different from the previous one. When Richter placed the pornographic photographs next to the concentration camp photographs, he established a relationship that would not otherwise exist. But when he built a verbal bridge between the concentration camp photographs and the RAF photographs, he ratified one that was already emphatically in place. Both groups of images show people who were physically isolated by the German state—in the former case through deportation and life or death in the camps and in the latter through arrest and internment.[54] Both sets of photographs also show us figures who were subjected to a symbolic sequestration—expelled from the category of the "human." The Nazis refused to acknowledge that their Jewish victims were people, and referred to their corpses as "*Figuren*," i.e., "dolls."[55] The townspeople of Stuttgart treated the terrorists in a similar way; they tried to prevent their bodies from being buried in the local cemetery. They were overruled by Manfred Rommel, the mayor of Stuttgart, who—perhaps because he was the son of Erwin Rommel, who was famous for having broken with Hitler near the end of the Third Reich, as well as for his military prowess during World War II—was able to see that the most terrible of histories was on the verge of repeating itself.[56] "I will not accept that there should be first class and second class cemeteries," he declared. "All enmity should cease after death."[57] But Rommel was powerless to prevent this foreclosure from being enacted at a psychic level, either in Stuttgart or in the rest of Germany. Finally,

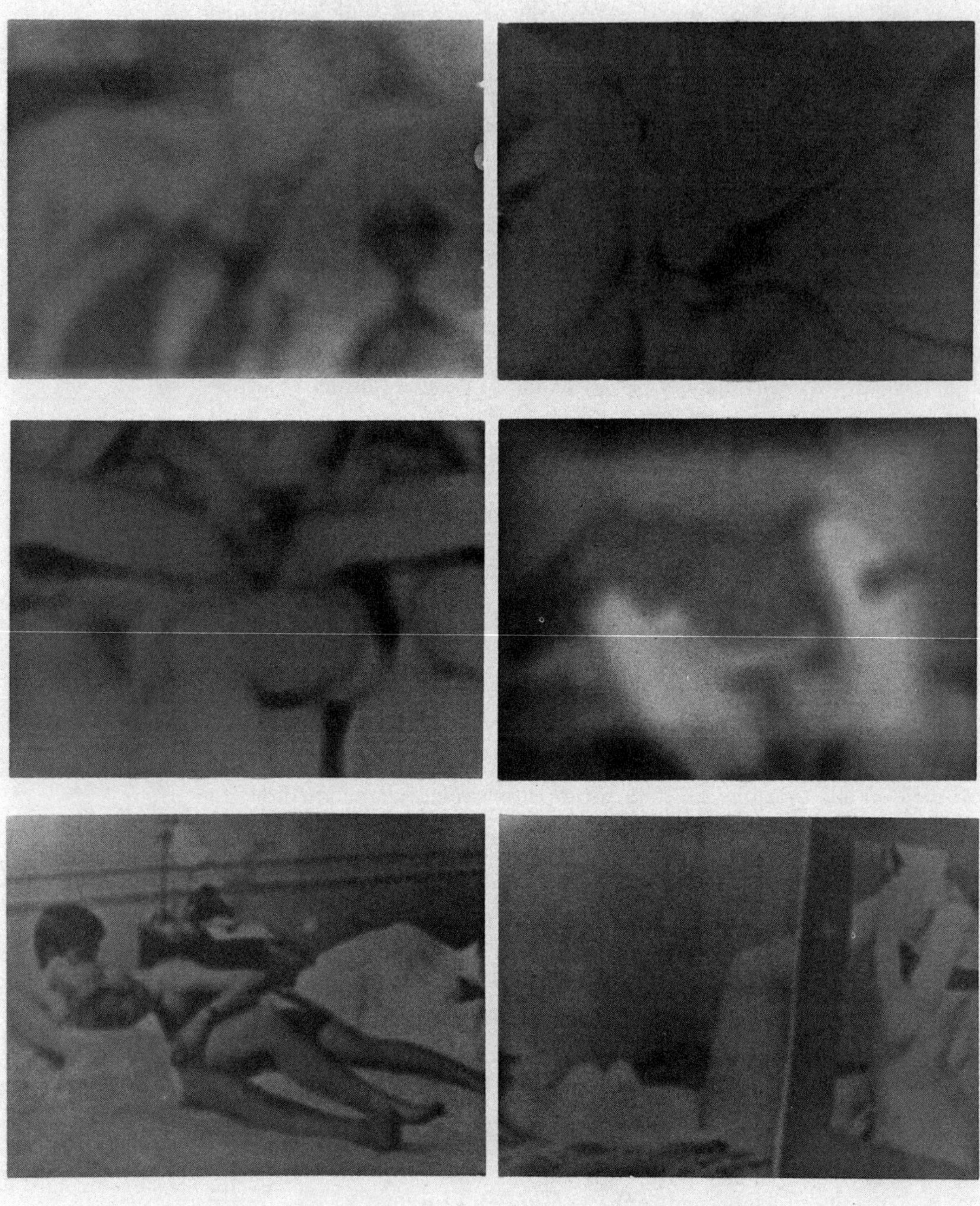

both groups of photographs cry out for the kind of thinking that would undo this sequestration: analogical thinking.

But when Richter first mentions the concentration camp photographs in his conversation with Prikker, he does not link them to the RAF photographs in any of the ways I have just enumerated. He invokes the former when speaking about the latter because he feared that the RAF photographs, like the concentration camp photographs, would turn out to be "unpaintable." And many of them in fact were, he tells Prikker: those showing the dead bodies of Ensslin, Meinhof, and Baader. These photographs were unpaintable because they held up a mirror into which he did not want to look—because they showed him, as he later put it, his "*own* end."[58] This was obviously the case with the concentration camp photographs as well. In 1968 Richter turned away from his mortality, taking his paintbox with him. But he was unable to escape the solicitation of the concentration camp photographs; their demand for an analogue kept ringing in his ears. He eventually answered this summons in the usual way: by putting someone else in his place. In so doing, he unwittingly aligned himself with those whose violence he found so terrible.

As the emaciated bodies and piles of corpses in the concentration camp photographs make clear, national socialism worked hard to establish death as something that happens elsewhere, and only to those who are not fully human. But there is a much subtler way of establishing the alterity of death, and one that often passes for sympathy: we can relate to it in the mode of an onlooker. In a richly ironic passage in "Thoughts for the Times on War and Death," Freud suggests that most of us are so accustomed to occupying this position that we automatically slip into it even when imagining our own death.[59] It was in an attempt to consolidate himself in his position that Richter juxtaposed the concentration camp photographs with the pornographic photographs. He chose the latter because of their specularity. Unlike the bodies in the concentration camp photographs, those in the pornographic photographs display themselves for a gaze. And unlike the look that witnessed the atrocities of the Nazis, the one for whom this spectacle is staged is protected from it by the fourth wall; the bodies that give themselves to be seen inhabit an image, but their spectator is real.

The pornographic photographs also permitted Richter to feminize death. Although the gaze for whose pleasure they were produced can obviously be instantiated—and thereby appropriated—by anyone who looks at them, it is symbolically male. And although there are men as well as women in these photographs, the women figure much more prominently. They play an even more central role in Richter's pornographic photo pictures. Since these latter paintings do not deal in an explicit way with death, they might seem to fall outside the scope of this discussion. They are, however, strangely non-erotic. The women in them often have a corpse-like pallor and languor. Some of them are also inexplicably horrifying.

The most striking example of this is *Student*, a photo picture from 1967. In it, a young woman sits on the floor, wearing nothing but stockings and garters. Her legs are spread, providing an unobstructed view of her genitals. But

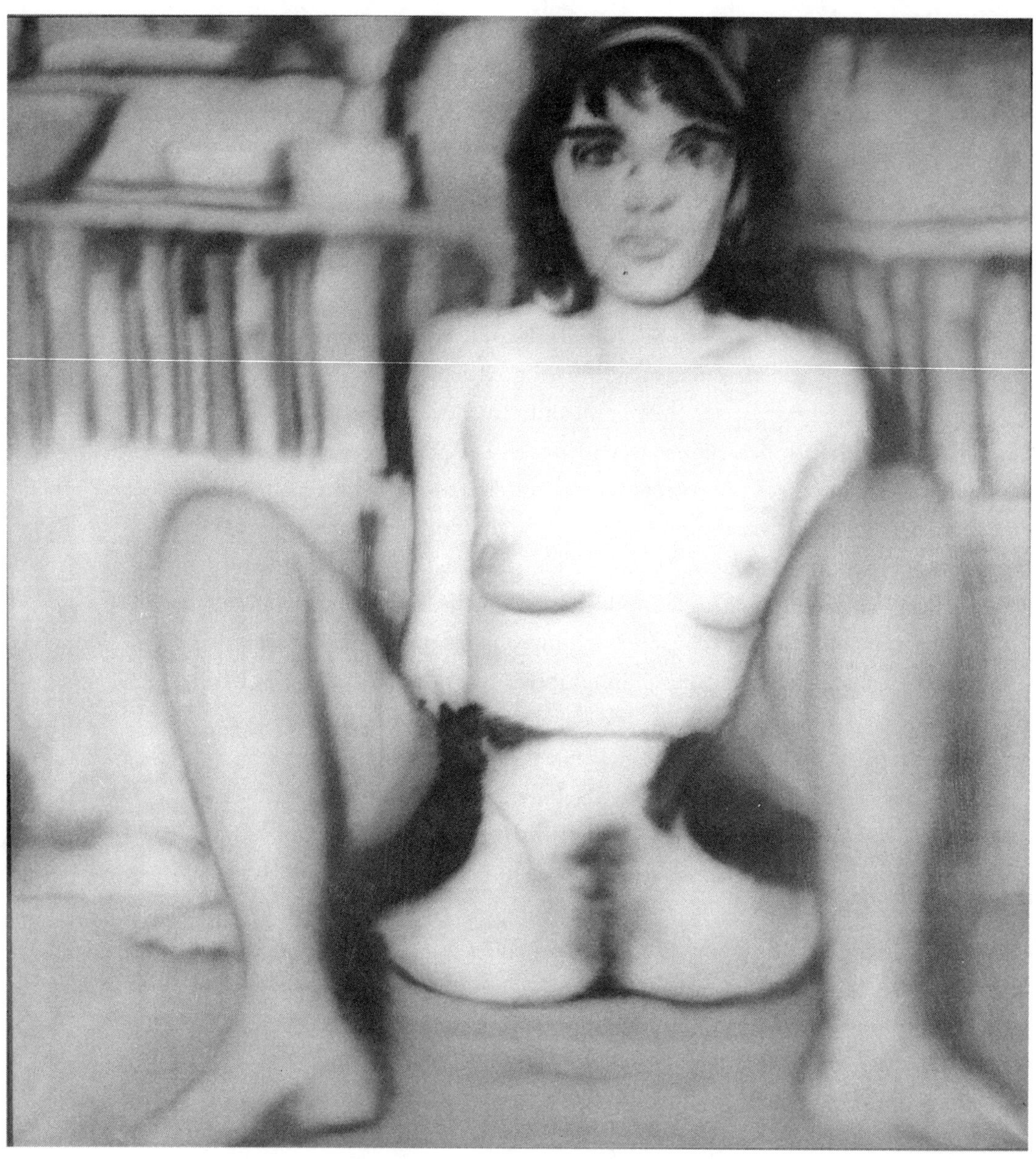

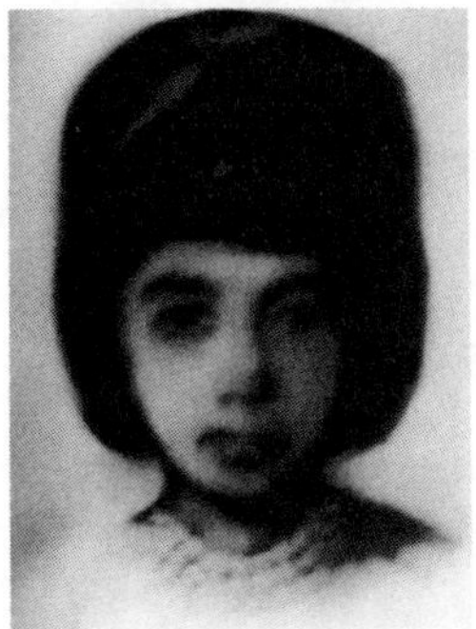
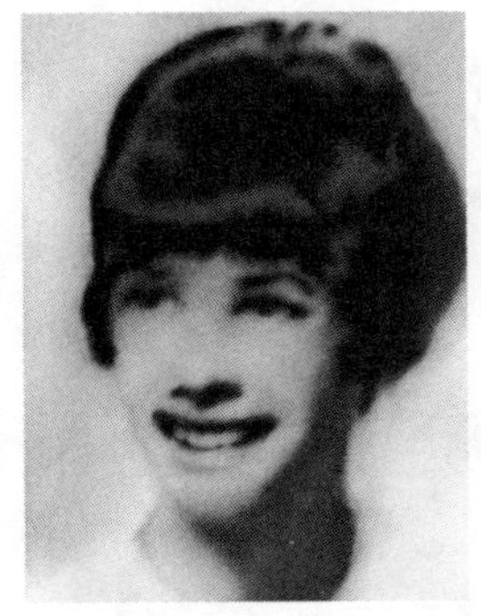
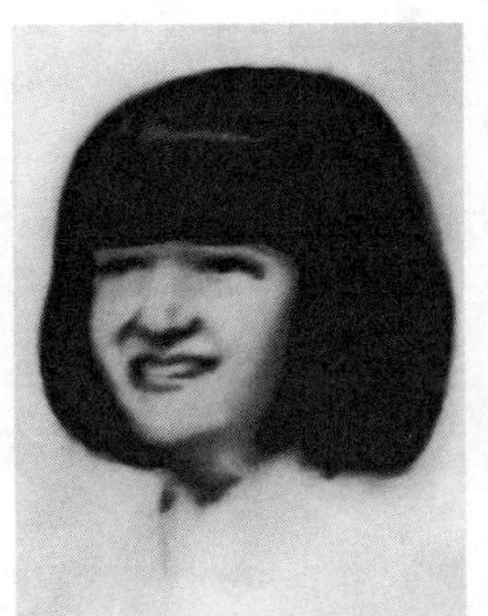
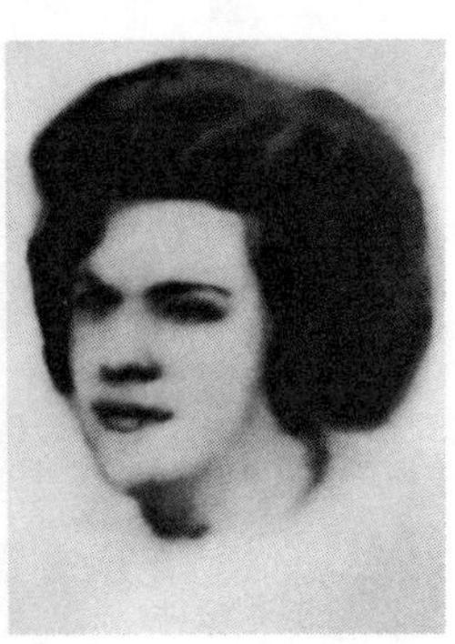

she looks directly back at us through thick glasses, which render her strangely threatening. There is also something unnerving about the bluntness and frontality of her self-presentation: she does not so much invite as challenge us to look at her vulva—and at our own risk. The fact that her body is riven into three parts by the preternatural whiteness of her torso makes looking at this photo picture even more disturbing. *Eight Student Nurses* (1966)—a series of canvases based on institutional photographs of the women killed by Richard Speck—elicits a similar response.

The word "horror" figures prominently in the interview in which Richter compares the concentration camp photographs and those documenting the arrest, imprisonment, and deaths of Meinhof, Ensslin, and Baader. It was the affect induced in him by both groups of photographs, he tells Prikker, and what made them unpaintable. In a number of his early photo pictures, as in the *Atlas*, Richter protects himself against the horror elicited in him by the concentration camp photographs by gendering death. Like the projection through which Freud's little boy defends himself against his own lack, this has the unintended—and perhaps even unwanted—consequence of making women themselves horrifying. It is not surprising that the photo picture that most vividly dramatizes the collapse of "death" and "femininity" should be so psychoanalytically resonant.[60] What is most horrifying about *Student* is finally the woman's genitalia, which represent not the origin of the world, as Gustave Courbet would have it,[61] but something more closely approximating its end.

IN 1982 AND 1983 Richter produced a series of still-life paintings of skulls and candles, sometimes in tandem and sometimes in isolation from each other. Although they draw on a devotional tradition, they are not religious paintings. They are the medium, rather, through which he attempted to confront his own mortality. It is obvious from the sheer number of them that he did not succeed.[62] This is hardly surprising, since when we confront something, it is in the

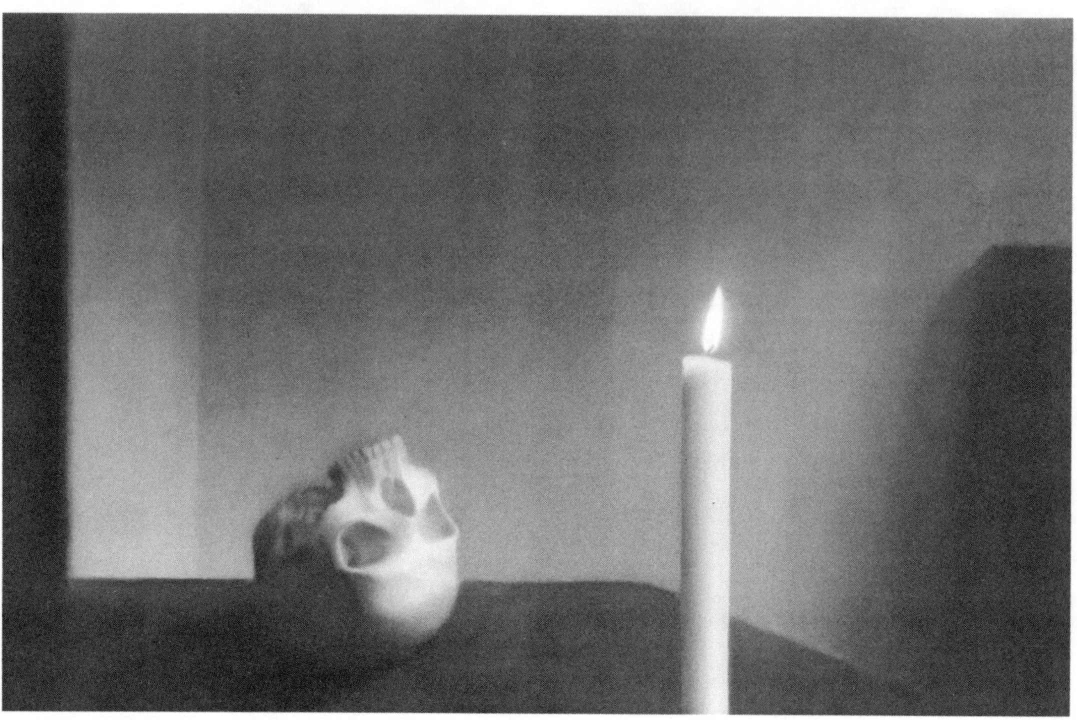

See also Plate 14 in color insert.

hope of mastering it. Richter's attempt resolutely to assume his finitude was consequently yet another evasion of it.[63]

This project foundered in part because it was such a dramatic departure from the artist's usual *modus operandi.* Richter has always profoundly distrusted his own will and often speaks about his desire to circumvent it by painting automatically, like a camera. He also gives as one of the reasons why he so frequently painted from photographs in the 1960s the fact that they permitted him to eliminate conscious thought—not to know, as he explains it, what he was doing.[64] In a note from 1985, Richter accounts for the color charts and the abstract paintings in a similar way: "At twenty: Tolstoy's *War and Peace* . . . the only thing that stayed with me, that struck me at the time, was Kutuzov's way of not intervening, of planning nothing, but watching to see how things worked out, choosing the right moment to put his weight behind a development that was beginning of its own accord. Passivity was that general's genius. (The Photo Pictures: taking what is there. . . . The Color Charts: the hope that this way a painting will emerge that is more than I could ever invent . . .). The Abstract Pictures: more and more clearly, a method of not having and planning the 'motif' but . . . letting it come." In the same passage, Richter emphasizes that none of these projects has anything to do with "chance painting, painting blind, drug painting."[65] They are, rather, forms of ontological openness.

This project also foundered for what might be called "generic" reasons. Most works in the *vanitas* tradition orient us away from this world to a "truer" and "higher" world by asserting the worthlessness of earthly things. They also render death abstract and anonymous. Although Richter's skull and candle paintings do not gesture toward another world, they do negate this one. They also treat mortality as a generalized abstraction—as something that everyone experiences in the same way. Being-towards-death does the opposite; it discloses us to ourselves and teaches us how to care about other creatures and things by *singularizing* our mortality.

Although he was a clergyman as well as a poet, and lived during the heyday of *vanitas* painting, John Donne was able to do what some of his more visually minded contemporaries could not: parse this paradox. He begins a 1624 meditation on the funereal sound of a death knell with the usual exteriorization of mortality: "Perchance he for whom this *bell* tolls, may be so ill, as that he knows not that it tolls for him." However, a moment later Donne does something extraordinary: he entertains the possibility that he himself might be this man. And the realization that the bell may be tolling for him, rather than for someone else, precipitates in him an understanding of his profound relatedness to all other human beings. "No man is an *island*, entire of itself," he exults near the end of the meditation; "every man is a piece of the *continent*, a part of the *main*; if a *clod* be washed away by the *sea*, *Europe* is the less, as well as if a *promontory* were . . . any man's *death* diminishes *me*, because I am involved in *mankind*."[66]

There is also a third reason why Richter fails to accomplish what he sets out to do in the skull and candle paintings. As we have seen, by juxtaposing the concentration camp photographs with the pornographic photographs, he linked "death" and "woman." In the pornographic paintings, and *Student Nurses*, he narrowed the distance between these two terms. In order to approach his own death, he had to move backward in time, to the scene of this crime. He also needed to acknowledge his complicity in this age-old murder, and to resurrect his victims. I say "age-old murder" because it did not begin with Richter; it has been occurring over and over again, since the beginning of time.

It was only in 1988, and in response to an external prompting, that the artist was able to make this journey. *October 18, 1977* was the result. Richter's initial plan for this series was, as he put it, to paint "the whole business, the world as it then was, the living reality"—"something big and comprehensive."[67] What he ended up painting, though, was death.[68] One of the forces driving him to do so was the photographs themselves, which not only appealed to him to paint them but also showed him what to paint. "The photographs just lie there for a very long time," he remarked in his conversation with Prikker, "and you look at them again and again, and . . . the choice gets smaller and smaller, the choice of paintings that might be paintable."[69]

But there was also another force determining his choice: one that, although it was beyond his conscious control, was nevertheless internal to his own psyche. "I am more and more aware of the importance of the unconscious process *that has to take place* while one is painting," he says in the same interview, "as if something were working away in secret. You can almost just stand by and wait until something comes" (195–196; my emphasis). The unconscious process to which Richter refers is of course the same one that makes it possible for us to dream, or to displace our desire for our mother onto a series of substitute objects: the exploration of the resemblances linking one thing to another.[70]

What Richter's unconscious pointed him toward was primarily Ulrike Meinhof and Gudrun Ensslin. Eight of the fifteen canvases in *October 18, 1977* are devoted to them: *Youth Portrait*, the three canvases bearing the title *Dead Person*,[71] *Hanged*, and *Confrontation 1*, *Confrontation 2*, and *Confrontation 3*. Richter produced two paintings of Andreas Baader's corpse, *Man Shot Down 1*, and *Man Shot Down 2*, and two others that evoke him, *Cell* and *Record Player*, but none in which he is alive. And although the source photographs for *Arrest 1* and *Arrest 2* show Holger Meins, this figure is not visible in the paintings themselves. Richter made a photo picture of Meins's corpse, as well as a third one of Baader's, but he later removed them from the series.[72]

In his conversation with Prikker, Richter says that he believes the women terrorists to have played a more important role than the male terrorists in this chapter of German history; indeed, for him the RAF was "primarily a women's movement."[73] This is a highly revisionist account of the Baader-Meinhof group; Andreas Baader presided over it like a primal father, and subjugated the female members of the organization in crudely gendered ways.[74] But although Richter's characterization of the RAF may not be historically accurate, it is conceptually "just," because Meinhof and Ensslin were the real ideologues in the group.[75]

But what "impressed" Richter about Ensslin and Meinhof was not simply the role they played in German society in the 1970s; it was also the elaborate constellation of analogies that linked them to his daughter, Betty. The artist had to wait a very long time for this constellation to form, and even longer for it to emerge into his consciousness. Like all of the complex networks of correspondences that our unconscious weaves, it arrived in bits and pieces. As a result, what Richter himself is able to see in *October 18, 1977* is constantly expanding.

SINCE THERE WAS A MORBID FASCINATION with the RAF, in Germany and elsewhere, countless photographs of its members were published during the 1970s, and the artist began collecting them early on.[76] For eleven years they haunted him as "unfinished business," but he was not able to paint them, or even to link them to the concentration camp photographs.[77] But Benjamin speaks in *The Arcades Project* about a not-yet-conscious knowledge (389), and something like that was clearly operative in Richter in 1977, because shortly after the deaths of Ensslin and Baader, he shot three photographs of his daughter, Betty, which he then transformed into two photo pictures. An astonishing number of details connect the photographs and the paintings to *October 18, 1977.*

Richter includes his mock-up of the three photographs of his daughter in the *Atlas*, thereby permitting us to see how he got from them to the 1977 *Betty*'s. At first glance, he seems to have positioned his daughter against a wall before shooting them. However, the fall of her hair and the relaxed position of her hand in the image on the upper right indicate that he placed her on a flat wooden surface—a floor or a table. In one of the photographs, Betty faces the camera, which her father has pointed down at her, but in the other two she inclines her head to either one side or the other. The photograph on the lower right provided the model for the first of the *Betty* paintings. As the mock-up of the three photographs shows, he turned it on its side before painting it. In so doing, he brought the affinities linking it to another image into focus.

See also Plate 15 in color insert.

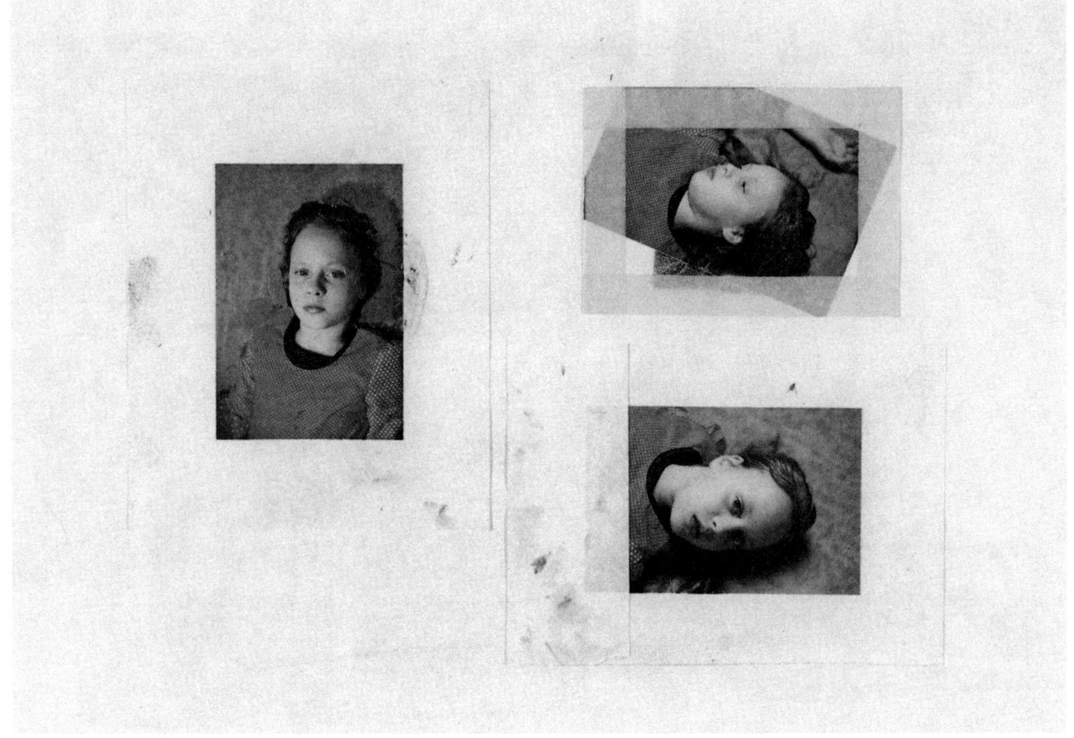

In 1976 the German magazine *Stern* published a photograph of Ulrike Meinhof's corpse. In it, Meinhof also lies on a flat surface, which appears to be a table in a morgue. The rope with which she hanged herself has left a prominent gash around her neck.[78] Meinhof's head fills the right side of the photograph, which shows us only her head and shoulders. The photograph itself is extremely grainy, and it subjects her body to the kind of photographic exposure that Barthes so feared: one that coarsens and cheapens.[79] Its function is purely evidentiary; it exists to prove that Meinhof is dead.

When Richter painted *October 18, 1977,* he used this photograph as the model for three different photo pictures, to all of which he gave the title *Tote.* The paintings are of varying sizes—the first is 24½" x 28¾"; the second is 24½" x 24½"; and the third is 13¾" x 15½". Each time I have seen them exhibited, they were hung so as to encourage the viewer to begin with the largest canvas and end with the smallest. When this prompt is followed, the paintings function as three glimpses of a disappearing image because Meinhof's head is less distinct in the second painting than it is in the first, and even fainter in the third.

These are important changes. The photograph on which Richter based the three *Dead Person* paintings kept Meinhof's corpse on view long after she was

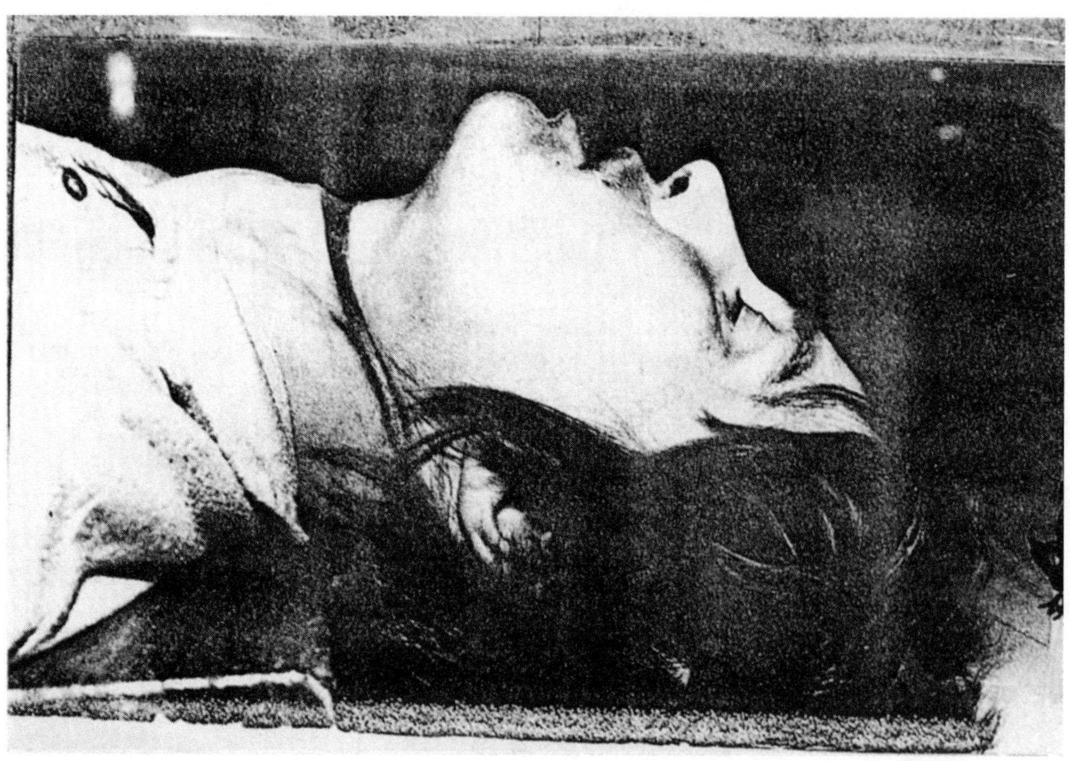

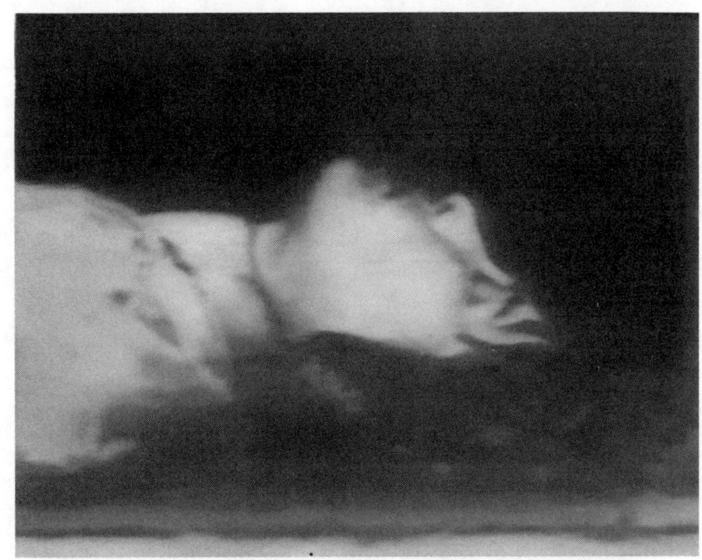

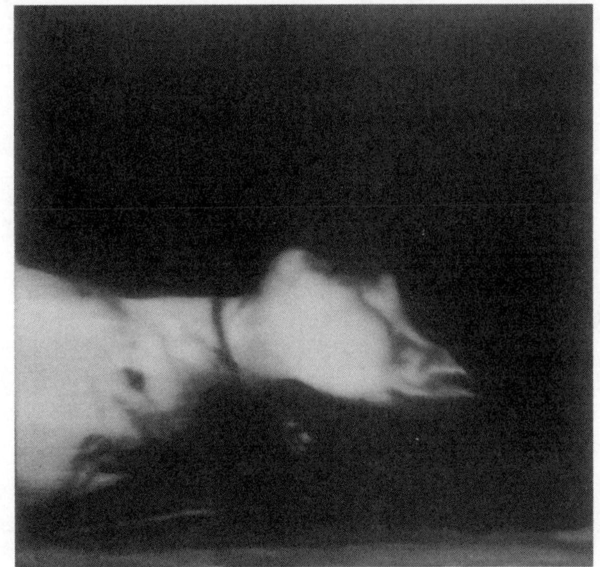

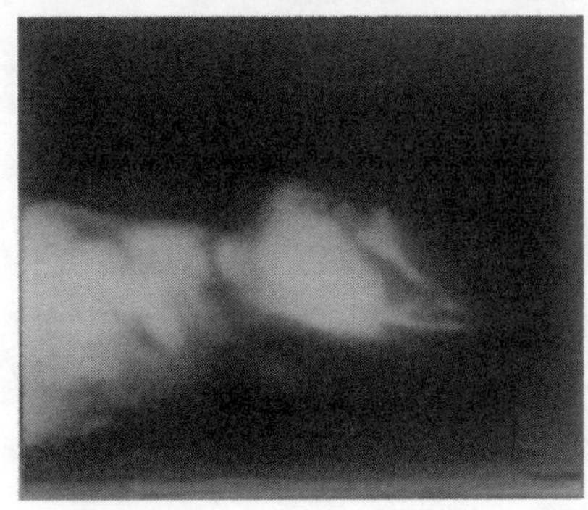

buried. It also encouraged those who looked at it to adopt a spectatorial relationship to death. By allowing her image to fade away, he releases her from this posthumous exposure. He also smoothes out the texture of her face and neck and darkens the background, thereby blurring the dividing line between life and death. But *Stern* did even more than put Meinhof's lifeless body into specular circulation; when it published the photograph of her corpse, it also spread it across two pages, so that the center fold divides her head from the rest of her body, slightly above the gash on her neck. It thereby hung her all over again. What made this act of violence possible was the rectangular size of the photograph. The first and third of the *Dead Person* paintings are also rectangular. In the second, though, Richter "squares" off against *Stern* by cropping off part of the left side of the image.

The artist reinforces the relationship between Meinhof and his daughter in the first of his *Betty* paintings. Again he places Betty on her back, on a flat surface, and shows only her head, neck, and shoulders; and again he positions her body—which extends into the frame from the left—horizontally. Now, though, he also diminishes the age gap between the two women by changing the girlish orange of Betty's lips and T-shirt to a bright red and sharpening her features.

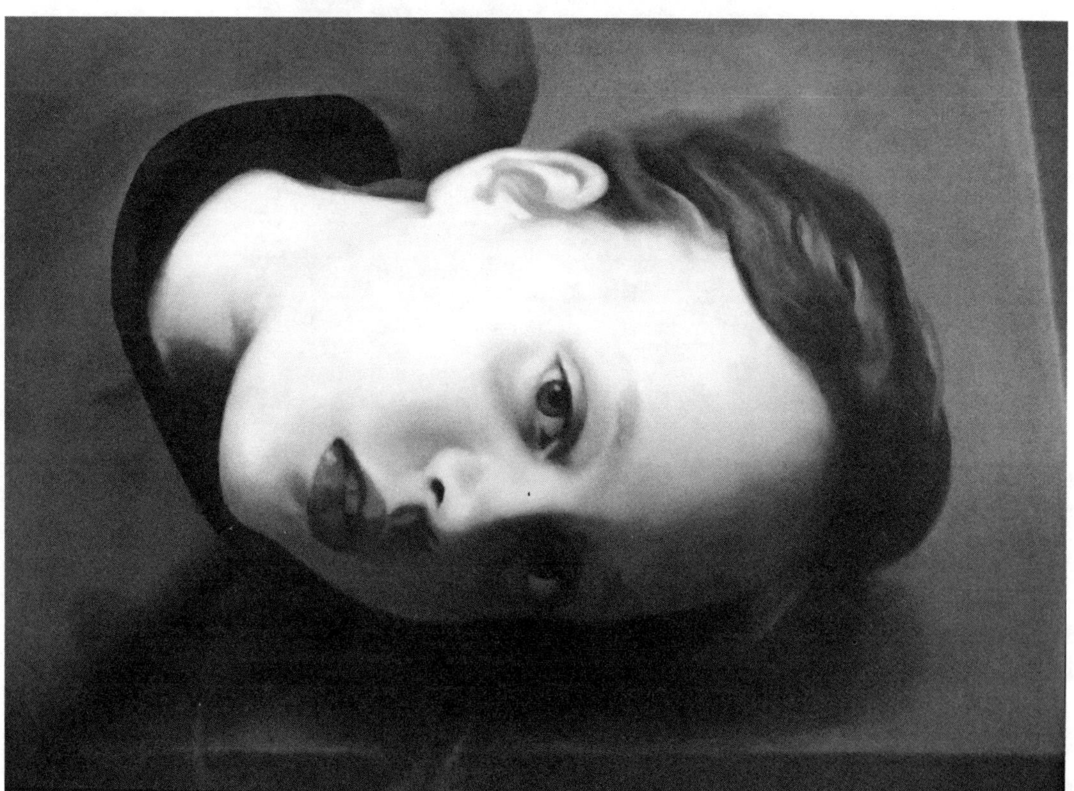

In addition, he transforms the wooden surface on which she is lying in the photograph into a butcher block by shrinking it into a rectangle that does not align with the larger rectangle of the painting. We can see him working out this idea with another image from the same photo shoot. As Bridget Alsdorf notes, it is approximately the same size as the smallest of the *Dead Person* paintings.[80] In all of these ways, Richter draws attention to the sacrificial dimensions of the Meinhof photograph. She must die, he in effect says, so that *we* will not have to. However, he does not repeat this sacrifice with his daughter; Betty's eyes are open, and she looks back at us.

This is an extremely complex analogy. In the notes he wrote for a 1988 press conference, Richter indicates that he painted *October 18, 1977* in order to establish what he did not have: an emotional relationship to the RAF.[81] This was one of the most polarized periods of German history. It was not only that for the state and many inhabitants of the FRG the members of the Baader-Meinhof group were scarcely even human; the RAF also mounted the same kind of attack from the other side. One of the most painful features of the story Aust recounts is the frequency with which the imprisoned terrorists referred to the police, those responsible for prosecuting them, those in positions of political authority, the prison guards who brought them their food and medicine, their own lawyers, and those on the left who were not prepared to sanction their violence as "swine."[82] Baader also bullied the other members of the RAF into submission by referring to them as "swine," "cunts," and "shits."[83] Not surprisingly, Richter's response to this opposition was once again to say "neither/nor." But by refusing to acknowledge that there was any relationship between himself, on the one hand, and the state and the RAF, on the other, he was also doing exactly what each of them was doing. He was saying: the death drive has nothing to do with me. He was also absenting himself psychically from a chapter of German history of which he was very much a part.

In the first of his *Betty* paintings, Richter finally begins the laborious process of reorienting himself affectively to the death of the Other, situating himself within the analogy of finitude, and assuming his position within German history. In this photo picture, he puts his daughter in Meinhof's place, which allows him for the first time to register the terribleness of what happened to her. As a result, what now horrifies is not Meinhof herself, but the violence to which she was subjected. By placing his daughter's head on a chopping block, Richter also exposes the similarities linking him to Meinhof's executioners.

He returns to the analogy between Betty and Meinhof in *October 18, 1977*, but this time he reverses its terms; instead of putting Betty in Meinhof's position, he puts Meinhof in Betty's. The agency of this reversal is *Youth Portrait*, a

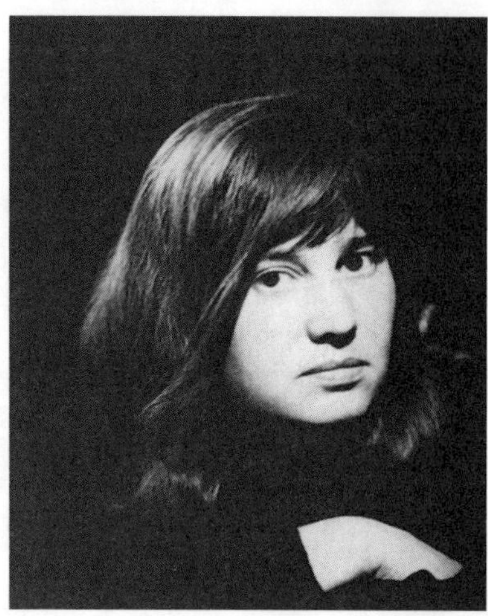

photo picture based on a studio photograph of the terrorist. This photograph was taken in 1970, when Meinhof was thirty-six.[84] Although she was already a well-known leftist writer, it depicts her as an unformed girl. Like the photographs that Richter used as the models for *Student Nurses*, it has the formal coordinates of those published in high school yearbooks.

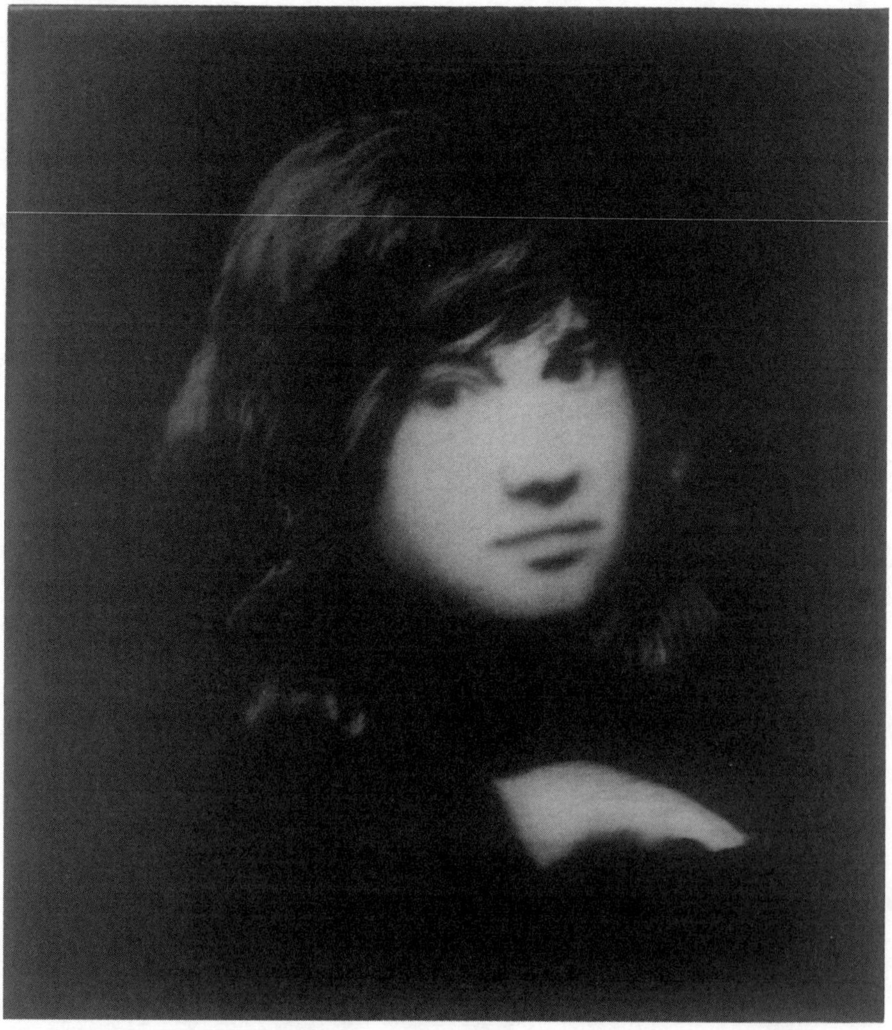

In the painting that Richter made from this photograph, he plays up both of these features. He also softens everything about the source image, thereby shearing even more years off Meinhof's age. Putting the older woman in Betty's place permits Richter to claim her. As a consequence, he is now able to experience her death not merely as a horror but also as a loss.

Richter based his second painting of Betty on the last of the photographs on the left side of the *Atlas* mockup. This time he upended the source photograph before painting it. In both it and the corresponding painting, he links his daughter to Gudrun Ensslin. The analogy is easy to miss, since its only trace is sartorial. In the source photographs for *Confrontation 1*, *2*, and *3*, Ensslin wears an institutional-looking tunic over a black shirt and stands against the murky backdrop of a prison wall.[85] In all of the photographs that Richter shot of Betty, she, too, wears two shirts, and the one closest to her body is black. In her upright position, she also appears to be standing in front of a wall. The figure in the second of the *Betty* paintings also stands upright, against an undifferentiated background.

Although both *Betty*'s prefigure *October 18, 1977*, they bear little resemblance to each other. Richter forgoes the squeegee in the first of these paintings. He also gives its outlines the sharpness of the axe that is about to land on Betty's neck, and its colors the blocklike solidity of the surface on which her head rests. In the second painting, on the other hand, he blurs the paint so painstakingly that everything has a spectral quality; looming out of a mist from which she is barely differentiated, Betty is no longer a living person but rather a ghost who has returned to haunt us.

The formal dimensions of this painting link it to the fourth of the Ensslin paintings in *October 18, 1977*: *Hanged*. This last photo picture is based on a photograph of Ensslin's lifeless body, still attached to the door of her cell. The

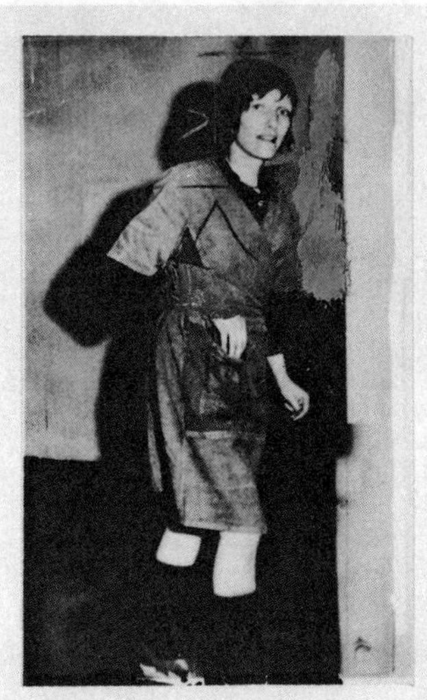

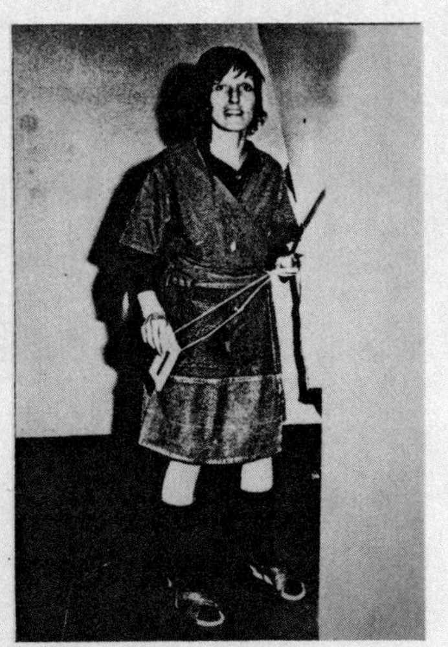

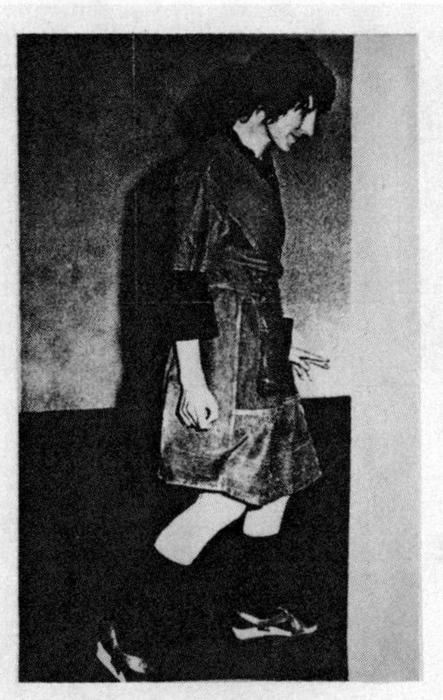

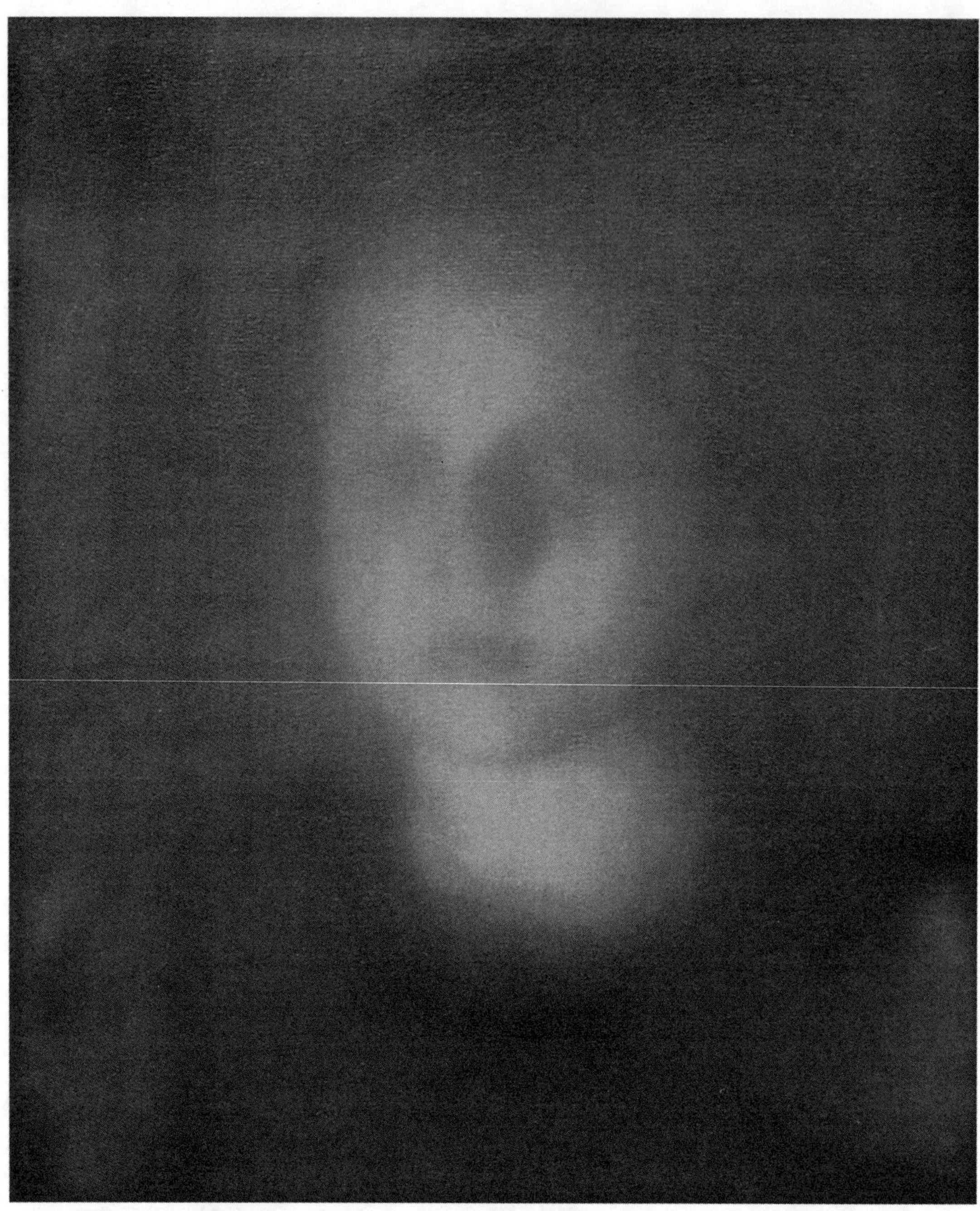

See also Plate 16 in color insert.

lighting in the source photograph is harsh and clinical, and it casts a cold eye on Ensslin's death. Her corpse is a heavy, inert object, powerless to resist this scrutiny. It still hangs from the door because—even posthumously—a prison is where Ensslin "belongs." We, on the other hand, are only visitors; although we must enter her cell in order to see her corpse, we do so in broad daylight, and in the company of prison "authorities." The photograph of Ensslin's corpse thus draws a firm line between seer and seen, the state and terrorism, and life and death.

Hanged undoes every one of these certitudes. The details and outlines of the original painting are so blurred that it is impossible to locate Ensslin, either spatially or temporally. Her head and torso make a ghostly appearance in the upper half of the canvas, but her legs appear to be fading away before our very eyes. And because there is no "bottom" to the image, it is obvious that the same thing could happen at any moment to our own. We consequently cannot look at Ensslin's corpse without realizing that we are suspended over a void—held out, as Heidegger would say, into the "nothing."[86]

Hanged is modeled as much on the second painting of Betty as it is on the photograph of Ensslin's corpse; it is, indeed, from the first of these works that it derives most of its formal properties. Once again, then, Richter reverses the analogy with which he begins. In the earlier work, he puts Betty in Ensslin's place. In the later, he treats Ensslin's body as if it were his daughter's. He also draws on another image of Betty in *Hanged.* In the photograph on the upper right side of the *Atlas* mockup, Betty looks to the left, away from the camera. In the source photograph for *Hanged,* Ensslin's head droops forward. In the painting itself, however, Ensslin does exactly what Betty does in the photograph I have just described: she looks to the left, away from the viewer. This change functions much as the dwindling sizes of the three *Dead Person* paintings do: it protects Ensslin from the objectifying gaze solicited by the photograph of her corpse, as well as by a number of Richter's early photo paintings of women.

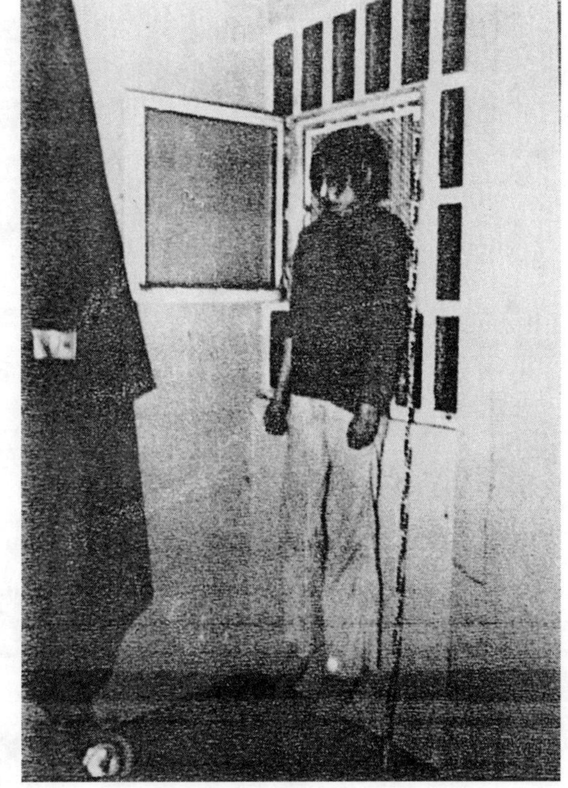

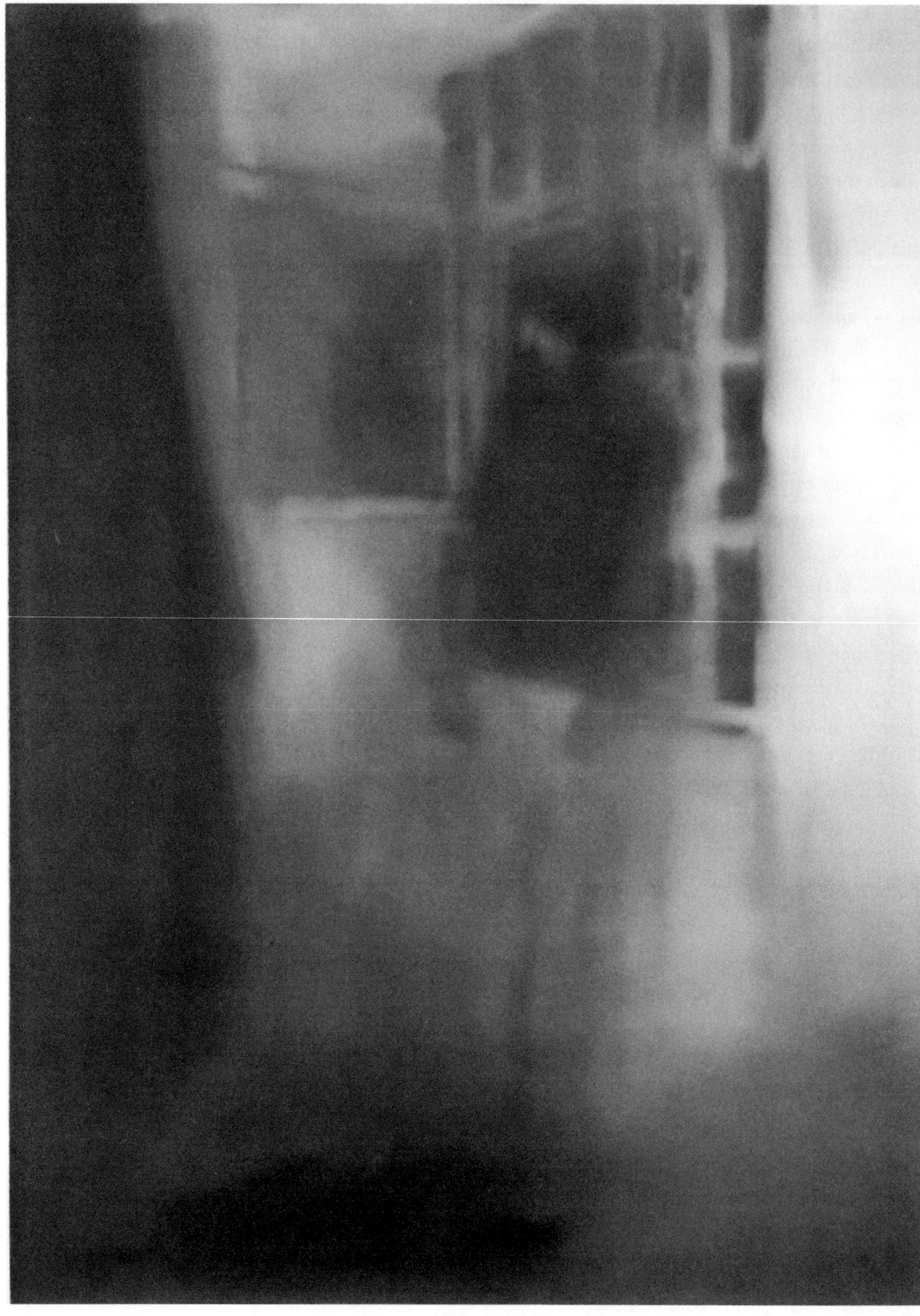

A PHOTOGRAPH FROM 1984 makes clear that the analogy between Betty and the two RAF women continued to preoccupy Richter long after he painted his 1977 portraits of her, and that he had not yet found a way of reversing it. Taken by Isa Genzken, Richter's second wife, and Betty's mother, it shows Betty pointing a gun in a practiced way at one of the walls of her father's studio. He watches her closely, and seems to be assessing her as an image. Richter published this photograph in *The Daily Practice of Painting*, immediately after identifying the death drive as the motor force behind "civilization" (126).[87]

But he then adds the following words: "I just wanted to put it on record that I perceive our only hope—or our one great hope—as residing in art. We must be resolute enough in promoting it." Richter also locates this hope in a surprising analogy. "I was interrupted just as I was detecting something like hope in the very realization that this cruelty is present in everyone," he writes, "—as if

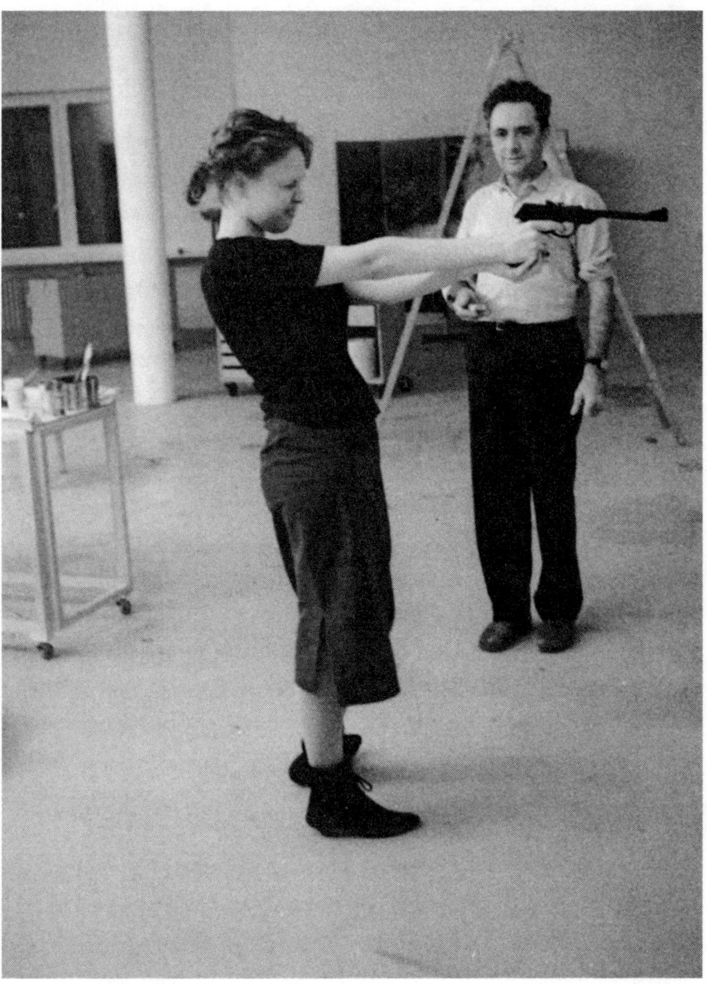

this very fact could be the starting-point of betterment, a key to the possibility of doing something" (125).

Richter was obviously thinking ahead to *October 18, 1977* when he wrote these words. Curiously, though, his initial response to the latter work was hopelessness, not hope. In the notes that he wrote for a 1988 press conference, Richter asked himself what he had painted in *October 18, 1977*. This was how he answered the question:

> Three times Baader, shot. Three times Ensslin, hanged . . . Three times Ensslin, neutral . . . Then a big, unspecific burial—a cell dominated by a bookcase—a silent, grey, record player—a youthful portrait, sentimental in a bourgeois way. . . . All the pictures are dull grey, mostly very blurred, diffuse. Their presence is the hard-to-bear refusal to answer, to give an opinion.[88]

Freud suggests in one of his meta-psychological essays that two people can communicate at an unconscious level.[89] The same is true, I would like to suggest, of history and the unconscious; unbeknownst to us, they are in constant dialogue with each other. However, until we consciously acknowledge the analogies through which this exchange occurs, they have no psychic purchase; it is as if they do not even exist. Richter was in this state of oblivion in 1988. He had already installed Meinhof in Betty's place in *Youth Portrait*, and treated Ensslin as if she were his daughter in *Hanged*, but he could not yet see that. He had consequently not yet taken either woman in his arms. Sometime between the completion of *October 18, 1977* and the autumn of the following year, the scales fell from his eyes. In an interview conducted late in 1989, he still associated the source photographs with "horror," but he now associated the paintings themselves with an altogether different affect: grief.[90] When, at a subsequent point in the same conversation, his interlocutor asked him to explain what *October 18, 1977* meant to him, the same word surfaced in his answer. "Grief," he replied, "compassion and grief." "Grief at what?" the interviewer queried. "That it is the way it is," was Richter's surprising response (200).

As must be evident by now, the artist places a strong emphasis on the affective dimensions of his work. He also attributes a redemptive function to them. This is because painting is more for Richter than an aesthetic practice. It is also a way of inhabiting the world, a mode of thinking, and a form of relationality. Let us eavesdrop again on his 1986 conversation with his most important and influential critic, Benjamin Buchloh:

> Buchloh: "[Y]ou're really trying to pursue both a rhetoric of painting and the simultaneous analysis of that rhetoric."

Richter: "If all this were just a display of matter—the way the yellow, tatter-edged area rises up against the blue-green background—how could it tell a story or set up moods?"

Buchloh: "A mood? You mean it really sets up an emotional experience?"

Richter: "Yes, and aesthetic pleasure, too."

Buchloh: "That's something different. Aesthetic pleasure I can see, but absolutely not a mood."

Richter: "So what is a mood?"

Buchloh: "A mood has an explicitly emotional, spiritual, psychological quality."

Richter: "That's exactly what is there."

Buchloh: "Fortunately only in the weakest parts."

Richter: "Surely you don't think that a stupid demonstration of brushwork, or of the rhetoric of painting and its elements, could ever achieve anything, say anything, express any longing."

Buchloh: "Longing for what?"

Richter: "For lost qualities, for a better world—for the opposite of misery and hopelessness."

Buchloh: "The longing to be able to present culture as a contemplative spectacle without losing credibility?"

Richter: "I might also call it redemption. Or hope—the hope that I can after all effect something through painting."

Buchloh: "Again, this is all so generalized: effect in what sense? Epistemological, emotional, psychological, political?"

Richter: "All [of the above] at once."[91]

In the original text of this interview, which took place in German, the word to which Richter constantly returns is not "*Emotion*," or "*Gefühl*," but rather "*Stimmung*."[92] Neither of the words chosen by the English translator—"mood," or "state of mind"—has an equivalent meaning. A mood, like a state of mind, is a subjective condition—something internal to a psyche. A *Stimmung*, on the other hand, is a relationship between the psyche and something exterior—the affective attunement of the former to the latter. It is through this attunement that we acknowledge the analogies that link us to other creatures and things, thereby actualizing their redemptive potential. Not all affects connect us to the world. Some—like horror—do the opposite; they provide the means through which we distance ourselves from it. Grief, however, constitutes one of the most profound forms that this emotional relatedness can take, because it is—as Richter puts it—"not partisan."[93] It may take sides politically, but it refuses to do so ontologically.

The importance of grief can best be understood by looking at the three portraits of Gudrun Ensslin in *October 18, 1977: Confrontation 1, 2,* and *3*. In English, we generally use the word "confrontation" in two contexts—when speaking about the face-off between two opposing positions and when referring to an encounter with our own mortality.[94] As I have already suggested, when we confront death, it is in an attempt to overcome it. When we confront another person, or group of people, it is with a similar goal: the negation of this Other. This is of course obvious when the confrontation takes the form of a war and corpses begin to pile up. But our battles are no less deadly when we attack the Other with words than when we pick up a gun, since what victory really means in both cases is not the physical annihilation of the Other but rather his or her *ontological nullification*. Grief undoes this nullification.

The most striking thing about *Confrontation 1, 2,* and *3* in the context of the present discussion is how nonconfrontational they are.[95] Even in the source

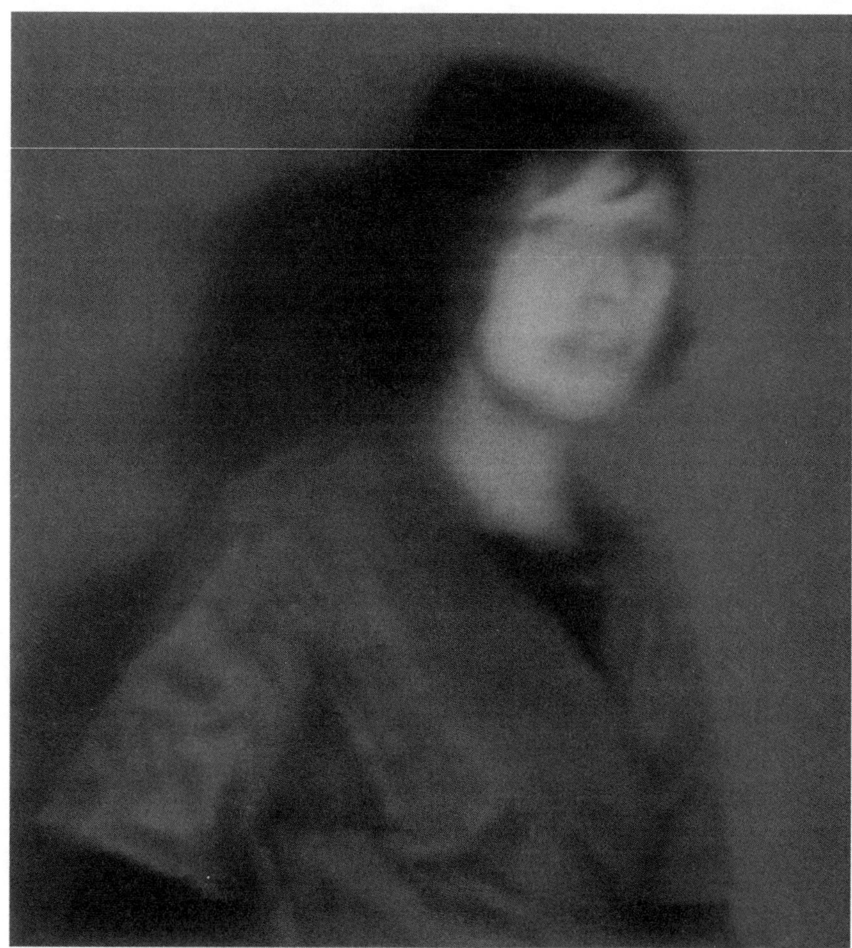

photographs, Ensslin bears little resemblance to the woman demonized by the Bundesrepublik. Her posture and demeanor communicate diffidence, not rage. The photographs themselves, however, throw up a wall between her and us. We would do almost anything to avoid being in such debased—and debasing—images. Richter dramatically transforms these photographs in the process of painting them. Instead of showing us Ensslin's whole body, surrounded by a lot of dead space, he paints only the upper third of her body. He also harmonizes her with the surrounding space by filling a significant amount of it with her shadow, and by coordinating its gray with the color of her tunic in the first two paintings. Richter rescues Ensslin from the harsh glare of the photographer's flashbulb by softening the outlines of her body and the details of her face. Finally, as in *Hanged*, he liberates her from prison. He thus creates the conditions under which Ensslin can approach us, which is exactly what she does in *Confrontation 2*.

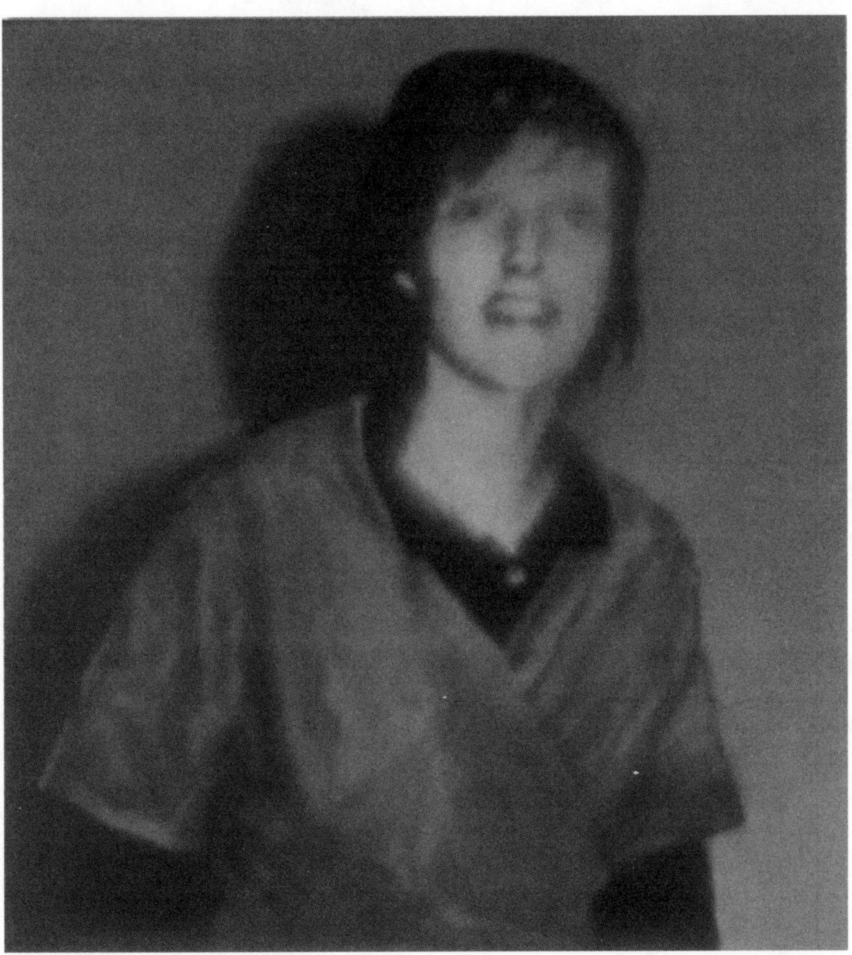

Richter indicates in his *Catalogue Raisonné* that he painted *Hanged* and the three *Dead Person* canvases before he painted either the *Confrontation* series or *Youth Portrait*.[96] If we read these works in the order in which they were produced, they could be said not only to bury the two women terrorists but also to resurrect them in another form. Meinhof and Ensslin die as beings and are reborn as Beings. But regardless of the order in which we look at the fifteen paintings in *October 18, 1977*, they show these two women to be flesh of our flesh and skin of our skin. They also teach us that our own capacity for destruction is as limitless as theirs.

Even more disturbingly, for those of us who are leftists, *October 18, 1977* foregrounds the similarities between us and the state. Richter derived a number of his source photographs from police files, and on two separate occasions—*Arrest 1* and *Arrest 2*—he obliges us to look from the structural position of a surveillance camera.[97] In his 1989 conversation with Prikker, which documents

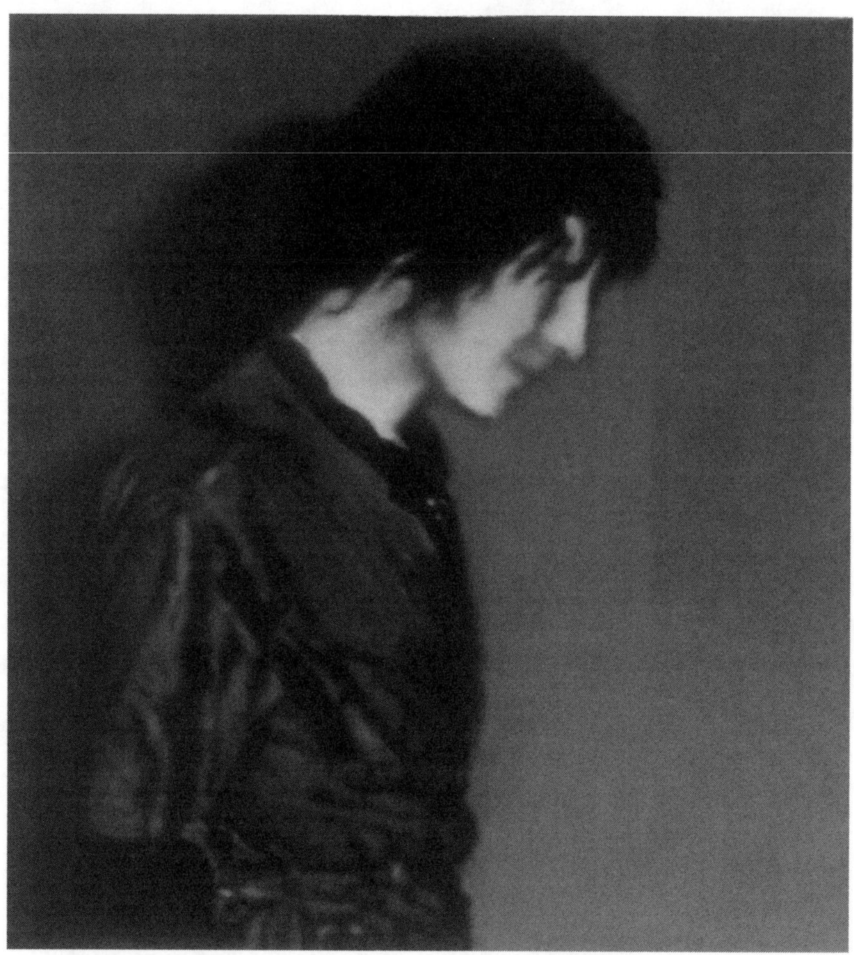

a number of the discoveries he has made about *October 18, 1977* since painting it, Richter talks about these last two analogies and how they make us feel: "This terrorism inside all of us, that's what generates the rage and fear, that's what I don't want, any more than I want the policeman inside myself—there's never just one side of us. We're always both: the State *and* the terrorist."[98] Although Richter begins this passage with the plural form of the first-person pronoun, he quickly reverts to the singular form. He does so because the viewer he is describing is in the first instance himself. Since Richter's response to the conflict between the RAF and the state was to distance himself emotionally from both of them, he was vulnerable to a dangerous fantasy: the fantasy that he was not a violent person. The fantasy was rampant during the 1960s and 1970s, both in Germany and in the United States, and it took a generational form. Unlike our parents, and their parents, those of us who came of age during the Vietnam War, and in opposition to it, imagined ourselves to be peace-lovers. We also believed that our peace would wipe the slate of history clean, permitting everything to begin anew. But far from opening up new libidinal channels, this fantasy guaranteed that nothing would change.

As many other scholars have already noted,[99] German men who were born in the 1940s and early 1950s were at particular risk of succumbing to this

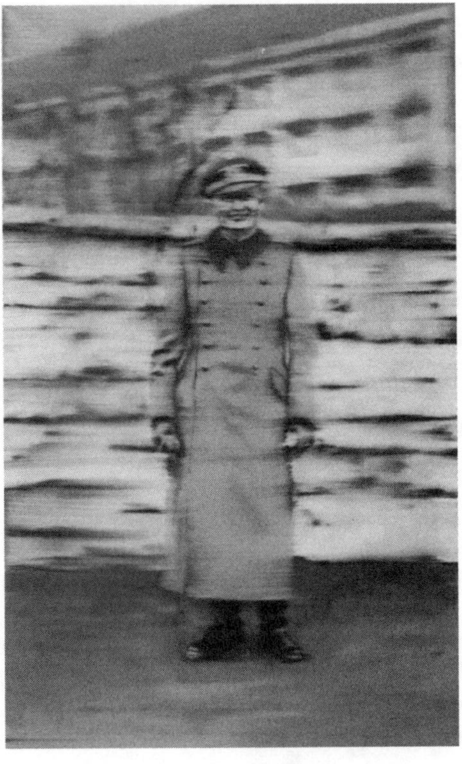

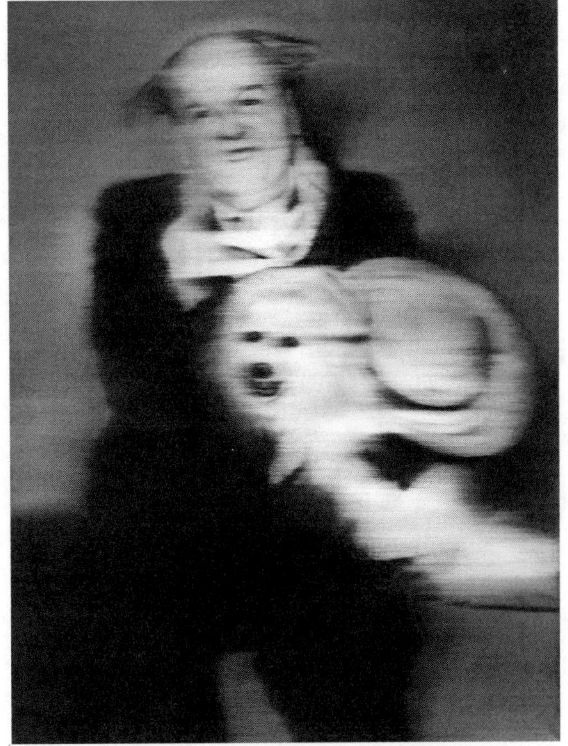

fantasy, because their country had been reduced to rubble and because it was difficult not to hold their fathers responsible for this destruction. This added an enormous amount of fuel to the Oedipal fire. It also made it virtually impossible to extinguish. The paternal legacy now meant defeat and guilt, not power and privilege, and few young men were prepared to assume this burden. The result was a widespread paternal dis-identification. I take the phrase "paternal dis-identification" from Buchloh, who uses it in the context of discussing Richter's *Forty-Eight Portraits* (1971–1972), as well as a work he coauthored with Blinky Palermo: *Two Sculptures for a Room by Palermo* (1971).[100] It is also the driving force, I believe, behind a number of the author's other early works, such as *Uncle Rudi* (1965), and *Horst and His Dog* (1965), the only painting he has ever produced of his father. And many of Richter's later paintings of his son, Moritz (2000–2001),[101] attest loudly to the fear and loathing he experienced when obliged to become father to a son.[102]

But one of the most important achievements of *October 18, 1977* is to render the very idea of a "generation" unthinkable. When Richter reverses the analogies he establishes between Betty on the one hand, and Meinhof and Ensslin on the other, he undoes chronological time. Meinhof, who was two years older than the painter, is reincarnated as a schoolgirl, and Ensslin rises like Lazarus from her grave. The past happens all over again, in a new way. Richter also paused in the middle of painting *October 18, 1977* to paint a third portrait of his daughter—and one that puts her in a generative relationship to him. This photo picture, which has increasingly come to "stand" for his work, introduces us to a new kind of analogy: one whose logic is additive, rather than comparative.

In a whole series of ways, the painting says "this *and* that." Betty sits on a bench, facing us, but she has twisted her head and torso around to look at something behind her. She wears girlish clothing, but her hairstyle is that of an adult woman.[103] The painting is unequivocally figurative, yet it makes room for abstraction. As we have already seen, Richter brings figuration and abstraction together in his early photo pictures by quite literally blurring the distinction between them. He paints a figurative analogy of a photograph, and then uses his squeegee to create an abstract analogy of this figurative analogy. Although "softer" in every way than his first painting of his daughter, Richter's third painting is clearly delineated. But what Betty turns around to look at is one of her father's abstract paintings, which fills the entire background of the canvas. Consequently, although abstraction and photographic figuration now stand at a new distance from each other, they still inhabit the same canvas.[104]

Since the canvas that fills the background of the 1988 *Betty* is one of the gray paintings, it also serves another function. For a long time now Richter has

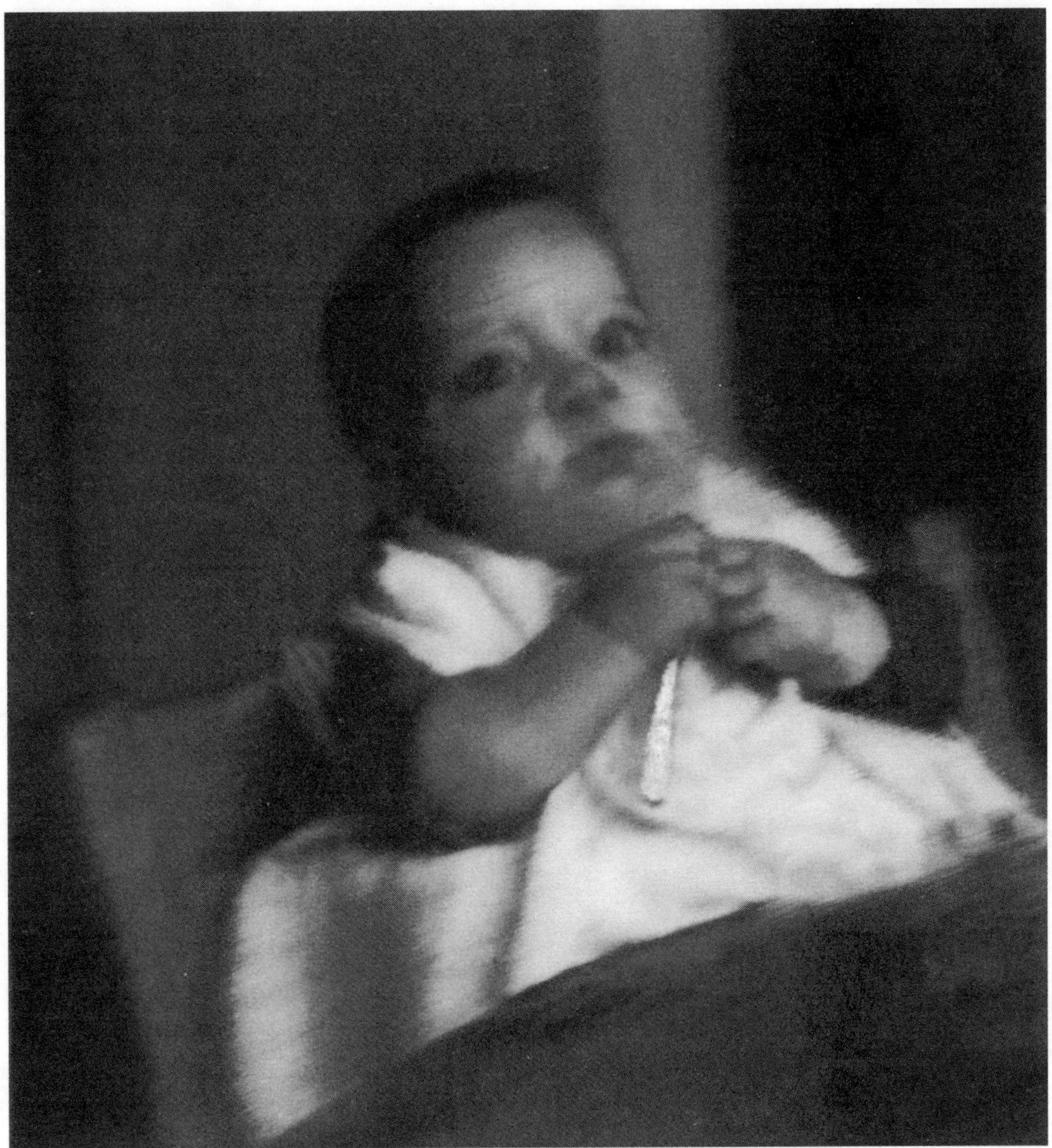

been opening up a space for analogy within his gray monochromes by constructing them out of reflective materials.[105] The monochrome toward which Betty looks, however, has been produced out of the most traditional of materials: canvas and paint. It is also bereft of distinguishing features. These attributes make it representative of those works in Richter's oeuvre that evoke neither "feelings" nor "associations." When Betty turns around to look at this painting, she therefore gestures toward that moment in her father's past in which he most emphatically abjured relationality.

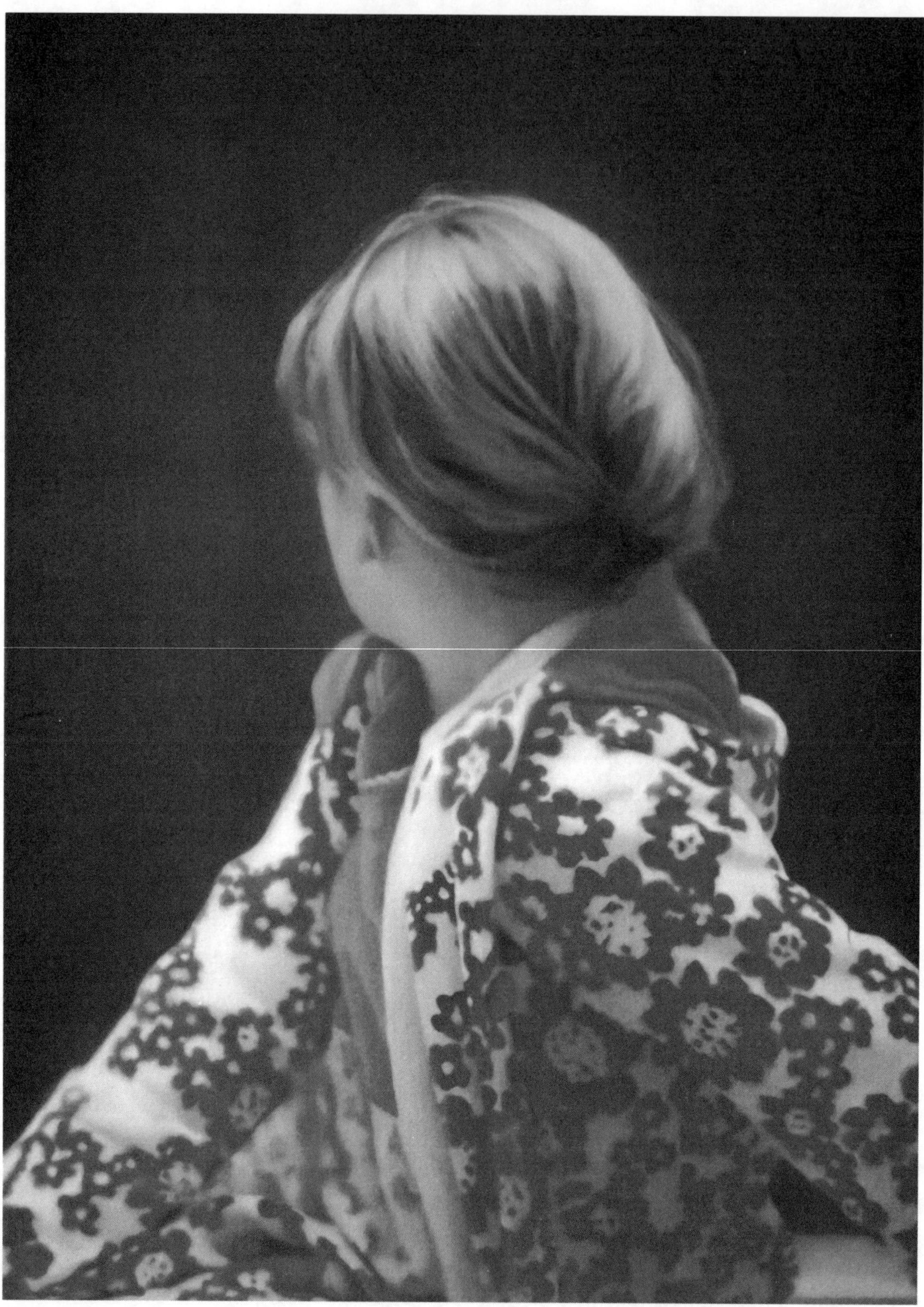

See also Plate 17 in color insert.

The 1988 *Betty* is in close dialogue with an important passage from Benjamin's "On the Concept of History." Although this is one of the most frequently-cited passages in twentieth-century thought, I will take the liberty of quoting it in its entirety:

> There is a picture by Klee called *Angelus Novus.* It shows an angel who seems about to move away from something he stares at. His eyes are wide, his mouth is open, his wings are spread. This is how the angel of history must look. His face is turned toward the past. Where a chain of events appears before *us, he* sees one single catastrophe, which keeps piling wreckage upon wreckage and hurls it at his feet. The angel would like to stay, awaken the dead, and make whole what has been smashed. But a storm is blowing from Paradise and has got caught in his wings; it is so strong that the angel can no longer close them. This storm drives him irresistibly into the future, to which his back is turned, while the pile of debris before him grows toward the sky. What we call progress is *this* storm. (392)

The most obvious link between this passage and the 1988 *Betty* is of course the action at the center of each: that of turning around, like Ovid's Orpheus, to face the past. But there are other resemblances as well. Both establish an analogical connection between philosophy and a painting, and both rely on a figural account of history.[106] Immediately before painting *October 18, 1977* and the 1988 *Betty*, Richter also made an entry in his diary whose metaphors are uncannily reminiscent of Benjamin's: "We have lost the great ideas, the Utopias, we have lost all faith, everything that creates meaning. Incapable of faith, hopeless to the utmost degree, we roam across a toxic waste dump in extreme peril; every one of those incomprehensible shards, these odds and ends of junk and detritus, menaces us, constantly hurts and maims us and sooner or later, inevitably kills us."[107]

Robert Storr takes this passage as proof of a new interest on the painter's part in Christianity.[108] However, in the world of Gerhard Richter, it is not belief that will redeem the past; it is affect. The artist stopped in the middle of producing *October 18, 1977* to paint his daughter as the angel of history because it was she who transformed his horror into grief. And because of the grief that he felt for two women who could have been his daughter, and were in fact flesh of his ontological flesh, Richter was finally able to respond to the solicitation of the concentration camp photographs. At the beginning of May 1989, he shot a series of self-portraits, to which he gave the name *Six Photos.*[109] They are gray and out of focus, like the concentration camp and the Baader-Meinhof photographs. In each of them, Richter also inhabits a confined space, which could be a prison cell, or the cramped quarters in which the Nazis housed camp inmates. Because the

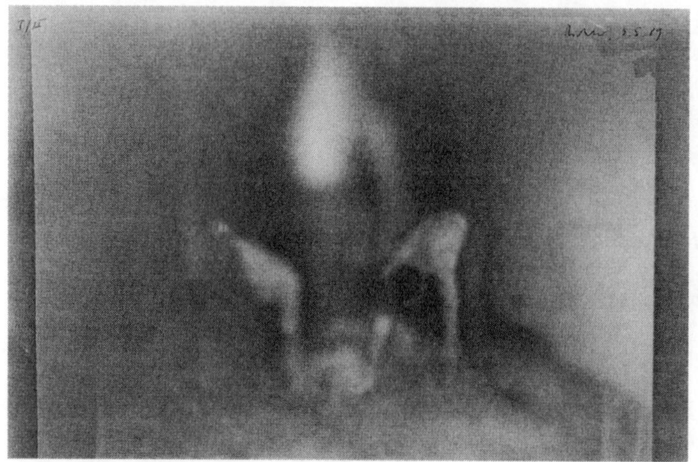

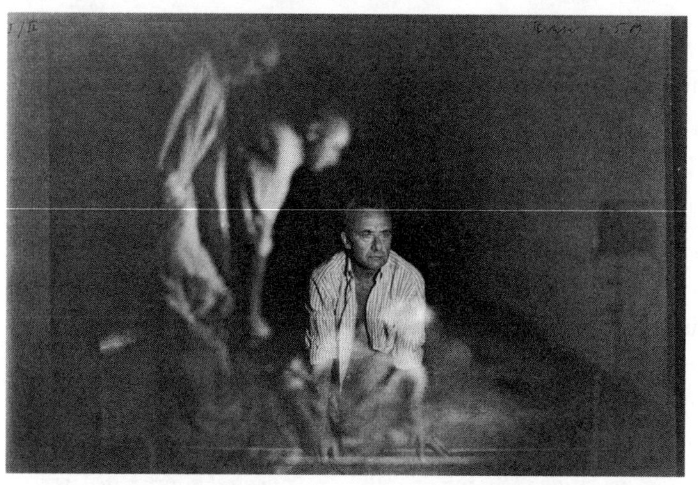

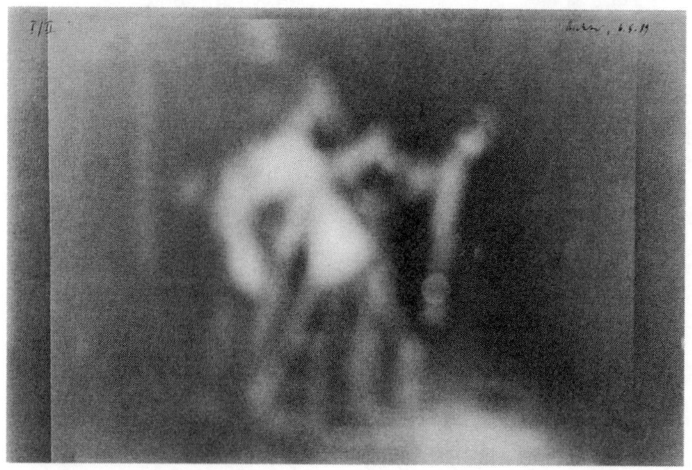

photographs are multiply exposed, Richter sometimes appears more than once. In one he wears a striped shirt, connecting him to those who had the dubious privilege of working in the camps instead of dying there.[110] In another, he evokes a guard as well as a prisoner, and in several others he joins hands with the dead.

The same year, Richter inserted the out-of-focus photographs of the Baader-Meinhof group into the *Atlas*, thereby foregrounding their relationship to the concentration camp photographs.[111] But although he did not know this at the time, there was also another reason why he paused in the middle of working on *October 18, 1977* to paint another portrait of his daughter. The mountainous pile of debris described by Benjamin was in imminent danger of mounting even higher. Betty turns around to look behind her because it is the only way of preventing this from happening.

EARLY IN 1989, Richter began painting what are in my view his greatest abstract works: *January*, *December*, and *November*. Each canvas in this triptych is powerfully evocative of the month after which it has been named.[112] But the three paintings also reference *October 18, 1977* in ways that are hard to ignore. Dramatic vertical strokes run down the center and right side of *January* and *December*. So far as I have been able to ascertain, the first time Richter uses this kind of facture is in *Cell*, where it plays a crucial role. The source photograph for the latter painting shows Baader's prison cell, filled with his many books and a few other personal possessions. In *Cell*, Richter creates a vertiginous analogy between the bookcases and his own paint strokes by using the latter to foreground the verticality of the former. This has a "liquifying" effect on the cell and its contents. Water seems to be running down the image, and dissolving it; the bottom is already devoid of representation. A ghostlike presence also hovers in the center of *November*. It is photographic in consistency, like the deer in *Stag*. It also points back to another "haunted" painting, *Hanged*, and—through that—to Richter's second painting of Betty.[113]

Richter painted these three works in reverse chronological order; he began with *January* and ended with *November*. If we look at them in this order, we quickly traverse the distance separating us from October, the month in which Ensslin and Baader died. Time is obviously crucial here. But so is place. Each of the canvases is so enormous—10 feet x 13 feet—that it would fill virtually any wall onto which it might be hung, and could even be a wall itself. Each also resembles a concrete surface onto which graffiti have been painted, and then rendered illegible through rain and snow. Finally, each work consists of two panels. In the first German exhibition of the series, which took place in December 1999, the panels were separated by an inch or two.[114] In the SFMOMA show, though,

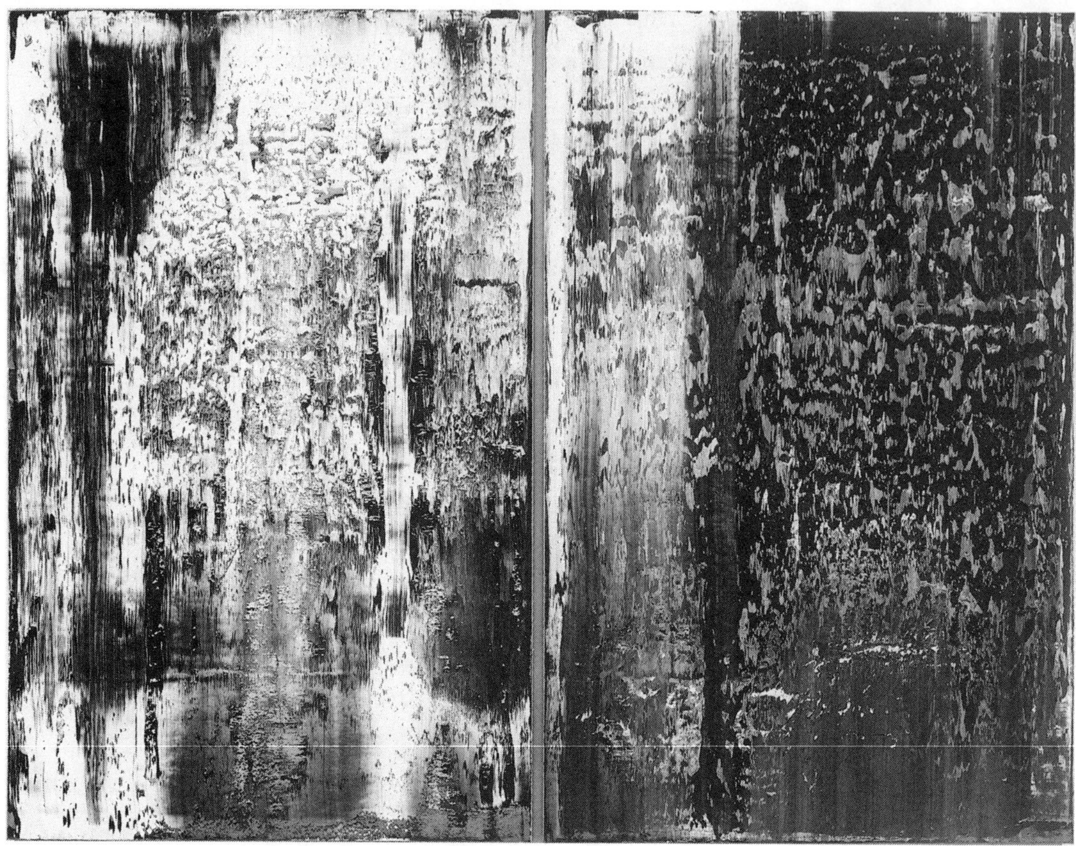

See also Plate 18 in color insert.

which opened in October 2002, they were flush with each other. In all of these ways, *January*, *December*, and *November* analogize both the Berlin Wall and what lies on either side of it.[115]

The GDR erected the Berlin Wall in 1961 to prevent further defections. As Richter points out, this made it a prison, much like Stammheim and the concentration camps.[116] In the fall of 1989, hundreds of thousands of East Germans escaped from this confinement by fleeing west through Hungary and Czechoslovakia, a flight made possible by the crumbling of the power structure in each of those countries. On November 9, 1989, the GDR lifted travel restrictions, allowing free access to the FRG. A few days later, people on both sides of the border began tearing down the wall itself. Richter painted *January*, *December*, and *November* months before any of these things occurred. But even if we were to impute to him the kind of prescience he has so often shown, it would be difficult to understand why he should offer such a bleak view of reunification. The Berlin Wall promoted the kind of oppositional thinking that Richter has always despised, and he left the GDR for the FRG the year it was built.

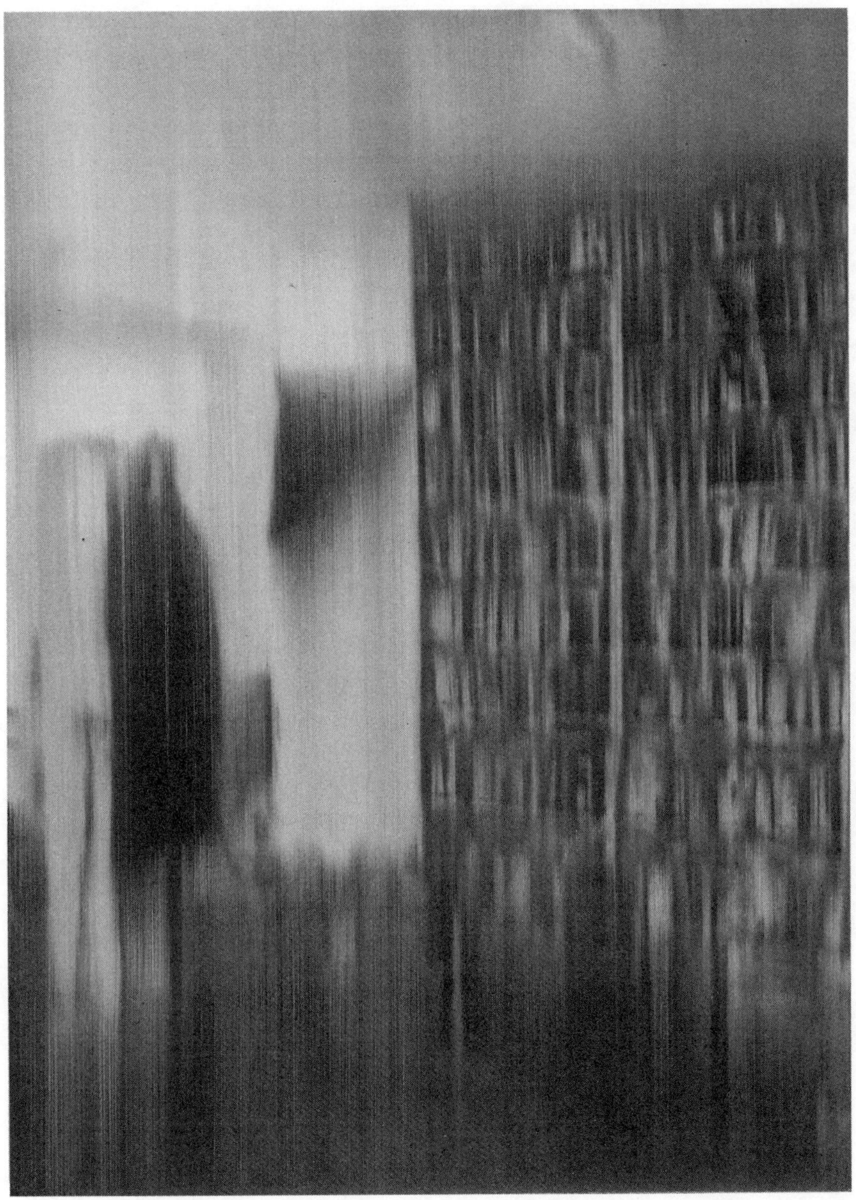

As we have already seen, Richter was initially interested in analogies in which similarity overwhelmed difference, and he found the model for this kind of analogy in photography. When he began painting color abstractions in the mid-seventies, he started making more room in his analogies for alterity. Over the next decade, similarity usurped the position earlier occupied by difference: it became the minimal term. What initially drew Richter to this kind of analogy was its potential for helping us think beyond our

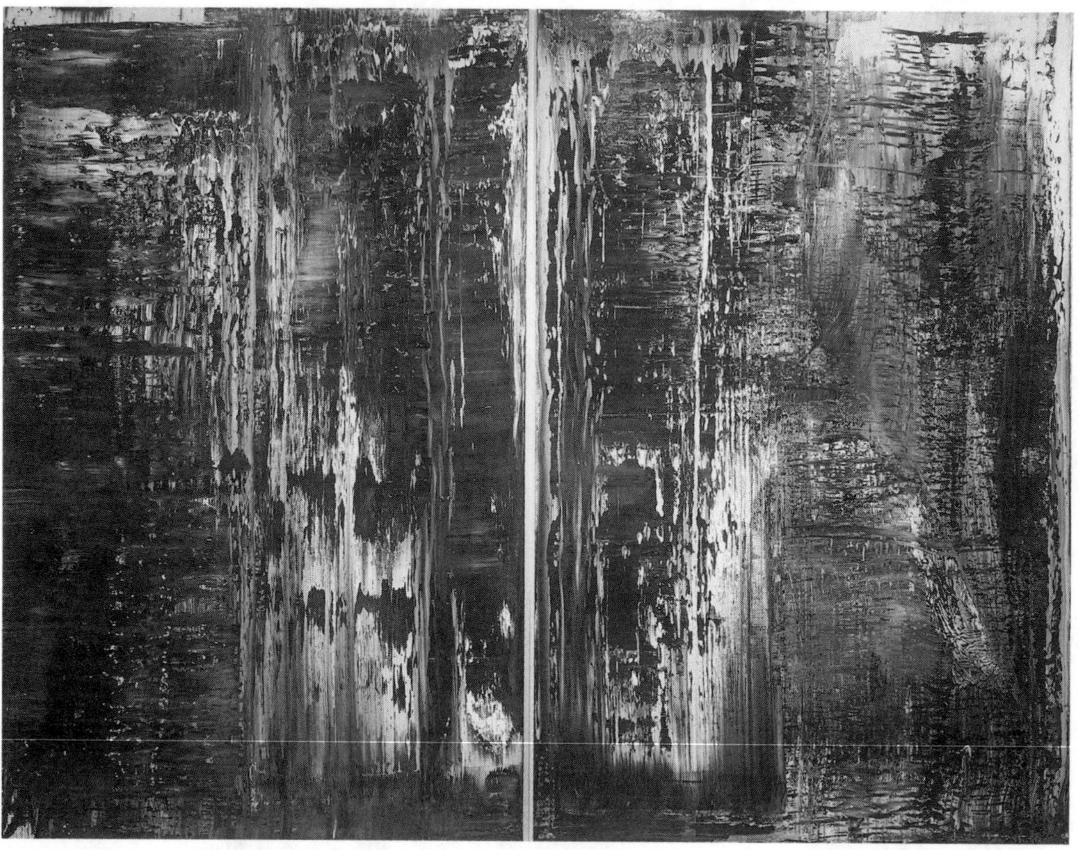

See also Plate 19 in color insert.

conceptual limits. "The lovelier, cleverer, madder, extremer, more visual and more incomprehensible the analogy, the better the picture," the artist wrote in 1982, in the text for a major exhibition of his color abstractions.[117] But in the middle of his 1986 conversation with Buchloh, he suddenly realized that the kind of analogies he had been working with also opened onto a new kind of sociality—one capable of accommodating an almost unimaginable degree of heterogeneity. They did so by mobilizing the same conjunction he uses in his third portrait of Betty: "and." "If I now think of your interpretation of Mondrian, in which pictures can partly be interpreted as models of society," Richter told Buchloh, "I can see my abstracts as metaphors in their own right, pictures that are about a possibility of social coexistence. Looked at this way, all that I am trying to do in each picture is to bring together the most disparate and mutually contradictory elements, alive and viable, in the greatest possible freedom. No Paradises."[118] In this passage, Richter anticipates the kind of Germany he would later paint: one that is neither double nor singular, but rather two-in-one.

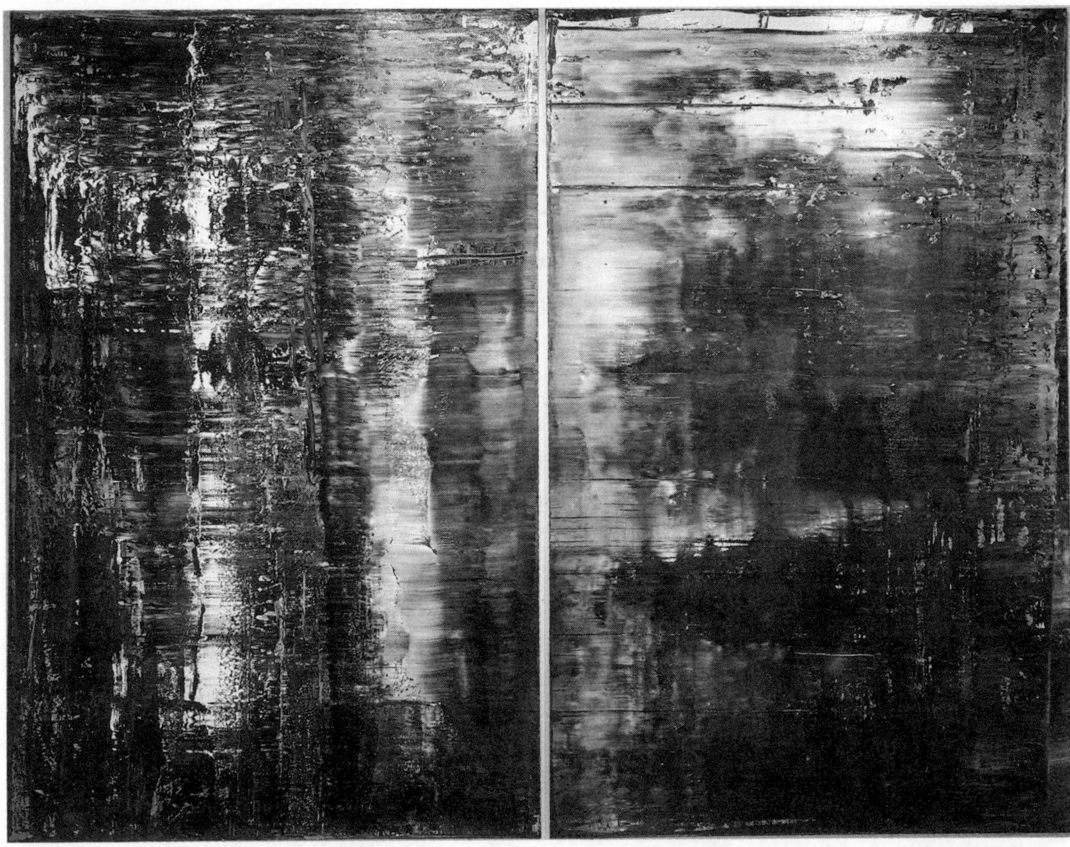

See also Plate 20
in color insert.

Shortly after the deaths of Ensslin, Meinhof, and Baader, the period of history commemorated by Richter in *October 18, 1977* was largely forgotten. This amnesia posed a grave threat, since the only way the GDR and the FRG could have entered into a relationship in which each was "alive" and "viable" was by reorienting themselves to the past. Richter painted *January*, *December*, and *November* not just for all of the reasons I have already explored but also to jog the memories of his countrymen and -women. Since oblivion, as Marguerite Duras once said, begins with the eyes,[119] and the first thing we lose the capacity to see is oblivion itself, he began this part of his project by dramatizing the process of erasure through which the RAF was removed from social consciousness. In *November*, one month after the burial of Baader and Ensslin, a thick mist already permeates everything, limiting what can be seen, but Ensslin's ghost still shines through. It also continues from the panel on the right to the panel on the left, linking two things that would otherwise remain separate. In *December*, the mist turns into rain, and then wet snow, dissolving everything it touches. By the time we reach *January*, the corpses of the RAF have been completely covered by snow.

But by painting and often hanging *January*, *December*, and *November* in reverse chronological order, Richter also turned the calendar back to October, giving his countrymen and -women the opportunity to make something different of the years that followed. He does something similar inside the works themselves. Like most of his abstract canvases, they have been laboriously built up, with layer upon layer of paint.[120] In a 1984 conversation with Wolfgang Pehnt, Richter encourages us to see each layer as a separate sheet of time by emphasizing the discontinuity of his own production process. "A picture like this is painted in different layers," he says, "separated by intervals of time."[121] For a long time now, Richter has used this kind of superimposition to build analogies across time. In *January*, *December*, and *November*, he also uses it to undo the past. In these works, each layer of paint does not adhere tightly to the one beneath it. Instead, unpredictable holes open up within the paint strokes, permitting us to see what lies behind.

THIS IS NOT, of course, the end of the story—nor will it conclude with this chapter. In January 1990, Richter produced two more series of self-portraits, again consisting of black-and-white photographs. In the earlier of these works, *Misty Self-Portrait*, the artist looms out of the darkness of a confined space, just as he

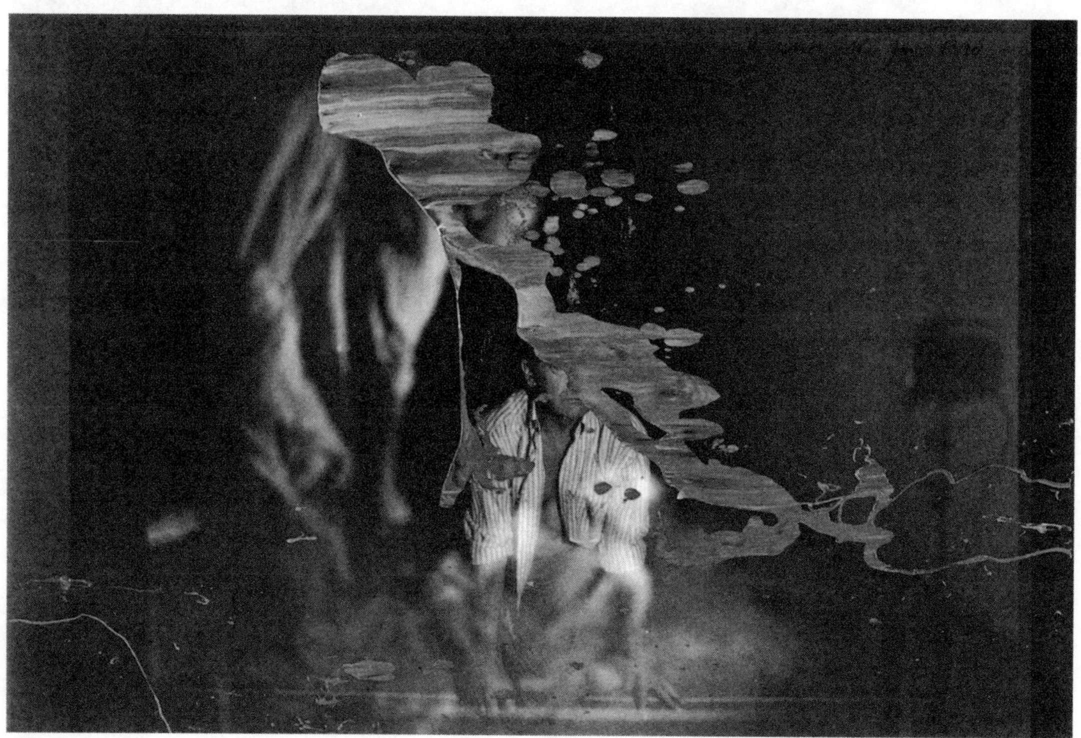

does in *Six Photos*. Again the space is unlocatable, but it is strongly evocative of a prison or a concentration camp.

The photographs in the later work—*Self-Portrait Times Three*—situate Richter in a recognizable venue: his studio. But although they permit us to say *where* he is, they, too, frustrate our attempts to situate him temporally. Richter produced the *Self-Portrait Times Three* by exposing their negatives three times and by occupying a different spot in the room on each occasion. His body has, as a result, a spectral quality,[122] reminiscent both of the second *Betty* and of *Hanged*. By triply exposing the photographs and titling them *Self-Portrait Times Three*, Richter also links them to *January*, *December*, and *November*. Finally, the artist spreads delicate tendrils of lavender paint across the black-and-white surfaces of *Misty Self-Portrait* and *Self-Portrait Times Three*, thereby returning us to the most foundational of his analogies.

A number of the works discussed in this chapter have also made their way to American soil, where they have entered into new alliances. In January 1990, Richter exhibited *October 18, 1977* in the United States, first at the Saint Louis Art Museum and then at the Grey Art Gallery and Study Center. Later in the same year, he sold *January*, *December*, and *November* to the former institution. In 1992 the Saint Louis Art Museum also purchased the 1988 *Betty*, and in

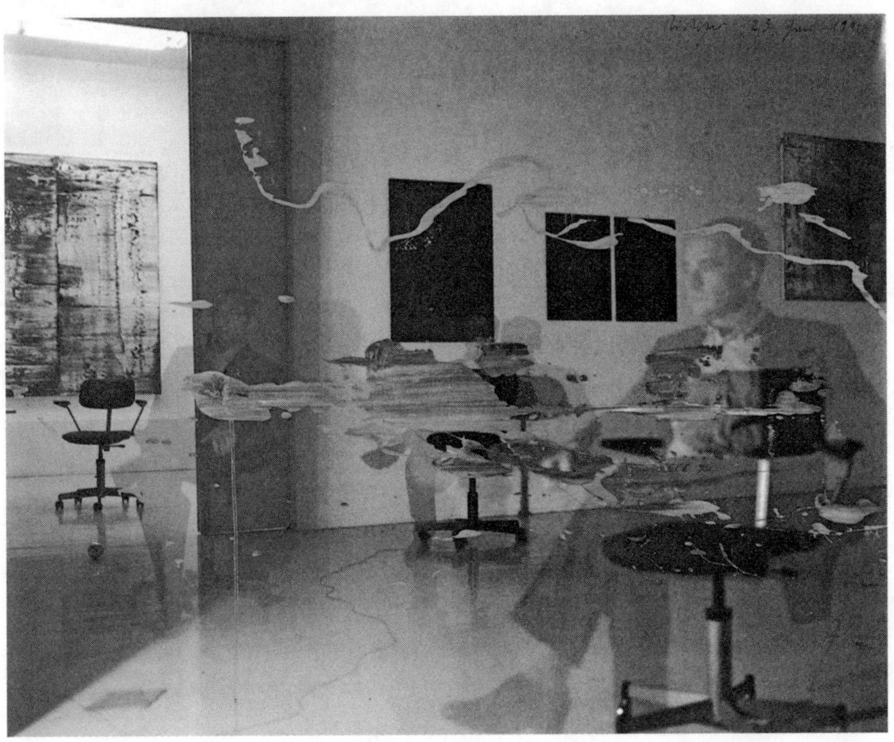

1995 New York MoMA bought the other major work in this constellation of paintings: *October 18, 1977*. This last sale caused a furor in Germany.[123] Richter seemed to be auctioning off a crucial chapter of German history, and to be doing so to a country that knew nothing about its players and that would therefore be incapable of understanding it.

For Richter, however, it was *October 18, 1977*'s German audience who misunderstood the series. Because they were "so affected by the [paintings'] subject matter," they viewed them in "almost exclusively political terms"—as grist, in other words, for the old state/terrorist binary.[124] Richter saw the transfer of these fifteen paintings from Germany to America as an opportunity for them to find a different kind of reception—one that, rather than holding them in

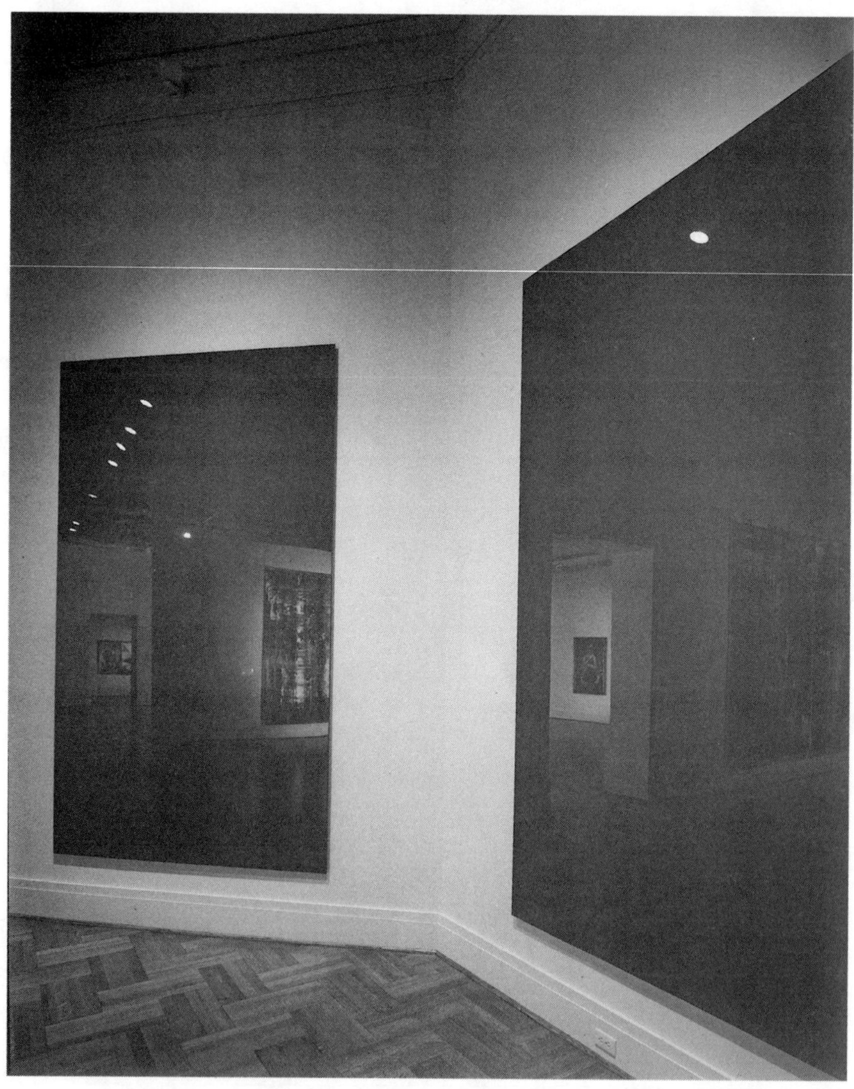

the vise of an unchanging past, would allow their "meanings" to "develop" into the future.[125] The artist had already paved the way for this reception of *October 18, 1977* three years earlier, by giving the Saint Louis Art Museum a work with the descriptive title *Gray Mirror* (1991). The product of an unusual collaboration—Richter "conceived" of it "in concert with the Museum"—it consists of four enormous glass panels, the reverse sides of which have been painted with gray enamel.[126] *Gray Mirror* hung for a while in the same room as *Betty* and *January, December*, and *November*, reflecting them and making a space within the same frame for us.[127]

In the same interview in which Richter expressed the hope that American viewers would be able to situate themselves within this figural network, he pointed to the similarities linking the student movement in the United States to its counterpart in Germany (36). But another transatlantic analogy would soon upstage this one. When MoMA purchased *October 18, 1977*, the work was still on loan at the Museum für Moderne Kunst in Frankfurt. As a result, it was not exhibited in its new home until November 2000—and by then the storm cloud of the twenty-first century had already begun to form over the city of New York. MoMA showed *October 18, 1977* again in early 2002, this time in the company of *January, December, November*, and two of the *Betty* paintings. The dust had just settled over Ground Zero.[128]

It was not only because Richter's contract with the Museum für Moderne Kunst expired in 2000 that *October 18, 1977* reached New York when it did. Its fifteen paintings came looking for us, just as the concentration camp photographs had earlier come looking for him. They traveled through time and space to find us, their brothers and sisters, hoping that our September would redeem their fall. Why were we unable to see them as our kin?

Notes

Introduction

1. Jacques Lacan, "The Mirror Stage as Formative of the *I* Function, as Revealed in Psychoanalytic Experience," in *Ecrits*, trans. Bruce Fink (New York: Norton, 2006), 76.

2. Jacques Lacan, "Aggressiveness in Psychoanalysis," in *Ecrits*, 82–102.

3. Michel Foucault, *The Order of Things: An Archaeology of the Human Sciences* (London: Tavistock, 1970), 17. In her book *Visual Analogy: Consciousness as the Art of Connecting* (Cambridge, Mass.: MIT Press, 2001), Barbara Maria Stafford also talks about the disfavor into which analogy has fallen and argues for its recuperation "as a general theory of artful invention and a practice of intermedia communication" (8). Although my approach differs from hers, I share her belief in the social importance of analogy. I am also in profound agreement with another of Stafford's claims—that analogy is "the vision of ordered relationships articulated as similarity-in-difference" and that "this order is neither facilely affirmative nor purchased at the expense of variety" (9).

4. Ovid, *The Metamorphoses*, trans. Michael Simpson (Amherst: University of Massachusetts Press, 2001), 256–257.

5. Because this part of *The Metamorphoses* is narrated by Numa and attributed to Pythagoras, some classical scholars do not believe that the ideas in it should be imputed to Ovid. Since I am not a classicist, I will not hazard an opinion on this topic. When I utter the name "Ovid," I am referring to the author projected by the text, rather than a biographical figure.

6. In *Leonardo da Vinci: The Rhythm of the World*, Rosetta Translations (New York: Konecky and Konecky, 1998), Daniel Arasse talks about the affinities between Leonardo's thought and Book XV of *The Metamorphoses*. For Leonardo, as for Ovid's Pythagoras, the world is "in a permanent state of flux." Instead of "sinking into depression or sorrow, Leonardo used this perception as a foundation for his researches" (17–18). He is less interested in form than in what Paul Klee calls "the formation beneath the form" (19). The notion of an "unfinished universality" also comes from Arasse.

7. Martin Heidegger, "The Age of the World Picture," in *The Question Concerning Technology and Other Essays*, trans. William Lovitt (New York: Harper and Row, 1977), 115–154.

8. René Descartes, *Discourse on Method and Meditations on First Philosophy*, ed. David Weissman (New Haven, Conn.: Yale University Press, 1996), 9.

9. Ibid., 66.

10. Arthur O. Lovejoy wrote the definitive book on the latter concept. See *The Great Chain of Being* (Cambridge, Mass.: Harvard University Press, 1964).

11. Lynn R. Wilkinson, *The Dream of an Absolute Language: Emanuel Swedenborg and French Literary Culture* (Albany: State University of New York Press, 1996), 62, 94–96.

12. Ibid., 147–216.

13. Wilkinson devotes most of the first chapter of *The Dream of an Absolute Language* to Swedenborg's influence on Constant, and chapter 5 to his influence on Baudelaire. For a discussion of Emerson's relationship to Swedenborg, see chapter 2 of Eric Wilson's book, *Emerson's Sublime Science* (New York: St. Martin's Press, 1999).

14. Ralph Waldo Emerson, "Fourierism and the Socialists," in *Uncollected Writings: Essays, Addresses, Poems, Reviews, and Letters* (New York: Lamb Publishing, 1912), 72.

15. Walt Whitman, *Leaves of Grass*, ed. Richard Maurice Bucke, Thomas R. Harned, and Horace L. Traubel (New York: Doubleday, 1902), 2:22.

16. Charles Darwin, *The Origin of Species* (New York: Random House, 1979), 454–455.

17. Wilkinson, *The Dream of an Absolute Language*, 9.

18. James Moore and Adrian Desmond provide a fascinating and extremely informative account of Darwin's relationship to slavery in their introduction to *The Descent of Man* (London: Penguin, 2004), xi–lviii.

19. See Betsy Erkkila, *Whitman the Political Poet* (New York: Oxford University Press, 1989), 47. Martin Klammer makes sense of Whitman's shifting views on slavery and race by positioning them against a historical backdrop in *Whitman, Slavery, and the Emergence of Leaves of Grass* (University Park: Pennsylvania State University Press, 1995).

20. Lacan, "Aggressiveness in Psychoanalysis," 98–101.

21. Jacques Lacan, "Some Reflections on the Ego," *International Journal of Psychoanalysis*, no. 34 (1953): 13; "Aggressiveness in Psychoanalysis," 84–86.

22. Ovid, *The Metamorphoses*, 163–167.

23. Charles Segal offers an overview of many of these appropriations in *Orpheus: The Myth of the Poet* (Baltimore: Johns Hopkins University Press, 1989), 155–198. For a more detailed account of Christian readings of the myth, see Eleanor Irwin, "The Songs of Orpheus and the New Song of Christ," in *Orpheus: The Metamorphosis of a Myth*, ed. John Warden (Toronto: University of Toronto Press, 1982), 51–62, and Patricia Vicari, "Sparagmos: Orpheus among the Christians," in *Orpheus: The Metamorphosis of a Myth*, 63–83. John Warden conducts a more in-depth study of Neoplatonic interpretations of the myth in "Orpheus and Ficino," in *Orpheus: The Metamorphosis of a Myth*, 85–110.

24. Mary Zimmerman's 1998 play, *Metamorphoses*, is a particularly striking example of this. Theodore Ziolkowski discusses its treatment of the Orpheus and Eurydice myth in *Ovid and the Moderns* (Ithaca: Cornell University Press, 2005), 203–205.

25. Timothy J. McGee, "Orfeo and Eurydice, the First Two Operas," in *Orpheus: The Metamorphosis of a Myth*, 163–181.

26. For illustrations of works by these and many other artists who have gravitated to the myth of Orpheus and Eurydice, see Dorothy M. Kosinski, *Orpheus in Nineteenth-Century Symbolism* (Ann Arbor: UMI Research Press, 1989).

27. Judith E. Bernstock discusses the Balanchine ballets and the Beckmann lithographs in her book *Under the Spell of Orpheus: The Persistence of a Myth in Twentieth-*

Century Art (Carbondale: Southern Illinois Press, 1991), 70–73, 55–69. She also talks about a number of other twentieth-century artists and writers who worked with the myth, including Franz Marc, Guillaume Apollinaire, Raoul Dufy, Giorgio de Chirico, Pablo Picasso, Paul Klee, and Oskar Kokoschka.

28. John Ashbery's "Syringa" and Muriel Rukeyser's "In Hades, Orpheus" can be found in *Orpheus and Company: Contemporary Poems on Greek Mythology*, ed. Deborah de Nicola (Hanover, N.H.: University Press of New England, 1999), 3–5, 36, along with many other recent poems about the myth. Margaret Atwood's three poems on this topic are included in her *Selected Poems II: 1976–1986* (Boston: Houghton Mifflin, 1987), 106–115, and Adrienne Rich's "I Dream I'm the Death of Orpheus" in her *Poetry and Prose* (New York: Norton, 1993), 43.

29. Patricia Vicari, "Sparagmos: Orpheus among the Christians," in *Orpheus: The Metamorphosis of a Myth*, 68–70.

30. Maurice Blanchot, "The Gaze of Orpheus," in *The Station Hill Blanchot Reader: Fiction and Literary Essays* (Barrytown, N.Y.: Station Hill Press, 1999), 437.

31. "The Orpheus: A Tragedy," in *A Translation of the Orpheus of Angelo Politian and the Aminta of Torquato Tasso*, trans. Louis E. Lord (Oxford: Oxford University Press, 1931), 100. I am quoting from the original version of the play.

32. Emmet Robbins, "Famous Orpheus," in *Orpheus: The Metamorphosis of a Myth*, 15; and Segal, *Orpheus: The Myth of the Poet*, 155–159.

33. Poliziano's *Orfeo* ends with this scene, Milton restages it in *Lycidas*, and many artists have depicted it, including Mantegna and Dürer. Patricia Vicari explores Milton's use of it in "The Triumph of Art, the Triumph of Death: Orpheus in Spenser and Milton," in *Orpheus: The Metamorphosis of a Myth*, 215–230. Aby Warburg describes Mantegna and Dürer's depictions of the death of Orpheus in "Dürer and Italian Antiquity" (*The Renewal of Pagan Antiquity*, trans. David Britt [Los Angeles: Getty Research Institute, 1999], 553–558).

34. My attention was drawn to Leonardo's drawings of the Orpheus machine by James Coleman, who included digital versions of them in his "intervention" in the Louvre's 2003 exhibition of Leonardo's drawings and manuscripts. I provide a detailed reading of this exhibition and Coleman's place within it in chapter 6.

35. This part of the meal is described in Matthew 26:17–30, Mark 14:12–25, and Luke 22:7–20. The first of these passages reads as follows in *The New Oxford Annotated Bible* (New York: Oxford University Press, 1994): "While they were eating, Jesus took a loaf of bread, and after blessing it he broke it, gave it to the disciples, and said, 'Take, eat; this is my body.' Then he took a cup, and after giving thanks he gave it to them saying, 'Drink from it, all of you; for this is my blood of the covenant, which is poured out for many for the forgiveness of sins.'" Freud claims that the Eucharist derives from the cannibalistic meal he describes in *Totem and Taboo* (*The Standard Edition of the Complete Psychological Works of Sigmund Freud*, trans. James Strachey [London: Hogarth Press, 1943–1974], 13:141–143). However, the author whom Freud invokes in support of this claim, Salomon Reinach, emphasizes the similarities between Christianity and Orphism (see *Orpheus: A History of Religions*, trans. Florence Simmonds [New York: Liverright, 1930], v–vii, 228–229).

36. 1882 is the publication date of the first edition of *The Gay Science*, and 1939 the publication date for the first British edition of *Moses and Monotheism*. The latter

book was published in Holland the year before, and two of its essays appeared earlier in the decade. 1965 was the year in which Richter painted *Motor Boat* and *Stag*, which I discuss in chapter 7, and 2003 was the date of Coleman's "intervention" in the Louvre's Leonardo exhibition, which I discuss in chapter 6.

37. Freud had the first of these operations in April 1923, and the one that impaired his speech and hearing six months later. He wrote "Some Psychical Consequences of the Anatomical Distinction between the Sexes" in 1925, "Fetishism" in 1927, "Female Sexuality" in 1931, and "Femininity" in 1932. He also had many other operations during this period.

38. See, for instance, Freud, "Some Psychical Consequences of the Anatomical Distinction between the Sexes," in *The Standard Edition*, 19:252–256.

39. Freud, *Moses and Monotheism*, in *The Standard Edition*, 23:7–137.

40. Lou Andreas-Salomé, *Looking Back*, ed. Ernst Pfeiffer, trans. Breon Mitchell (New York: Marlowe, 1995), 10–11.

41. Salomé describes the act of turning around to see the "partner" one has left behind as a psychoanalytic undertaking in her *Freud Journal*, trans. Stanley A. Leavy (New York: Basic Books, 1964), 192–193.

42. Salomé, *Looking Back*, 30–32. See also 159, n. 28.

43. Rainer Maria Rilke, *Letters: 1910–1926*, trans. Jane Bannard Greene and M. D. Herter Norton (New York: Norton, 1969), 46–49.

44. Rainer Maria Rilke, *Sonnets to Orpheus*, Part 1, Sonnet XII, in *Ahead of All Parting: The Selected Poetry and Prose of Rainer Maria Rilke*, trans. Stephen Mitchell (New York: Modern Library, 1995), 433.

45. Rilke, *Letters: 1910–1926*, 373.

46. Ibid., 41–45.

47. In a 1923 letter, Rilke wrote that the *Sonnets to Orpheus* "impos[ed] themselves on [him]," and that they were "the most enigmatical dictation" he had ever "sustained and achieved" (*Letters: 1910–1926*), 327.

48. Ibid., 109–110.

49. Ibid., 381–382.

50. Ibid., 47–49.

51. Friedrich Nietzsche, *Thus Spoke Zarathustra*, ed. Adrian del Caro and Robert Pippin, trans. Adrian del Caro (Cambridge: Cambridge University Press, 2006), p. 110.

52. Dorothy M. Kosinski, *Orpheus in Nineteenth-Century Symbolism* (Ann Arbor: UMI Research Press, 1989), 159.

53. Marcel Proust, *In Search of Lost Time*, Vol. 1, *Swann's Way*, trans. C. K. Scott Moncrieff, Terence Kilmartin, and D. J. Enright (New York: Modern Library, 2003), 1–9.

54. Rilke talks about these issues in a series of letters written in December 1911 and January 1912. See his *Letters: 1910–1926*, 32–51.

55. Paul Valéry, "Solitude," *Poems*, trans. David Paul, in *The Collected Works of Paul Valéry*, vol. 1 (Princeton, N.J.: Princeton University Press, 1971), 319, and two very different versions of a poem called "Orpheus," the first of which was published in 1891 and the second of which was published in 1926 (see Valéry, *Poems*, 435–436, and Valéry, *Oeuvres*, Bibliothèque de la Pléiade, vol. 1 [Paris: Gallimard, 1957], 1540–1541).

56. Kosinksi provides a very helpful—and lavishly illustrated—account of these

works in *Orpheus in Nineteenth-Century Symbolism*, 159–162. She includes both a front and a rear view of *Orpheus* (1892), the statue with the severed hand. See also Albert E. Eisen with Rosalyn Frankel Jamison, *Rodin's Art*, ed. Bernard Barryte (New York: Oxford University Press, 2003), 331–335.

57. Proust, *In Search of Lost Time*, Vol. 6, *Time Regained*, 262–263.

58. Josef Breuer and Sigmund Freud, *Studies on Hysteria*, in *The Standard Edition*, 2:302–303.

59. Martin Heidegger, "What Are Poets For?" in *Poetry, Language, Thought*, trans. Albert Hofstadter (New York: Harper and Row, 1971), 91–142.

60. The act of turning around figures prominently in Benjamin's famous passage about the angel of history. See "On the Concept of History," in Walter Benjamin, *Selected Writings*, ed. Howard Eiland and Michael W. Jennings (Cambridge, Mass.: Harvard University Press, 2003), 392–393.

61. Walter Benjamin, *The Arcades Project*, trans. Howard Eiland and Kevin McLaughlin (Cambridge, Mass.: Harvard University Press, 1999), 462–464, 473.

62. Ibid., 475.

63. Ibid., 474.

64. Ibid.

65. Benjamin, "On the Concept of History," 392.

66. Martin Heidegger, "What Is Metaphysics?" in *Pathmarks*, ed. William McNeill (Cambridge: Cambridge University Press, 1998), 82–96.

67. Freud, "Leonardo da Vinci and a Memory of His Childhood," in *The Standard Edition*, 11:63–137.

68. This phrase comes from Coleman's wall text.

Chapter 1

1. Friedrich Nietzsche, *The Gay Science*, ed. Bernard Williams, trans. Josefine Nauckhoff and Adrian del Caro (Cambridge: Cambridge University Press, 2001), 119. Nietzsche published the first version of the book in 1882 and a second, longer edition in 1887.

2. As Lou Andreas-Salomé puts it in *Friedrich Nietzsche: The Man in His Works*, which is published in a book entitled *Nietzsche*, trans. Siegfried Mandel (Urbana: University of Illinois Press, 2001): "The Zarathustra figure represents Nietzsche's own transformation, mirroring the transformation of his vitality into a godlike photograph" (123).

3. Friedrich Nietzsche, *Thus Spoke Zarathustra*, ed. Adrian del Caro and Robert Pippin, trans. Adrian del Caro (Cambridge: Cambridge University Press, 2006), 18.

4. Freud is extremely evasive on the topic of his relationship to Nietzsche. In "On the History of the Psycho-Analytic Movement," he writes: "In later years I have denied myself the very great pleasure of reading the works of Nietzsche, with the deliberate object of not being hampered in working out the impressions received in psycho-analysis by any sort of anticipatory ideas. I had therefore to be prepared—and I am so, gladly—to forgo all claims to priority in the many instances in which laborious psycho-analytic investigation can merely confirm the truths which the philosopher recognized by intuition" (*The Standard Edition of the Complete Psychological Works of Sigmund Freud*, trans. James

Strachey [London: Hogarth Press, 1943–1974], 14:15–16). He repeats this claim in a later text, "Autobiographical Study" (*The Standard Edition*, 20:60). Ronald Lehrer writes that Freud's contemporaries often remarked upon the similarities between his writings and Nietzsche's, and that he responded in the same way to these comments (*Nietzsche's Presence in Freud's Life and Thought: On the Origins of a Psychology of Dynamic Unconscious Mental Functioning* [Albany: SUNY Press, 1995], 103–105, 254–255). However, there are numerous references to Nietzsche in Freud's work. He quotes phrases or lines from the philosopher three times in *The Interpretation of Dreams* (*The Standard Edition*, 4:330, 5:549, 655); once in *Notes Upon the Case of an Obsessional Neurosis* (*The Standard Edition*, 10:184); and once in "Some Character-Types Met with in Psycho-Analytic Work" (*The Standard Edition*, 14:333). Freud also refers indirectly to him in "The Uncanny" (*The Standard Edition*, 17:234), and mentions him in *Group Psychology and the Analysis of the Ego* (*The Standard Edition*, 18:123). Nietzsche casts a long shadow over Freud's discussion of repetition in *Beyond the Pleasure Principle* (*The Standard Edition*, 18:7–64), and the late topography in *The Ego and the Id* (*The Standard Edition*, 19:13–59). Freud also refers to Salomé's relationship with Nietzsche in a commemorative essay ("Lou Andreas-Salomé," *The Standard Edition*, 23:297), and her book about him in one of his letters to her (Sigmund Freud and Lou Andreas-Salomé, *Letters*, ed. Ernst Pfeiffer, trans. William and Elaine Robson-Scott [New York: Norton, 1966], 198). And this is by no means a comprehensive list. Lehrer provides an encyclopedic account of Freud's relationship to Nietzsche in *Nietzsche's Presence in Freud's Life and Thought*. For a more philosophical and closely reasoned discussion of this relationship, see Paul-Laurent Assoun, *Freud and Nietzsche*, ed. Richard L. Collier (London: Athlone Press, 2000). Assoun is more interested in exploring the dialogue between psychoanalysis and philosophy than in questions of priority and influence.

5. Sigmund Freud, *Totem and Taboo*, in *The Standard Edition*, 13:140–143.

6. Freud, "On Narcissism," in *The Standard Edition*, 14:91.

7. Freud, *Civilization and Its Discontents*, in *The Standard Edition*, 21:91–92.

8. Although Freud claims that reason is antithetical to the omnipotence of thoughts in *Totem and Taboo* and *The Future of an Illusion*, he later acknowledged that all "advances in intellectuality have as their consequence that the individual's self-esteem is increased, that he is made proud—that he feels superior to other people who have remained under the spell of sensuality" (*Moses and Monotheism*, in *The Standard Edition*, 23:115).

9. Freud relates to the reader much as he describes President Schreber relating to his doctor in his famous case history of the judge. See his *Psycho-Analytic Notes on an Autobiographical Account of a Case of Paranoia*, in *The Standard Edition*, 12:38.

10. Nietzsche, *The Gay Science*, 119.

11. Lou Andreas-Salomé, *Looking Back*, ed. Ernst Pfeiffer, trans. Breon Mitchell (New York: Marlowe, 1995), 2.

12. Jacques Lacan, "The Mirror Stage as Formative of the *I* Function, as Revealed in Psychoanalytic Experience," in *Ecrits*, trans. Bruce Fink (New York: Norton, 2006), 75–81.

13. In one of the two chapters of *Looking Back* that she devotes to Freud, Salomé writes that the "'extra' quality which distinguishes us from everything we deal with con-

sists precisely in the consciousness of that which allows us entry into the brotherhood of all things" (102).

14. See, for instance, Salomé's May 20, 1927, letter to Freud (Freud and Salomé, *Letters*, 165–168).

15. Rainer Maria Rilke, *Letters: 1910–1926*, trans. Jane Bannard Greene and M. D. Herter Norton (New York: Norton, 1969), 84.

16. I am relying here on Angela der Lippe's translation of this passage, which she quotes in the introduction to her translation of Salomé's *You Alone Are Real to Me: Remembering Rainer Maria Rilke* (Rochester, N.Y.: BOA Editions, 2003), 24. For a quite different translation of the same lines, which irons out some of their ambiguity, see *Looking Back*, 85.

17. Salomé, *Looking Back*, 10.

18. Ibid., 4–6.

19. Ibid., 10–11.

20. Rilke, *Letters: 1910–1926*, 315.

21. Ibid., 324–325.

22. Rilke, *Sonnets to Orpheus*, Part 1, Sonnet VII, lines 3–4, in *Ahead of All Parting: The Selected Poetry and Prose of Rainer Maria Rilke*, trans. Stephen Mitchell (New York: Modern Library, 1995), 423.

23. Rilke, *Sonnets to Orpheus*, 1, XIII, in *Ahead of All Parting*, 487.

24. See Freud and Salomé, *Letters*, 171–172, 182–184, 206–207.

25. Ibid., 183.

26. Salomé, *Looking Back*, 102.

27. Leo Bersani provides a very different reading of this concept in *The Freudian Body: Psychoanalysis and Art* (New York: Columbia University Press, 1986), 13–25. He suggests that the oceanic feeling may conceal "a considerable amount of destructive aggression toward the world" (15). However, in a later book, he and Ulysse Dutoit describe Being in terms that are very close to my own, and which I see as the basis of this feeling. "We are not cut off from anything," they write in *Caravaggio's Secret* (Cambridge, Mass.: MIT Press, 1998). "[N]othing escapes connectedness, the play of and between forms. . . . In a sense, there is nothing 'to know,' only the consciousness of the movement in which we participate" (72).

28. This letter, which was written on December 5, 1927, is included in the appendix to William B. Parsons's book, *The Enigma of the Oceanic Feeling: Revisioning the Psychoanalytic Theory of Mysticism* (New York: Oxford University Press, 1999), 174, along with the rest of the surviving correspondence between Freud and Rolland. In the first four chapters of his book, William Parsons provides a very illuminating account of the relationship between Freud and Rolland, to which I am much indebted.

29. Parsons, *The Enigma of the Oceanic Feeling*, 77.

30. This footnote is also present in the German edition. It reads: "Ja, aus der Welt werden wir nicht fallen. Wir sind einmal darin" (*Das Unbehagen in der Kultur*, in *Studienausgabe*, vol. 9 [Frankfurt: S. Fischer Verlag, 1989], 198).

31. Freud, *The Interpretation of Dreams*, in *The Standard Edition*, 4:196.

32. The German text reads: "Aus dieser Welt können wir nicht fallen" (*Das Unbehagen in der Kultur*, 198).

33. Parsons, *The Enigma of the Oceanic Feeling*, 174.

34. Ernest Jones, *The Life and Works of Sigmund Freud* (New York: Basic Books, 1957), 3:97.

35. Parsons, *The Enigma of the Oceanic Feeling*, 178.

36. Ibid.

37. Ibid., 171.

38. Ibid., 172.

39. Ibid., 171.

40. Sigmund Freud, *Psychoanalysis and Faith: Dialogues with the Reverend Oskar Pfister*, ed. Heinrich Meng and Ernst L. Freud (New York: Basic Books, 1963), 48.

41. Freud, *Three Essays on the Theory of Sexuality*, in *The Standard Edition*, 7:135–243.

42. Freud, *Beyond the Pleasure Principle*, in *The Standard Edition*, 18:49.

43. The English translation of the last part of this passage adheres closely to the German, which reads: "Warum das geschehen müsse, wissen wir nicht; das sei eben das Werk des Eros. Diese Menschen-mengen sollen libidinös aneinander gebunden werden" (*Das Unbehagen in der Kultur*, *Studienausgabe*, 9:249).

44. Freud and Salomé, *Letters*, 21.

45. See Freud, *Beyond the Pleasure Principle*, 18:49; and *Civilization and Its Discontents*, 21:122, both in *The Standard Edition*.

46. See Freud, *Civilization and Its Discontents*, in *The Standard Edition*, 21:122.

47. Freud, *The Ego and the Id*, in *The Standard Edition*, 19:41–47.

48. Freud, "Why War?" in *The Standard Edition*, 22:203–15.

49. Barbara Low, *Psychoanalysis: A Brief Account of the Freudian Theory* (London: George Allen and Unwin, 1920), 73.

50. Parsons, *The Enigma of the Oceanic Feeling*, 98.

51. Ibid., 174.

52. Ibid., 98.

53. Freud, *Beyond the Pleasure Principle*, in *The Standard Edition*, 18:12–14.

54. In their *Studies on Hysteria*, Freud and Josef Breuer write that "hysterics suffer mainly from *reminiscences*" (in *The Standard Edition*, 2:7).

Chapter 2

1. Robert Hendrickson, *The Literary Life and Other Curiosities* (New York: Viking, 1981), 107.

2. G. W. F. Hegel, *Phenomenology of Spirit*, trans. A. V. Miller (New York: Oxford University Press, 1977), 111–119. The part of this passage that is devoted to the slave or "bondsman," is—however—fully caught up in the dream of self-overcoming. "In fear, the being-for-self is present in the bondsman himself," Hegel writes there. "[I]n fashioning the thing, he becomes aware that being-for-self belongs to him, that he himself exists essentially and actually in his own right. . . . Through this rediscovery of himself by himself, the bondsman realizes that it is precisely in his work wherein he seemed to have only an alienated existence that he acquires a mind of his own" (118–119).

3. Friedrich Nietzsche, *The Gay Science*, ed. Bernard Williams, trans. Josefine Nauckhoff and Adrian del Caro (Cambridge: Cambridge University Press, 2001), 53.

4. Marcel Proust, *In Search of Lost Time*, Vol. 1, *Swann's Way*, trans. C. K. Scott Moncrieff, Terence Kilmartin, and D. J. Enright (New York: Modern Library, 2003), 1.

5. Rainer Maria Rilke, *Letters, 1910–1926*, trans. Jane Bannard Greene and M. D. Herter Norton (New York: Norton, 1969), 257.

6. Rainer Maria Rilke, *Letters, 1892–1910*, trans. Jane Bannard Greene and M. D. Herter Norton (New York: Norton, 1969), 84.

7. See in particular her January 10, 1915, letter to Freud, in Sigmund Freud and Lou Andreas-Salomé, *Letters*, ed. Ernst Pfeiffer, trans. William and Elaine Robson-Scott (New York: Norton, 1966), 22–26.

8. Freud, "Leonardo da Vinci and a Memory of His Childhood," in *The Standard Edition of the Complete Psychological Works of Sigmund Freud*, trans. James Strachey (London: Hogarth, 1943–1974), 11:63–137.

9. Lou Andreas-Salomé, *Friedrich Nietzsche: The Man in His Works*, in *Nietzsche*, trans. Siegfried Mandel (Chicago: University of Illinois Press, 2001), 5. Salomé takes this phrase from one of Nietzsche's letters. In the same letter, which Salomé includes in her book, he tells her that he agrees with her approach to his work: "Your idea of reducing philosophical systems to the personal records of their originators is truly an idea arising from a 'brother-sister brain'" (3). Salomé uses a similar passage from Nietzsche's *Human, All Too Human* as the epigraph to *Looking Back* (ed. Ernst Pfeiffer, trans. Breon Mitchell [New York: Marlow, 1995]): "Life is the return of investment in life: A person may preen himself ever so much with his knowledge and flatter himself as ever so objective; in the final tally, he comes away with nothing more than his own biography" (1).

10. Freud, "Creative Writers and Day-Dreaming," in *The Standard Edition*, 9:150.

11. Salomé, *Looking Back*, 50.

12. Lou Andreas-Salomé, *The Freud Journal*, trans. Stanley A. Leavy (New York: Basic Books, 1964), 192–193.

13. The same word appears in the German text. "War man sonst so rasch und stark in den Partner eingedrungen," reads the clause in question. See Lou Andreas-Salomé, *In der Schule bei Freud: Tagebuch eines Jahres* (Zürich: Max Niehans, 1958), 223.

14. As Mieke Bal explains in *Lethal Love: Feminist Literary Readings of Biblical Love Stories* (Bloomington: Indiana University Press, 1987), 114–119, and Daniel Boyarin has also stressed in a private conversation with me, the Hebrew text differs from these later interpretations, because it does not impute a subordinate status to "helper."

15. *The New Oxford Annotated Bible*, ed. Bruce M. Metzger and Roland E. Murphy (New York: Oxford University Press, 1991), 4.

16. Ibid.

17. Ibid., 5.

18. Ibid., 4n.

19. *The Compact Oxford English Dictionary* (Oxford: Clarendon, 1991), 1280.

20. *The Complete Letters of Sigmund Freud to Wilhelm Fliess, 1887–1904*, trans. Jeffrey Moussaieff Masson (Cambridge, Mass.: Harvard University Press, 1985), 364.

21. Lou Andreas-Salomé, *Mein Dank an Freud: Offener Brief an Professor Sigmund Freud zu seinem 75. Geburtstag* (Vienna: Internationaler Psychoanalytischer Verlag, 1931), 13.

22. I am using Biddy Martin's excellent translation of this passage in *Women and*

Modernity: The (Life)styles of Lou Andreas-Salomé (Ithaca: Cornell University Press, 1991), 228.

23. Salomé, *Mein Dank an Freud*, 14.

24. Sigmund Freud, *Project for a Scientific Psychology*, in *The Standard Edition*, 1:353–359.

25. Josef Breuer and Sigmund Freud, *Studies on Hysteria*, in *The Standard Edition*, 2.

26. Genesis 3:19 (*The New Oxford Annotated Bible*, 6).

27. Sigmund Freud, *Totem and Taboo*, in *The Standard Edition*, 13:143.

28. Martin Heidegger, *Nietzsche*, trans. David Farrell Krell (San Francisco: Harper and Row, 1991), vols. 3 and 4.

29. Freud develops this account of analogy in *The Interpretation of Dreams* (*The Standard Edition*, vols. 4 and 5).

30. Sigmund Freud, *The Interpretation of Dreams*, *The Standard Edition*, 4:176.

31. Freud, *Studies on Hysteria*, in *The Standard Edition*, 2:304.

32. Ibid., 302.

33. Freud, *The Interpretation of Dreams*, in *The Standard Edition*, 5:654.

34. In *Studies on Hysteria*, Breuer and Freud write that "*hysterics suffer mainly from reminiscences*" (7; their emphasis).

35. Salomé, *Looking Back*, 97.

36. Salomé, *The Freud Journal*, 116.

37. See Walter Benjamin, "On the Concept of History," in *Selected Writings*, ed. Howard Eiland and Michael W. Jennings (Cambridge, Mass.: Harvard University Press, 2003), 4:389–400; and *The Arcades Project*, trans. Howard Eiland and Kevin McLaughlin (Cambridge, Mass.: Harvard University Press, 1999), 456–488.

38. Benjamin, *The Arcades Project*, 474.

39. *The Georgics* were probably composed in 29 BC, thirty years before Ovid began writing *The Metamorphoses* (Ovid, *The Metamorphoses*, trans. Michael Simpson [Amherst: University of Massachusetts Press, 2001], 360; translator's note).

40. The myth is, however, much older. Emmet Robbins writes that the "first literary mention of the name of Orpheus occurs in the mid-sixth-century poet Ibycus," and that there are even earlier visual representations of him ("Famous Orpheus," in *Orpheus: The Metamorphosis of a Myth*, ed. John Warden [Toronto: University of Toronto Press, 1982], 5). Orpheus was a musician, a shaman, and sometimes a religious teacher, but not a lover (Robbins, ibid., 4; Patricia Vicari, "Sparagmos: Orpheus among the Christians," in *Orpheus: The Metamorphosis of a Myth*, 63). Although there are references to Eurydice in Aeschylus, Euripides, Apollonius, and Plato, she was a late addition, and the emphasis on romantic love and the unhappy ending were probably Virgil's innovations (Robbins, "Famous Orpheus," 15–17; Charles Segal, *Orpheus: The Myth of the Poet* [Baltimore: Johns Hopkins University Press, 1989], 16–17, 23).

41. I do not purport to know what either of these authors intended to say, or how they were originally read. I will be approaching their accounts of the myth the same way I approach Freud's account of religion: as a history of the present.

42. Virgil, *Eclogues, Georgics, Aeneid* 1–6, trans. H. R. Fairclough and G. Goold (Cambridge, Mass.: Harvard University Press, 1999), 251–259.

43. W. S. Anderson provides a very different reading of this story in his essay "The

Orpheus of Virgil and Ovid: flebile nescio quid" (*Orpheus: The Metamorphosis of a Myth*). In his view, Virgil "minimizes the role of Eurydice by not naming her [when describing her death] and by avoiding qualifying details other than calling her 'a girl doomed to die'" (28). Orpheus is also "a victim of madness and love together, pardonable by human standards but unpardonable here where gods were judging, of irrationality and the failure to remember the penalty" (29). Orpheus mourns excessively, and he compares negatively in this respect to Aristaeus (36). Segal emphasizes Orpheus's madness and Aristaeus's contrasting moderation in the first chapter of *Orpheus: The Myth of the Poet* (20–21), but in a later chapter he writes that both men have "some measure of control over and independence from nature, both are united as parts of nature's realm in their participation of the renewal of life, the most mysterious and least humanly controllable (as both learn) of nature's processes" (50).

44. As Segal observes, Virgil "shows us the relation of man and nature from the point of view of nature, not man." His Orpheus gives "animate nature" a "voice" (*Orpheus: The Myth of the Poet*, 46).

45. There is considerable disagreement about how this sentence is to be read. Anderson writes that "the adjective 'satis' ["enough"] is damning, no matter how you view it" (40); Simpson thinks that Ovid and Orpheus are simply "eager to get to where Eurydice is" (361); and Segal claims that the word "*satis*" is an ironic comment on Virgil's Orpheus, who grieves too much (59).

46. Scholars also disagree about this speech. Anderson maintains that Orpheus "works with cheap, flashy, and specious rhetoric," and that "almost every phrase" in the lines he devotes to death was "a commonplace for Roman ears, the trite baggage of expectable words" (40–41). Adolf Primmer thinks that it is "the greatest song of the greatest mythical singer," because Orpheus is so overwhelmed "when face-to-face with the powers of death and of love" that he loses his "skill in speaking" ("Das Lied des Orpheus in Ovids 'Metamorphosen,'" 129–130; quoted by Simpson, 362); and Segal thinks that Orpheus's "anti-rhetoric" may actually be extremely "rhetorical" (82–83).

47. As Anderson points out, this is the first time the word "love" is used in this story, and Ovid "presents it as a chilly abstract noun" (40).

48. David West offers a contrary interpretation of this passage. For him, Ovid's Orpheus is a "lover," and "that explains all" ("Orpheus and Eurydice," *Joint Association of Classical Teachers Review* 4 [1986]:10).

49. Ovid scholars find this complex simile perplexing, in part because it involves unknown myths and in part because they assume that the comparison of Orpheus and Eurydice to Lethaea and Olenos proceeds along standard gender lines. See Anderson, "The Orpheus of Virgil and Ovid," 43; Segal, *Orpheus: The Myth of the Poet*, 62; and Simpson, *The Metamorphoses*, 363. What happens in the coda is therefore not as significant to them as it is to me.

50. Shadi Bartsch says that "desiring" would be a better translation of the Latin text than "loving." I want to thank her for offering me a word-by-word translation of Ovid's version of the myth.

51. Robbins, "Famous Orpheus," 11–13.

52. The scholar is W. K. C. Guthrie. Robbins discusses the strengths and weaknesses of this reading in "Famous Orpheus," 10–14.

53. Giuseppe Scavizzi, "The Myth of Orpheus in Italian Renaissance Art, 1400–1600," in *Orpheus: The Metamorphosis of a Myth*, 117.

54. Ibid., 118.

55. Vicari, "The Triumph of Art, the Triumph of Death: Orpheus in Spenser and Milton," in *Orpheus: Metamorphosis of a Myth*, 223; and Segal, *Orpheus: The Myth of the Poet*, 2–5.

56. Vicari, "Sparagmos: Orpheus among the Christians," 64–66.

57. Segal provides an extended discussion of these two traditions in *Orpheus: The Myth of the Poet.*

58. Vicari, "Sparagmos: Orpheus among the Christians," 68–69.

59. Ibid., 66–68, 70; Segal, *Orpheus: The Myth of the Poet*, 166–168.

60. This is also true of a much later allegorization of the myth: that found in Maurice Blanchot's essay "The Gaze of Orpheus" (*Station Hill Blanchot Reader: Fiction and Literary Essays*, trans. Lydia Davis [Barrytown, N.Y.: Station Hill Press, 1999], 437–442).

61. "The Orpheus: A Tragedy," in *A Translation of the Orpheus of Angelo Politian and the Aminta of Torquato Tasso*, trans. Louis E. Lord (Oxford: Oxford University Press, 1931), 71–103. It was first printed in 1496, and in a revised version in a 1776 edition.

62. Ibid., 96. All quotations from this text are taken from the original version.

63. Aby Warburg, "Dürer and Italian Antiquity," in *The Renewal of Pagan Antiquity*, trans. David Britt (Los Angeles: Getty Research Institute, 1999), 555.

64. Warburg also invokes this play a number of times in "Sandro Botticelli's Birth of Venus and Spring." See *The Renewal of Pagan Antiquity*, 121–122, 124–125.

65. Indeed, Freud makes them first about the story itself. After recounting it, he writes that the "totem meal" was "the beginning of so many things—of social organization, of moral restrictions and of religion" (142).

66. Freud may also have dipped into another of this scholar's books. In the preface to *Orpheus: A History of Religions* (New York: Liveright, 1930), Reinach asserts that Orpheus was "the theologian par excellence, founder of those mysteries which ensured the salvation of mankind," and that "not only did Orphism enter deeply into the literature, philosophy and art of the ancient world; it survived them. The figure of Orpheus charming the beasts with his lyre is the only mythological motive which appears and recurs in the Christian paintings of the catacombs. The fathers of the church . . . saw in him a type—or rather a *prototype*—of Jesus" [my emphasis].

67. Aby Warburg, "Memories of a Journey through the Pueblo Region," in Philippe-Alain Michaud, *Aby Warburg, and the Image in Motion*, trans. Sophie Hawkes (New York: Zone Books, 2004), 307. This is—of course—not all there is to be said on this topic. The Indian novels mentioned in this anecdote anticipated Warburg's journey to the Pueblo region, and that journey led him to a different part of the myth. I will discuss Warburg's project in my next book, "The Miracle of Analogy."

68. I take this information from one of Stephen Mitchell's notes in *The Selected Poetry of Rainer Maria Rilke*, trans. Stephen Mitchell (New York: Vintage, 1989), 336.

Chapter 3

1. See Sigmund Freud, *Fragment of an Analysis of a Case of Hysteria*, in *The Standard Edition of the Complete Psychological Works of Sigmund Freud*, trans. James Strachey (London: Hogarth, 1943–1974), 7:7–122, and *Three Essays on the Theory of Sexuality*, in *The Standard Edition*, 7:130–243. Freud published both of these works in 1905. In *Three Essays*, he argues that every subject is both male and female, and has the capacity to be heterosexual, homosexual, or bisexual. He thus comes close to conceptualizing the relationship between "man" and "woman" as an analogy instead of a binary opposition. Freud was clearly led to this account of gender by the story he recounts in *Fragment of an Analysis*, which turns upon Dora's desire for Frau K. In 1908 Freud published an essay called "Hysterical Phantasies and Their Relation to Bisexuality," in which he explicitly links female hysteria to bisexuality and once again construes bisexuality both as a kind of androgyny and as the capacity to love both women and men (*The Standard Edition*, 9:159–166).

2. Sigmund Freud, "Psychopathic Characters on the Stage," in *The Standard Edition*, 7:305–310. This essay was not published until 1942.

3. "[Women] don't know what they're saying—that's the whole difference between them and me," Lacan writes in *On Feminine Sexuality: The Limits of Love and Knowledge, 1972–1973*, trans. Bruce Fink (New York: Norton, 1998), 73.

4. Sigmund Freud, "Creative Writers and Day-Dreaming," in *The Standard Edition*, 9:143–153.

5. Sigmund Freud, *The Future of an Illusion*, in *The Standard Edition*, 21:17–20.

6. Sigmund Freud, *Delusions and Dreams in Jensen's 'Gradiva'*, in *The Standard Edition*, 9:7–95.

7. I will return to *Delusions and Dreams in Jensen's 'Gradiva'* in chapter 4.

8. This account of art is very close to that proposed by Freud's contemporary Aby Warburg. See his book *The Renewal of Pagan Antiquity*, trans. David Britt (Los Angeles: Getty Research Institute, 1999).

9. Lou Andreas-Salomé, *Nietzsche: The Man in His Works*, in *Nietzsche*, trans. Siegfried Mandel (Chicago: University of Illinois Press, 1998).

10. Sigmund Freud and Lou Andreas-Salomé, *Letters*, ed. Ernst Pfeiffer, trans. William and Elaine Robson-Scott (New York: Norton, 1966), 22–26.

11. Lou Andreas-Salomé, *Mein Dank an Freud: Offener Brief an Professor Sigmund Freud zu seinem 75. Geburtstag* (Vienna: Internationaler Psychoanalytischer Verlag, 1931), 14. I am drawing on Ernst Pfeiffer's translation of this passage, which serves as an epigraph to Lou Andreas-Salomé, *Looking Back*, ed. Ernst Pfeiffer, trans. Breon Mitchell (New York: Marlowe, 1995).

12. In another passage in *Looking Back*, Salomé says that she has simply signed her signature at the bottom of a text that was "dictated" to her (18).

13. Rainer Maria Rilke and Lou Andreas-Salomé, *The Correspondence*, trans. Edward Snow and Michael Winkler (New York: Norton, 2006), 175–178.

14. Ibid., 184.

15. Biddy Martin, *Woman and Modernity: The (Life)styles of Lou Andreas-Salomé* (Ithaca: Cornell University Press, 1991), 45–46.

16. Rilke and Salomé, *The Correspondence*, 247.

17. The letters Rilke wrote Franz Xaver Kappus in 1903 and 1904 are a striking instan-

tiation of his ability to help others accomplish what he himself was unable to do. See Rainer Maria Rilke, *Letters to a Young Poet*, trans. Stephen Mitchell (New York: Vintage, 1984).

18. Ibid., 348.

19. Lou Andreas-Salomé, *You Alone Are Real to Me: Remembering Rainer Maria Rilke*, trans. Angela von der Lippe (Rochester, N.Y.: BOA Editions, 2003), 127.

20. Rainer Maria Rilke, *Letters, 1910–1926*, trans. Jane Bannard Greene and M. D. Herter Norton (New York: Norton, 1969), 43.

21. Eric Torgersen, *Dear Friend: Rainer Maria Rilke and Paula-Modersohn-Becker* (Evanston, Ill.: Northwestern University Press, 1998), 60.

22. Ibid.

23. Rilke, *Letters, 1910–1926*, 309.

24. Ibid., 327.

25. Rainer Maria Rilke, *Letters, 1892–1910*, trans. Jane Bannard Greene and M. D. Herter Norton (New York: Norton, 1969), 19.

26. Ibid., 84.

27. Matthew von Unwerth, *Freud's Requiem: Mourning, Memory, and the Invisible History of a Summer Walk* (New York: Penguin, 2005), 117–118.

28. Rilke, *Letters, 1910–1926*, 308.

29. Ibid., 334.

30. W. G. Sebald, *Austerlitz*, trans. Anthea Bell (New York: Modern Library, 2001), 258.

31. Marcel Proust, *In Search of Lost Time*, Vol. 1, *Swann's Way*, trans. C. K. Scott Moncrieff, Terence Kilmartin, and D. J. Enright (New York: Modern Library, 2003), 64.

32. Rilke, *Letters, 1910–1926*, 109–110.

33. Proust, *In Search of Lost Time*, Vol. 6, *Time Regained*, 274.

34. Ibid., 322.

35. Rilke, *Letters, 1910–1926*, 279.

36. Rilke, *Letters, 1892–1910*, 10.

37. I am referring here to Rilke's extraordinary poem "Turning-Point," which I discuss later in this chapter.

38. Rilke, *Letters, 1910–1926*, 38.

39. Ibid., 41–42.

40. Ibid., 44–45.

41. Ibid, 47–48.

42. Salomé, *You Alone Are Real to Me*, 33.

43. I will be relying throughout this discussion upon Stephen Mitchell's evocative translation of "Orpheus. Eurydice. Hermes," in Rainer Maria Rilke, *Ahead of All Parting: The Selected Poetry and Prose*, ed. and trans. Stephen Mitchell (New York: Modern Library, 1995), 55–59.

44. I take the concept of "focalization" from Mieke Bal, who uses it to theorize the optic through which a story is told. She provides an especially rich account of this concept in her book *The Mottled Screen: Reading Proust Visually*, trans. Anna-Louise Milne (Stanford, Calif.: Stanford University Press, 1997).

45. Rilke, *Letters to a Young Poet*, 75–78.

46. Eric Torgersen, *Dear Friend*, 111, 118–120, 128, 134.

47. Rilke, *Letters, 1892–1910*, 150.

48. For a detailed account of the early stages of Rilke's relationship with Paula Becker and Clara Westhoff, see Torgersen, *Dear Friend*, 60–109.

49. Paula Modersohn-Becker, *The Letters and Journals*, ed. Günter Busch, Liselotte von Reinken, Arthur S. Wensinger, and Carole Clew Hoey (New York: Taplinger, 1983), 189, 226, 276, 342, 369–370.

50. Ibid., 344–345, 392, 400, 408.

51. Modersohn was with her for approximately four months of this period. He arrived at the end of October 1906, and they returned to Worpswede in March 1907.

52. Rilke wrote this letter in response to a letter Paula wrote to Clara. Both letters are included in Modersohn-Becker, *The Letters and Journals*, 269–270.

53. Torgersen, *Dear Friend*, 69, 79, 229.

54. Gillian Perry provides a useful overview of Becker's artistic career in *Paula Modersohn-Becker* (London: Women's Press, 1979).

55. Becker discovered Cézanne in 1900 and showed some of his paintings to Clara Westhoff. In the "Recollection" Westhoff wrote about this experience, she observes: "In her own way, Paula had discovered him and this discovery was an unexpected confirmation of her own artistic search" (Modersohn-Becker, *The Letters and Journals*, 173). Rilke's engagement with Cézanne came much later. In 1907 he wrote Clara an extraordinary series of letters about the painter's work, which she shared with Becker shortly before Becker's death. In his foreword to these letters, Heinrich Wiegand Petzet writes: "Paula Modersohn-Becker had experienced the master's work 'like a great thunderstorm,' years before Rilke—and it was thanks to her that at a decisive moment his eyes were opened to its message. 'Perhaps I am being unfair—but all I saw was Cézanne,' he wrote to her in the days of his most intense emotion" (Rainer Maria Rilke, *Letters on Cézanne*, trans. Joel Agee [Farrar, Strauss, and Giroux, 1985], xxiv). As Petzet points out, there are also important connections between these letters and *Requiem for a Friend*, a point to which I will return in chapter 5.

56. Modersohn-Becker, *The Letters and Journals*, 278.

57. Rilke, *Letters, 1892–1910*, 316.

58. Modersohn-Becker, *The Letters and Journals*, 274.

59. Perry, *Paula Modersohn-Becker*, 1.

60. Modersohn-Becker, *The Letters and Journals*, 285.

61. Ibid., 384.

62. Ibid., 401. Torgersen also notes this coincidence in *Dear Friend*, 191.

63. Torgersen, *Dear Friend*, 182–207.

64. This passage has been edited out of the letter in Rilke, *Letters, 1892–1910*, but is quoted by Torgersen in *Dear Friend*, 213–214.

65. Torgersen, *Dear Friend*, 69.

66. He began looking seriously at her work in 1905, and shortly before she moved to Paris, he and Westhoff bought one of her paintings, *Infant with Its Mother's Hand* (1903). Becker wrote Rilke a letter on February 17, 1906, thanking him for his enthusiastic response to this painting (Modersohn-Becker, *The Letters and Journals*, 383–384).

67. In his brilliant introduction to *Rainer Maria Rilke: The Selected Poetry* (New York: Vintage, 1982), ed. and trans. Stephen Mitchell, Robert Hass writes: "All the evidence of

[Rilke's] life is that he fled relationships, that he was always attracted by the first flaring of eros and terrified of its taking root. What was hard for *him*, as Louise Gluck has observed, was holding on; and she believes that there is a certain amount of bad faith in his pretending otherwise" (xxxii). Hass is one of the few authors who doesn't turn Eurydice into a signifier for something else.

68. Rilke, *Letters, 1910–1926*, 38.

69. Torgersen, *Dear Friend*, 239.

70. Rilke, *Letters, 1910–1926*, 329–330.

71. Rainer Maria Rilke, *The Notebooks of Malte Laurids Brigge: A Novel*, trans. Stephen Mitchell (New York: Vintage, 1985), 99.

72. This is Torgersen's elegant formulation (*Dear Friend*, 12).

73. Torgersen quotes this passage in *Dear Friend*, 66. He does not cite its source, but I am assuming that it comes from Rilke's *Tagebücher aus der Frühzeit*.

74. Quoted by Torgersen in *Dear Friend*, 85.

75. Snow and Winckler, introduction to Rilke and Andreas-Salomé, *The Correspondence*, xvi.

76. I am quoting here from Mitchell's translation of the *Duino Elegies* (Rilke, *Ahead of All Parting*, 331–407).

77. Ovid, *The Metamorphoses*, trans. Michael Simpson (Amherst: University of Massachusetts Press, 2001), 166.

78. I am also using Mitchell's translation of this poem. See *Ahead of All Parting*, 127–129.

79. Rilke, *Letters, 1910–1926*, 374.

80. Mitchell recounts this story in a footnote on page 336 of *The Selected Poetry of Rainer Maria Rilke*. This drawing is reproduced in Chapter 2.

81. I will be relying throughout my discussion of the *Sonnets to Orpheus* on Mitchell's translation of the sequence. See *Ahead of All Parting*, 410–519.

82. I have substituted my own translation of these last four words for Mitchell's, so as to bring the meaning of this line closer to the German text ("und ein Mund der Natur").

83. Rilke, *Letters, 1910–1926*, 284.

84. Ibid., 289.

85. Ibid., 373.

86. Mitchell quotes this in a note in Rilke, *The Selected Poetry*, 336–337.

87. Rilke, *Letters, 1910–1926*, 373.

88. Ibid.

89. See letter from April 12, 1923, quoted by Mitchell on p. 336.

90. Rilke, *Letters, 1910–1926*, 373.

Chapter 4

1. What follows is indebted in several ways to Eric Torgersen, who also explores the relationship between these two paintings and *Requiem for a Friend* in his book *Dear Friend: Rainer Maria Rilke and Paula Modersohn-Becker* (Evanston, Ill.: Northwestern University Press, 1998), 191–195.

2. As Gillian Perry points out, "In formal terms [this and related works] would

have been inconceivable without [Becker's] Paris sojourn of 1906–7" (*Paula Modersohn-Becker* [London: Women's Press, 1979], 58).

3. Rilke, *Requiem for a Friend, Ahead of All Parting: The Selected Poetry and Prose of Rainer Maria Rilke*, trans. Stephen Mitchell (New York: Modern Library, 1995), 83.

4. Lou Andreas-Salomé, *Looking Back*, ed. Ernst Pfeiffer, trans. Breon Mitchell (New York: Marlowe, 1995), 84. See also Salomé, *The Freud Journal*, trans. Stanley A. Leavy (New York: Basic Books, 1964), 178–179.

5. Rainer Maria Rilke, *Letters: 1892–1910*, trans. Jane Bannard Greene and M. D. Herter Norton (New York: Norton, 1969), 147.

6. Rainer Maria Rilke, *Letters: 1910–1926*, trans. Jane Bannard Greene and M. D. Herter Norton (New York: Norton, 1969), 257.

7. Eric Torgersen, *Dear Friend*, 199.

8. Rilke, *Letters: 1910–1926*, 46.

9. Salomé, *Looking Back*, 1–11.

10. Rainer Maria Rilke and Lou Andreas-Salomé, *The Correspondence*, trans. Edward Snow and Michael Winkler (New York: Norton, 2006), 12.

11. Ibid., 14.

12. Ibid., 23.

13. Ibid., 38.

14. Ibid., 39.

15. Ibid., 41–42.

16. Rainer Maria Rilke, *The Notebooks of Malte Laurids Brigge*, trans. Stephen Mitchell (New York: Vintage, 1990), 75.

17. David Kleinbard also discusses Rilke's "fantasy of a perfectly empathic, selflessly responsive, undemanding woman" in his extremely interesting book, *The Beginning of Terror: A Psychological Study of Rainer Maria Rilke's Life and Work* (New York: New York University Press, 1993). Kleinbard points out that "only a mother attuned to her infant, completely identified with him, expecting nothing for herself, an ideal parent created by a narcissistic mind, could fulfill such needs" (64). However, he approaches this topic through object-relations psychoanalysis and attributes Rilke's difficulties to bad mothering (68–109). He also regards the poet's solitary existence during the last years of his life as a positive accomplishment (240).

18. Rilke, *Letters: 1892–1910*, 140.

19. This is a Lacanian pun, created through the amalgamation of the French words "l'homme" and "l'omelette."

20. Salomé, *Looking Back*, 3.

21. Rilke, "Self-Portrait, 1906," in *Ahead of All Parting*, 47. My attention was drawn to this connection by Torgersen, *Dear Friend*, 202.

22. Rilke, "Antistrophes," in *The Selected Poetry of Rainer Maria Rilke*, trans. Stephen Mitchell (New York: Vintage, 1989), 221–223. This poem straddles an enormous temporal divide; Rilke wrote lines 1–4 several months after this exchange of letters, and the rest on February 9, 1922, shortly after learning of the death of Vera Knoop, the girl celebrated in *Sonnets to Orpheus*.

23. Rilke uses this phrase to describe himself and his contemporaries in a 1912 letter. See his *Letters: 1910–1926*, 48.

24. Marcel Proust, *In Search of Lost Time*, Vol. 2, *Within a Budding Grove*, trans. C. K. Moncrieff, Terence Kilmartin, and D. J. Enright (New York: Modern Library, 2003), 335. For an excellent discussion of the exorbitance of Marcel's desire for his grandmother, see Serge Doubrovsky, *Writing and Fantasy in Proust: La Place de la Madeleine*, trans. Carol Mastrangelo Bové (Lincoln: University of Nebraska Press, 1986), 18–23.

25. Proust, *In Search of Lost Time*, vol. 3, *The Guermantes Way*, 173–178.

26. For a fuller reading of the photographic dimensions of this passage, see Mieke Bal, *The Mottled Screen: Reading Proust Visually*, trans. Anna-Louise Milne (Stanford, Calif.: Stanford University Press, 1997), 198–200, and my article "Je Vous," which engages with Bal's book (*Art History*, nos. 30–33 [June 2007]: 451–467).

27. Sigmund Freud, *Beyond the Pleasure Principle*, in *The Standard Edition of the Complete Psychological Works of Sigmund Freud*, trans. James Strachey (London: Hogarth, 1943–1974), 18:15.

28. Through one of those uncanny coincidences that point to a profound ontological connection, Freud's daughter and Rilke's mother had the same birth name.

29. In "A Child Is Being Beaten," which he wrote shortly before *Beyond the Pleasure Principle*, Freud argues that the figure who stands to one side of the beating scene, watching it, is actually internal to the fantasy itself (*The Standard Edition*, 17:190–191). He makes the same claim in *From the History of an Infantile Neurosis*, which he began in 1914 but published in 1918. This case history contains his most extended discussion of the primal scene (*The Standard Edition*, 17:29–47), the first instantiation of which occurred when the "wolfman" was one and a half—the same age as the little boy in the *fort/da* story.

30. Jacques Lacan, *Four Fundamental Concepts of Psychoanalysis*, trans. Alan Sheridan (New York: Norton, 1978), 62.

31. The Oedipus complex does not depend upon the physical presence of an actual father; it can occur fantasmatically, and even retroactively, through a paternal proxy.

32. I developed this section of my argument in an earlier essay in which I discuss an important work by Eija-Liisa Ahtila, *Anna, Aki, and God*. See "How to Stage the Death of God," in English and Finnish, in *Eija-Liisa Ahtila: Fantasized Persons and Taped Conversations* (Helsinki: Museum of Contemporary Art Kiasma, 2002), 182–196.

33. Freud, *Beyond the Pleasure Principle*, in *The Standard Edition*, 18:20; "Female Sexuality," in *The Standard Edition*, 21:234; *The Future of An Illusion*, in *The Standard Edition*, 21:24.

34. This phrase is the first entry under "*Mutter*" in the volume titled *Sexuelleben*. See Freud, *Studienausgabe*, vol. 5 (Frankfurt am Main: S. Fischer Verlag, 1972), 320.

35. *The Orpheus of Politian and the Aminta of Tasso*, trans. Louis E. Lord (London: Oxford University Press, 1931), 71.

36. Ibid.

37. Appignanesi and Forrester, *Freud's Women* (London: Other Press, 2001), 397.

38. As I will show in chapter 7 of this book, this is how Gerhard Richter conceptualizes analogy.

39. Freud, "Thoughts for the Times on War and Death," in *The Standard Edition*, 14:289–292.

40. Matthew von Unwerth makes a strong case for this in *Freud's Requiem: Mourning, Memory, and the Invisible History of a Summer Walk* (New York: Riverhead Books, 2005).

41. Sigmund Freud, "On Transience," in *The Standard Edition*, 14:305.

42. Freud, *Beyond the Pleasure Principle*, 38.

43. Ernest Jones, *The Life and Works of Sigmund Freud* (New York: Basic Books, 1957), 3:279.

44. Ibid., 2:184, 196. Earlier in his life, he was certain that he would die in his forties "from rupture of the heart" (ibid., 1:310).

45. Freud, *The Interpretation of Dreams*, in *The Standard Edition*, 4:111–112.

46. Ibid., 5:583.

47. Freud, "The Theme of the Three Caskets," in *The Standard Edition*, 12:292.

48. Jones, *The Life and Work of Sigmund Freud*, 3:94–95.

49. Ibid., 3:145. Freud related in a similar way to Martha during their engagement. Since he could not be certain that she was "really his unless he could perceive his 'stamp' on her," Jones writes, he demanded "complete identification with himself, his opinions, his feelings and his intentions" (*The Life and Work of Sigmund Freud*, 1:122).

50. This is my metaphor.

51. Freud, *The Interpretation of Dreams*, in *The Standard Edition*, 4:107. Madelon Sprengnether explores the relationship between Freud's cancer and the dream of Irma's injection in "Mouth to Mouth: Freud, Irma, and the Dream of Psychoanalysis," *American Imago* 60, no. 3:259–284.

52. Freud, *The Interpretation of Dreams*, in *The Standard Edition*, 4:107.

53. A similar dynamic is at work in the following story. In spring 1935, Jones recounts, he and his two children visited Freud. Freud gave some antiquities to Jones's son, who was then thirteen, and urged him to become an archaeologist, but "surprised" his daughter, who was then five, "by taking hold of her nose between two fingers," a gesture Jones calls "castrating" (*The Life and Work of Sigmund Freud*, 3:196).

54. Jones, *The Life and Work of Sigmund Freud*, 3:112.

55. Freud, "The Theme of the Three Caskets," 301.

56. For a fuller discussion of the parallels between Freud's relationship to Anna and Lear's relationship to Cordelia, see Appignanesi and Forrester, *Freud's Women*, 11–12, 272–306.

57. Jones, *The Life and Work of Sigmund Freud*, 3:138, 99, 148.

58. Freud, "Postscript to the Second Edition," in *The Standard Edition*, 9:95.

59. Although psychoanalysis has not traditionally paid very much attention to the category of siblings, that is beginning to change. Juliet Mitchell published a book on this topic several years ago, *Siblings* (London: Polity, 2003).

60. The novel is available in English in a volume with the unwieldy title *Gradiva by Wilhelm Jensen and Delusion and Dream in Wilhelm Jensen's Gravida by Sigmund Freud*, trans. Helen M. Downey (Los Angeles: Sun and Moon Press, 1993).

61. Strachey replaces these names with "Edwin" and "Angelina."

62. The English translator of *Gradiva* uses Henry King's translation of these lines.

63. Ovid, *The Metamorphoses*, trans. Michael Simpson (Amherst: University of Massachusetts Press, 2001), 183.

64. Jensen uses the same word in the German text (see *Gradiva: Ein pompajanisches Phantasiestück* [Dresden and Leipzig: Verlag von Carl Reissner, 1913], 29).

65. Ovid, *The Metamorphoses*, 183.

66. Freud, *Delusions and Dreams in Jensen's 'Gradiva,'* in *The Standard Edition*, 9:7–10.

67. In his introduction to this work, James Strachey suggests that this was an abiding interest: "Freud was fascinated by the analogy between the historical fate of Pompeii (its burial and subsequent excavation) and the mental events with which he was so familiar—burial by repression and excavation by analysis" (4–5).

68. Jones, *The Life and Work of Sigmund Freud*, 2:393.

69. Ibid., 3:318.

70. Ibid., 2:381.

71. Since the circumstances of this patient's death are very similar to those that Freud earlier imputes to Mathilde, she may be the same person.

72. This term derives from Josef Breuer, who uses it to describe Anna O's "absences" (see Breuer and Freud, *Studies on Hysteria*, in *The Standard Edition*, 2:26–27).

73. Freud, *The Psychopathology of Everyday Life*, in *The Standard Edition*, 6:264–266.

74. Freud, "Psychical (or Mental) Treatment," in *The Standard Edition*, 7:297.

75. Jensen, *Gradiva*, 108.

76. Virgil, *Eclogues, Georgics, Aeneid*, 1–6, trans. H. R. Fairclough and G. Goold (Cambridge, Mass.: Harvard University Press, 1999), 255.

77. I am relying here on Simpson's translation of this passage. In Shadi Bartsch's reading, it is Eurydice who seizes "empty air," as she tries to hold and be held by Orpheus.

78. Lou Andreas-Salomé, *The Freud Journal*, 192–193.

79. This is a close paraphrase of a sentence from Jensen, *Gradiva*, 45.

Chapter 5

1. Heidegger also identifies the poem as "Bread and Wine." Martin Heidegger, "What Are Poets For?" in *Poetry, Language, Thought*, trans. Albert Hofstadter (New York: Harper and Row, 1971), 91.

2. Ibid., 116.

3. The notion of a "saving power" comes from Hölderlin's poem "Patmos." The passage in question, which Heidegger discusses in "What Are Poets For?" (118), reads as follows in Michael Hamburger's translation: "Near is / And difficult to grasp, the God. / But where danger threatens / That which saves from it also grows" (Friedrich Hölderlin, *Poems and Fragments* [London: Anvil Press, 2004], 551).

4. Martin Heidegger, "The Turning," in *The Question Concerning Technology*, trans. William Lovitt (New York: Harper and Row, 1977), 44.

5. Terrence Malick, *The Essence of Reasons* (Evanston, Ill.: Northwestern University Press, 1969). I am using the title this essay has in the English translation of Heidegger's *Pathmarks*, ed. William McNeill (Cambridge: Cambridge University Press, 1998), 97–135: "On the Essence of Ground."

6. Heidegger, "On the Essence of Ground," in ibid., 121.

7. I will henceforth refer to this company simply as "Charlie Company."

8. *The Thin Red Line*, www.foxmovies.com/thinredline/htmls, 1.

9. See, for instance, Kenneth Turan, "*A Thin Red Line*: A Distant Epic," *Los Angeles Times*, December 22, 1998, and Richard Natale, "The 'Thin Red' Battleground," *Los Angeles Times*, December 16, 1998. Oddly, Natale seems not yet to have seen the film when he wrote this review. Martin Flanagan provides a fascinating discussion of the film's critical reception in "'Everything a Lie': The Critical and Commercial Reception of Terrence Malick's *The Thin Red Line*," in *The Cinema of Terrence Malick: Poetic Visions of America*, ed. Hannah Patterson (London: Wallflower Press, 2003), 123–136. He writes that positive reviewers "slanted their approaches . . . towards the implications of Malick's personal return" and that "this return was celebrated not only as the rediscovery of a singular talent, but as a heraldic moment for the eventual restoration of the kind of directorial autonomy and free expression last observed in the Hollywood of the 1970s" (128–129).

10. See James Jones, *The Thin Red Line* (New York: Dell, 1962).

11. This is also a highly sentimentalized account of Jones's war experiences.

12. Stacy Peebles Power, "The Other World of War: Terrence Malick's Adaptation of *The Thin Red Line*," in *The Cinema of Terrence Malick*, 158.

13. As Michel Chion points out, the film "deliberately gives us no assessment . . . of the [actual] historical impact of the battle or of the importance later accorded to the events for the course of World War II. In watching the film, we, like the characters, are plunged into the events in the present; we do not know in advance what is important and what is not" (*The Thin Red Line* [London: BFI, 2004], 22–23).

14. In their wonderful reading of *The Thin Red Line*, Leo Bersani and Ulysse Dutoit write: "This is his first war, *his* war; he fights not mainly for enemy territory, but for the war itself, his most precious property. The notion of property contaminates all relationality. In *The Thin Red Line*, the insistent 'propertizing' of human relations is presented in familial terms: my sons, my brothers, my wife" (*Forms of Being: Cinema, Aesthetics, Subjectivity* [London: BFI, 2004], 137).

15. Martin Heidegger, "What Is Metaphysics?", *Pathmarks*, 95.

16. This phrase plays a crucial role in Heidegger's 1929 account of Being. See "What Is Metaphysics?," 85–89.

17. Martin Heidegger, *Being and Time*, trans. John Macquarrie and Edward Robinson (San Francisco: Harper and Row, 1962), 310.

18. Ibid., 308.

19. Ibid., 231. See also the next few pages of *Being and Time* and "What Is Metaphysics?" 88–93.

20. See Heidegger, *Being and Time*, 317–335.

21. Ibid., 225–228.

22. Heidegger advances this claim in ibid., 284.

23. I am indebted to Steve Choe for this attribution.

24. It is unusual for Malick to use synchronization in this way. Witt's subsequent meditations on finitude take the form of voice-over monologues, and his voice mingles with the disembodied voices of many other characters to create what Chion calls "a single text," or "shared reading" (57).

25. The second of Bell's flashbacks takes place after Charlie Company arrives in Guadalcanal, but since it is linked to Witt rather than to him, I will wait until later in this chapter to discuss it.

26. Doll also links Welsh to her by glancing in her direction as he and the other soldiers march by the cemetery.

27. Willam B. Parsons publishes the letters that Rolland and Freud exchanged in an appendix to his book *The Enigma of the Oceanic Feeling: Revisioning the Psychoanalytic Theory of Mysticism* (Oxford: Oxford University Press, 1999), 170–179.

28. I don't know whether Malick has read Freud and Rolland's epistolary exchange, but he is clearly familiar with the passages in which Freud discusses it, because there are many references in *The Thin Red Line* to this section of *Civilization and Its Discontents.* The two contending powers that Witt projects onto nature at the beginning of the film sound like Eros and Thanatos; the crocodile that crawls into the water in the opening shot alludes to a passage in which Freud attempts to think beyond this opposition; and the scene in which Witt watches the Melanesian woman bathe her child is a response to Freud's dismissive reading of the oceanic feeling (see *The Standard Edition of the Complete Psychological Works of Sigmund Freud,* trans. James Strachey [London: Hogarth Press, 1943–1974], 21:122–123, 68, 64–73). I discuss the Freud/Rolland exchange at considerable length in chapter 1.

29. Lou Andreas-Salomé, *Looking Back,* ed. Ernst Pfeiffer, trans. Breon Mitchell (New York: Marlowe, 1995), 17.

30. For Heidegger, "fallenness" signifies not a permanent lapse out of innocence into sinfulness but rather *Dasein*'s normal, everyday state, out of which it rises to more "authentic" forms of Being, and to which it inevitably returns; see *Being and Time,* 220. "Fallenness" has much the same significance for Malick.

31. The opposition of "love" and "strife" comes from Empedocles, and is also mentioned by Freud in one of the passages where he talks about the drives. In "Analysis Terminable and Interminable," he equates the first of these categories with Eros and the second with Thanatos. See *The Standard Edition,* 23:245–247.

32. Dale is also on the outgoing ship, and listens with impassive eloquence as a younger soldier talks in rosy terms about his future.

33. As Bersani and Dutoit point out in *Forms of Being,* faces also play a central role in the film's account of looking. "The soldiers in Malick's 'war film' are individuated not as personalities but as perspectives on the world," they write. " . . . [T]heir faces . . . manifest their perspective on the world; their world is inscribed on their faces" (146). They provide virtuoso readings of two of the film's faces: Welsh's and Witt's (149–151 and 158–165).

34. In this passage Benjamin himself quotes Proust: "That Proust was quite familiar with the problem of the aura needs no emphasis. It is nonetheless notable that he sometimes alludes to it in concepts that comprehend its theory: 'People who are fond of secrets occasionally flatter themselves that objects retain something of the gaze that has rested on them.' (The objects, it seems, have the ability to return the gaze.) 'They believe that monuments and pictures appear only through a delicate veil which centuries of love and reverence on the part of so many admirers have woven about them'" ("On Some Motifs in Baudelaire," in Walter Benjamin, *Selected Writings,* ed. Howard Eiland and Michael W. Jennings [Cambridge, Mass.: Harvard University Press, 2003], 4:338–339. The Proust passage comes from *Le temps retrouvé.* A different English translation of this passage can be found in *In Search of Lost Time: Time Regained,*

trans. Andreas Major, Terence Kilmartin, and D. J. Enright (New York: Modern Library, 2003), 283–284.

Chapter 6

1. Paul Valéry, *Poems*, trans. David Paul, in *The Collected Works of Paul Valéry* (Princeton, N.J.: Princeton University Press, 1971), 1:319. For more information about this poem, see the editor's note on 478–479.

2. I draw here on both the editorial note to this poem in Valéry, *Poems*, 435–436, and research done for me by Sonja Bertucci.

3. Paul Valéry, *Œuvres*, Bibliothèque de la Pléiade (Paris: Gallimard, 1957), 1:1540–1541. I am using Bertucci's translation of the poem.

4. Paul Valéry, "To Rainer Maria Rilke," in *Masters and Friends*, trans. Martin Turnell, in *The Collected Works of Paul Valéry* (London: Routledge and Kegan Paul, 1968), 9:290. I quote more from this essay in the first epigraph to chapter 2.

5. Paul Valéry, *Poems*, 9. I am using Bertucci's more literal rendition of the poem.

6. All these essays are published in Paul Valéry, *Leonardo, Poe, Mallarmé*, trans. Malcolm Cowley, in *The Collected Works of Paul Valéry* (Princeton, N.J.: Princeton University Press, 1972), 8:3–157.

7. There are deep and abiding similarities between Leo Bersani's work and my own—but also enough differences to prevent our friendship from turning into a monologue. Our thinking diverges most on the topic of impersonality. This concept plays an important role in a number of his books, including the most recent, which he coauthored with Adam Phillips: *Intimacies* (Chicago: University of Chicago Press, 2008).

8. Valéry, "Solitude," in *Poems*, 319.

9. Sigmund Freud, "Leonardo da Vinci and a Memory of His Childhood," in *The Standard Edition of the Complete Psychological Works of Sigmund Freud*, trans. James Strachey (London: Hogarth, 1943–1974), 11:63–107.

10. Maurice Merleau-Ponty, "Cézanne's Doubt," in *The Merleau-Ponty Aesthetics Reader*, ed. Galen A. Johnson (Evanston, Ill.: Northwestern University Press), 70.

11. Rainer Maria Rilke, *Letters, 1910–1926*, trans. Jane Bannard Greene and M. D. Herter Norton (New York: Norton, 1969), 381–382.

12. This was a category created by the curators of the exhibition.

13. For a recent photographic documentation of *Spiral Jetty*, see Eve Meltzer, "Now You See It: Robert Smithson's *Spiral Jetty*," in *Frieze Magazine*, no. 72 (January 2003): 48–49. George Baker provides a brilliant discussion of Smithson's own filmic documentation of the work in "The Cinema Model," in *Robert Smithson: The Spiral Jetty*, ed. Lynne Cooke and Karen Kelly (New York: Dia Art Foundation with the University of California Press, 2005), 79–113.

14. I take the notion of a paternal legacy from Jacques Lacan, who discusses it in "Function and Field of Speech and Language in Psychoanalysis," in *Ecrits*, trans. Bruce Fink (New York: Norton, 2006), 197–268.

15. See Claude Lévi-Strauss, *Elementary Structures of Kinship*, trans. James Harle Bell and John Richard von Sturmer (Boston: Beacon, 1969); Luce Irigaray, *This Sex Which Is Not One*, trans. Catherine Porter (Ithaca, N.Y.: Cornell University Press, 1985), 170–197; and Gayle Rubin, "Traffic in Women: Notes on the 'Political Economy' of Sex,"

in *Toward an Anthropology of Women*, ed. Rayna Raiter (New York: Monthly Review Press, 1975), 157–210. I am emphasizing the phallic meaning of "transmission," in spite of the fact that it is not part of the semantic field of "*diffuser*," because this meaning was operative at so many other points in the exhibition.

16. Gregg M. Horowitz, *Sustaining Loss: Art and Mournful Life* (Stanford, Calif.: Stanford University Press, 2001), 13.

17. Douglas Crimp discusses a number of other contemporary artists who have a contestatory relationship to the museum in his important book, *On the Museum's Ruins* (Cambridge, Mass.: MIT Press, 1993).

18. Lacan, "Function and Field of Speech and Language in Psychoanalysis," 230.

19. This is from an entry in the *Codex Urbanus* that has the heading "How the painter is master of all sorts of people and of all things." See Leonardo da Vinci, *Leonardo on Art and the Artist*, ed. André Chastel (New York: Dover, 2002), 51.

20. Françoise Viatte, "The Early Drapery Studies," in *Léonard de Vinci: Dessins et manuscrits* (Paris: Musée du Louvre, 2003), 111–112. Françoise Viatte and Varena Forcione were the curators of the Louvre exhibition.

21. The drawing to which I refer, Inv. 6632, is in the collection of Frits Lugt. I asked for permission to reproduce it, but my request was denied.

22. I am quoting the text as it is presented in William Shakespeare, *The Sonnets: Poems of Love* (New York: St. Martin's Press, 1980).

23. Kenneth Clark, *Leonardo da Vinci* (London: Penguin Books, 1959), 106–107, 171–172. It also seems safe to say that Leonardo would have been unperturbed if one of his apprentices had later outstripped him; he observes in one of his manuscripts that it is "a poor pupil who does not surpass his master" (*Leonardo on Art and the Artist*, 86).

24. *Leonardo on Art and the Artist*, 86.

25. Ibid., 84.

26. Ibid., 193.

27. Ibid., 90.

28. Ibid., 50.

29. "The things of the mind that have not passed through the senses are vain and only give rise to invisible truths," Leonardo observes in one of his anatomical notebooks (Ibid., 125).

30. This was also a category created by the curators of the exhibition.

31. For an excellent analysis of this relationship, see Jeff Wall, "Four Essays on Ken Lum," in exhibition catalogue, *Ken Lum* (Winnipeg and Rotterdam: Winnipeg Art Gallery and Witte de With Center for Contemporary Art, 1990), 25–76.

32. This passage comes from the *Codex Urbanus* (*Leonardo on Art and the Artist*, 81–82).

33. Pietro C. Marani, "Leonardo's *Last Supper*," in *Leonardo: The Last Supper*, trans. Harlow Tighe (Chicago: University of Chicago Press, 2001), 10.

34. "'*Scrittura infinita*' (infinite writing) meant that there were no boundaries between forms of expression, languages, intellectual disciplines, and experience," Carlo Vecce observes in "Word and Image in Leonardo's Writings," but "it also meant . . . not recognizing the act of separation that constituted the closing of a text, the conclusion

of the argument, the final word" (*Leonardo da Vinci: Master Draftsman*, ed. Carmin C. Bambach [New York: Metropolitan Museum/Yale University Press, 2003], 75).

35. *Leonardo on Art and the Artist*, 92.

36. Ibid., 149–150.

37. Ibid., 38; "Leonardo and the Philosophers," in *Leonardo, Poe, Mallarmé*, 112.

38. Valéry, "Notes and Digression," in *Leonardo, Poe, Mallarmé*, 85.

39. This is a line from Cézanne, that Merleau-Ponty quotes in "Cézanne's Doubt," 67. I invoke it here because of the close affinities between Merleau-Ponty's reading of Cézanne, and the passage I am about to quote from Valéry.

40. Valéry, "Introduction to the Method of Leonardo," *Leonardo, Poe, Mallarmé*, 18.

41. Merleau-Ponty. "Cézanne's Doubt," 74.

42. Ibid., 75.

43. Daniel Arasse provides a helpful summary of a number of the scholarly arguments that have been made against Freud's essay in *Leonardo da Vinci: The Rhythm of the World*, trans. Rosetta Translations (New York: Konecky and Konecky, 1997), 488–493.

44. Freud, *Beyond the Pleasure Principle*, *The Standard Edition*, 14–16.

45. Ibid., 15.

46. D. W. Winnicott, *Playing and Reality* (London: Tavistock, 1977), 10–11.

47. Quoted by A. Richard Turner in *Inventing Leonardo* (Berkeley: University of California Press, 1992), 92–93.

48. Pietro C. Marani, *Leonardo da Vinci: The Complete Paintings*, trans. A. Lawrence Jenkins (New York: Harry N. Abrams, 2000), 163–165.

49. Quoted by Arasse in *Leonardo da Vinci*, 115.

50. I quote here from the *New Revised Standard Edition of the Oxford Annotated Bible* (New York: Oxford University Press, 1994), 155.

51. Marani, *Leonardo da Vinci: The Complete Paintings*, 228; Marani, "Leonardo's *Last Supper*," 22.

52. Turner, *Inventing Leonardo*, 89–93; Marani, "Leonardo's *Last Supper*," 1–57.

53. This information derives from Coleman, who visited the room behind the fresco when shooting the photographs for his digital *Last Supper*.

54. Marani, "Leonardo's *Last Supper*," 35.

55. Ibid., 27, 35.

56. Leo Steinberg, *Leonardo's Incessant "Last Supper"* (New York: Zone Books, 2001), 150.

57. Ibid., 19–29; Arasse, *Leonardo da Vinci*, 362–383. In *Leonardo on Art and the Artist*, Chastel also suggests that *The Last Supper* registers and makes visible "the imperceptible movement of the organs and the play of emotions" (124).

58. Ovid, *The Metamorphoses*, trans. Michael Simpson (Amherst: University of Massachusetts Press, 2001), 257.

59. Freud, *The Ego and the Id*, in *The Standard Edition*, 19:26.

60. Coleman alerted us to this dimension of his "intervention" in his wall text. He "presented" some works that were not "present" in the exhibition through a "numerical projection."

Chapter 7

1. Gerhard Richter, *The Daily Practice of Painting: Writings, 1962–1993,* ed. Hans-Ulrich Obrist, trans. David Britt (Cambridge, Mass.: MIT Press, 1995), 146. This is not the only time that I will part company with Buchloh on the topic of Richter's work. However, I owe him a debt of gratitude, both because the pressure that he exerts on Richter's thought has been so consistently productive and because it was while talking with him and reading his work that I began formulating my own thoughts about the artist.

2. Although Richter based some of his earlier paintings on photographs, he regards *Mouth* (1963) as the first of his photo paintings (*The Daily Practice of Painting,* 22).

3. I say "for which Warhol is most famous" because I do not regard all of the artist's silk screens as ironic. Many of them entertain a complex emotional relationship with the images from which they derive.

4. Richter, *The Daily Practice of Painting,* 38.

5. For the sake of consistency, I will refer throughout this chapter to the device with which Richter works over the wet paint of his photo paintings as a "squeegee." In fact, though, it is only one of a range of implements deployed for this purpose. For a discussion of these implements, and the different uses to which the artist has put them, see Robert Storr's text in *Gerhard Richter: Forty Years of Painting* (New York: Museum of Modern Art, 2002), 43–44.

6. When discussing the status of photography in Richter's work, Luc Lang remarks that it is as if "photography were . . . the origin of all images and had begun to exist before a form of painting that could only explore its tekhné with criteria inherited from photography" ("The Photographer's Hand," in Gertrud Koch, Luc Lang, and Jean-Philippe Antoine, *Gerhard Richter* [Paris: Editions Dis Voir, 1995], 32). Later in the same essay he adds that "painting rediscovers its power by exploring the photographic image and its margins" (38). For a helpful overview of the different uses to which Richter has put the photographic image, see Stefan Gronert, "Pictorial (Re)Production," in *Gerhard Richter: Editions 1965–2004* (Ostfildern-Ruit, Germany: Hatje Cantz Verlag, 2004), 85–106.

7. Richter, *The Daily Practice of Painting,* 211.

8. Martin Hentschel, "On Shifting Terrain: Looking at Richter's Abstract Paintings," in *Gerhard Richter 1998* (London: Anthony d'Offay Gallery, 1998), 15.

9. Gerhard Richter, *128 Details from a Picture* (Halifax: Editions CR, 1978).

10. Gerhard Richter, *Abstract Painting 825–II: 69 Details* (Zurich: Scalo, 1996).

11. This analogy operates on many different levels. David Frankel describes two of them. The "surfaces" of Richter's abstract paintings, he notes, can be "almost as slick and shiny as a Cibachrome." They can also "evoke photographic film" as images, "as though the chemical conversions of the developing bath had printed as rippled color" ("Gerhard Richter," *Artforum* 37, no. 6 (February 1999): 89.

12. See, for instance, Gerhard Richter, *Florence 1999/2000,* ed. Dietmar Elger (Ostfildern-Ruit, Germany: Hatje Cantz Verlag, 2001).

13. This has since been published in two different forms. The first appeared in 1997, under the title *Atlas of the Photographs, Collages, and Sketches,* ed. Helmut Friedel and Ulrich Wilmes (New York: Distributed Art Publishers), and is the version with which I

will be working. The second appeared in 2006, under the title *Atlas*, ed. Helmut Friedel (New York: Distributed Art Publishers). Buchloh explores the relationship between the earlier of these two versions of the *Atlas* and the archival projects of Aby Warburg, Bernhard and Hilla Becher, and Christian Boltanski in his illuminating and informative essay "Gerhard Richter's *Atlas*: The Anomie Archive," *October*, no. 88 (1999): 117–147.

14. Richter, *The Daily Practice of Painting*, 73. Peter Osborne discusses this passage at length in "Painting Negation: Gerhard Richter's Negatives" (*October*, no. 62 [1992]: 103–113). He claims that "photo-painting" is "an affirmation of photography by painting" but also of painting "in the face of photography" (106–107). David Green argues that Richter uses painting to undo certain aspects of the photographic image, particularly its indexicality, its temporality, and its legibility ("Reflections on the Work of Gerhard Richter," in *History Painting Reassessed*, ed. David Green and Peter Seddon [Manchester: Manchester University Press, 2000], 31–49).

15. Several other writers have also identified analogy as one of the organizing principles of Richter's work. See Dietmar Elger, "Landscape as a Model," in *Gerhard Richter: Landscapes* (Ostfildern-Ruit, Germany: Cantz Verlag, 1998), 8–38; Michael Danoff, *Gerhard Richter: Paintings* (London: Thames and Hudson, 1988), 49–50, 79, 110; and Richard Cork, "Through a Glass Darkly: Reflections on Gerhard Richter," in *Gerhard Richter: Mirrors* (London: Anthony d'Offay Gallery, 1991), 11, 15.

16. Richter, *The Daily Practice of Painting*, 119.

17. As Storr points out, he not only spent sixteen years in the GDR, but he also spent thirteen years in Nazi Germany (*Gerhard Richter: October 18, 1977*, ed. Robert Storr [New York: Museum of Modern Art, 2000], 98).

18. André Bazin, "The Ontology of the Photographic Image," in *What Is Cinema?* trans. Hugh Gray (Berkeley: University of California Press, 2004), 1:9–16, and Roland Barthes, *Camera Lucida: Reflections on Photography*, trans. Richard Howard (New York: Hill and Wang, 1981).

19. This account of photography is by now so firmly entrenched that it belongs at the same time to everyone and to no one. Therefore, rather than attempting to document its sources, I will simply quote from a text in which it is presented with particular lucidity. "Photography captures an aspect of reality which is only ever the result of an arbitrary selection, and, consequently, of a transcription," Pierre Bourdieu writes in "The Social Definition of Photography." "[A]mong all of the qualities of the object, the only ones retained are the visual qualities which appear for a moment and from one sole viewpoint; these are transcribed in black and white, generally reduced in scale and always projected on to a plane. In other words, photography is a conventional system which expresses space in terms of the law of perspective (or rather of one perspective). . . . Photography is considered to be a perfectly realistic and objective recording of the visible world because (from its origin) it has been assigned social uses that are held to be 'realistic' and 'objective'" (*Photography: A Middle-Brow Art*, trans. Shaun Whiteside [Stanford, Calif.: Stanford University Press, 1990], 73–74).

20. Richter, *The Daily Practice of Painting*, 63. "Ich möchte versuchen, das zu verstehen, was ist. Wir wissen sehr wenig, und ich versuche es so, dass ich Analogien shaffe. Analogie ist eigentlich fast jedes Kunstwerk. Wenn ich etwas abbilde, so ist das auch

eine Analogie zu dem Bestehenden" (Gerhard Richter, *Text: Schriften und Interviews*, ed. Hanns-Ulrich Obrist [Frankfurt am Main: Insel Verlag, 1996], 58).

21. Ibid., 33. One of the reasons the photograph is invisible is that it has been subsumed since the moment of its invention to the index and treated as a form of evidence. (As Jean-Philippe Antoine points out, Richter cancels this aspect of the photographs he paints by blurring their outlines ["Photography, Painting, and the Real," in Antoine, Koch, and Lang, *Gerhard Richter*, 63–64]).

22. "To have an ideology means having rules and guidelines; it means killing those who have different rules and guidelines," Richter wrote in 1964–1965. "What is the good of that?" (*The Daily Practice of Painting*, 39). "I pursue no objectives, no system, no tendency; I have no programme, no style, no direction," he added a year later (ibid., 58).

23. Ibid., 37.

24. I am not suggesting that monochrome painting necessarily spells the end of difference. As David Batchelor argues—and as Richter's later art practice spectacularly shows—the monochrome often contains within itself "all or many of the discontinuities, tensions, divisions, polarities, splits, and conflicts of other genres of art" ("In Bed with the Monochrome," in *From an Aesthetic Point of View*, ed. Peter Osborne (London: Serpent's Tail, 2000), 156.

25. Richter, *The Daily Practice of Painting*, 82.

26. Ibid., 70.

27. Quite the contrary; as of 2002, Richter had painted one hundred gray monochromes—not counting his mirror paintings (Storr, *Gerhard Richter: Forty Years of Painting*, 56).

28. In a 1975 letter to Edy de Wilde, Richter wrote: "When I first painted a number of canvases gray all over . . . I did so because I did not know what to paint, or what there might be. . . . As time went on, however, I observed differences of quality among the gray surfaces—and also that they betrayed none of the destructive motivation that lay behind them. The pictures began to teach me. . . . Destitution became a constructive statement; it became relative perfection, beauty, and therefore painting" (*The Daily Practice of Painting*, 82).

29. This passage derives from "'I Ask Myself, What Does It Mean?'," Shapiro's preface to *Gerhard Richter: Paintings, Prints, and Photographs in the Collection of the Saint Louis Museum* (Saint Louis Art Museum 1992 Summer Bulletin), 14.

30. This is how Richter himself describes them (*The Daily Practice of Painting*, 88).

31. Storr, *Gerhard Richter: Forty Years of Painting*, 303.

32. As Gertrud Koch notes, one of the things evoked by Richter's abstract paintings is perspectival depth ("The Open Secret," in Antoine, Koch, and Lang, *Gerhard Richter*, 26).

33. Richter, *The Daily Practice of Painting*, 98. The German text reads "lebt zwar von den *Ähnlichkeiten* mit natürlichen Gefügen" (my emphasis). The word "*Analogie*" figures prominently in this entry.

34. See Richter, *Atlas*, 92–105, and *Werkübersicht Catalogue raisonné, 1962–1993* (Ostfildern-Ruit, Germany: Cantz Verlag, 1993), 345–1, 345–2, and 345–3.

35. Richter, *The Daily Practice of Painting*, 98. The translation of this passage conforms closely to the original, which reads: "Malerei ist die Schaffung einer Analogie zum

Unschaulichen und Unverständlichen, das auf diese Weise Gestalt annehmen und verfügbar werden soll. Deshalb sind gute Bilder auch unverständlich" (*Text*, 91).

36. Ibid., 100.

37. I quote here from T. S. Eliot's poem *The Waste Land*, line 76 of which reads: "You! Hypocrite lecteur!—mon semblable,—mon frère!" Eliot is himself quoting from the last line of Charles Baudelaire's poem "To the Reader," which appears in the preface to *Les Fleurs du Mal*. Eliot places these words at the end of the stanza including the all-important exclamation "I had not thought death had undone so many." The work from which the latter derives—Dante's *Inferno*, III.55–57—is of course also centrally concerned with mortality.

38. Gregg M. Horowitz offers a radically different account of photography in *Sustaining Loss: Art and Mournful Life* (Stanford, Calif.: Stanford University Press, 2001), a book with which I often disagree but admire enormously. In a photograph, he writes, "looking becomes fixed, immune to change. . . . [T]he object is used to send its own look into the future, by a past which seeks to predetermine its own reception" (142, 144). Horowitz develops this account of photography in a chapter devoted to Richter's *October 18, 1977* (133–169).

39. "Photographs . . . drop onto our doormats, almost as uncontrived as reality, but smaller," Richter told an interviewer in 1989, in the middle of a discussion of the images that gave rise to *October 18, 1977* (*The Daily Practice of Painting*, 187).

40. For a discussion of the dialectical image, see Walter Benjamin, "On the Concept of History," in Benjamin, *Selected Writings*, ed. Michael W. Jennings (Cambridge, Mass.: Harvard University Press, 2003), 4:389–400; and *The Arcades Project*, trans. Howard Eiland and Kevin McLaughlin (Cambridge, Mass.: Harvard University Press, 1999), 456–475.

41. This metaphor was inspired by the following passage from Benjamin: "One can read the real like a text. And that is how the nineteenth century will be treated here. We will open the book of what happened" (*The Arcades Project*, 464).

42. Ibid., 474.

43. "On the Concept of History," 390. In his wonderful book *Words of Light: Theses on the Photography of History* (Princeton, N.J.: Princeton University Press, 1997), which intersects with this chapter at many points, Eduardo Cadava talks about how central photography is to Benjamin's *own* thinking about history.

44. Freud introduces the notion of a death drive in *Beyond the Pleasure Principle*, in *The Standard Edition of the Complete Psychological Works of Sigmund Freud*, trans. James Strachey (London: Hogarth Press, 1943–1974), 18:7–64. It casts a long shadow over all of his later works.

45. *The Daily Practice of Painting*, 125. *Civilization and Its Discontents*—which is included in volume 21 of *The Standard Edition*—is full of similar passages. See, for instance, 111–112, as well as many of the passages quoted from this book in chapter 1.

46. Heidegger provides his most important account of human finitude in "What Is Metaphysics?," in Martin Heidegger, *Pathmarks*, ed. William McNeill (Cambridge: Cambridge University Press, 1998), 82–96. However, this essay should be read along with *Being and Time*, trans. John Macquarrie and Edward Robinson (San Francisco: HarperCollins, 1962), 274–488.

47. Richter, *Atlas*, 16–20.

48. The first to do so was of course Theodor Adorno, who decreed there to be no lyric poetry after Auschwitz. In 1986 Buchloh asked Richter if he agreed with this pronouncement. The latter responded: "No. There is lyric poetry after Auschwitz" (*The Daily Practice of Painting*, 148). Three years later he came close to suggesting that there *must* be lyric poetry after—and also *about*—Auschwitz, since the avoidance of this topic permits us to sweep mortality and violence under the carpet. "Death and suffering always have been an artistic theme," he told another interviewer. "Basically, it's *the* theme. We've eventually managed to wean ourselves away from it, with our nice, tidy life-style" (ibid., 186).

49. Richter, *Atlas*, 21–23. Gertrud Koch claims that "the photographs in *Atlas* . . . constitute the decomposition of history" ("The Richter-Scale of Blur," *October*, no. 62 [1992]: 140). I will be arguing that although the *Atlas* may indeed do away with the continuum of time, it facilitates the establishment of another kind of history: a figural history.

50. Richter, *The Daily Practice of Painting*, 185.

51. Heinrich Böll, "Will Ulrike Gnade oder freies Geleit?" *Der Spiegel*, Week 2, Hamburg, 1972, 52. Cited by Rainer Usselmann in "*18. Oktober 1977*: Gerhard Richter's Work of Mourning and Its New Audience," *Art Journal* 61, no. 1 (Spring 2002): 7.

52. See Stefan Aust, *The Baader-Meinhof Group: The Inside Story of a Phenomenon*, trans. Anthea Bell (London: Bodley Head, 1987), 231–552. I am also drawing here on Storr, *Gerhard Richter: October 18, 1977*, 41–67; and Usselmann, "*18. Oktober 1977*: Gerhard Richter's Work of Mourning and Its New Audience."

53. Storr, *Gerhard Richter: October 18, 1977*, 57.

54. The RAF were the first to note these parallels, but they did so only in order to construct a binary opposition between themselves and the state (see Aust, *The Baader-Meinhof Group*, 542–543). There was nothing analogical about their thought. "Either a pig or a human being / either survival at any price / or a fight to the death / either a problem or a solution / nothing in between," Holger Meins declared shortly before dying.

55. For a discussion of the dehumanization to which the Nazis subjected their Jewish prisoners not only when they were alive but also after they had died, see Primo Levi, *The Drowned and the Saved*, trans. Raymond Rosenthal (New York: Random House, 1989), 36–69; and Giorgio Agamben, *Remnants of Auschwitz: The Witness and the Archive*, trans. Daniel Heller-Roazen (New York: Zone Books, 1999), 41–86.

56. Usselmann, "*18. Oktober 1977*: Gerhard Richter's Work of Mourning and Its New Audience," 23.

57. Aust, *The Baader-Meinhof Group*, 542.

58. Richter, *The Daily Practice of Painting*, 187.

59. Freud, "Thoughts for the Times on War and Death," in *The Standard Edition*, 14:289.

60. In "Some Psychical Consequences of the Anatomical Distinction between the Sexes," Freud maintains that the prototypical male subject responds to the sight of the female genitals either with "horror of the mutilated creature, or triumphant contempt" (*The Standard Edition*, 19:252).

61. I am of course referring here to Courbet's notorious painting *The Origin of the World* (1866).

62. Horowitz notes that although there is a chair in one painting in this series, *Skull with Candle* (1983), it is unoccupied, "so the picture is not an act of contemplating death." It is, rather, "a narrative picture visibly lacking the central action of its narrative" (*Sustaining Loss*, 156–157),

63. As my language is meant to suggest, Heidegger provides an important reference point here. In *Being and Time*, he defines death as "the possibility of the absolute impossibility of Dasein," and maintains that it "is not to be outstripped" (294). He nevertheless calls upon Dasein "resolutely" to "anticipate" the moment at which it will cease to be (304–348). In "What Is Metaphysics?" Heidegger breaks dramatically with this account of what it means to live "toward" death. "The human being [is] a lieutenant of the nothing," he writes there. "We are so finite that we cannot even bring ourselves originally before the nothing through our own decision and will. So abyssally does the process of finitude entrench itself in Dasein that our most proper and deepest finitude refuses to yield to our freedom" (93). It is also only by finding ourselves within the midst of "beings as a whole" that we are able to approach the "nothing" that defines us (90).

64. Richter, *The Daily Practice of Painting*, 30.

65. Ibid., 119–120.

66. John Donne, "Meditation XVII," in *Devotions on Emergent Occasions* (Philadelphia: Folcroft Library Editions, 1972), 96–98.

67. Richter, *The Daily Practice of Painting*, 186.

68. Ibid., 186, 209.

69. Ibid., 183.

70. Freud offers his fullest discussion of this associative logic in *The Interpretation of Dreams*, in *The Standard Edition*, vols. 4 and 5. I explore its relationship to care in *World Spectators* (Stanford, Calif.: Stanford University Press, 2000).

71. The original title of these three works is *Tote.* The usual English translation, *Dead*, treats this word as an adjective, but almost all of the titles in the series are nouns that have been rendered nonspecific through the elimination of the article [e.g., *Gegenüberstellung* (*Confrontation*), *Zelle* (*Cell*), *Beerdigung* (*Funeral*)], and *Tote* seems to me to function in the same way. I have discussed the title with Harun Farocki, who thinks that *Tote* is the equivalent within the domain of mortality of "Sleeper" within the domain of sleep, or "Dancer" within the domain of dance. Because English has no noun that generalizes the condition of being dead, I am using the admittedly awkward construction *Dead Person.* Although I follow convention with the title of another work in this series, Erhängte, and translate it as "*Hanged*," it also appears to function in this way.

72. See Richter, *The Daily Practice of Painting*, 175, and Storr, *Gerhard Richter: October 18, 1977*, 95–96.

73. Richter, *The Daily Practice of Painting*, 190.

74. Aust, *The Baader-Meinhof Group*, 131–133, 275–277, 278, 280. In *Baader-Meinhof: Pictures on the Run*, 67–77 (Zurich: Scalo, 1998), Astrid Proll, who was also a "Red Army Faction activist" (007), mordantly observes that "after Baader was arrested . . . [he] was always the center of attraction. From that point of view the RAF was a FBA, a 'Free Baader Faction'" (009–010).

75. Aust, *The Baader-Meinhof Group*, 253–255, 280; Storr, *Gerhard Richter: October 18, 1977*, 51–53.

76. Shapiro, preface to *Gerhard Richter: Paintings, Prints, and Photographs*, 17; Storr, *Gerhard Richter: October 18, 1977*, 99.

77. Richter, *The Daily Practice of Painting*, 183.

78. Storr suggests that what I am calling a "gash" is the ligature of the rope through whose agency Meinhof died (*Gerhard Richter: October 18, 1977*, 108).

79. Barthes, *Camera Lucida*, 10–15.

80. I initially began to think about the relationship between this painting and the three *Dead Person* canvases with Bridget Alsdorf, during a graduate seminar on Richter. I can no longer remember who said what during our many conversations about it, but I know that her thoughts shaped mine in all kinds of ways. Subsequently, Alsdorf wrote a fine essay about this group of paintings, which constitutes the "prompt" for this note. In her essay, to which I am also profoundly indebted, she offers a detailed account of the temporal changes Richter introduced into *Youth Portrait*, the 1988 *Betty*, and the photo picture currently under discussion.

81. Richter, *The Daily Practice of Painting*, 173–174.

82. Aust, *The Baader-Meinhof Group*, 16, 262–263, 306, 313.

83. See, for instance, ibid., 131.

84. Storr reproduces this photograph in *Gerhard Richter: October 18, 1977*, 106.

85. Storr also includes these photographs in ibid., 108–109.

86. Heidegger, "What Is Metaphysics?" 91.

87. In the German edition of *The Daily Practice of Painting*, the photograph of Betty appears in the middle of this note, instead of at the end (Gerhard Richter, *Text*, 117).

88. Richter, *The Daily Practice of Painting*, 175.

89. Freud, "The Unconscious," in *The Standard Edition*, 14:194.

90. Richter, *The Daily Practice of Painting*, 189.

91. Ibid., 156–157.

92. Richter, *Text*, 147.

93. Richter, *The Daily Practice of Painting*, 203.

94. The word that Richter uses in the German titles is "*Gegenüberstellung*," which means "the placement of something over and against something else."

95. Storr also remarks upon this in his discussion of the paintings (*Gerhard Richter: October 18, 1977*, 107).

96. Gerhard Richter, *Catalogue Raisonné, 1962–1993* (Bonn: Cantz Verlag, 1993), vol. 3, paintings 667–1 to 674–2.

97. I say "structural position" because these photographs were shot by a television camera, not a police camera. See Storr, *Gerhard Richter: October 18, 1977*, 105.

98. Richter, *The Daily Practice of Painting*, 186.

99. Eric Santner provides both an excellent survey of what has been written on this subject and an especially compelling account of it in his book *Stranded Objects: Mourning, Memory, and Film in Postwar Germany* (Ithaca, N.Y.: Cornell University Press, 1990). This topic also figures centrally in the New German Cinema, most particularly the films of Rainer Werner Fassbinder and Wim Wenders. Thomas Elsaesser offers a perceptive discussion of the responses of German filmmakers to "the fatherless society" in chapter 8 of *New German Cinema: A History* (New Brunswick, N.J.: Rutgers University Press, 1989), which references a range of other scholars.

100. Benjamin Buchloh, "Divided Memory and Post-traditional Identity: Gerhard Richter's Work of Mourning," *October*, no. 75 (Winter 1996): 75. Buchloh elaborates this concept through a definitive reading of *Two Sculptures for a Room by Palermo, 48 Men*, and *Uncle Rudi*.

101. Buchloh reads this painting as a self-portrait in "Archaeology to Transcendence: A Random Dictionary for/on Gerhard Richter," in *Gerhard Richter* (New York: Marian Goodman Gallery, 2001), 15.

102. Richter has himself become one of the most eloquent critics of his generation's refusal of the paternal legacy. In a 2001 interview with Storr, he observed that "the absence of the father is a typical German problem," since after the war, "nobody wanted [their fathers]" (*Gerhard Richter: Forty Years of Painting*, 301, 19). (The first of these remarks is included in the abridged version of the interview that appears in the book, but the second is only quoted by Storr in his prefatory text.) Intriguingly, the artist also mentioned in the same interview that "it wasn't until Moritz was born that I started to know what a father is" (62). When I first read this last comment, I assumed it to reflect negatively on Richter's relationship to his daughter, Betty. Later, however, I realized that it was the artist's wry acknowledgment of the crisis into which he was thrown when forced into an identification with his own father. No matter how fraught a father's relationship might be with his daughter, it still stands outside the history from which Richter's generation attempted to remove itself. Storr also comments on the "paternal apprehension" that is registered in Richter's paintings of Moritz (*Gerhard Richter: Forty Years of Painting*, 81–82), but he denies that the artist's work constitutes a "manifesto of disidentification," and makes this denial the launching point for a virulent attack on Buchloh (64).

103. This is not the painting's only temporal equivocation. Richter shot the photograph on which he based it when his daughter was twelve, but did not produce the work itself until she was twenty-two (Shapiro, preface to *Gerhard Richter: Paintings, Prints, and Photographs*, 19). And although the artist characterizes it at one point as a parental "leave-taking" (he makes this remark in an interview with Storr, "The Day Is Long," *Art in America* 90, no. 1 [January 2002]: 121), he kept the canvas in his possession, unexhibited, until 1991 (Shapiro, preface to *Gerhard Richter: Paintings, Prints, and Photographs*, 19).

104. As Robin Clark observes in a note on the painting, it "embodies Richter's insistence on a practice that weds, without blurring, the abstract and the representational" (*German Art Now* [St. Louis: Saint Louis Art Museum, 2003], 91).

105. As Dr. Tessen von Heydebrech notes in his preface to *Gerhard Richter: Eight Gray* (Berlin: Guggenheim Museum Foundation, 2002), the reflective monochromes gesture not only toward the museum space but also toward "the world outside" (9), much as the color abstractions do. But these works also reference the spectator, a point to which I will return later.

106. Every time I look at the second *Betty* I am also struck by the similarities between it and Klee's *Angelus Novus*. Both paintings have a similar shading in the upper-left-hand corner, depict faint figures that are frontally positioned, and seem to be the source of their own illumination.

107. Richter, *The Daily Practice of Painting*, 171–172.

108. See *Gerhard Richter: October 18, 1977*, 97–98, where Storr quotes and discusses this passage. He pushes this argument much further in *Gerhard Richter: Forty Years of Painting*, 79–89.

109. Richter shot these photographs after painting *January, December*, and *November*.

110. Other Richter scholars have also noted the penal atmosphere of these photographs. See, for instance, Shapiro, preface to *Gerhard Richter: Paintings, Prints, and Photographs*, 19 and 25; and Storr, *Gerhard Richter: October 18, 1977*, 116 n.

111. Richter, *Atlas*, 470–479. Armin Zweite also notes the relationship between these panels and those devoted to the concentration camp photos ("Gerhard Richter's 'Album of Photographs, Collages, and Sketches,'" in B. H. D. Buchloh, J. F. Chevier, A. Zweite, and R. Rochlitz, *Photography and Painting in the Work of Gerhard Richter* (Barcelona: MACBA, 1998), 72.

112. For an evocative description of this dimension of the paintings, see Shapiro, preface to *Gerhard Richter: Paintings, Prints, and Photographs*, 22–24.

113. Other scholars have also suggested that these two series of paintings are somehow related. Storr describes *January, December*, and *November* as a "coda" to *October 18, 1977* (*Gerhard Richter: Forty Years of Painting*, 78), and Shapiro comments on their affective affinities (Shapiro, preface to *Gerhard Richter: Paintings, Prints, and Photographs*, 18, 24).

114. Shapiro, preface to *Gerhard Richter: Paintings, Prints, and Photographs*, 25–26.

115. Catharina Manchanda also suggests that there may be a link between the triptych and these events (*German Art Now*, 93).

116. Richter, *The Daily Practice of Painting*, 180–181.

117. Ibid., 100.

118. Ibid., 166. This passage also provides a moving account of the friendship between Richter and Buchloh.

119. *Hiroshima, Mon Amour: Text by Marguerite Duras for the Film by Alain Resnais*, trans. Richard Seaver (New York: Grove, 1961), 80.

120. Shapiro maintains that there are three layers of paint in *January, December*, and *November* (preface to *Gerhard Richter: Paintings, Prints, and Photographs*, 22). If this is indeed the case, these layers could be read as an analogy for the three moments of German history they bring together: national socialism, the conflict of the RAF and the Bundesrepublik, and the fall of the Berlin Wall.

121. Richter, *The Daily Practice of Painting*, 112.

122. As Cork notes, these figures "seem far less 'real' than the abstractions displayed behind them" ("Through a Glass Darkly," 13).

123. I am drawing here upon Storr's account of the German response to the sale in *Gerhard Richter: October 18, 1977*, especially 33–37.

124. Richter issued this complaint during an interview with Hubetis Butin (*Neue Zürcher Zeitung* [October 23, 1995], 25. Quoted by Storr in *Gerhard Richter: October 18, 1977*, 35.

125. Usselmann describes one way in which this might work: "Perhaps, dislocated as they are now from their original *telos*, Richter's *Oktober* cycle could continue to release cathectic energies and be transformed into a nonspecific work of mourning. In

a society that is marked by ever-more-frequent outbursts of violence, by murder and state executions, this role could not be more appropriate. . . . Could we not all mourn, together, the fate of the anonymous death-row inmate or the senseless killing of loved ones as we have been mourning our failings in the Baader-Meinhof trauma?" (25).

126. Shapiro, preface to *Gerhard Richter: Paintings, Prints, and Photographs*, 27. Buchloh provides a helpful account of the technical process Richter uses to impart color to glass in "Between *Vorschein* and *Glanz*," in *Gerhard Richter: Eight Gray* (New York: Guggenheim Museum, 2002), 19 n.

127. As Buchloh observes in "Between *Vorschein* and *Glanz*," Richter's reflective monochromes "situate the production of inscription entirely within the range of the reader/spectator. Now it is in fact the spectators' movement alone, the reflection of their random acts performed in front of these mirrors or in the ambient spaces that surround them, that is . . . recorded as 'marks' within the mirrors' immaculate surface" (20).

128. Fascinatingly, when talking about the sale of *October 18, 1977*, Richter remarked that "the address was certainly a decisive issue" (quoted by Storr in *Gerhard Richter: October 18, 1977*, 35).

Index

Page numbers in italics refer to illustrations.

Adorno, Theodor, 252n48
Agamben, Giorgio, 252n55
Ahtila, Eija-Liisa, 240n32
aesthetic reception, 140, 149, 152, 220–21, 251n38. *See also* transmission
affects, 110, 113, 202–203; anxiety 110–11; grief, 203–204; guilt, 17–18, 19–20, 42, 85, 111; hope, 202; horror, 181, 187, 197, 202–203; and Richter, 181, 202–204, 211; wonder, 111. *See also Stimmung*
Alsdorf, Bridget, 195, 254n80
analogy, 65, 74, 223n3; in the analytic relationship, 41, 44; in Benjamin, 179, 181; Christian, 1; in Coleman, 156, 166–67; in Darwin, 3; in Donne, 189; in Freud, 11, 36, 44, 62, 96, 98, 100; in Genesis, 40; in Leonardo, 2, 152–54, 155, 166; in Ovid, 1–2; Platonic, 1; in Proust, 65–66; in Richter, 13–14, 173–79, 181, 183–84, 194–95, 215–16, 249n15, 249n20, 250n33; in Salomé, 45; as socially transformative, 3; Swedenborgian, 2; in Valéry, 134–35, 153–54; in Whitman, 3. *See also* Benjamin: the dialectical image; correspondences; photography; similarity
the analytic relationship, 41, 44–45
Anderson, W.S., 232n43, 233n45–47, 233n49
Andreas-Salomé, Lou. *See* Salomé, Lou Andreas-
Antoine, Jean-Philippe, 248n6, 250n21
Appignanesi, Lisa, 96, 98, 240n37, 241n56
Arasse, Daniel, 223n6, 247n43
Ashbery, John, 225n28
Assoun, Paul-Laurent, 227n4
Atwood, Margaret, 225n28
Aust, Stefan, 183, 195, 252n52

Baader, Andreas, 190, 195, 253n74. *See also* the Baader-Meinhof group; RAF
the Baader-Meinhof group, 181–185, 190, 192, 194, 195, 217, 252n54, 253n74. *See also* Baader, Andreas; Ensslin, Gudrun; Meinhof, Ulrike; Meins, Holger; RAF
Baker, George, 245n13
Bal, Mieke, 231n14, 236n44, 240n26
Barthes, Roland, 249n18
Bartsch, Shadi, 233n50, 242n77
Batchelor, David, 250n24
Bazin, André, 249n18
Becker, Paula Modersohn-, 70–74, 237n49, 237n51, 237n54; *The Letters and Journals*, 237n52, 237n55, 237n66; *Portrait of Rainer Maria Rilke*, 86, 89, *87*; *Reclining Mother and Child*, 89–90, *89*; *Self-Portrait on her Sixth Wedding Anniversary*, 83–85, *84*;

Becker, Paula Modersohn- (*continued*)
Self-Portrait with Amber Necklace, 81–83, *82*
beings as a whole, 12, 126
Being-towards-death, 25, 189
Benjamin, Walter, 11, 46, 132; *The Arcades Project*, 11, 190, 227n60, 232n37, 251n41; the dialectical image, 179, 181, 251n40; "On Some Motifs in Baudelaire," 244n34; "On the Concept of History," 11, 211, 227n60, 232n37
Berenson, Bernard, 165
Bernstock, Judith E., 224n27
Bertucci, Sonja, 245n2–3, 245n5
Bersani, Leo, 229n27, 243n21, 244n33, 245n7
the Bible, 39–40, 225n35, 231n15, 247n50
Blanchot, Maurice, 6, 225n30, 234n60
Boethius, Anicius Manlius Severinus, 5, 53
Böll, Heinrich, 252n51
Bourdieu, Pierre, 249n19
Boyarin, Daniel, 231n14
Breuer, Josef, 227n58, 230n54, 232n25, 232n34, 242n72
Buchloh, Benjamin, 168, 202–203, 208, 216, 248n1, 252n48, 255n100–101, 257n126–127

Cadava, Eduardo, 251n43
Chastel, André, 246n19, 247n57
Chion, Michel, 243n22
Cima da Conegliano, Giovanni Battista, *57*
Clark, Kenneth, 246n23
Clark, Robin, 255n104
Coleman, James, 13, 136–141, 156–164, 166–167, 225n34, 225n36, 227n68, 247n53, 247n60
The Compact Oxford English Dictionary, 231n19
Cork, Richard, 249n15, 256n122
correspondences, 2, 3, 11, 40, 90, 174, 190. *See also* analogy; Benjamin: the dialectical image; similarity
Courbet, Gustave, *The Origin of the World*, 252n61
Crimp, Douglas, 246n17

Darwin, Charles, 224n18; *The Origin of Species*, 3, 224n16
the death drive, 33–35, 83, 181, 183, 195, 201, 251n44
the death of God, 17–18, 19–20, 23–24, 38, 240n32
Danoff, Michael, 249n15
da Vinci, Leonardo, 136, 142–146, 147, 246n29; and analogies, 2; Battle of Anghiari drawings, 164; *A Cloudburst of Material Possessions*, 157, 161, 163–164, *163*; *Codex Ashburnham*, 149; *Codex Atlanticus*, 149; *Codex Urbanus*, 246n19, 246n32; *Divided Skull*, 157, 159–161, *160*; drapery studies, 142–143, *142*, *143*; "grotesques," 151, *151*; *Head of a Young Woman*, 149; *Interior of a Skull*, 157, 159–161, *159*; *The Last Supper*, 6, 13, 136–138, 157, 163, 164–166, *165*; *Leda and the Swan*, 164; *Codex Leicester*, 152; *Leonardo on Art and the Artist*, 246n19, 246n23; Louvre exhibition in 2003, 136–139, *137*, 141–152, *147*, 156–164, 166–167; *Madonna on the Rocks*, 150; the *Mona Lisa*, 155; *The Musician*, 157, 158, 161, *162*, 166; and Orpheus and Eurydice 6; Orpheus Machine, 6, 157–159, *158*, 225n34; *Portrait of Isabelle d'Este*, *148*, 149; *Studies of horsemen, dragons, horses, and a dog*, *150*; *The Virgin and Child*, *144*; *Virgin and Child with Saint Anne*, 6, 13, 136, 144–146, *145*, 151, 152, 155–156, 161, 166; *Virgin and Child with Saint Anne and John the Baptist*, 146
der Lippe, Angela, 229n16
Descartes, *Meditations*, 2, 223n8

Desmond, Adrian, 224n18
Donne, John, 189, 253n66
Doubrovsky, Serge, 240n24
Duras, Marguerite, 217, 256n119
Dürer, Albrecht, 52, 54, *55*, 225n33
Dutoit, Ulysse, 229n27, 243n21, 244n33

Eisen, Albert E., 226n56
Elger, Dietmar, 249n15
Eliot, T.S., 251n37
Elsaesser, Thomas, 254n99
Emerson, Ralph Waldo, 224n13–14
Ensslin, Gudrun, 190, 197, *197*, 199, *199*, 204–206. *See also* the Baader-Meinhof group; RAF
Entz, Sophie (Phia), 88
Erkkila, Betsy, 224n19
the eternal recurrence, 18–19, 42
Eurydice's absence, 11, 52, 53, 57, 232n40, 232n43
Eve as helper, 39–40

fallenness, 129–130, 244n30
the father, 94–95; and aesthetic transmission, 141, 147; in Christianity, 22, 95; in Freud, 8, 19–22, 30, 55, 95; in Malick, 129. *See also* Freud: parricide; Freud: the primal father; God; Oedipus complex; the paternal legacy; transmission
finitude, 4, 41–42, 94, 141, 146, 204; and Freud, 7, 21, 24–25, 61, 97; and Heidegger, 11, 108–109, 110, 251n46, 253n63; as inimical to narcissism, 4, 21, 111–12; and Leonardo, 147, 156; and Malick, 12, 111–32; and Nietzsche, 7, 25; and Richter, 12, 181, 185, 187–89, 195–197; and Rilke, 8, 28, 75; and Salomé, 8, 27–28; and Shakespeare, 146–147, and Winnicott, 156
Flanagan, Martin, 243n9
flesh, 2–3, 4–5, 12, 14, 40–41, 43, 53, 78, 90, 152, 161, 206, 211. See also Whole
Forrester, John, 96, 98, 240n37, 241n56
the *fort-da* game, 92–93, 155, 167; and matricide, 93
Foucault, Michel, *The Order of Things*, 1, 223n3
Frankel, David, 248n11
Freud, Anna, 98–100
Freud, Sigmund: "Analysis Terminable and Interminable," 244n31; "Autobiographical Study," 227n4; *Beyond the Pleasure Principle*, 33, 35–36, 44–45, 92–93, 95–104, 155, 227n4, 240n27, 247n44; cancer treatments, 7, 98–99, 226n37, 241n51; castration, 7–8, 95, 154–55; "A Child Is Being Beaten," 240n29; *Civilization and Its Discontents*, 23, 29, 30, 35, 228n7, 229n30, 229n32, 230n43; *The Complete Letters of Sigmund Freud to Wilhelm Fliess, 1887–1904*, 231n20; "Creative Writers and Day-Dreaming," 60–61, 231n10, 235n4; the death drive (Thanatos), 33–35, 251n44; *Delusions and Dreams in Jensen's 'Gradiva'*, 61–62, 102–103, 235n6, 242n66; dream of Irma's injection, 97–98; dream of mother's death, 98; *The Ego and the Id*, 34, 166, 227n4, 247n59; Eros, 32–34, 244n31; "Female Sexuality," 7, 95, 99, 226n37; "Femininity," 7, 99, 226n37; "Fetishism," 226n37; and fetishism, 61; and the *fort/da* game, 92–93, 155; *Fragment of an Analysis of a Case of Hysteria*, 234n1; *From the History of an Infantile Neurosis*, 240n29; *The Future of an Illusion*, 21–24, 29, 95, 97, 99, 235n5; *Group Psychology and the Analysis of the Ego*, 227n4; "Hysterical Phantasies and Their Relation to Bisexuality," 234n1; *The Interpretation of Dreams*, 30, 36, 44, 98, 227n4, 232n33, 241n45; lack, 7, 94–95, 99, 154–55, 187;

Freud, Sigmund (*continued*)
"Leonardo da Vinci and a Memory of His Childhood," 154–55, 227n67, 231n8, 245n9; *Letters*, with Salomé, 227n4, 231n7, 235n10; letter to Albert Einstein, 34–35, 230n48; and literature, 59–62; "Lou Andreas-Salomé," 227n4; *Moses and Monotheism*, 6, 7, 225n36, 228n8; and Nietzsche, 6, 7, 19, 20, 23, 24, 25, 30, 227n4; nirvana, 35; *Notes Upon the Case of an Obsessional Neurosis*, 227n4; the omnipotence of thought, 19–20, 228n8; "On Narcissism," 21, 228n6; "On the History of the Psycho-Analytic Movement," 227n4; "On Transience," 96–97, 241n41; and Orpheus and Eurydice, 10; negative hallucination, 103–104; parricide, 19; the primal father, 19–21, 55; *Project for a Scientific Psychology*, 42, 232n24; *Psychical (or Mental) Treatment*, 242n74; *Psychoanalysis and Faith*, 230n40; *Psycho-Analytic Notes on an Autobiographical Account of a Case of Paranoia*, 228n9; "Psychopathic Characters on the Stage," 59–60, 235n2; *The Psychopathology of Everyday Life*, 103, 242n73; and reason, 23, 228n8; *Sexuelleben*, 240n34; "Some Character-Types Met with in Psycho-Analytic Work," 227n4; "Some Psychical Consequences of the Anatomical Distinction between the Sexes," 7, 99, 226n37–38, 252n60; *Studies on Hysteria*, 42, 103, 227n59, 230n54, 232n25, 232n34; "The Theme of the Three Caskets," 98, 99–, 241n47; "Thoughts for the Times on War and Death," 96, 97, 185, 240n39, 252n59; *Three Essays on the Theory of Sexuality*, 32, 230n41, 234n1; *Totem and Taboo* 7–8, 19–20, 55, 225n35, 228n5, 234n66; on trauma, 36; "The Uncanny," 227n4; "Why War?" 230n48

Genesis, 39–43, 58, 232n26
Giovanni, Bertoldo di, 52
God, 22, 39–40, 42, 64, 95, 108, 156. *See also* the death of God; the father; Freud: parricide; Freud: the primal father; Oedipus complex; the paternal legacy; Salomé: "The God Experience"
Goethe, Johann Wolfgang von, 157
Green, David, 249n14
Gronert, Stefan, 248n6
guilt,17–18, 19–20, 42, 85, 111. *See also* affects; finitude: and Richter
Guthrie, W.K.C., 233n52

Hass, Robert, 73, 237n67
Heidegger, Martin, 2, 11, 107–111, 223n7; *Being and Time*, 110, 111, 243n15, 244n30, 251n46, 253n63; beings as a whole, 12, 110, 126, 131; Being-towards-death, 111; care, 111; "On the Essence of Ground," 108, 242n5; and the Holocaust, 111; *Nietzsche*, 232n28; on Nietzsche, 43; *Stimmung*, 110; "The Turning," 108, 109, 242n4; "What Are Poets For?" 107, 109, 227n59, 242n1; "What Is Metaphysics?" 109, 111, 227n66, 242n14, 251n46, 253n63
Hegel, Georg Wilhelm Friedrich, 37; *The Phenomenology of Spirit*, 37, 230n2
Hendrickson, Robert, 230n1
Hentschel, Martin, 172, 248n8
the heterosexual couple, 9, 10, 69, 100, 124
Heydebrech, Tessen von, 255n105
Hölderlin, Friedrich, 242n3
Horowitz, Gregg, 141, 246n16, 251n38, 253n62

impersonality, 135, 153
Irigaray, Luce, 245n15
Irwin, Eleanor, 224n22

Jamison, Rosalyn Frankel, 226n56
Jensen, Wilhelm, 100–102, 241n60, 241n64
Jones, Ernest, 97, 241n43, 241n49, 241n53
Jones, James, 109, 243n10

Key, Ellen, 64
Klammer, Martin, 224n19
Klee, Paul, 255n106
Kleinbard, David, 239n17
Klossowska, Balladine (Merline), 56, 77
Koch, Gertrud, 248n6, 250n32, 252n49
Kosinski, Dorothy M., 10, 226n52, 226n56

Lacan, Jacques, 1, 4, 60, 223n1–2, 224n21, 228n12, 235n3, 239n19, 240n30, 245n14, 246n18. *See also* the mirror stage; the paternal legacy
Lang, Luc, 248n6
Lehrer, Ronald, 227n4
the Léonardesques, 146
Levi, Primo, 252n55
Lévi-Strauss, Claude, 245n15
Lovejoy, Arthur O., 224n10
Low, Barbara, 35, 230n49

Malick, Terrence, 12, 108–132; *The Essence of Reasons*, 242n5; and Heidegger, 108–109, 110, 130; *The Thin Red Line*, 12, 109–132, 242n8, 243n24, 243n28
Manchanda, Catharina, 256n115
Mantegna, Andrea, 52
Marani, Pietro C., 165–166, 246n33, 247n48
Martin, Biddy, 231n22, 235n15
matricide, 86–100
McGee, Timothy J., 224n25
Meinhof, Ulrike, 190, 192, 194, 195–197. *See also* the Baader-Meinhof group; RAF
Meins, Holger, 190, 252n54. *See also* the Baader-Meinhof group; RAF
Meltzer, Eve, 245n13
Merleau-Ponty, Maurice, 136, 153, 154–155; "Cézanne's Doubt," 136, 153, 245n10, 247n39
metaphor, 173. *See also* analogy; similarity
Milton, John, 225n33
the mirror stage, 1, 26, 228n12
Mitchell, Juliet, 241n59
Mitchell, Stephen, 234n68, 236n43, 238n80
Modersohn-Becker, Paula. *See* Becker, Paula Modersohn-
Moore, James, 224n18
mortality. *See* finitude
the mother, 93–94; and Freud, 92–93, 95, 98, 99; and Leonardo, 144–46, 154–56; and Malick, 114–16, 125; and Proust, 90–92; and Rilke, 81, 83, 85–90, 239n17; and Winnicott, 156. *See also* the *fort/da* game; the paternal legacy; turning away from the other

Nachträglichkeit, 42, 43, 46
narcissism, 4; Christian, 25; crisis of, 23; and Freud, 99; infantile, 7, 27, 30, 60, 86; and literature, 61–62; maternal, 94; and parental, 21; and Rilke, 86; as wounded by finitude, 4, 21, 111–12. *See also* the solitary male subject
Natale, Richard, 243n9
The New Oxford Annotated Bible, 39–40, 225n35, 231n15
The New Revised Standard Edition of the Oxford Annotated Bible, 247n50
Nietzsche, Friedrich: the eternal recurrence, 18–19; *The Gay Science*, 6, 17–18, 24–25, 37, 43, 225n36, 227n1, 230n3; self-overcoming, 18;

Nietzsche, Friedrich (*continued*)
Thus Spoke Zarathustra, 10, 18–19, 56–58, 226n51, 227n3

the oceanic feeling, 30–32, 35, 113, 124–25, 229n27–28, 243n28
Oedipus complex, 8, 20, 44, 45, 55, 94–95, 141, 143, 161, 208, 240n31
Oedipus myth, 54, 58
Orpheus and Eurydice myth, 46–58, 232n40; adaptations of, 5, 52, 224n23–27, 225n28–34; in Boethius, 5; in Blanchot, 6, 234n60; in Coleman, 136; in Freud 6–7, 10–11, 55, 95–96, 104; in Heidegger, 108; in Jensen, 100–102; in Leonardo, 6, 136, 223n6; in Nietzsche, 6; in the Ovidians, 5; in Poliziano, 6, 95–96; in Proust, 91–92; in Rilke, 8–10, 68–70, 76, 77–79, 90; in Rodin, 10; in Salomé, 8, 10, 12, 46–59, 104; in Valéry, 133–34; in Virgil, 47–48, 232n42–43, 233n44–45. *See also* Ovid: *The Metamorphoses*
Orphic Mysteries, 52
Osborne, Peter, 249n14
Ovid, *The Metamorphoses*, 1–2, 4–5, 48–52, 76, 78, 79, 80, 223n4–5, 232n39, 233n45, 233n48–50, 238n77, 241n63, 247n58

Parsons, William B., 229n28, 244n27
the paternal legacy, 13, 94, 147, 208, 245n14, 255n102. *See also* the father; Freud: parricide; Freud: the primal father; God; Oedipus complex; transmission
Perry, Gillian, 237n54, 238n2
Petzet, Heinrich Wiegand, 237n55
Pfeiffer, Ernst, 235n11
Pfister, Oskar, 32, 230n40
photography, 11, 12, 13, 14, 168–221
Poliziano, Angelo, *Orfeo*, 6, 53–54, 95–96, 157–58, 159, 225n31, 234n61, 240n35
Power, Stacy Peebles, 109, 243n12
Prikker, Jan Thorn, 181, 185, 187, 189–190, 206–207
Primmer, Adolf, 233n46
Proll, Astrid, 254n74
Proust, Marcel, 9, 10, 90–92, 226n53, 231n4, 236n31; *Swann's Way*, 65, 74; *Time Regained*, 66, 244n34; *Within a Budding Grove*, 240n24

RAF (Red Army Brigade), 181–85, 190, 192, 194, 195, 217, 252n54, 253n74. *See also* Baader, Andreas; the Baader-Meinhof group; Ensslin, Gudrun; Meinhof, Ulrike; Meins, Holger; RAF
reason, 23, 29
redemption, 43, 127, 179, 181, 202–203, 221
Reinach, Salomon, 55, 225n.35, 234n66
relationality, 4, 11, 94; and Benjamin 11; and Freud, 34; and Genesis, 40; and Heidegger 11; and Leonardo, 149, 156; and Malick, 111; and Proust, 10; and Richter, 174–75, 202; and Rilke, 70; and Salomé, 26
Rich, Adrienne, 225n18
Richter, Gerhard, 13–14, 169–221, 252n48; *128 Details from a Picture*, 248n9; *Abstract Painting 825-II*, 248n10; *Abstract Picture, 178*; *Arrest 1* and *Arrest 2*, 206; *Atlas*, 13, 173, 181, *182*, 183, *184*, 190, *191*, 199, 213, 248n13; *Betty* paintings, *191*, 191, *194*, 194, 195–197, *198*, 199, 208–209, *210*, 211, 255n103, 255n106; *Blanket*, 173; *Catalogue Raisonné*, 206; *Cell*, 213, *215*; color abstractions, 176, 178; concentration camp photographs, 181–85, 211, 213; *Confrontation 1, 2*, and *3*, 197, 204–205, *204, 205, 206*; conversation with Benjamin Buchloh, 168, 202–203, 216; conversation with Jan Thorn Prikker, 181, 185, 187, 189–90, 206–207;

The Daily Practice of Painting, 179, 201, *201*, 248n1, 249n20, 250n22, 250n28, 250n33, 250n35, 251n39, 254n87; *Dead Person*, *194*, 192, 194, 199, 253n71; and death, 185–87; and the death drive, 183, 195, 201; *Eight Student Nurses*, 187, *187*; *Florence*, 248n12; gray monochromes, 175–76, *176*, 208, 250n27–28; and grief, 202–204, 256n125; *Hanged*, 199, *200*; and hope, 201; *Horst and His Dog*, *207*, 208; and the ineffable, 178–79; *January*, *December*, and *November*, 14, 173, 213–14, *214*, *216*, *217*, 217–18, 256n113, 256n120; *Marian*, *177*; *Mirror Painting (Gray)*, 221, *220*, 257n127–128; *Misty Self-Portrait*, 218–19, *218*; *Moritz*, 208, *209*; *Motor Boat*, 170–71, *170*, 225n36; *October 18, 1977*, 14, 189–92, 194–97, 199, 202, 204–208, 256n113; and paternal dis-identification, 208, 255n102; pornographic photographs, 183–86; and the RAF, 181–85, 190–92, 194–97; *Self-Portrait Times Three*, 219, *219*; *Six Photos*, 211, *212*, 213, 255n109–110; *Stag*, *171*, 172, 225n36; *Stimmung*, 203; *Student*, 186–87, *186*; *Uncle Rudi*, *207*, 208; and United States museums, 219–21, 257n128; *vanitas* series, 187–89, *188*, 253n62; *Werkübersicht Catalogue raisonné*, 250n34; *Youth Portrait*, 195–97, *196*

Rilke, Clara. *See* Westhoff, Clara.

Rilke, Rainer Maria 8, 26, 28, 56, 62–80, 81–90, 97, 226n43–44, 226n54; "Antistrophes," 90, 239n22; and Cézanne, 71, 237n55; *The Correspondence*, with Salomé, 235n13, 239n10; *Duino Elegies*, 9, 63, 64, 75–76, 79, 88; *Letters: 1892–1910*, 231n6, 236n5, 239n5; and Knoop, Gertrude Ouckama, 79; and Knoop, Vera, 79–80, 239n22; *Letters: 1910–1926*, 229n15, 231n5, 236n20, 239n6, 239n23, 245n11; *Letters on Cézanne*, 237n55; *Letters to a Young Poet*, 235n17; and love 9; *The Notebooks of Malte Laurids Brigge*, 74–75, 88, 238n71, 239n16; "Orpheus. Eurydice. Hermes," 8, 56, 68–70, 236n43; *Requiem for a Friend* 8, 56, 64, 70, 72, 73, 81–86, 90, 239n3; "Self-Portrait, 1906," 90, 239n21; *Sonnets to Orpheus* 8–9, 55, 64, 78–80, 81, 86, 108, 226n47, 229n22, 238n81; *Stories of God*, 64; "Turning Point" ("Wendung"), 76–77, 236n37

Rilke, Sophie. *See* Entz, Sophie (Phia)

Robbins, Emmet, 52, 225n32, 232n40, 233n52

Rodin, Auguste, *ii*, 10, 37

Rolland, Romain, 29–32, 35–36, 124–25, 229n28

Rommel, Manfred, 183

Rubin, Gayle, 245n15

Salomé, Lou Andreas-, 8, 25–29, 62–, 85–88; *The Correspondence*, with Rilke, 235n13, 239n10; and Freud, 28–29; the *Freud Journal*, 8, 39, 40–43, 45–46, 58, 85, 226n41, 231n12–13; "The God Experience," 25–28; "identification," 26, 28, 43; *Letters*, with Freud, 227n4, 231n7, 235n10; *Looking Back*, 8, 38, 45, 62, 85, 88, 226n40, 228n11, 228n13–14, 229n16, 231n9, 235n11–12, 239n4, 244n29; *Mein Dank an Freud*, 41, 231n21, 235n11; *Nietzsche: The Man in His Works*, 38, 227n2, 231n9, 235n9; and reverence, 28; and Rilke, 26–27, 62–63, 85–88; *You Alone Are Real to Me*, 236n19. *See also* Orpheus and Eurydice myth

Santner, Eric, 254n99

Scavizzi, Giuseppe, 52, 234n53

Schütz, Sabine, 172

Sebald, W.G., 236n30
Segal, Charles, 224n23, 232n40, 232n43–44, 234n57
Shakespeare, William, 99, 146–47, 246n22
Shapiro, Michael Edward, 176, 250n29, 256n113, 256n120
Silverman, Kaja, 253n70
similarity, 1–2, 3, 4, 7, 36, 44, 65, 96, 152, 173–75, 215–16, 223n3. *See also* analogy, correspondences, metaphor
Simpson, Michael, 232n39
Smithson, Robert, *Spiral Jetty*, 139, 245n13
Snow, Edward, 235n13, 238n75
the solitary male subject, 9–10; and Adam, 39; and Nietzsche, 37–38; and Proust 9, 37; and Rilke 9, 39, 66–68, 75, 90; and Valéry, 133
Sprengnether, Madelon, 241n51
Stafford, Barbara Maria, 223n3
Steinberg, Leo, 166, 247n56
Stimmung, 111, 203. *See also* affect
Storr, Robert, 211, 248n5, 249n17, 252n52, 256n113, 256n123
Strachey, James, 242n67
Swedenborg, Emanuel, 2–3, 224n13

Torgerson, Eric, 86, 236n21, 237n48, 238n1
transmission, 140–41, 146–47, 152, 155, 245n15. *See also* aesthetic reception
Turan, Kenneth, 243n9
turning around, 53; in Benjamin, 11, 211, 227n60; in Freud, 10–11, 104; in Heidegger, 11; in Richter, 211; in Salomé, 45–46; in Virgil, 47
turning away from the other, 42, 53, 95, 104, 115

Unworth, Matthew von, 236n27, 240n40
Usselmann, Rainer, 252n51–52, 256n125

Valéry, Paul, 56, 133–36, 153–54, 226n55; "Introduction to the Method of Leonardo," 134–35; "Leonardo and the Philosophers," 133; *Leonardo, Poe, Mallarmé*, 245n6; *Poems*, 245n1; "Note and Digression," 134, 153–54; *Oeuvres*, 245n3; "Orpheus," 133, 134; "Paradoxe sur l'architecte," 133–36; "Solitude," 133; "To Rainer Maria Rilke," 245n4
the *vanitas* tradition, 189
Vecce, Carlo, 150, 246n34
Viatte, Françoise, 142–143, 246n20
Vicari, Patricia, 52, 224n23, 225n29, 225n33, 232n40, 234n55
Virgil, 47–48, 232n39, 232n42–43, 242n76

Wall, Jeff, 246n31
Warburg, Aby, 54, 56, 225n33, 234n63–64, 234n67, 235n8
Warden, John, 224n23
Warhol, Andy, 169, 248n3
West, David, 233n48
Westhoff, Clara, 66, 70, 71, 72, 75, 237n55
Whitman, Walt, 3, 224n14, 224n19
Whole, 4, 7, 8, 11, 12, 27, 30, 41, 45, 62, 65, 68, 78, 83, 111, 112, 119, 125, 126, 131, 135. *See also* analogy, flesh, similarity
Wilkinson, Lynn R., 224n11, 224n13
Wilson, Eric, 224n13
Winckler, Michael, 235n13, 238n75
Winnicott, D.W., 156, 247n46

Zimmerman, Mary, 224n24
Ziolkowski, Theodore, 224n24
Zoppo, Marco, 52
Zweite, Armin, 256n111

Illustration Captions and Credits

1. Auguste Rodin. *Orpheus and Eurydice.* 1893. Marble. Height 50 in. (27 cm); width 30 in. (76.2 cm); depth 28 in. (71.1 cm). The Metropolitan Museum of Art, N.Y., Gift of Thomas F. Ryan, 1910 (10.63.2) Image © The Metropolitan Museum of Art. ii

2. Albrecht Dürer. *The Death of Orpheus.* 1494. Pen and brown ink. 11.4 in. x 8.9 in. (28.9 x 22.5 cm). Inv. 23006. Hamburger Kunsthalle, Hamburg, Germany. Photo: Christoph Irrgang. Photo credit: Bildarchiv Preussischer Kulturbesitz / Art Resource, N.Y. 55

3. Giovanni Battista Cima da Conegliano (b.1459/60–d.1517/18). *Orpheus.* Ink on paper. Uffizi, Florence, Italy. Photo credit: Alinari / Art Resource, N.Y. 57

4. Paula Modersohn-Becker. *Self-Portrait (Semi-Nude with Amber Necklace and Flowers)* (*Selbstbildnis Halbnakt mit Bernsteinkette II*). 1906. Oil on board. 24 x 19.7 in. (61 x 50 cm). Inv. 1748. Credit: Kunstmuseum Basel. Photo credit: Martin Bühler. 82

5. Paula Modersohn-Becker. *Self-Portrait on Her Sixth Wedding Anniversary* (*Selbstbildnis am sechsten Hochzeitstag*). 1906. Oil on board. 40 x 27.6 in. (101.5 x 70.2 cm). Paula Modersohn-Becker Museum, Bremen. Permission of museum. 84

6. Paula Modersohn-Becker. *Portrait of Rainer Maria Rilke* (*Porträt des Rainer Maria Rilke*). 1906. Oil on board. 12.7 x 10 in. (32.3 x 25.4 cm). Roselius House, Bremen. Permission of museum. 87

7. Paula Modersohn-Becker. *Reclining Mother and Child* (*Liegende Mutter mit Kind*). 1906. Oil on canvas. 32.3 x 49.1 in. (82 x 124.7 cm). Paula Modersohn-Becker Museum, Bremen. Permission of museum. 89

8. © Fox Home Video 113

9. © Fox Home Video 115

10. © Fox Home Video 116

11. © Fox Home Video 116

12. © Fox Home Video 118

13. © Fox Home Video 119

14. © Fox Home Video 119

15. © Fox Home Video 120

16. © Fox Home Video 120

17. © Fox Home Video 121

18. © Fox Home Video 123

19. © Fox Home Video 124

20. © Fox Home Video 126

21. © Fox Home Video 127

22. © Fox Home Video 129

23. © Fox Home Video 130

24. © Fox Home Video 131

25. © Fox Home Video 131

26. Leonardo Exhibition Floor Plan (detail 1). Architectural Drawing from James Coleman's Archive. Musée du Louvre/Cabinet Wilmotte-Paris, architect. Permission of James Coleman and the Louvre. 137

27. Leonardo da Vinci. *Drapery for a Seated Figure.* Distemper with white highlights. 10.5 x 9.2 in. (26.6 x 23.3 cm). Inv. 2255. Photo: Thierry Le Mage. Louvre, Paris, France. Photo credit: Réunion des Musées Nationaux / Art Resource, N.Y. 142

28. Leonardo da Vinci. *Study for Drapery of a Seated Figure.* Point of brush and tempera, heightened with white on linen. 12.6 x 8.6 in. (31.9 x 21.8 cm). Inv. RF 4105. Photo: J. G. Berizzi. Louvre, Paris, France. Photo credit: Réunion des Musées Nationaux / Art Resource, N.Y. 143

29. Leonardo da Vinci. *The Virgin and Child,* called *The Virgin of Fruits.* 1475–85. Pen and brown ink. 14 x 10 in. (33.5 x 25.3 cm). Inv. RF486, recto. Louvre, Paris. Photo credit: Réunion des Musées Nationaux / Art Resource, N.Y. 144

30. Leonardo da Vinci. *Virgin and Child with Saint Anne* (*La Vierge et l'Enfant avec sainte Anne et un agneau dans un paysage*). 1508. Oil on wood, 66.1 x 51.2 in. (168 x 130 cm). Inv. 776. Louvre, Paris, France. Photo credit: Réunion des Musées Nationaux / Art Resource, N.Y. 145

31. Leonardo Exhibition Floor Plan (detail 2). Architectural Drawing from James Coleman's Archive. Musée du Louvre / Cabinet Wilmotte-Paris, architect. Permission of James Coleman and the Louvre. 147

32. Leonardo da Vinci. *Portrait of Isabella d'Este* (Portrait d'Isabelle d'Este). 1519. Black and red chalk. 24.8 x 18.1 in. (63 x 46 cm). Inv. MI 753 recto. Photo: Thierry Le Mage. Louvre, Paris, France. Photo credit: Réunion des Musées Nationaux / Art Resource, N.Y. 148

33. Leonardo da Vinci. *Studies of horsemen, dragons, horses, and a dog.* Pen and brown ink. Photo: Arnaudet. 7.6 x 4.8 in. (19.2 x 12.3 cm). Inv. 781 D.R. Louvre, Paris, France. Collection Edmond der Rothschild. Photo credit: Réunion des Musées Nationaux / Art Resource, N.Y. 150

34. Leonardo da Vinci. *Head of Man in Profile Facing to the Left.* 1490–1494. Pen and brown ink over charcoal or black chalk. 4⅝ x 2¹⁄₁₆ in. (11.7 x 5.2 cm). Rogers Fund, 1909 (10.45.1). The Metropolitan Museum of Art, N.Y. Photo credit: Image Copyright ©The Metropolitan Museum of Art / Art Resource, N.Y. 151

35. Leonardo da Vinci. *Orpheus Machine.* 1508–1518. Arundel 263, f.22. British Library, London. ©All Rights Reserved. The British Library Board. Licence Number: UNICAL21. 158

36. Leonardo da Vinci. *Interior of a Skull.* 1489. Pen and brown ink over traces of leadpoint. 7 7/16 x 5½ in. (18.9 x 13.9 cm). Inv. 19058 recto. Royal Library, Windsor Castle. The Royal Collection ©2008 Her Majesty Queen Elizabeth II. 159

37. Leonardo da Vinci. *Divided Skull.* 1489. Pen and brown ink over black chalk or leadpoint. 7 7/16 x 5½ in. (18.9 x 13.9 cm). Inv. 19058 verso. Royal Library, Windsor Castle. The Royal Collection ©2008 Her Majesty Queen Elizabeth II. 160

38. Leonardo da Vinci. *Portrait of a Musician.* 1490. Oil on panel. 16 15/16 x 12 3/16 in. (43 x 31 cm). Pinacoteca Ambrosiana, Milan, Italy. Photo credit: Scala / Art Resource, N.Y. 162

39. Leonardo da Vinci. *A Cloudburst of Material Possessions.* Circa 1510. Inv. 12698 recto. Royal Library, Windsor Castle. The Royal Collection ©2008 Her Majesty Queen Elizabeth II. 163

40. Leonardo da Vinci. *Study for the Last Supper.* 1493–95. Pen and golden brown ink, soft black chalk or charcoal. 10½ x 8 7/16 in. (26.6 x 21.4 cm). Inv. 12542 recto. Royal Library, Windsor Castle. The Royal Collection ©2008 Her Majesty Queen Elizabeth II. 165

41. Gerhard Richter. *Motor Boat*, first version (*Motorboot* 1. Fassung). 1965. Oil on canvas. 66 15/16 x 66 15/16 in. (170 cm x 170 cm). GR 79-a. Öffentliche Kunstsammlung, Basel, Switzerland. Permission of artist. 170

42. Gerhard Richter. *Stag* (*Hirsch*). 1963. Oil on canvas. 59 x 78¾ in. (150 x 200 cm). GR 7. Private collection. Permission of artist. 171

43. Gerhard Richter. *Gray* (*Grau*). 1973. Oil on canvas. 35 7/16 x 25⅝ in. (90 x 65 cm). GR 348/7. Private collection. Permission of artist. 176

44. Gerhard Richter. *Marian.* 1983. Oil on canvas. 78¾ x 78¾ in. (200 x 200 cm). GR 554-2. Collection Maria Sandtretto. Permission of artist. 177

45. Gerhard Richter. *Abstract Picture* (*Abstraktes Bild*). 1977. Oil on canvas. 88⅝ x 78¾ in. (225.1 x 200.5 cm). GR 417. Art Gallery of Ontario. Permission of artist. 178

46. Gerhard Richter. *Atlas*, Panel 19. 1967. 5 black and white cuttings. 26 5/16 x 20⅜ in. (66.7 x 51.7 cm). Permission of artist. 182

47. Gerhard Richter. *Atlas*, Panel 21. 1967. 6 black and white cuttings. 26.3 x 20.4 in. (66.7 x 51.7 cm). Permission of artist. 184

48. Gerhard Richter. *Student* (*Studentin*). 1967. Oil on canvas. 41⅜ x 37 7/16 in. (105 x 95 cm). GR 149. Private collection. Permission of artist. 186

49. Gerhard Richter. *Eight Student Nurses* (*Acht Lernschwestern*). 1966. Detail. Oil on 8 canvases, each 36⅛ x 27 9/16 in. (95 x 70 cm). GR 130. Kunstmuseum Winterthur. Permission of artist. 187

50. Gerhard Richter. *Skull with Candle* (*Schädel mit Kerze*). 1983. Oil on canvas. 39 7/16 x 59 1/16 in. (100 x 150 cm). GR 547-2. Neues Museum Weserburg, Bremen, Germany. Permission of artist. 188

51. Gerhard Richter. *Atlas*, Panel 394. 1978. 3 color photographs (partly over-painted and pasted up, individually mounted). 14 7/16 x 20 7/16 in. (36.7 x 51.7cm). Permission of artist. 191

52. Ulrike Meinhof, dead, May 9th, 1976. Published in *Stern*, June 16, 1976. Photographic model for the three *Dead Person* paintings. From artist's notebook. Permission of artist. 192

53. Gerhard Richter. *Dead* (*Tote*). 1988. Oil on canvas. 24½ x 28¼ in. (62 x 73 cm). GR 667-1. Photo: Friedrich Rosenstiel. Museum of Modern Art, New York. Permission of artist. 193

54. Gerhard Richter. *Dead* (*Tote*). 1988. Oil on canvas. 24½ x 24½ in. (62 x 62 cm). GR 667-2. Photo: Axel Schneider. Museum of Modern Art, New York. Permission of artist. 193

55. Gerhard Richter. *Dead* (*Tote*). 1988. Oil on canvas. 13¾ x 15½ in. (35 x 40 cm). GR 667-3. Photo: Axel Schneider. Museum of Modern Art, New York. Permission of artist. 193

56. Gerhard Richter. *Betty*. 1977. Oil on canvas. 11 13/16 x 15 ¾ in. (30 x 40 cm). GR 425-4. Photo: Friedrich Rosenstiel. Private collection. Permission of artist. 194

57. Portrait of Ulrike Meinhof, circa May 1970. Photographic model for *Youth Portrait*. From artist's notebook. Permission of artist. 196

58. Gerhard Richter. *Youth Portrait* (*Jugendbildnis*). 1988. Oil on canvas. 26 7/16 x 24½ in. (67 x 62 cm). GR 672-1. Photo: Axel Schneider. Museum of Modern Art, New York. Permission of artist. 196

59. Photos of Gudrun Ensslin, 1972. Models for *Confrontation 1*, *2*, and *3*, with hand notations by the artist. From the artist's notebook. Photo: Franz Ruch. Permission of artist. 197

60. Gerhard Richter. *Betty*. 1977. Oil on canvas; 19 11/16 x 15 11/16 in. (50 x 40 cm). GR 425.5. Private collection. Permission of artist. 198

61. Gudrun Ensslin, hanged in her Stammheim cell, October 18th, 1977. Photographic model for *Hanged*. From artist's notebook. Permission of artist. 199

62. Gerhard Richter. *Hanged* (*Erhängte*). 1988. Oil on canvas. 78¾ x 55⅛ in. (200 x 140 cm). GR 668. Photo: Friedrich Rosenstiel. Museum of Modern Art, New York. Permission of artist. 200

63. Isa Genzken, *Betty with the Air-pistol*, 1984. Black-and-white photograph. Permission of Gerhard Richter. 201

64. Gerhard Richter. *Confrontation 1* (*Gegenüberstellung 1*). 1988. Oil on canvas. 44 x 40¼ in. (112 x 102 cm). GR 671-1. Photo: Friedrich Rosenstiel. Museum of Modern Art, New York. Permission of artist. 204

65. Gerhard Richter. *Confrontation 2* (*Gegenüberstellung 2*). 1988. Oil on canvas. 44 x 40¼ in. (112 x 102 cm). GR 671-2. Museum of Modern Art, New York. Permission of artist. 205

66. Gerhard Richter. *Confrontation 3* (*Gegenüberstellung 3*). 1988. Oil on canvas. 44 x 40¼ in. (112 x 102 cm). GR 671-3. Photo: Friedrich Rosenstiel. Museum of Modern Art, New York. Permission of artist. 206

67. Gerhard Richter. *Uncle Rudi* (*Onkel Rudi*). 1965. Oil on canvas. 34¼ x 19 11/16 in. (87 x 50 cm). GR 85. Czech Museum of Fine Arts, Prague. Permission of artist. 207

68. Gerhard Richter. *Horst and His Dog* (*Horst mit Hund*). 1965. Oil on canvas. 31½ x 23⅝ in. (80 x 60 cm). GR 94. Private collection. Permission of artist. 207

69. Gerhard Richter. *Moritz.* 2000. Oil on canvas. 20⅛ x 18⅛ in. (51 x 46 cm). GR 863-1. De Pont Museum voor hedendaagse kunst, Tilburg, The Netherlands. Permission of artist. 209

70. Gerhard Richter. *Betty.* 1988. Oil on canvas. 40⅛ x 28 7/16 in. (102 x 72 cm). GR 663-5. Saint Louis Art Museum. Permission of artist. 210

71. Gerhard Richter. *Six Photos* (*Sechs Fotos*). 1991. Portfolio with six black-and-white photographs on resin-coated paper; 20 x 23⅝ in. (50.9 x 60 cm). Editions CR: 74B. Artist's collection. Permission of artist. 212

72. Gerhard Richter. *Six Photos* (*Sechs Fotos*). 1991. Portfolio with six black-and-white photographs on resin-coated paper; 20 x 23⅝ in. (50.9 x 60 cm). Editions CR: 74C. Artist's collection. Permission of artist. 212

73. Gerhard Richter. *Six Photos* (*Sechs Fotos*). 1991. Portfolio with six black-and-white photographs on resin-coated paper; 20 x 23⅝ in. (50.9 x 60 cm). Editions CR: 74E. Artist's collection. Permission of artist. 212

74. Gerhard Richter. *January* (*Januar*). 1989. Oil on canvas. 2 panels, overall 125 x 156½ in. (320 x 400 cm). GR 699. Saint Louis Art Museum. Funds given by Mr. and Mrs. James E. Schneithorst, Mrs. Henry L. Freund, and the Henry L. and Nathalie Edison Freund Charitable Trust; and Alice P. Francis, by exchange. Permission of artist. 214

75. Gerhard Richter. *Cell* (*Zelle*). 1988. Oil on canvas. 78½ x 55⅛ in. (200 cm x 140 cm). GR 670. Photo: Friedrich Rosenstiel. Museum of Modern Art, New York. Permission of artist. 215

76. Gerhard Richter. *December* (*Dezember*). 1989. Oil on canvas. 2 panels, overall 125 x 156½ in. (320 x 400 cm). GR 700. Saint Louis Art Museum. Funds given by Mr. and Mrs. Donald L. Bryant Jr., Mrs. Francis A. Mesker, George and Aurelia Schlapp; Mr. and Mrs. John E. Simon, and the estate of Mrs. Edith Rabushka in memory of Hyman and Edith Rabushka, by exchange. Permission of artist. 216

77. Gerhard Richter. *November* (*November*). 1989. Oil on canvas. 2 panels, overall 125 x 156½ in. (320 x 400 cm). GR 701. Saint Louis Art Museum. Funds given by Dr. and Mrs. Alvin R. Frank and the Pulitzer Publishing Foundation. Permission of artist. 217

78. Gerhard Richter. *Misty Self-Portrait 18.1.90.* 1990. Oil on photograph. 13 7/16 x 20 in. (34.9 x 50.8 cm). Private collection. Permission of artist. 218

79. Gerhard Richter. *Self-Portrait Three Times 23.1.90* (*Dreifaches Selbstportrait* 23.1.90). 1990. Oil on photograph. 20 x 23⅝ in. (50.8 x 60 cm). Private collection. Permission of artist. 219

80. Gerhard Richter. Installation view of *Gray Mirror* (*Grauer Spiegel*). 1991. Glass, enamel, and paint. 4 panels: 1: 299.9 x 175.4 cm; 2: 299.9 x 175.4 x 0.5 cm; 3: 299.9 x 175.1 cm; 4: 299.7 x 175.3 cm. Saint Louis Art Museum. Gift of Gerhard Richter. Permission of artist. 220